I0794788

Washburn®

Prewar Instrument Styles

Guitars, Mandolins, Banjos and Ukuleles 1883-1940

by Hubert Pleijsier

Cover and book design by Design Associates

ISBN 13: 978-1-57424-227-0
ISBN 10: 1-57424-227-X
SAN 683-8022

CENTERSTREAM

Copyright © 2008 CENTERSTREAM Publishing LLC
P.O. Box 17878 – Anaheim Hills, CA 92817

All rights for publication and distribution are reserved.
This book is in no way intended to infringe on the intellectual property rights of any party. All products, brands, and names represented are trademarks or registered trademarks of their respective companies; information in this book was derived from the author's independent research and was not authorized, furnished or approved by other parties.
No part of this book may be reproduced in any form or by any electronic or mechanical means including information storage and retrieval systems without permission in writing from the publisher, except by reviewers who may quote brief passages in review.

Contents

Introduction

When Lyon & Healy of Chicago launched their first line of Washburn guitars in the late 1800s, the company already was a dominant force in the musical instrument retail and wholesale business in the United States and abroad, and well on its way towards becoming one of the world's biggest and most influential instrument manufacturers. Sadly, not much remains today of the rich history of the former music industry giant. Those who have endeavored to find facts about the company and its musical instrument lines before 1940, which feature many original and groundbreaking designs, must have been amazed by the lack of available information. A major drawback for researchers is that the company archives of this period –such as ledger books, correspondence, accounts and other records- are missing. These documents are not in the possession of the present-day Lyon & Healy Harps, Inc., established during the late 1920s as a successor to the original company, but have disappeared at an unknown point in time and may never surface again.

In view of the prominent role of Lyon & Healy during the last decades of the 19th century through the early 1900s as the self-proclaimed but undisputed largest music house in the world, one would expect to find many historical materials in the public archives in Chicago, home ground of the company since its inception until today. Not so. Apart from a few old merchandise catalogs little information is available from notable institutions as the Chicago Public Library and the Chicago Historical Society. The most detailed account of Lyon & Healy's prewar years comprises not more than twenty pages of a booklet commissioned by the company on the occasion of its centennial in 1964.[1]

A prime source of information regarding the prewar instruments are the annual musical merchandise catalogs that were published during a number of decades since the 1870s by Lyon & Healy and Tonk Bros Co., who acquired the distribution rights for the Washburn instruments in 1928. Original catalogs are rare and command prices of up to hundreds of dollars, which also has spawned a small market for reprinted versions. Unfortunately the catalogs can only solve part of the puzzle. After studying surviving instruments and comparing these to original catalog data, it only becomes too clear that the catalogs were not always complete and up to date at the time of their publication, and that artist impressions of the instruments and instrument descriptions are often inaccurate.

Most of the interest in Lyon & Healy and their instruments by vintage instrument collectors and players has been sparked by the company's flagship brand for stringed instruments, Washburn, which was inaugurated in 1883. 'Washburn' was also the middle name of George W. Lyon, co-founder of the firm of Lyon & Healy that had been established in 1864. The Washburn lines represented in most cases the highest quality instruments that Lyon & Healy was capable of making and rivaled the premium products of most competitors in quality and also in price, due to their high production totals that could be achieved by the use of specially developed instrument building tools and machinery.

The purpose of the research carried out for this book is to provide detailed instrument descriptions for the more than 450 Washburn guitar, mandolin, banjo and ukulele styles that were offered between 1883 and 1940, to reconstruct the various serial numbering schemes used during this period, and to estimate approximate production totals. The information about specific instrument parts, labels and other relevant data provides additional clues that will hopefully enable Washburn owners to identify their instruments and to date these within one or two years from their actual manufacturing dates. Due to the absence of company archive materials, most dates and serial number information, based on research data assembled from over 2,000 prewar Washburn instruments, must necessarily remain approximations. The instrument descriptions may in a few cases contain assumptions regarding materials or individual parts, as not all instrument styles and catalogs for every year were available for inspection.

1 *A Century of Music in Chicago – the Story of Lyon-Healy's First One Hundred Years 1864-1964 (1964).*

Acknowledgments

I am greatly indebted to John Bernunzio (Bernunzio Vintage Instruments), Jay Scott and Ron Middlebrook for their support and encouragement. Many thanks also to Stan Werbin (Elderly Instruments), who graciously forwarded instrument descriptions from the Elderly sales archives and went out of his way to provide photos and to get me in touch with collectors, Fred Oster (Vintage Instruments) for letting me copy data from his sales archive, Lynn Wheelwright for researching the Gibson ledger data, Peter Kohman (Retrofret), Scott Freilich, Frank Ford, Richard Myers, Mark Demaray, Jim Garber, John King, Bernice Gunderson and George Gruhn (Gruhn Guitars) for kindly allowing me to photocopy catalog materials at his store and sending me the 1913 banjo catalog section. Special thanks to Lesley Martin at the Chicago Historical Society for the help in researching the Lyon & Healy factory buildings in Chicago, to Canadian luthier and bowlback mandolin expert Neil Russell for the many catalog pages and enlightening discussions, and to all Washburn owners and vintage instrument dealers who willingly provided pictures and information about their instruments.

About the Author

Hubert Pleijsier is a Dutch national. Inspired by his older brother, a professional guitarist, he developed an interest in vintage guitars in the 1970s. During a four-year job secondment in the late 1990s to New York and Chicago he bought a beat up Washburn parlor guitar at a vintage guitar show and became fascinated by it. Prompted by the lack of available information regarding prewar Washburns and original maker Lyon & Healy, he started doing research about the company and set up a database containing particulars of more than 2,000 surviving Washburn guitars, mandolins, banjos and ukuleles. He also visited many reputable vintage instrument dealers throughout the U.S., who encouraged him to publish his findings. The author lives in The Hague, the Netherlands, with his wife and two children.

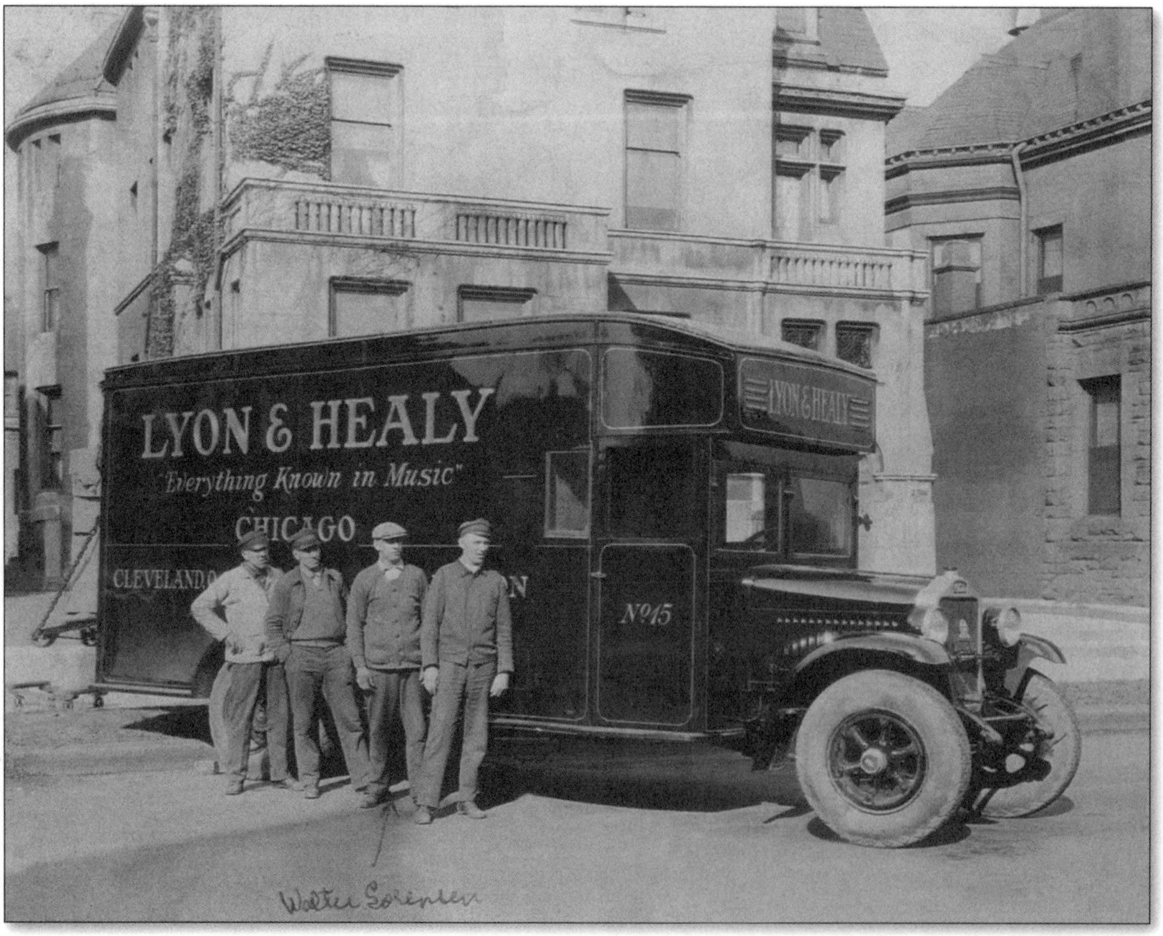

1920s Lyon & Healy delivery truck

CHAPTER ONE

A brief history of Lyon & Healy and the 'Washburn' brand

The house of Lyon & Healy was founded in Chicago in 1864 by Patrick Joseph Healy and George Washburn Lyon. Lyon, born in July 1825 in Northboro, Massachusetts, was a veteran of the music business.[2] He had been an employee of The Oliver Ditson Co., a long-standing Boston-based music publishing company and musical instrument retailer, and took a great interest in instrument design. Patrick Healy was born on March 17, 1840 on a farm near Burnfort, Ireland. When he was ten years old his family emigrated to the U.S. and settled in Boston. After having attended public schools there Healy started working at the store of music publisher George P. Reed, where he distinguished himself as an ambitious and hard working young man.[3]

George Washburn Lyon, 1882
(Craig Pfannkuche - Memory Trail Research)

Near the end of the Civil War, Oliver Ditson sent for him and Lyon and offered them the charge of establishing a western outlet for his company. After having considered a few other major cities as possible store locations the partners decided to start up business in Chicago, where they arrived in May, 1864. Lyon & Healy's first store in the Windy City, located at Washington and Clark Streets, opened in October of the same year. The firm concentrated on selling sheet music and books, as well as small musical instruments and cabinet organs. Business grew rapidly, and in January 1870 Lyon & Healy moved to larger premises in the Drake Building, which was situated a few blocks down the road at the corner of Washington Street and Wabash Ave.

On September 4, 1870 a flash fire destroyed the entire block and reduced the Lyon & Healy store to ashes. Healy suffered a nervous breakdown, and for a time his life was feared for. After his recovery the two partners decided to reopen their business on a new location at 150 S. Clark Street. In the spring of 1871 Lyon & Healy became the sole Chicago representative for Steinway & Sons through the acquisition of the piano business of Smith & Nixon, thus adding great prestige to the name of the young firm. George Lyon headed the fast growing piano department and would remain in charge of it for the next eighteen years.

Patrick Joseph Healy, around 1900

Another staggering blow came when the new store burned down in the Great Chicago Fire of October 8, 1871, which ravaged large parts of the city and swept out many businesses. Once more, Lyon & Healy showed their perseverance. The partners managed to recoup eighty-five percent of their losses through insurance proceeds and immediately secured a temporary store at 287 W. Madison Street. Shortly thereafter they moved into a little church building at Wabash Avenue and 16th Street in order to keep business going while the debris of the disaster was being cleared away.[4]

---

2 20th century company literature and other contemporary sources incorrectly state 1820 as Lyon's birth year.

3 Other sources state that Healy worked at the Henry Tolman Co., another renowned Boston music publishing house. According to his obituary, George Lyon had also been an employee of the Tolman Co. after having worked for Ditson.

4 In spite of claims that Lyon & Healy also suffered a third large fire during the 1900s which allegedly destroyed all company files, this event likely never occurred (see chapter 6).

Lyon & Healy's persistence paid off. In 1872 they opened up permanent headquarters on the ground floor of a building in downtown Chicago at the corner of State and Monroe Streets.[5] In the next twenty-two years during which the firm was situated at this location business flourished more than ever, and Lyon & Healy ended up occupying the whole building. Patrick Healy showed himself a visionary by his novel and imaginative use of advertising in promoting the company and its products.[6] Early on he invested large sums in long-term ad campaigns that proved successful and made Lyon & Healy a household name within the United States. In keeping with Healy's ambitious goals to expand the firm's product range and become the largest music house in the world, a six-story instrument factory and warehouse was opened in the early 1880s at Michigan Avenue and Madison Street. The first 'Washburn' brand guitars and mandolins were manufactured here.

The company store at State and Monroe Streets, pictured at the occasion of the opening of Chicago's cable car transportation system in January 1882

The Washburn name was first used on a line of guitars introduced in November 1883. These fairly expensive instruments were meant to compete in quality and price with the products of the leading guitar manufacturers at the time, in particular C.F. Martin & Co. A few years later a line of Washburn bowlback mandolins and zithers was launched, followed by banjos around 1892. The Washburn instruments were an immediate success and the product lines were expanded throughout the 1890s.

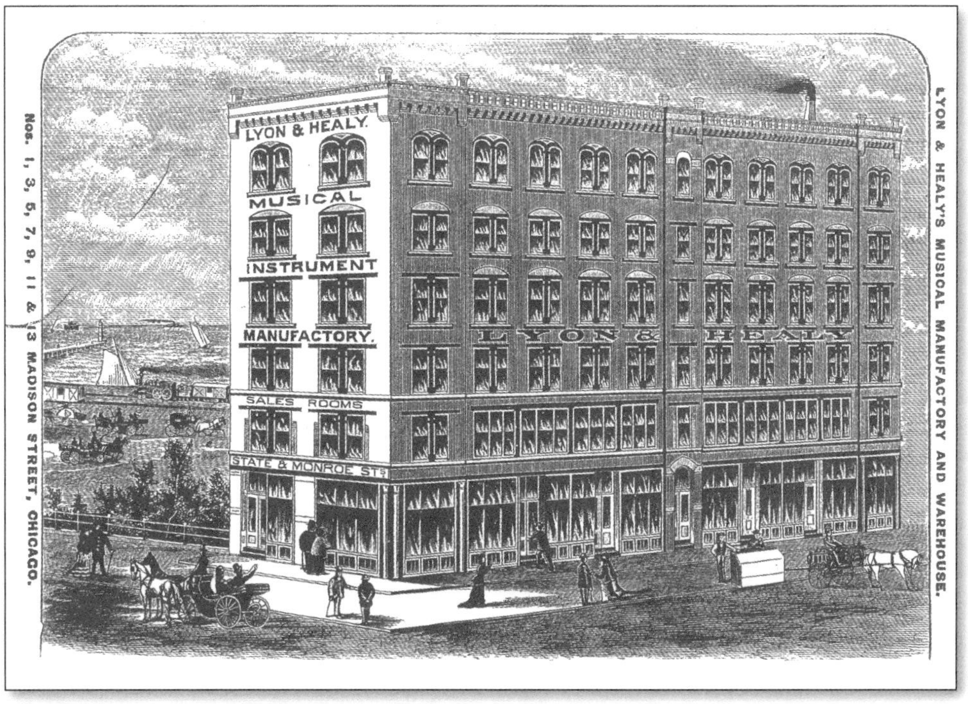

Lyon & Healy's first instrument factory and warehouse (1885 catalog)

The corner of Chicago's State and Madison Streets, shortly after the Great Fire of 1871. This intersection, situated a few blocks up the road from Lyon & Healy's South Clark Street store, has been the starting point of the city's street numbering system (100 numbers to a block, eight blocks to a mile) since almost a decade. It was devised in 1901 by Edward P. Brennan, a superintendent of Lyon & Healy, and finally adopted in 1908 (Chicago Historical Society)

5 The church building at Wabash Avenue remained in use at least until the mid 1920s as a wholesale outlet.

6 George Lyon has sometimes been incorrectly credited with the company's advertising policies (*Gruhn & Carter (I)*, p. 31).

Frame and Scale of the Lyon & Healy Patent Upright Piano.

This cut shows the Full Iron Frame, arrangement of the Strings, Pressure Plate, and Lyon's Patent Resonator.

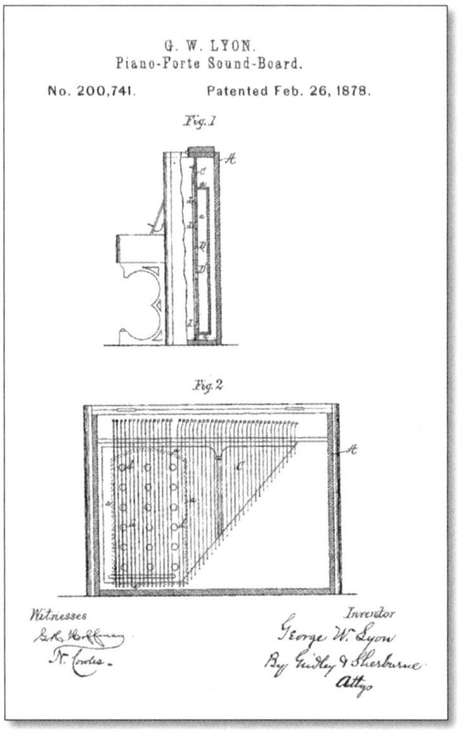

Two of the piano and guitar patents by George Lyon. The guitar (overleaf) has a tone chamber similar in function to the 'Virzi tone producer' that was installed in a number Gibson guitars and mandolins and patented in 1922

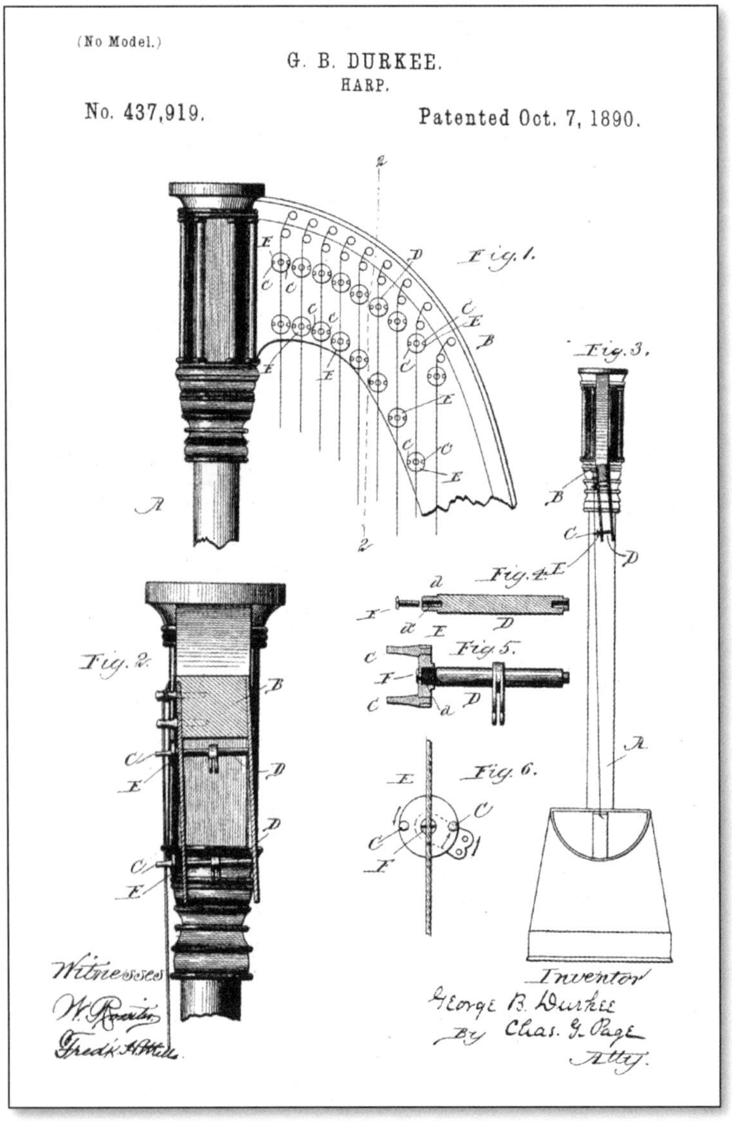

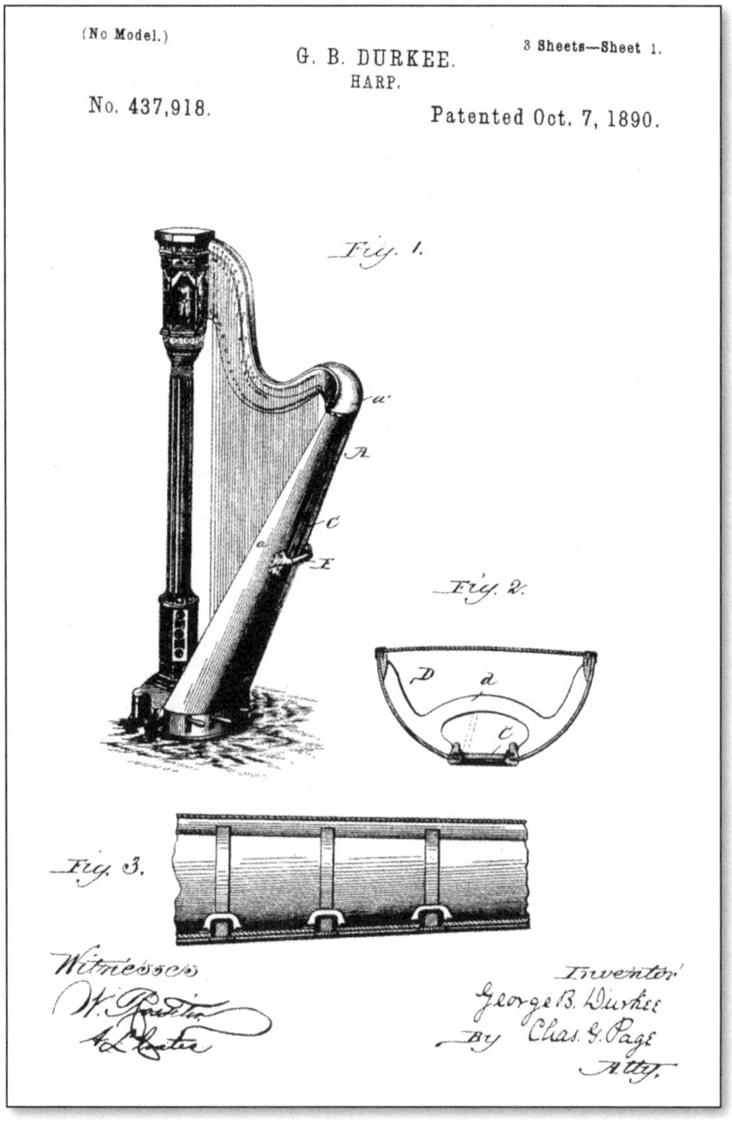

Drawings for some of George Durkee's harp patents

In October 1889 George Lyon, the firm's senior partner, retired. His parting with Patrick Healy was not amicable. Lyon, an accomplished musician who was the author of a number of instrument designs,[7] had since a long time objected to the firm's aggressive expansion led by Healy. By the end of the 1880s Lyon began to actively oppose further growth of the company and declined all retirement offers made to him. At the same time, he requested to occupy one of the main offices for life. A break with Healy was unavoidable. Eventually a deal was struck and a large sum was paid to Lyon for the use of his name in addition to the value of his partnership share in the firm.[8] Lyon thereafter formed Lyon & Potter with his new business partner E.A. Potter. This Chicago-based firm acquired the rights to sell Steinway pianos, likely as part of the settlement with Healy. A line of guitars and mandolins was also marketed briefly under the George W. Lyon name. These instruments may well have been manufactured by Lyon & Healy.[9] Lyon remained with Lyon & Potter until his death on January 12, 1894. Ironically, the company was acquired by Lyon & Healy in 1898.

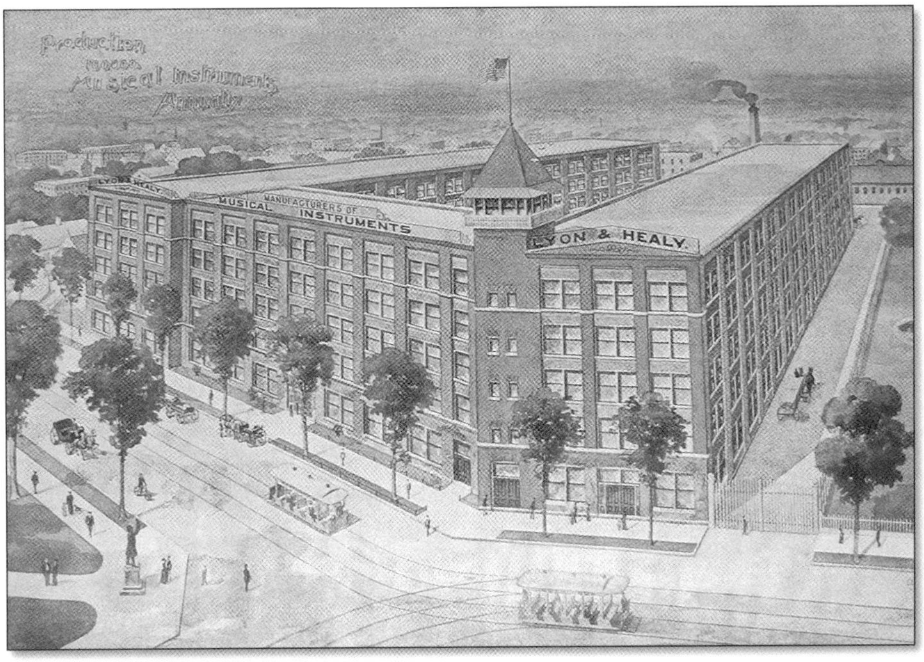

Lyon & Healy's Union Park factory (1903 catalog)

Harp ad from 1904

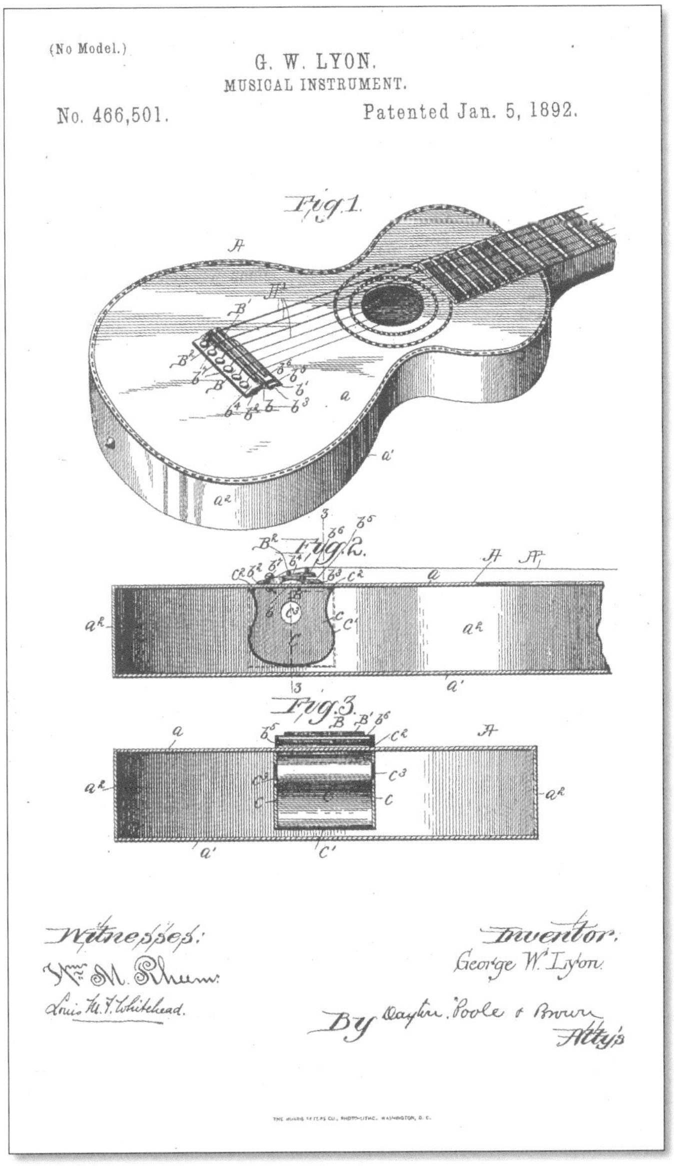

The year 1889 turned out to be pivotal for Healy and the company. Upon Lyon's departure Lyon & Healy was incorporated, with Healy being appointed as its first president. In the same year a large new five-story factory was opened at the corner of Randolph Street and Ogden Avenue opposite Union Park, providing the workmen with an unusual outlook upon flowerbeds and miniature lakes dotted with swans. Here one of Healy's long-cherished dreams was realized - to build the finest harp the world had ever seen. Based on designs of factory foreman George Durkee that incorporated significant improvements on the inventions of Sebastian Érard dating back to the 1810s, the Lyon & Healy harp debuted in its final form in 1889 after a few years of trials. It became an instant success with orchestras around the world, and is still recognized today as an industry standard.

7 His patents include a resonance-increasing soundboard for pianos (patent number 200,741, (1878), which was improved in 1884), a design for an upright piano with a supplemental top (patent number D19,302, 1889), and a guitar with a built-in tone chamber (patent number 466,501, registered in 1892).

8 Some of the historical details included in this chapter were derived from Healy's biography *Patrick Joseph Healy, founder of the house of Lyon & Healy – an appreciation (1907)*, likely commissioned by Lyon & Healy.

9 A surviving mandolin shows much similarity to the instruments made by Lyon & Healy at the time.

1897 and 1900 Christmas catalogs, 1898 catalog

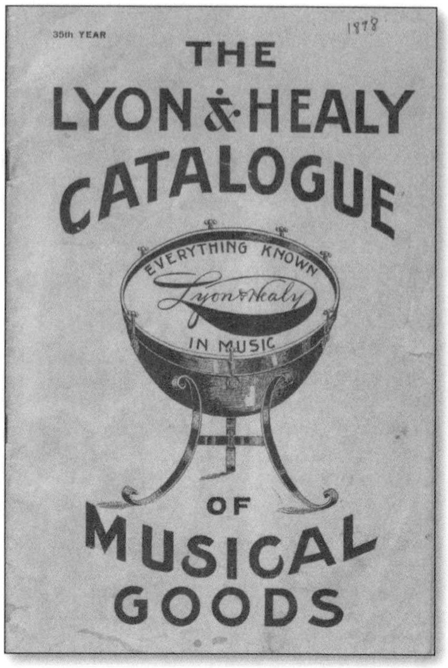

1911

1891

Washburn 'parlor' or reed organ, 1890s catalog

Within a year after its opening the annual output of the new Lyon & Healy factory was claimed to be 100,000 instruments or, as Healy put it, "a musical instrument every other working minute". During the early 1890s the company expanded further and received universal recognition as the largest music house in the world, which it would arguably remain for the next decades. Its sales representatives continuously visited the major cities in the United States, Canada, Europe, South America, Australia, China and Japan. Sales were boosted also by the large and lavishly illustrated musical merchandise catalogs that Lyon & Healy made available to dealers since the 1870s. Catalogs for band instruments and uniforms - which had been added to the company's product range early on - were published separately. Those interested in the Washburn instrument lines could request an illustrated souvenir catalog free of charge, which contained many endorsements by leading artists of the time. Even though the company chose not to offer musical merchandise to the public on a mail-order basis,[10] a network consisting of many thousands of dealers across the U.S. and abroad ensured that every item could be delivered to even the most remote customers.

The Battle Creek organ factory on a period postcard

Display at the 1894 Antwerp Exposition (Michael Holmes, Mugwumps Online)

In 1890 Lyon & Healy announced that they had imported a collection of rare old violins and bows from Europe, including instruments by Stradivari, Amati, Guarneri, Bergonzi, Stainer and a host of other famous makers. Many important instruments and collections were acquired and sold through the years, establishing Lyon & Healy's violin department as the foremost source for rare old violins in the world.[11] In the early 1890s the company also entered the field of pipe organ building. Healy, a deeply religious man, did not expect to make much profit out of this venture that merely appealed to him for sentimental reasons. Two organ factories were acquired, including the Compensating Pipe Organ Co. located in Battle Creek, Michigan. A small lithograph of this factory was printed on the company stationary for a few years during the early 1900s. A short-lived line of Washburn reed organs was introduced as well.[12] The Battle Creek factory was sold again around 1910.

Lyon & Healy's pavilion at the 1893 World's Columbian Exposition - a woodworker's dream (Michael Holmes, Mugwumps Online)

The 1893 World's Columbian Exposition held in Chicago gave Lyon & Healy a unique opportunity to showcase their product lines to a large public. In the ornamental two-story pavilion and two other large display cases specially erected for this purpose over 1,000 instruments were exhibited and concerts were performed during a six-month period. Among the many prizes carried off by Lyon & Healy was an award given to the Washburn instruments for 'supreme excellence'. The company garnered another diploma for excellence for

10 Only band instruments could be ordered by mail.

11 Among the Stradivarius violins acquired and sold by Lyon & Healy were the 'Kreisler', the 'Earl', the 'Bott', the 'Jansa', the '1697', the 'Healy', the 'Colossus', the 'Duke of Edinburgh', the 'Ludwig', the 'Nelson', the 'Wieniawski', the 'Czar Nicholas II/Kochansky', the 'Reynier' and the 'Spanish', and the 'Piatti' cello.

12 Around 1890, Lyon & Healy also bought New York reed and pipe organ maker Peloubet & Co. Surviving large church organs built by Lyon & Healy include those in Chicago's Lake View Presbyterian Church (1898), St Vincent de Paul (1901) and Our Lady of Sorrows Basilica (1902). The organ built for Chicago's Orchestra Hall (1905) was diagnosed in 1967 as damaged beyond repair, but the design of the new organ that replaced it in 1981 copied the façade of the Lyon & Healy instrument.

the Washburn line during the 1894 Universal Exposition in Antwerp, Belgium. Both feats were proudly mentioned on the labels of Washburn instruments until the mid 1920s.

The Wabash/Adams Street store, around 1900

Later in 1893 the stock market crashed, causing a widespread financial panic and the bankruptcy of 15,000 businesses. Fortunately, the financial affairs of Lyon & Healy were in excellent shape and the company continued to prosper during the remainder of the decade. In 1894 the company's headquarters were moved to a larger building located on the corner of Wabash Avenue and Adams Street, which would house Lyon & Healy's retail and wholesale businesses until 1916. Period photographs illustrated the luxurious appointments of the reception and sales rooms, displaying vaulted ceilings with painted frescoes, wood paneling and Persian carpets galore.

Sales and piano rooms (postcards from the early 1900s)

The revised Washburn instrument lines introduced in 1896 were marketed intensively during the late 1890s in frequent ad campaigns. The most memorable ad, which appeared in various versions between 1898 and 1903, pictured four 'Washburn babies' happily strumming away on their instruments. Among the active endorsers of the Washburn instruments at the time were such famous virtuosos as guitarist William Foden, mandolin players Valentine Abt and Samuel Siegel and the banjo duo Mays & Hunter. Various small merchandising items carrying the Washburn name were also offered, such as picks, envelopes, decks of playing cards and guitar and mandolin tutors. After 1905, when a new trimmed down Washburn model line was presented, the efforts of the company to promote their premium fretted instrument brand were only a fraction of what they had been during the 1890s. The economic downturn during the first decade of the 20th century, which included the severe market crashes of 1901-1903 and 1906-1907, may have prompted Lyon & Healy to cut down on advertising costs for the expensive Washburn lines.

The famous 'Washburn babies', from an 1898 lithograph by artist Gaston de Herbert

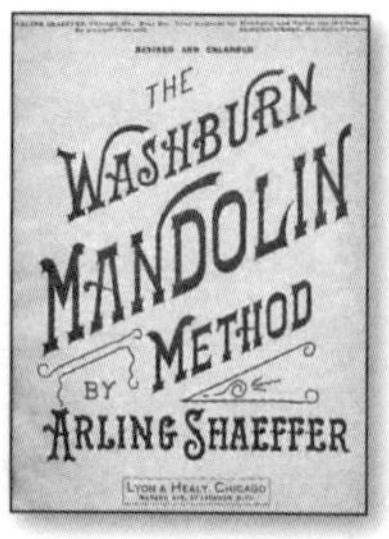

Arling Shaeffer, author of the Washburn guitar and mandolin tutors, was a well known guitar, mandolin and banjo teacher and performer in Chicago around the turn of the 20th century. He also briefly marketed a banjo under his own name, and is pictured here with a Style 303 Washburn showing the correct (at left) and the wrong way of holding the guitar - Keith Richards never saw this.

Patrick J. Healy died on April 3, 1905, shortly after his sixty-fifth birthday. He had actively managed the company for forty years and seen the small Washington Street store develop into a music industry giant that sold an unequaled assortment of merchandise to dealers and customers all over the world.[13] Among the later presidents of Lyon & Healy were two of his sons, Paul J. Healy (1911-1915) and Marquette A. Healy (1921-1927). During Paul Healy's presidency a new big fireproof factory was built at Fullerton and Crawford Avenues, which opened in 1914. But that was not all. Paul Healy wanted to create another monument to his father's outstanding business genius, and plans were made for a building of unprecedented luxury where the company's headquarters and sales rooms would be located. It was designed by Marshall and Fox, a well known architectural firm that was also responsible for Chicago's illustrious Drake Hotel. After Healy stepped down as president in 1915 the building activities were supervised by his younger brother Marquette, then the company's vice-president. The new Lyon & Healy Building, situated in downtown Chicago at the corner of Jackson Boulevard and Wabash Avenue, was completed and occupied in May 1916. A special booklet published for this occasion boasted of the lavish features of the stunning nine-story building, including its façade covered with pink granite and gray terra cotta, entrances finished in walnut, marble, gold leaf and white enamel, corridors adorned with Toanazzo marble wainscoting and marble floor tiles and walnut woodwork throughout.[14] In a concert hall situated on the first floor daily free concerts were performed and broadcasted. In the 1920s the building was also equipped with a professional recording studio. The structure has survived to the present day and has been used by DePaul University since the early 1980s.

The Fullerton or 'Healy Station' factory on a postcard from the mid 1910s. The Lyon & Healy truck was also featured in period catalogs from the Packard Motor Car Company of Detroit

Lyon & Healy's Wabash Avenue store and headquarters (1916)

2006

Lyon & Healy introduced a new dressed-down line of Washburn instruments around 1915. During the following years and after the beginning of the First World War the company managed to consolidate its leading position. The loss of a part of foreign sales and imports was compensated by large government orders from the U.S. Military. One hundred twenty-five employees served in the war, and all of them were welcomed back to their jobs upon their return from service.[15] During the 1920s the coming of the 'jazz age', aided by favorable economic conditions, caused an increased demand for banjos, drums and band instruments. The company quickly capitalized on this trend and actively promoted the popular instruments of the day in various ad

1918

13 Two of the honorary pallbearers at Healy's funeral were Charles H. Steinway, president of Steinway & Sons, and John C. Haynes, a former Ditson associate and president of the Boston-based John C. Haynes Co. (1861-1900), a musical instrument manufacturer mostly known for the Bay State, Wm. B .Tilton and Haynes Excelsior brand instruments.

14 *Everything Known in Music, a souvenir of the new home of the world's foremost music house* (Lyon & Healy, 1916).

15 Guy W. Bilsland, *Music Makers for the World,* in *Golden Rule Magazine*, March 1925 (reprint).

campaigns. Lyon & Healy's band instrument factory in LaPorte, Indiana, turned out large numbers of trumpets, horns and saxophones.[16] The newly designed Washburn instruments of 1922/3, which included an updated banjo line, were also moderately successful. A new stringed instrument factory was occupied in 1926.

In 1927 fifty-year old Raymond E. Durham became president of Lyon & Healy. Unlike all of his predecessors he had not been a longtime employee with the company. Durham, son in law of former company president Robert B. Gregory, had managed a number of businesses in Chicago before joining Lyon & Healy. He strongly believed that the company could increase its profits by catering to the fast growing suburban areas across the U.S. Durham's goal was to create a national chain of music stores bearing the company name, and to discontinue all of its manufacturing and wholesale activities except for the making of harps. This strategy led to the closing down of the Chicago and LaPorte factories in May 1928. A former warehouse right behind the 1889 Union Park factory provided accommodation for the company's harp division. The factory and headquarters of Lyon & Healy Harps, Inc. are still located at this site today.[17]

In May 1928 the machinery and all dies, jigs and patent rights for the Washburn instruments were sold to the J.R. Stewart Co., a Chicago based manufacturer of musical instruments. Stewart also acquired Lyon & Healy's new South Side factory at Rockwell and 22nd Streets.[18] Period publications stressed the fact that the features of the Washburn instrument lines would remain unchanged. It was agreed that Lyon & Healy would remain the exclusive distributor for the Washburn line, thus providing Stewart access to the company's unrivaled dealer network. Unfortunately for Stewart this was to be a short-lived association. Just a few months later, in August 1928, it was announced that Lyon & Healy had sold their wholesale small goods department to Tonk Bros. Co. of Chicago. Tonk, established

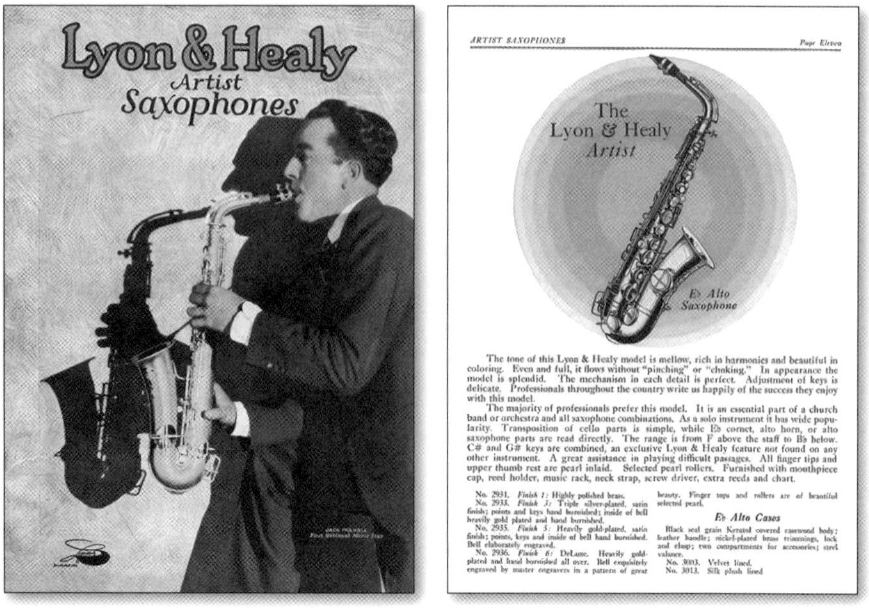

Saxophone catalog, 1926 (Glen Richards)

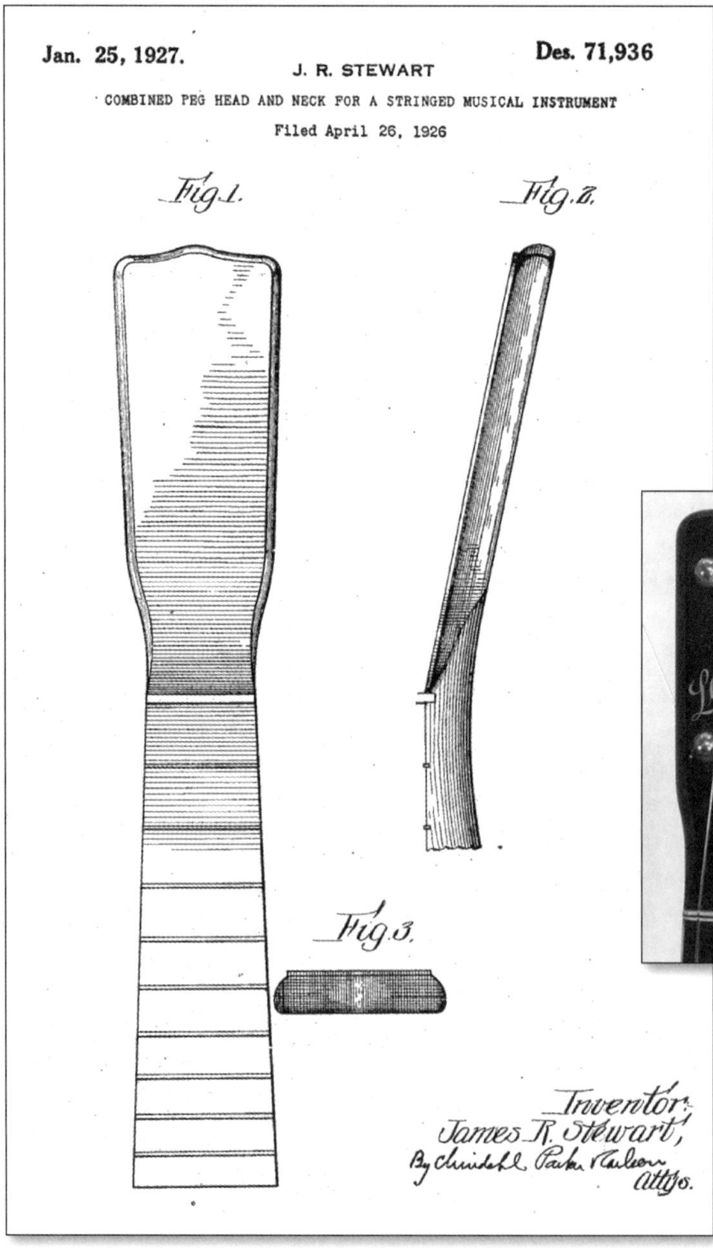

Patented headstock design of LeDomino uke by J.R. Stewart (Frank Ford)

16 The LaPorte factory, formerly named E.A. Couturier Ltd, had been acquired in 1923.
17 See chapter 6. After his Durham's death in 1952 one of his two sons, R. Gregory Durham, served as president of Lyon & Healy until his retirement in 1977.
18 Late 1920s publications announced that Stewart had acquired a new factory of 22,500 square feet at Rockwell and 22nd Streets, but did not mention that this was the former Lyon & Healy stringed instrument factory. Since the Rockwell factory was a three-story building of 60,000 square feet , Stewart may have only occupied the ground floor.

in 1893 and one of the company's major competitors in the wholesale music business, also took over the exclusive distribution rights for the Washburn line.

Then the Great Depression came, bringing tough times for Lyon & Healy. After 1929 annual sales declined about 20% for four years in a row until the mid 1930s, when business began to pick up slowly. The J.R. Stewart Co. was less fortunate. It fell victim to the profound economic downturn following Black Friday and went bankrupt in March 1930. At the ensuing receiver's sale Tonk Bros purchased the remaining stock and all trade names owned by Stewart. Around May 1930 the production of Washburns was taken over by the Regal Musical Instrument Co., with Tonk remaining the exclusive distributor for the various lines. This arrangement would continue throughout the 1930s. During the late thirties until around 1940 Gibson also manufactured small numbers of guitars and mandolins carrying the Washburn name for Tonk Bros, which was possibly prompted by the decision of Regal in 1938 to start selling instruments directly to dealers.[19]

Around the start of the Second World War Tonk Bros decided to discontinue the entire Washburn instrument line. The Washburn brand, which had stood for first class musical instruments since 1883, would not be resurrected until the early 1970s.[20] At that time a new line of Japanese-made guitars bearing the Washburn name emerged. The company that owned the trade name, Beckmen Musical Instruments, Inc., a Los Angeles based distributor, had no affiliation with any of the companies involved with the production of Washburns prior to 1940. The first new Washburn guitars were basically Martin knock-offs whose designs were in no way inspired by their prewar counterparts. A few Washburn models introduced during later years after the brand name was acquired the predecessor of the current owner, U.S. Music Corporation, incorporated some design features of the original Washburns. Though these instruments were more of a nod to the past than accurate reissues of prewar models, they kept part of the Lyon & Healy legacy alive.

Two designers: George Durkee and Walter Kirk

Many of the classic stringed instrument designs created between the 1880s and the 1920s that are now associated with Lyon & Healy were the brainchild of two of the company's chief designers, George B. Durkee and Walter I. Kirk.

George Durkee joined Lyon & Healy as factory superintendent in 1885, a few years after the firm's partners had decided to enter the field of instrument manufacturing. He had been a mechanical engineer for twenty five years and was responsible for creating the Washburn guitar, mandolin and banjo lines introduced between the late 1880s and the early 1910s. These included many eye-catching designs, such as the lavishly decorated 1896 guitar and mandolin styles, the groundbreaking Contra Bass Guitar, the unique lyre-shaped terz guitar and the presentation banjos of the early 1890s. More importantly, Durkee was the designer of the first Lyon & Healy harp, which incorporated a number of patented inventions and received wide international acclaim.

Durkee was a prodigious inventor whose instrument designs for Lyon & Healy received at least twenty patents relating to guitar, mandolin, banjo, harp, piano, drum, zither and violin construction between 1887 and 1896, even though some of his inventions were rather short-lived on the Lyon & Healy instrument

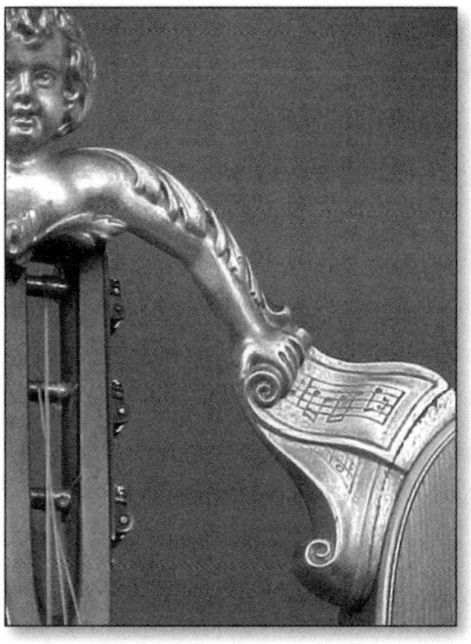

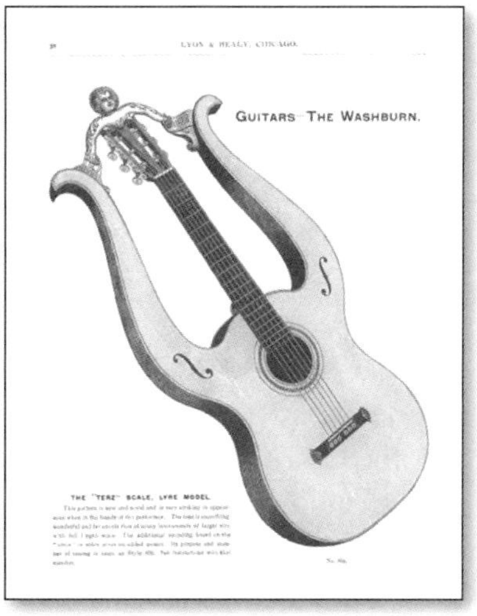

Two of George Durkee's creations: the Washburn Lyre Terz Guitar, and a Washburn Style 430 Presentation banjo (Frank Ford / Elderly)

19 *Wheeler*, p. 325.

20 A few cheap student guitars likely dating from the 1950s or 1960s era carrying the Washburn brand have turned up, possibly made by Regal, or the Harmony Co. The appointments of these instruments are not identical to prewar Washburn styles.

lines.[21] The guitar bridge that was referred to in the Lyon & Healy catalogs as "Durkee's patent" was a beautiful design but turned out to be fragile. The new cross bracing that was a feature of the 1889 Washburn mandolin line did not last long and was replaced by more traditional construction methods in 1896. The same happened to the disc-fitted rims introduced in 1892 on some models of the first Washburn banjo line. Durkee remained with Lyon & Healy until his death in 1913 at the age of 77, though it is not certain if he was still actively involved in the company's instrument designs during the last years of his life.

Walter Kirk (b 1867) began his career with the company in the early 1890s. He was likely trained by George Durkee and oversaw Lyon & Healy's harp and fretted instrument designs after Durkee's death. He designed the rather understated 1915 guitar and mandolin lines, which included the first flatback mandolins marketed by Lyon & Healy. Kirk's design genius combined technical improvements with original and elegant instrument shapes and designs. His masterpiece was the Lyon & Healy Style A mandolin, which he created around 1916. It featured a carved top and back and classy looks that were inspired by the violin, and is still considered a favored instrument by many of today's classical mandolinists and vintage instrument enthusiasts. Kirk was also responsible for the 1922/3 Washburn instrument line, which represented a refreshing departure from the earlier more traditional designs. The stylish 'smile' bridge, the raised soundhole ring and gold leaf designs were new and striking features of the new Washburn guitars and ukuleles. The 'donut' tone ring on the new open back banjos was not only extremely rigid but enhanced the sonic properties of the instruments as well –and it looked good, too! The last of Kirk's patent applications was submitted in 1923 for the successful Camp Uke, a cheap but serious musical instrument sold in large numbers by Lyon & Healy. It is not certain if Kirk, who was the author of at least thirty-four guitar, banjo, mandolin, piano, harp and ukulele patents during his association with Lyon & Healy,[22] was also behind the unusual 'Bell' and 'Shrine' instruments that made their appearance between the mid and late twenties.

Lyon & Healy Style A mandolin and Washburn Style A guitar, both designed by Walter Kirk (Kieron Seamons/Lowell Levinger, Players Vintage Instruments)

It is not certain who designed Lyon & Healy's instrument lines during the 1910-1915 period. Surprisingly, no patent applications for fretted musical instruments were filed by the company in the two

21 Apart from the 'Durkee bridge' for guitars (see page 2.3.2) and a hinged tailpiece for mandolins (3.3.2) Durkee's patents included among others the cross bracing for mandolins and the jig specially developed therefor (patent numbers 368,461 and 370,732, respectively), a banjo tailpiece (with co-inventor Charles N. Post, patent number 355,337), a banjo neck-adjustment construction that eliminated the need for a dowel stick (patent number 447,947), six patents regarding harp construction (patent numbers 437,917, 438,918, 437,919, 485,737, 509,022 and 538,038), mechanical tuning pegs for violins and other musical instruments (patent number 554,057) and an apparatus for forming violin case covers (patent number 370,731). He likely also invented the special banjo rim of the 1892 banjo line (see page 4.3.1).

22 Patents which list Kirk as inventor include among others the body, neck and pickguard shape and the tailpiece of the Style A mandolin (patent numbers D49,540, D52,661 and 1,301,059, respectively), a banjo tailpiece (patent number 1,367,526), improved banjo brackets (patent number 1,437,379), the 'donut' tone ring (patent number 1,575,212), a soundhole ring for guitars and ukuleles (patent number 1,559,108), the Camp Uke (patent number 1,757,577) and one of its earlier incarnations (patent number 1,750,843), and thirteen patents relating to harp construction (patent numbers 1,134,207, 1,153,232, 1,153,317, 1,167,504, 1,173,811, 1,220,430, 1,269,718, 1,295,759, 1,301,060, 1,301,061 1,301,062, 1,352,814, and 1,501,907).

decades between 1896 and 1916[23]. The only truly new Washburn line that was introduced during this era, the 1913 banjos with their 'patent truss' shell, was based on a five-year old patent of an inventor not affiliated with Lyon & Healy.[24] Amidst the cheaper instrument styles marketed by the company at this time were nonetheless intriguing new designs such as the Lakeside Jumbo, arguably the world's first real 'dreadnought' guitar, the College Line 'Monster Bass' guitar, twelve-string guitars with one or two necks, etc.[25] So who created these instruments? Some of the less expensive guitars and mandolins sold by the company were identical to instruments offered or made by the Regal Musical Instrument Co.[26] Did Lyon & Healy outsource part of its manufacturing activities to Regal? By all accounts there had been close ties between the two companies since the early 1900s. After the Regal Manufacturing Co. went bankrupt in 1904, Lyon & Healy bought the Regal trade name plus a large number of instruments in different stages of completion as well as parts and raw materials.[27] It is likely that Lyon & Healy used these for their new College Line brand instruments that were introduced in 1905 and catalogued until 1908, in which year the Regal Musical Instrument Co. of Chicago was incorporated. That Lyon & Healy kept a business interest in the new company can be derived from the fact that the 'Regal' trademark, registered in November 1906 for use with guitars and mandolins, was not transferred to the Regal Musical Instrument Co. until 1924.[28]

In a 1916 publication the activities of the new Fullerton factory were described as "absorbing the entire output of other factories operated according to the specifications of Lyon & Healy."[29] This statement confirms that other manufacturers had in fact been making instruments for Lyon & Healy, probably after the Union Park factory had reached its maximum production capacity during the early 1900s. It also seems to imply that these instruments were still being designed by Lyon & Healy. The cosmetic features of most guitars, mandolins and banjos that the company offered between 1910

40 LYON & HEALY, CHICAGO
AMERICAN MODEL MANDO
STYLE NO. G2325

Regal 'reverse scroll' mandolin, 1920s. This popular and cheap model was also marketed by Lyon & Healy under the "Guydyu" brand (see detail photo and 1921 catalog page). The patent notice on the label suggests that Lyon & Healy created this typical instrument, but the 1914 patent documentation shows that it was designed by Frank Kordick, president of the Regal Musical Instrument Co. to whom the patent was granted. This also evidences the close ties between the two Chicago instrument makers (Don Kingery, Frank Ford)

23 One patent was filed in 1905 by John Brandt and assigned to Lyon & Healy for a peculiar violin-shaped mandolin, but this was marketed under the 'Brandt' name, not under any of Lyon & Healy's brands.
24 See 4.3.1.
25 See 2.3.4.
26 This also applies to the Washburn flatback mandolin styles introduced in 1915.
27 *Teagle*, p. 36/7. The Regal Mfg Co. (1901-1904) was a successor to the original maker of the Regal brand instruments, Wulschner & Son Co. of Indianapolis.
28 See U.S. trademark registration numbers 51,372 (1906) and 246,164 (1929). Lyon & Healy were not among the subscribers for the stock of the Regal Musical Instrument Co.
29 See note 14.

and 1915, including the Washburn lines of 1910 and the cheaper Lyon & Healy guitars, mandolins and banjos of this period are much reminiscent of George Durkee's earlier designs. These may well have been among the last instruments that he created for the company.

The innovative tradition that was characteristic of many instruments designed and made by Lyon & Healy came to an end with the closing down of the Fullerton Factory and the sale of the Washburn name and manufacturing rights in 1928. The new Washburn models introduced in and after the mid 1930s were designed by Regal, although the Gibson-made Washburn styles of this era were not identical to their Regal counterparts. The models from this era were quality instruments as before, but their construction, features and looks followed existing trends and were not as distinctive or innovative as many of the pre 1930s Washburns.

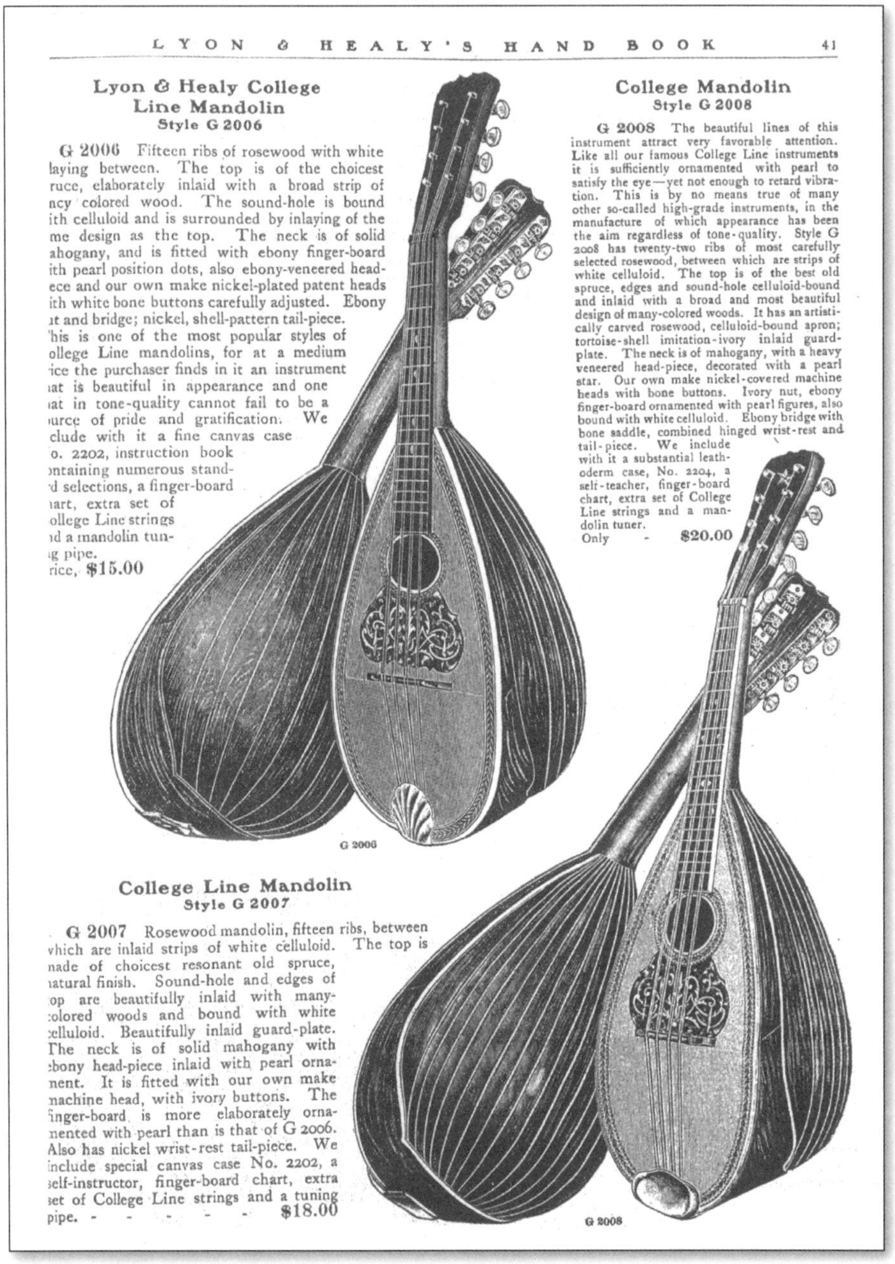

LYON & HEALY'S HAND BOOK 41

Lyon & Healy College Line Mandolin
Style G 2006

G 2006 Fifteen ribs of rosewood with white laying between. The top is of the choicest ruce, elaborately inlaid with a broad strip of ncy colored wood. The sound-hole is bound ith celluloid and is surrounded by inlaying of the me design as the top. The neck is of solid ahogany, and is fitted with ebony finger-board ith pearl position dots, also ebony-veneered head-ece and our own make nickel-plated patent heads ith white bone buttons carefully adjusted. Ebony it and bridge; nickel, shell-pattern tail-piece. 'his is one of the most popular styles of ollege Line mandolins, for at a medium ice the purchaser finds in it an instrument iat is beautiful in appearance and one iat in tone-quality cannot fail to be a iurce of pride and gratification. We clude with it a fine canvas case o. 2202, instruction book ontaining numerous stand-d selections, a finger-board iart, extra set of ollege Line strings id a mandolin tun-ig pipe.
rice, **$15.00**

College Mandolin
Style G 2008

G 2008 The beautiful lines of this instrument attract very favorable attention. Like all our famous College Line instruments it is sufficiently ornamented with pearl to satisfy the eye—yet not enough to retard vibration. This is by no means true of many other so-called high-grade instruments, in the manufacture of which appearance has been the aim regardless of tone-quality. Style G 2008 has twenty-two ribs of most carefully selected rosewood, between which are strips of white celluloid. The top is of the best old spruce, edges and sound-hole celluloid-bound and inlaid with a broad and most beautiful design of many-colored woods. It has an artistically carved rosewood, celluloid-bound apron; tortoise-shell imitation-ivory inlaid guard-plate. The neck is of mahogany, with a heavy veneered head-piece, decorated with a pearl star. Our own make nickel-covered machine heads with bone buttons. Ivory nut, ebony finger-board ornamented with pearl figures, also bound with white celluloid. Ebony bridge with bone saddle, combined hinged wrist-rest and tail-piece. We include with it a substantial leatherderm case, No. 2204, a self-teacher, finger-board chart, extra set of College Line strings and a mandolin tuner.
Only - **$20.00**

G 2006

College Line Mandolin
Style G 2007

G 2007 Rosewood mandolin, fifteen ribs, between vhich are inlaid strips of white celluloid. The top is nade of choicest resonant old spruce, iatural finish. Sound-hole and edges of op are beautifully inlaid with many-colored woods and bound with white celluloid. Beautifully inlaid guard-plate. The neck is of solid mahogany with ebony head-piece inlaid with pearl orna-nent. It is fitted with our own make nachine head, with ivory buttons. The inger-board is more elaborately orna-nented with pearl than is that of G 2006. Also has nickel wrist-rest tail-piece. We include special canvas case No. 2202, a self-instructor, finger-board chart, extra set of College Line strings and a tuning pipe. - - - - - **$18.00**

G 2008

College Line mandolins, 1905 catalog

Regal guitar (early 1920s). The marquetry, subtle fingerboard binding and snowflake inlay patterns on this instrument are very similar to the top of the line Washburns of this period (Retrofret.com)

The Washburn 'one price system'

1915 ad for the Gibson 'teacher-agent' plan. Gibson was an equal opportunity employer in the early 1900s! (Frank Ford)

Lyon & Healy were determined to take good care in promoting and protecting their new premium instrument brand. In doing so the company relied on its extensive dealer network. In a two-page preface to the 1903 merchandise catalog entitled "a word in regard to the mail order business", Lyon & Healy emphasized that the company would stick to its existing policy of not selling directly to customers by mail order, and of referring all inquiries for instrument sales except band instruments back to local dealers. In the closing paragraph this business adage was phrased as follows: "In a word we consider our success and the success of the local dealer identical". Of course this arrangement did not prevent Lyon & Healy from selling large numbers of instruments directly to customers through the company stores in downtown Chicago. In order to prevent the prestigious Washburn lines from being sold at bargain prices, a standard sales contract for these instruments was submitted to dealers since the late 1880s. Every dealer was required to sign the agreement prior to the delivery of Washburn instruments. It stipulated minimum retail prices for all available styles, and also forbid dealers to throw in free articles such as cases and books with the purchase of Washburns. According to the company this policy effectively provided the dealers with means to "control the prices and protect the trade" and also safeguarded them from competition of "some shortsighted rival with a weakness for doing business for nothing" as the period merchandise catalogs tersely put it. The only discount allowed with regard to the minimum retail prices was for sales to professional teachers, up to a maximum of 20%. The Washburn Premium Plan was another sales incentive specially directed at teachers and introduced by Lyon & Healy during the 1890s. The program awarded free instruments as a bonus to teachers for ordering Washburns for their pupils through local dealers. Likely inspired by the approach of its senior Chicago rival, Gibson also recognized the key role of the teacher in selling instruments and took Lyon & Healy's initiative a step further with its 'teacher-agent' plan of the early 1900s, which awarded the exclusive right to sell Gibsons to music teachers recruited by the company for this purpose.

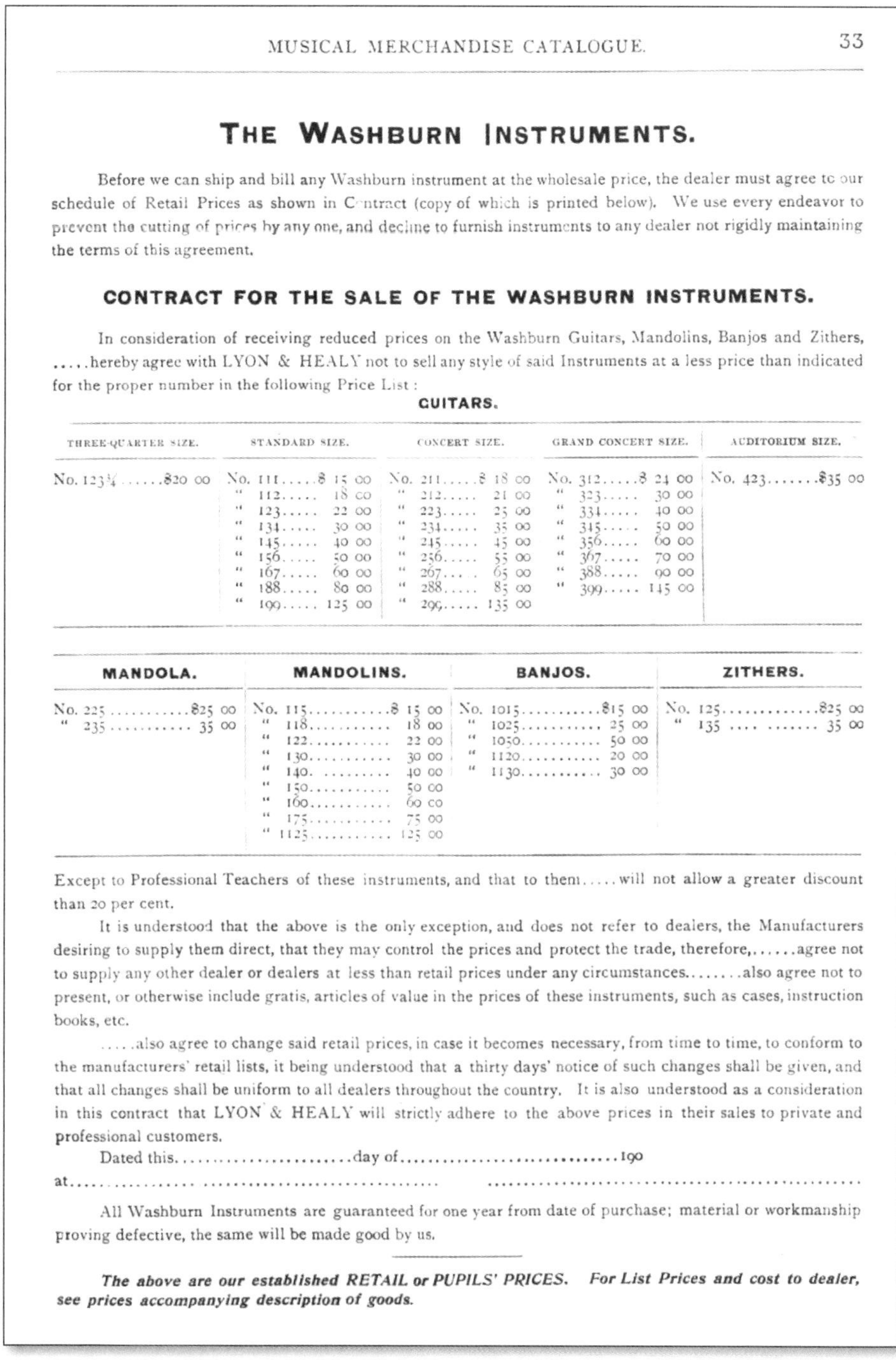

MUSICAL MERCHANDISE CATALOGUE. 33

THE WASHBURN INSTRUMENTS.

Before we can ship and bill any Washburn instrument at the wholesale price, the dealer must agree to our schedule of Retail Prices as shown in Contract (copy of which is printed below). We use every endeavor to prevent the cutting of prices by any one, and decline to furnish instruments to any dealer not rigidly maintaining the terms of this agreement.

CONTRACT FOR THE SALE OF THE WASHBURN INSTRUMENTS.

In consideration of receiving reduced prices on the Washburn Guitars, Mandolins, Banjos and Zithers, ...hereby agree with LYON & HEALY not to sell any style of said Instruments at a less price than indicated for the proper number in the following Price List:

GUITARS.

THREE-QUARTER SIZE.	STANDARD SIZE.	CONCERT SIZE.	GRAND CONCERT SIZE.	AUDITORIUM SIZE.
No. 123¾......$20 00	No. 111.....$ 15 00	No. 211.....$ 18 00	No. 312.....$ 24 00	No. 423.......$35 00
	" 112..... 18 00	" 212..... 21 00	" 323..... 30 00	
	" 123..... 22 00	" 223..... 25 00	" 334..... 40 00	
	" 134..... 30 00	" 234..... 35 00	" 345..... 50 00	
	" 145..... 40 00	" 245..... 45 00	" 356..... 60 00	
	" 156..... 50 00	" 256..... 55 00	" 367..... 70 00	
	" 167..... 60 00	" 267..... 65 00	" 388..... 90 00	
	" 188..... 80 00	" 288..... 85 00	" 399..... 145 00	
	" 199..... 125 00	" 299..... 135 00		

MANDOLA.	MANDOLINS.	BANJOS.	ZITHERS.
No. 225...........$25 00	No. 115..........$ 15 00	No. 1015..........$15 00	No. 125............$25 00
" 235........... 35 00	" 118.......... 18 00	" 1025.......... 25 00	" 135 .... 35 00
	" 122.......... 22 00	" 1050.......... 50 00	
	" 130.......... 30 00	" 1120.......... 20 00	
	" 140. .... 40 00	" 1130.......... 30 00	
	" 150.......... 50 00		
	" 160.......... 60 00		
	" 175.......... 75 00		
	" 1125.......... 125 00		

Except to Professional Teachers of these instruments, and that to them.....will not allow a greater discount than 20 per cent.

It is understood that the above is the only exception, and does not refer to dealers, the Manufacturers desiring to supply them direct, that they may control the prices and protect the trade, therefore,......agree not to supply any other dealer or dealers at less than retail prices under any circumstances........also agree not to present, or otherwise include gratis, articles of value in the prices of these instruments, such as cases, instruction books, etc.

.....also agree to change said retail prices, in case it becomes necessary, from time to time, to conform to the manufacturers' retail lists, it being understood that a thirty days' notice of such changes shall be given, and that all changes shall be uniform to all dealers throughout the country. It is also understood as a consideration in this contract that LYON & HEALY will strictly adhere to the above prices in their sales to private and professional customers.

Dated this.......................day of..............................190

at............... ....

All Washburn Instruments are guaranteed for one year from date of purchase; material or workmanship proving defective, the same will be made good by us.

The above are our established RETAIL or PUPILS' PRICES. For List Prices and cost to dealer, see prices accompanying description of goods.

Washburn dealer contract, early 1900s

CHAPTER TWO

Guitars

"It was the most important day in my life, the day the Lord put something in my hands so I could take care of myself."

(Reverend Gary Davis, upon being presented with an $18 Washburn guitar for his eighth birthday)

Carl Sandburg with a style 5271 'Bell' guitar (NPS Photograph, Courtesy of Carl Sandburg House, NHS, Flat Rock, NC)

2.1 Dating of Washburn guitars

The dating of prewar Washburn instruments is facilitated by the serial numbers that were factory stamped inside most instruments. All of the fretted instrument types manufactured by Lyon & Healy were separately numbered. The numbering systems used by Lyon & Healy and by Tonk Bros for their various instrument lines are not continuous, but were restarted a few times throughout their production period. This means that besides the serial number other features –such as labels and stamps– need to be examined in order to establish the approximate year of manufacture of a particular instrument. That said, the following guidelines might prove helpful in attempting the task of dating a Washburn guitar.

If there is a label inside the instrument, check under "Guitar labels" during which period it was used. Then look for the serial number of the instrument and match it with the serial number ranges of this period under "General appointments" and "Serial numbers and estimated production totals" (chapter 7). If there is no label, the manufacturing period can be determined on the basis of the stamps inside the guitar by comparing these to the data listed under "Guitar stamps" and "General appointments". If there is neither a serial number nor a label, the instrument may be a very early guitar. Lastly, it is advisable to verify if the various instrument parts match the descriptions stated under "Guitar styles" and "Construction / general remarks". Many old instruments have been repaired or modified and have non-original parts such as replacement bridges and fingerboards, added tailpieces, pickguards etc.

When identifying Washburn guitars on the basis of the style descriptions listed below it should be noted that custom orders for instruments were taken as early as the late 1880s, as evidenced by the 1889 Washburn catalog which offered to supply instruments inlaid with "special designs, monograms, or sketched figures of any nature". All Washburn instruments should either have a Washburn logo or name stamp, a Washburn label, or both.[30] Nonetheless many old parlor guitars and mandolins that do not have a brand or maker's stamp inside are incorrectly advertised by dealers or private sellers as Washburns.

In general, Washburn instruments manufactured around the time of the introduction of new lines and shortly thereafter sometimes show characteristics of both old and new styles. These hybrids are obviously not custom ordered models but were partly or wholly constructed from leftover parts, and usually have a serial number. To add to the confusion these instruments sometimes received a style stamp indicating a standard catalog model, or a unique style number not found in any of the catalogs. It is also not unusual to find instruments sold as 'new old stock' sometime after their respective styles were dropped from the catalog. This is evident from the 'newer' serial numbers that were found on these instruments. Lastly, the specifications of and materials used for the instruments made in the mid to late 1910s may vary from year to year due to unstable supplies during the wartime years.

30 The most expensive guitars of the 1922-1925 line did not have a 'Washburn' stamp, but are identifiable by an oval metal logo with the Washburn name attached to the back of the headstock (see 2.4.1)

2.2 Guitar labels

Mid to late 1896 until 1905:
Small round white paper warranty label with black lettering stating "the material and workmanship of this Washburn instrument / No.____ / fully guaranteed for the term of one year from the date of original purchase provided this label is not mutilated", serial number of instrument is handwritten on label.

1896-1905 warranty label (Florence Keel)

1903 until 1915:
Oval white and black (around 1906-1907 changed to white, black and red) label stating "The Washburn, Best in The World, Highest awards at World's Columbian Exposition, Chicago 1893, Gold Medal and Diploma of Honor, Antwerp 1894 / The material and workmanship of this Washburn instrument, fully guaranteed for the term of one year from date of original purchase provided this label is not mutilated".

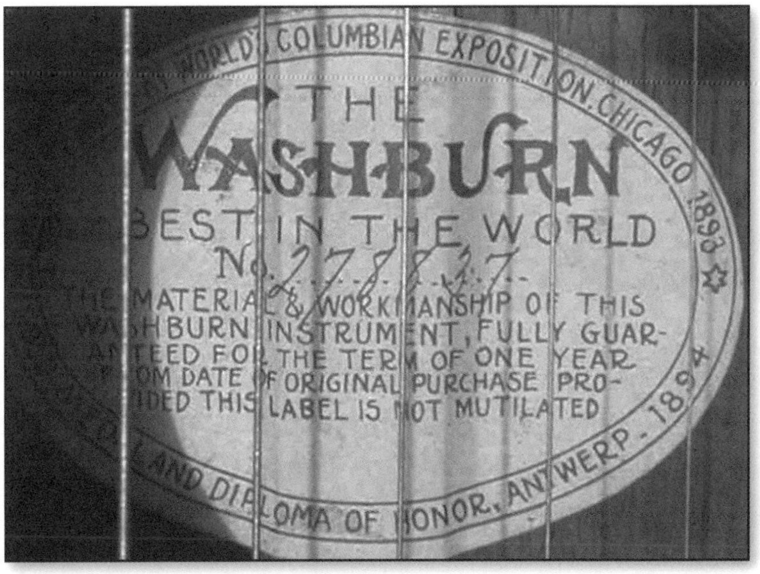

Approximately 1903-1906/7 (Randy Peterson)

1915 until 1923:
Oval label, crown shaped at top (white, black and red) stating "No. ____ Style ____ / Material and workmanship fully guaranteed for one year from date of original purchase providing this label has not been mutilated / Model 1915 / Highest award World's Columbian Exposition Chicago - 1893 - Gold Medal and Diploma Antwerp - 1894 ", number and style designations are ink stamped or handwritten on label.

1923 until 1925:
Oval white, black and red label, crown shaped at top, stating "No. __ Style __ / Material and workmanship fully guaranteed for one year from date of original purchase providing this label has not been mutilated / Model 1923-24", number and style designations are ink stamped or handwritten on label.

1925 until 1928:
Oval light yellow label w text "Made and guaranteed by / (Lyon & Healy signature logo) / Worlds largest music house / Chicago, USA / WASHBURN / No ___ Style" ____, number and style designations are ink stamped or handwritten on label.

1934/5 until 1940:
Oval white/light yellow label stating "Genuine Washburn, Style No.____ Serial No.____ / Made of choicest materials by workmen of exceptional skill, knowledge and experience / Tonk Bros. Co. Chicago / Exclusive Distributors (changed around 1936 to "Exclusive Wholesale Distributors"), number and style designations are typewritten or ink stamped on label.

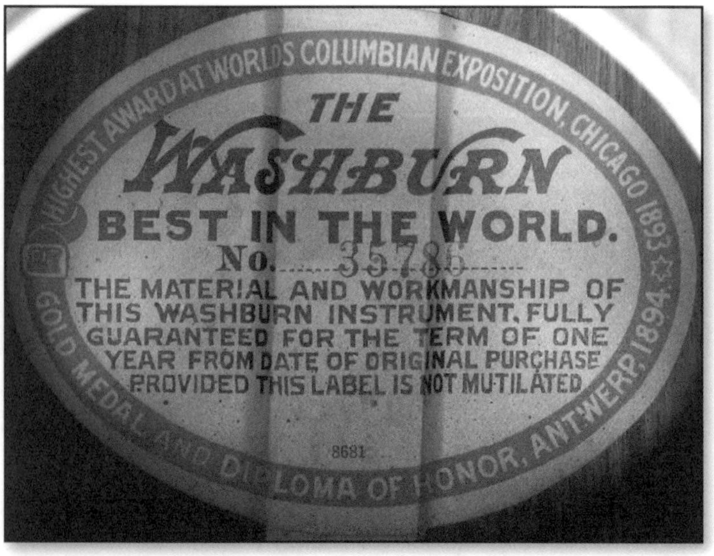

1906/7-1915 (Ryan Maloney)

1915-1922 (Bid Brothers)

1925-1926/7 (Lawrence Foster)

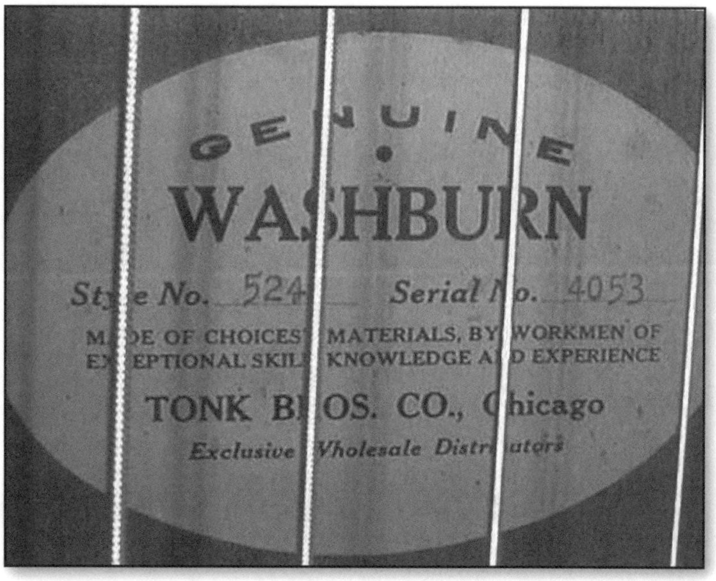

1934/5-1940 - the earlier labels state "Exclusive Distributors
(Mark Demaray)

2.2.2 Guitar stamps

1883/4-1922:
Branded Washburn logo stamp inside instrument picturing a belt encircling a guitar with name "George Washburn" on belt.

1886/7-1905:
Branded stamp inside instrument stating "NEW MODEL".

Mid to late 1896:
Branded stamp inside instrument stating "1896 STYLE".

Late 1896-1905:
Branded stamp inside instrument stating "1897 STYLE".

1922-1928/9:
Branded stamp inside instrument stating "Lyon & Healy / Makers / Chicago / USA".

1922-1925 (most guitars):
Impressed stamp on back of headstock stating "STYLE _", indicating style of instrument (sometimes preceded by an "X", which stands for "X-bracing"). On certain instruments only the letter of the style (e.g. "G") is stamped, not the word "style".

1922-1930 (some guitar styles):
Impressed stamp on back of headstock stating "WASHBURN".

1922-1928 (some guitars):
Impressed stamp on back or upper end of headstock stating "PAT APL'D FOR".

1928/9-1934/5, and during late 1930s:
Branded stamp inside instrument stating "genuine / WASHBURN / Tonk Bros. Co. / Chicago / sole distributors".

1883/4-1886/7

1886/7 -1896 - added "new model" stamp

1896-1905. A stamp stating "1896 style" was used on guitars for a few months during 1896.

2.3 General appointments

1883/4-1889:
A Washburn logo picturing a belt encircling a guitar is branded on the center strip. Guitars have no fingerboard inlays or position markers and a small neck heel, and sometimes have initials stamped on the neck block (e.g. AD, OO, VD). A more slender upper and lower bout (8″ instead of 8 ¾″ and 12″ instead of 12 ½″) and a rosewood bridge are typical for some of the earliest standard sized guitars. Around 1887 (or earlier) the words 'new model' are branded on the center strip next to the Washburn logo and consecutive serial numbers starting at 1 are ink stamped on the neck block. Between 1885 and 1887 some guitar styles are available with a headstock sporting mechanical friction peg tuners.

1889-1896:
All standard guitar styles from 1889 until 1920 have slotted headstocks with Brazilian rosewood or ebony overlay, Brazilian rosewood backs and sides and ebony fingerboards and bridges, except for the fanciest styles (Style 188 [1896-1905], Styles 150 and 175 [1905-1915]) which came with a pearl fingerboard, and the lower end Style 1115 (1915-1922) which had a rosewood fingerboard. All guitars have Spanish cedar necks and pearl position markers, with the possible exception of some of the Contra Bass Guitars (Style 503, 1889-1892) and two terz scale guitars (Styles 802 and 804, 1892-1896) which are pictured in the catalogs with a plain ebony fingerboard without position markers.[31] Around the start of 1889 the ink stamped serial numbers are in the low 10,000s range, around mid to late 1896 numbers are in the high 90,000s.

Mid to late 1896-1905:
The Washburn belt/guitar logo plus the words '1896 style' (around 1897 changed to '1897 style') and 'new model' are branded on the center strip. Numbering continues from the low 100,000s (1897) up to the 270,000s (1905), ink stamped on the neck block and also handwritten on a small round warranty label inside the instrument. From 1896-7 until 1905 the style and serial numbers are often also stamped in the wood on the upper end of the headstock. Starting around the 235,000s number range serial numbers are also handwritten on a larger oval white and black label stating 'Washburn, Best In The World' inside the instrument.

1905-1907:
Serial numbers continue from the mid 270,000s (1905) to the 316,000s (around 1907) and are ink stamped on the neck block and handwritten on an oval white and black label inside the instrument (changed to white, black and red starting around the 300,000s number range) stating 'Washburn, Best In The World'. The small round warranty label and the branded stamps '1897 style' and 'new model' (1896-1905) are discontinued. The Washburn logo is branded on the center strip. Around 1907 serial numbers reach the 316,000s.

1907-1915:
Serial numbers start again around 1907 with 1 running into the 20,000s (around 1910) and from the 20,000s up to the 36,800s (around 1915), ink stamped on the neck block and handwritten on a white/black/red label stating 'Washburn, Best In The World' inside the instrument. Serial numbers in the 1-35,000s range are preceded by "A or A-".

1915–1922:
Numbering runs from the 36,800s (around 1915) to the low 42,000s (around 1920) and continues into the high 44,000s / low 45,000s (around 1922), serial numbers are ink stamped on the neck block. Serial and style numbers are also ink stamped or handwritten and on a white, black and red Washburn label inside the instrument stating '1915 model', oval shaped with a crown on top. The Washburn logo is branded on the center strip. The A- prefix for serial numbers on the label is dropped in or shortly before 1915.

---

31 Some photos of lyre terz guitars show a fingerboard with dot inlays at the 5th, 7th and 9th fret, and the sole Contra Bass Guitar that was reported has 5th, 7th and 10th fret fingerboard inlays.

1922-1925:

Serial numbers start again with 1. Between 1922 and 1926-7 batch numbers are also stamped in instruments. The branded Washburn belt/guitar logo is discontinued in 1922. Styles A-E (1922-1925) do not have a label and are stamped inside the body "Lyon & Healy, Makers, Chicago, USA", and usually have a letter indicating the style stamped in the back of the headstock. Between 1923 and 1925 Styles F and G have a white, black and red Washburn label stating '1923-24 model', oval shaped with a crown on top, with ink stamped serial numbers in the 45,000-47,000 range. Many guitars made between 1922 and 1925 have a number stamped in the wood on the back of the headstock that represents the serial number, and a different inked serial number on the neck block indicating the batch number.[32]

1925-1930:

Starting around 1925 guitars have a yellow oval label stating "Made and guaranteed by" / "Worlds largest music house" / "Chicago USA", "WASHBURN", "No" (likely indicating the batch number!) and "Style" (indicating model designation), with another set of digits (likely indicating the serial number) stamped on the neck block. After mid 1928, when the Washburn instrument manufacturing facility was sold to the J.R. Stewart Co., the yellow Washburn label and the "Lyon & Healey, Makers" stamp are discontinued. After late 1928 or early 1929 guitars no longer have a label inside but are branded on the center strip "Genuine WASHBURN Tonk Bros. Co. Chicago Sole Distributors". Between around 1926-7 and 1930 the style number (52XX) is ink stamped on the neck block (until 1928 or later often preceded by "1., 2., 3. or 6."). Batch numbers (9,000s up to the high 14,000s range) are impressed in the back of the headstock, while serial numbers are no longer stamped in the instruments.

1930-mid 1934:

From 1930 onwards Washburn guitars and mandolins share the same numbering sequence. Serial numbers start again with 1 into the low 2,000s. Guitars have no label, and batch numbers are not stamped on the instruments. Usually the style number (52XX) is printed on the neck block. Serial numbers are stamped in the back of the headstock and sometimes also inked on the neck block together with the style number. The center strip is usually branded "genuine Washburn Tonk Bros. Co Chicago sole distributors" (on some guitars this text is branded on a diamond shaped piece of wood inlaid in the center strip, while some guitars do not have a stamp).

Mid 1934-1940:

Serial numbers start again with 1 into the low 7,000s, ink stamped on a white/yellow oval label stating "Genuine Washburn, Style No.___ Serial No.___, made of choicest materials by workmen of exceptional skill, knowledge and experience, Tonk Bros. Co. Chicago, Exclusive Distributors (in 1936 changed to: "Exclusive Wholesale Distributors")", while the center strip is usually branded "genuine Washburn Tonk Bros. Co Chicago sole distributors". Serial and style numbers are often both printed on the neck block, sometimes the neck block does not contain any numbers. Some of the Gibson-made Washburns (1938-1940) have a factory order number (FON) inked on the neck block consisting of a batch number followed by a letter (D stands for 1938, E for 1939 etc.), and another set of digits indicating the number of the instrument within the specific batch.

32 This is evidenced by instruments bearing the same neck block number, such as three Style A guitars with respective headstock numbers #1297, #1298 and #1301, and the same number (7356) on the neck block. This would also mean that one batch consisted of at least five instruments, but possibly many more. Some of Gibson's batches in the 1920s contained close to 200 instruments.

2.4 Construction / general remarks

The Washburn guitar line appeared for the first time in an 1884 Lyon & Healy merchandise catalog.[33] Eight styles were available, all with rosewood back and sides. The sizes of the guitars were described as 'Large', 'Extra Large' and 'Extra Large Concert'. The 'Large' model with its 12" lower bout was comparable to a Size 2 Martin, but had a smaller upper bout (8" vs. 8 ½"). The earliest Washburns are generally characterized by a somewhat cruder look and show more variation in their individual parts, measurements and workmanship compared with the instruments made after the mid 1880s. New or revised lines were launched in 1889, 1896-7, 1905, 1910, 1915, 1920, 1922,[34] 1925, 1928, 1934/5, 1937 and 1939.

Lyon & Healy had already sold many guitars before the introduction of their Washburn line. Their 1880 merchandise catalog listed no less than twenty-six available guitar styles priced between $4 and $72. Six of these guitars were blatantly described as "Copy of Martin". Ironically, Lyon & Healy would soon share the same fate as Martin. The 1889 Washburn catalog warned the public against a "mushroom growth of would be imitators" that had sprung up due to the "wonderful popularity of the Washburn".

Washburn guitar in Lyon & Healy's 1885 'Musical Holiday Goods' catalog. The neck of the pictured instrument has 20 frets, a feature that would not be introduced on the Washburn guitar line until 1930

The manufacturer of these pre-Washburn guitar lines was not identified in the 1880 catalog. The company usually emphasized in its sales and promotion materials which instruments or other products were 'own make'. Since Lyon & Healy did not possess their own instrument factory until the early 1880s, the guitars listed in the catalogs that predated the opening of the factory were manufactured by other makers. These instruments were most likely imports from the large manufacturing community of Markneukirchen, Germany, which at the time churned out scores of copies of the products of well-known makers, including Martin.[35]

In the early 1870s Lyon & Healy had been one of the largest accounts of C.F. Martin & Co. until a falling out over a 40% standard discount requested by Lyon & Healy soured relations between the companies. The rift with Martin may have been one of the reasons for the Chicago music house to develop its own line of premium guitars that could compete with Martin's products.[36] A few decades later Lyon & Healy would offer Martin guitars to the public in their merchandise catalogs.

33 The original 1887 trademark application for the "Washburn' brand name stated that it had been in use since November 1883.
34 No 1922 Lyon & Healy or Washburn catalogs were available to verify this assumption, which is based on the 1921 patent applications filed for certain guitar and ukulele features introduced on the new lines.
35 Philip F. Gura, *C.F. Martin and His Guitars*, 1796-1873 p. 178. For decades Lyon & Healy' had a warehouse at Markneukirchen.
36 See previous note, p. 180, with citations of the correspondence between the two companies. After the disagreement with Martin Lyon & Healy continued to order guitars from the Nazareth guitar maker.

CATALOGUE OF MUSICAL MERCHANDISE. 19

SMALL GUITARS WITH ORDINARY PATENT HEADS.

No.		Each.
9	**One-Half Size** — Dark red color, inlaid purfling around sound hole and edges, varnished top, good quality and finish	$6 50
11	**Three-Quarter Size** — Dark red color, inlaid purfling around sound hole and edges, varnished top, good quality and finish	7 25

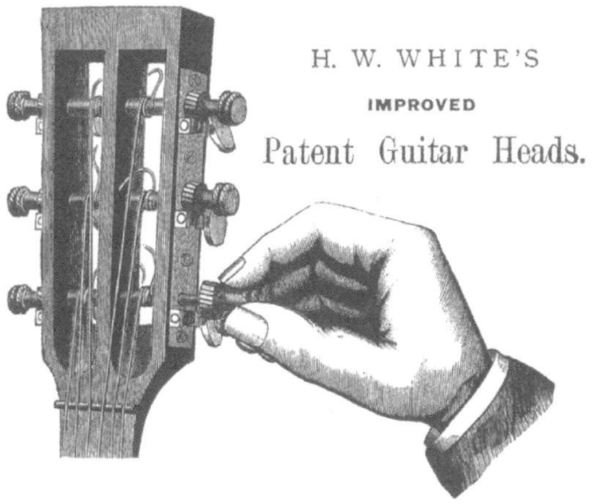

The following advantages will be apparent to the dealer as well as to every guitar player in the use of **White's Improved Patent Heads.**

When the string is first inserted, the head-pin, to which the cog-wheel is attached, is so arranged that the latter can be drawn out beyond the threads of the screw (as seen by above illustration), thus giving the player the advantage of as quickly winding the string as upon a violin peg. After pushing back the head-pin, which carries the cog-wheel back to its connection with the screw, he has but to give one or two turns to the ivory button to find the new string perfectly in tune, thus avoiding the delay and annoyance always experienced in the use of the ordinary kind of heads when putting on new strings or tuning. It being the only improvement ever made in Guitar Patent Heads, and meeting a long felt want by the players of this instrument, it must commend itself highly to the music trade. With the exception of the cheaper grades, all of our Guitars are furnished with **White's Improved Heads,** and the patent being owned and controlled exclusively by us, the instruments and heads can only be obtained through our establishment. Prices and descriptions will be found on following pages.

Extra heads can be supplied for any style of Guitar. See page 96.

20 CATALOGUE OF MUSICAL MERCHANDISE.

GUITARS WITH H. W. WHITE'S IMPROVED PATENT HEADS.

No. 38. No. 507.

No.		Each.
100	**Maple** — Fine Imitation of Rosewood, light colored edges, colored wood inlaying around sound hole, finely finished	$10 00
38	" Fine Imitation of Rosewood, light colored edges, Pearl and Jet ornamented sound hole, finely finished	12 00
43	" Dark red color, black and white cord rimmed edges, Pearl and Jet ornamented sound hole, finely finished	12 00
93	" Fine Imitation of Rosewood, light colored edges, Pearl and Jet ornamented sound hole, "Star Pattern," finely finished	16 00
166	" Silver color, *concert size*, Rosewood bound edges, fancy inlaid purfling around sound hole and edges, highly polished and finished	23 00
98	**Rosewood Veneered** — White bound and inlaid purfled edges, variegated wood inlaying around sound hole, finely finished	13 20
108	" " White bound edges, variegated wood inlaying around sound hole and edges, finely finished	16 50
109	" " Inlaid purfling around sound hole and edges, *plain model, highly polished and finished*	18 00
51	**Solid Rosewood** — Copy of Martin, fancy inlaid purfled edges, variegated wood inlaying around sound hole, highly polished and finished	20 00
484	" " Copy of Martin, *large size*, inlaid purfled edges and sound hole, *plain model, highly polished and finished*	24 00
490	" " Copy of Martin, *large size*, variegated wood inlaying around sound hole and edges, highly polished and finished	24 50

Pages from an 1880 catalog, showing a part of Lyon & Healy's guitar line. The more expensive guitars – likely imports from Germany – sported H.W. White's nifty heads that allowed for speedy tuning (patent # 155,352)

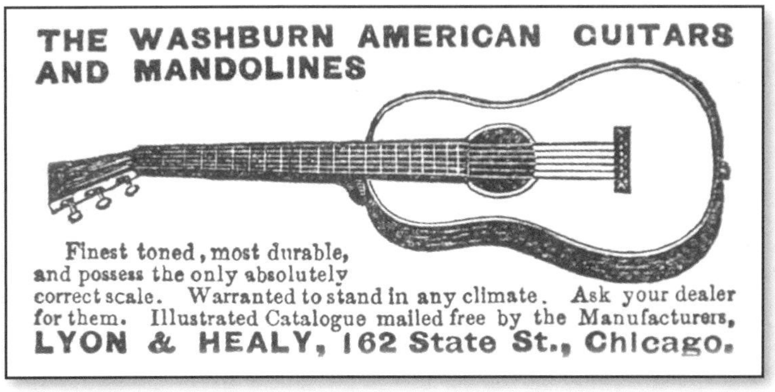

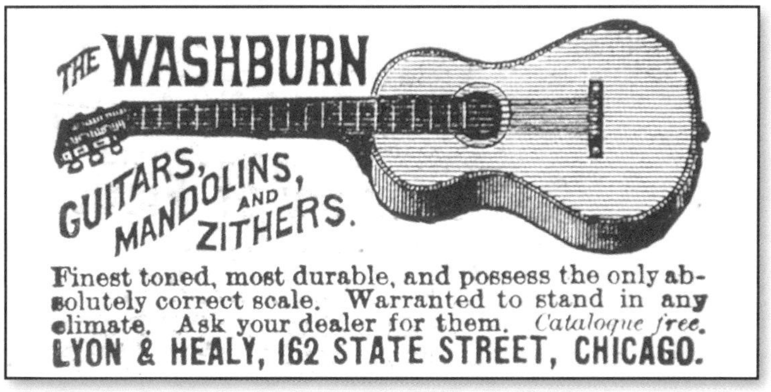

Two early advertisements for Washburn guitars (April 1887 and July 1888)

Different animals: the tenor guitar and the octo-chorda

Two entirely new guitar variants that were invented by Lyon & Healy failed to achieve lasting success. The tenor guitar, introduced in the mid 1920s, had four strings and was tuned like a tenor banjo, the most popular instrument of the day.[37] It was meant to offer the hordes of banjo players an easy alternative to the standard six-string guitar. Back in the 1890s the company had introduced a six-string banjo with a standard guitar scale and tuning, intended for guitar players who "lack the time and inclination to learn the system of banjo playing", but the instrument was not a success. Although the tenor guitar proved to be a more practical concept, it never caught on big. Various manufacturers took up the idea and made small numbers of tenor guitars in acoustic or electric versions. Washburn tenor guitars remained in the catalogs until the late 1930s.

Sam Moore (left) and his musical partner, pianist Carl Freed, pictured in a 1925 Washburn banjo catalog (Brian Lydford)

Endorsement picture of Roy Smeck playing a Washburn Style A banjo, 1925 catalog. A Style A mandolin and guitar are at his feet (Brian Lydford)

Another more obscure instrument was the octo-chorda, basically an eight-string Hawaiian guitar with a different tuning. It was invented around the late 1910s by Harry Skinner, an employee of Lyon & Healy. Sam Moore, a well-known entertainer at the time, played it regularly in public performances.[38] The octo-chorda was featured prominently on Moore's biggest hit, "Laughing Rag" of 1921, and also on a few period recordings by ukulele wizard and multi-instrumentalist Roy Smeck. Moore and Smeck also recorded together, and were endorsers for the Washburn banjo line during the mid twenties. Martin also made at least one octo-chorda, but the unusual instrument did not become a hit and quickly disappeared from sight.

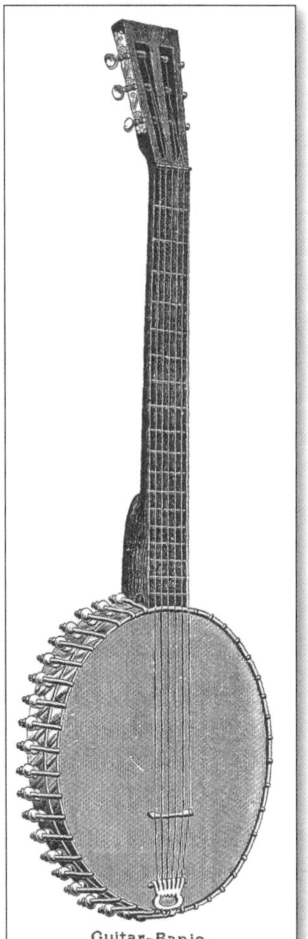

Guitar-Banjo.

Guitar Banjo from 1895 catalog

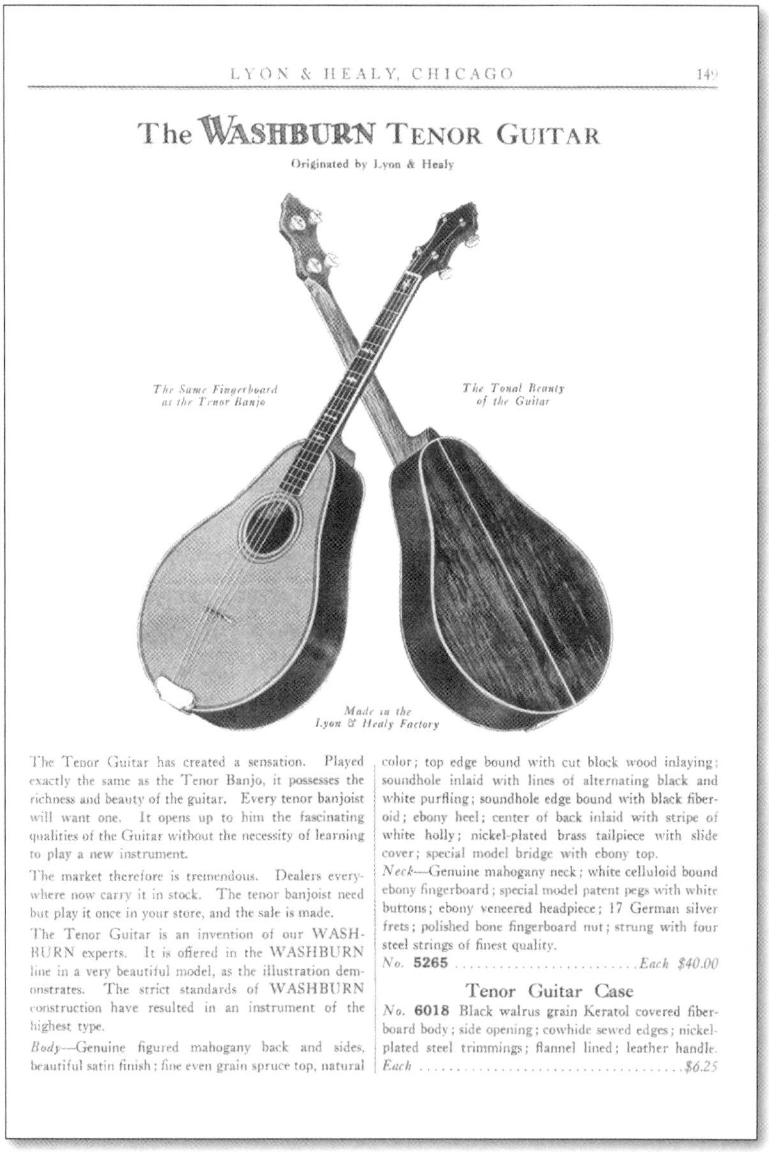

LYON & HEALY, CHICAGO 149

The WASHBURN TENOR GUITAR

Originated by Lyon & Healy

The Tenor Guitar has created a sensation. Played exactly the same as the Tenor Banjo, it possesses the richness and beauty of the guitar. Every tenor banjoist will want one. It opens up to him the fascinating qualities of the Guitar without the necessity of learning to play a new instrument.

The market therefore is tremendous. Dealers everywhere now carry it in stock. The tenor banjoist need but play it once in your store, and the sale is made.

The Tenor Guitar is an invention of our WASHBURN experts. It is offered in the WASHBURN line in a very beautiful model, as the illustration demonstrates. The strict standards of WASHBURN construction have resulted in an instrument of the highest type.

Body—Genuine figured mahogany back and sides, beautiful satin finish; fine even grain spruce top, natural color; top edge bound with cut block wood inlaying; soundhole inlaid with lines of alternating black and white purfling; soundhole edge bound with black fiberoid; ebony heel; center of back inlaid with stripe of white holly; nickel-plated brass tailpiece with slide cover; special model bridge with ebony top.

Neck—Genuine mahogany neck; white celluloid bound ebony fingerboard; special model patent pegs with white buttons; ebony veneered headpiece; 17 German silver frets; polished bone fingerboard nut; strung with four steel strings of finest quality.

No. **5265** .... *Each $40.00*

Tenor Guitar Case

No. **6018** Black walrus grain Keratol covered fiberboard body; side opening; cowhide sewed edges; nickel-plated steel trimmings; flannel lined; leather handle. *Each* *$6.25*

1925

37 Regal also claimed the design of the tenor guitar, *Teagle* p. 76.
38 Allan R. Sutton, *Rediscovering Sam Moore*, http://www.mainspringpress.com/moore.html.

Lyon & Healy, J.R. Stewart, Regal and Gibson-made instruments

Much can be said about the differences –or the lack thereof- between the Washburns made by Lyon & Healy (until 1928), J.R. Stewart Co. (May 1928- April 1930) and Regal (after May 1930). Though the pre-1928 guitar line remained for most part unchanged until 1935, certain appointments are characteristic for each of these manufacturing periods. All guitars manufactured by Lyon & Healy and Stewart have 18 or 19 frets (see under 'number of frets' for certain exceptions), while Regal- made guitars have 20 frets. There are only subtle constructional and cosmetic differences between the late 1920s Lyon & Healy and Stewart era guitars. However, most (but not all) of the Stewart-made instruments carry a 'Tonk Bros' stamp on the center strip whereas the guitars manufactured by Lyon & Healy have a 'Lyon & Healy, Makers' stamp. In general the Regal era is also characterized by a 9th fret fingerboard position marker as opposed to the 10th fret markers on most of the late 1920s Lyon & Healy and Stewart guitars (but see also 2.4.1).

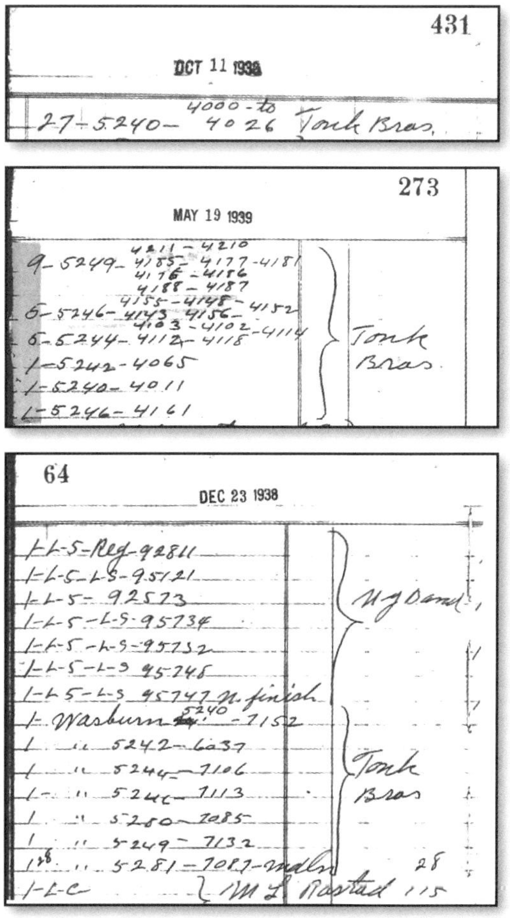

Gibson's late 1930s shipping ledgers listing various Washburn guitar styles. The numbering seems to be all over the place – the two ledger excerpts from October 11 and December 23, 1938 respectively show numbers in the 4,000 and 7,000 range, the third from May 19, 1939 again 4,000s numbers (Lynn Wheelwright)

Washburn guitars, mandolins, banjos and ukuleles made by J.R. Stewart between 1928 and 1930 can be found in the high 13,000s-14,000s batch number range.[39] The few post 1930 guitars manufactured by Regal wholly or partly with Stewart-made parts have serial numbers from 1 up to the 2,000s range.

Gibson manufactured small numbers of Washburn guitars and mandolins between 1938 and 1940. This is evidenced by Gibson's factory shipping ledgers.[40] In view of inconsistencies between examined late 1930s instruments bearing the same style number, it is certain that Regal and Gibson were both manufacturing Washburns for Tonk Bros at the same time. A possible explanation for this could be the change of Regal's marketing strategies in 1938,[41] which may have affected Regal's capacity to manufacture guitars for third parties like Tonk Bros, or could have led to less favorable contract terms offered by Regal to Tonk. The serial numbers of these rare Gibson-made Washburns start exactly at 4,000 and continue up to the low 7,000s serial number range. Many of these instruments will also have a Gibson factory order number used at the time, consisting of a batch number followed by a letter (with D indicating 1938, E 1939, and F 1940), ink stamped on the neck block. The serial numbers alone provide no clue as to the maker of the instrument, since both Regal-made and Gibson-made Washburns carry numbers within the 4,000-7,000 range.

39 The highest batch number recorded to date is in the 14600s range. A ukulele with batch number 13690 came with an original factory warranty certificate dated February 2, 1928, three months before the acquisition by Stewart.

40 *Gruhn & Carter (II)* (based on research carried out by Lynn Wheelwright, who estimates that between 35 and 50 examples of each Washburn model were shipped, except for Style 5240 with over 100 units made), also Carter, p. 136.

41 See chapter 1.

William Foden – the Foremost Early American Guitar Virtuoso

William Foden (1896 catalog)

The most famous name among the early endorsers of Washburn guitars was without doubt that of William Foden. Born in 1860 in St Louis, Missouri, Foden originally studied the violin. By the time he was sixteen he had organized his own orchestra, which became quite popular in his native city. After having been introduced to the guitar by a friend, he fell in love with it and practically taught himself to play. In the following decades he performed on the guitar in all major cities throughout the U.S. during extensive concert tours and established himself as the greatest guitarist that America had ever known. Foden was one of the first performers to include arrangements of light classical music in his concert programs. He also contributed to the guitar literature with many original compositions and transcriptions of classical pieces. His "Grand Method", a two-part treatise on guitar techniques, was hailed as the most comprehensive learning method since Carcassi's famous etudes of a century earlier. In 1911 Foden formed a trio with two other musical greats of the time, Giuseppe Pettine on mandolin and Frederic Bacon on banjo, quickly nicknamed "the Big Trio" by the music press, and toured the U.S. with phenomenal success. By this time he was no longer playing Washburns. Foden's portrait with his claim that "the Washburn instruments have no equal" was pictured in Washburn and Lyon & Healy catalogs between 1892 and the early 1900s, but around the turn of the century he apparently changed his mind and started ordering Martin guitars for himself and his students. Martin made a number of 'Foden Special" models between 1912 and 1917 that were designed in collaboration with the guitarist. Foden died in 1947.

2.4.1 Necks, headstocks, fingerboards

Headstock and neck design

Almost all Washburn guitars made from the 1880s until 1934/5 have slotted headstocks with three on a side strip mounted tuners, also known as 'patent heads'. Some of the mid to late 1880s Washburns were available with a solid headstock and mechanical friction pegs. Although these 'peghead' guitars have a number of characteristics of the very early Washburns, they likely did not form part of the 1884 line since their workmanship does not display the 'cruder' look of the earliest guitars. The new mechanical 'Champion' friction tuners that are featured on these instruments –likely a first on guitars- had been introduced in 1885.[42] The Champion tuners quickly became an industry standard for banjos and, later, for ukuleles. Since no guitars with friction pegs were listed in the 1884, 1887 and 1889 Washburn catalogs, these instruments may have been manufactured between 1885 and 1887. The four string tenor guitars of the 1920s and 1930s also had a solid headstock.

Style and serial number stamp on a Style 123, around 1899

From 1889 through 1905 most guitar necks were made of Spanish cedar.[43] Starting with the 1905 model line, mahogany necks became standard for the Washburns. Cedar necks were reintroduced on the cheapest models made between 1922 and 1928. Until 1934/5 all guitar necks joined the body at the 12th fret except the tenor guitar Styles 5265, 5225 and 5226, which had 14 frets clear of the body, and Style 503 where the neck/body join was located between the 10th and 11th fret.[44]

The small neck heel of the early guitars (see top instrument) was enlarged around 1887

A very small neck heel characterized the necks on the Washburns made prior to 1887. Another typical feature of some of the earliest guitars is that the headstock slots are often slightly wider than those on later instruments, and that they are equipped with thicker brass tuner plates that were engraved on the more upscale styles. Starting around 1935 all guitars were designed with solid headstocks and 14 frets to the body except the entry level Style 5200 ('Inspiration'), which from 1935-1937 sported a slotted headstock and a 12-fret neck.

Around 1926-7 a new and unique headstock shape was introduced on the then current guitar styles. This headstock was characterized by three small domes protruding at the upper end of the headstock, one in the middle and two extended 'ears' on both sides. Its profile is somewhat like a sailor's cap. This original shape, combined with the pearl deco-style Washburn name inlaid in pearl, contributed to the oriental touch of the new design. Around 1928 it was replaced by a more conservative mustache shaped headstock with one small dome in the middle. This classic shape was used throughout the 1930s until the end of production. U.S. Music Corporation, the current owner of the

42 According to the 1913 trademark registration the Champion brand had been in use since 1.1.1885. A patent for the Champion tuner was not registered until 1888.
43 The 1884 Lyon & Healy catalog specified necks as being made of mahogany, the 1887 catalog stated that these were made either of cedar or mahogany.
44 Style 5265, a tenor guitar introduced in 1925, was one of the first flat top guitars with a 14-fret neck. The 1921 patent application for a neck truss rod invented by Gibson President Ted McHugh shows a drawing of a 14-fret neck acoustic guitar with a round soundhole, but it is unknown if similar flattop models actually existed at the time.

Around 1886 - solid headstock with 'Champion' friction tuners

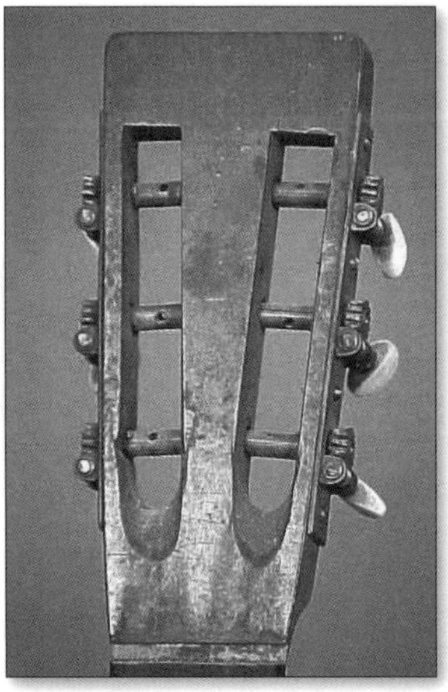

1884 - thin headstock sides, square headstock slots (Elderly)

Around 1886 - rounded headstock slots and arrow-shaped volute

Early style engraved brass tuner plates (late 1880s)

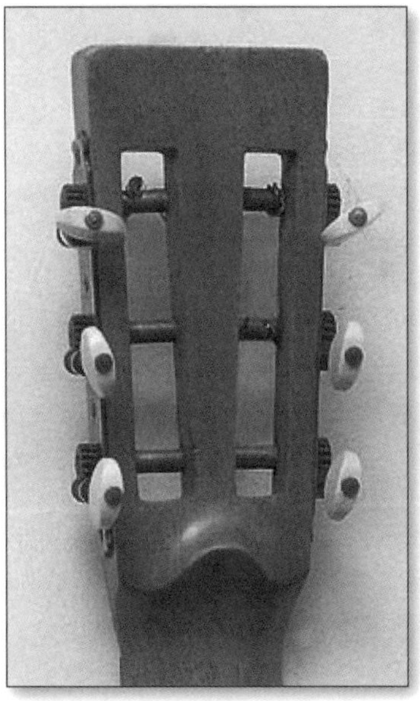

1889 - rounded volute (Style 104)

1896 (Style 167) (Laguitare.com)

1922 (Style A), missing gold plated tuners (Lowell Levinger, Players Vintage Instruments)

1927 - the sort-lived "sailor's cap" headstock

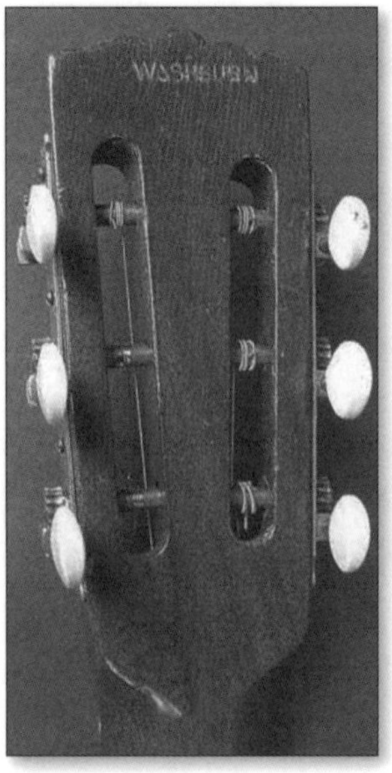

1928 (Style 5236) (Folkway Music, Canada)

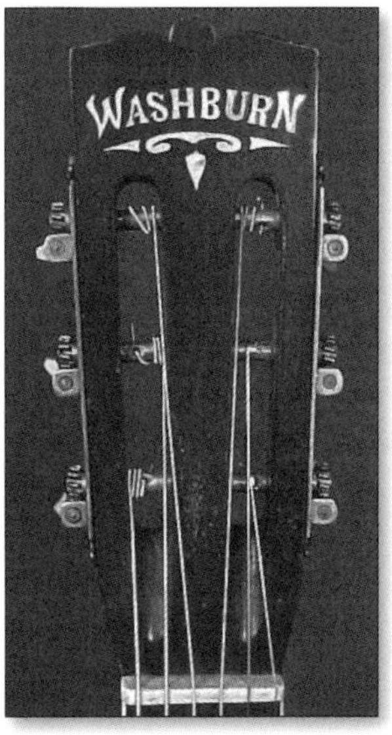

1928 (Elderly)

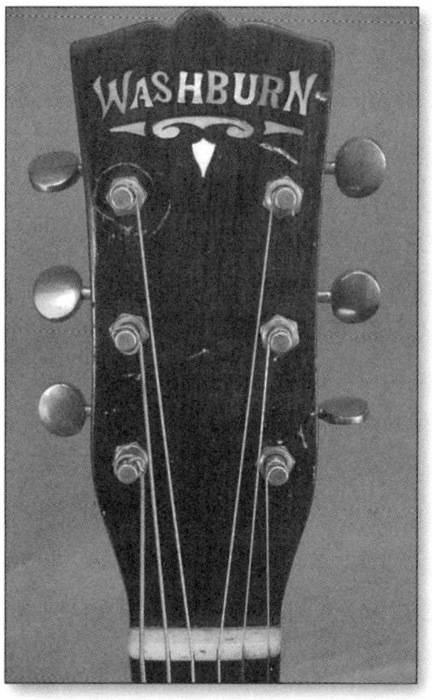

1934/5 - Style 5246, Regal-made
(Frank Ford)

1990s headstock

Headstock of guitar stamped
'Washburn' and 'J.R. Stewart'
inside, possibly prototype
(London Resonator Centre)

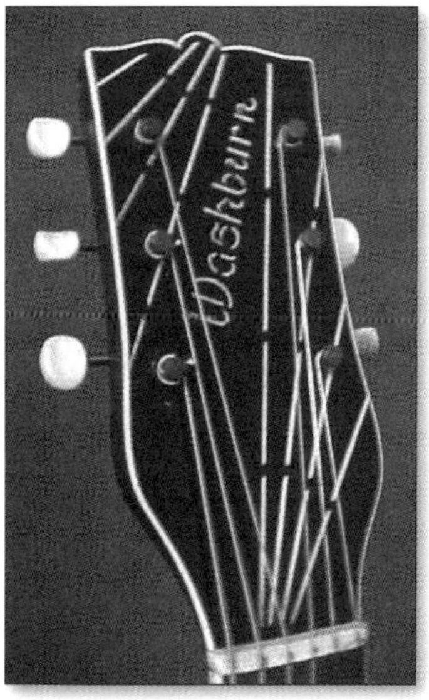

Late 1930s Regal (left, Style 5241) and Gibson (style 5242) headstocks - note differences in shape, tuner placement, script lines, top center dome (Elderly)

Gibson-made Style 5240, SN 4008
(Frank Ford)

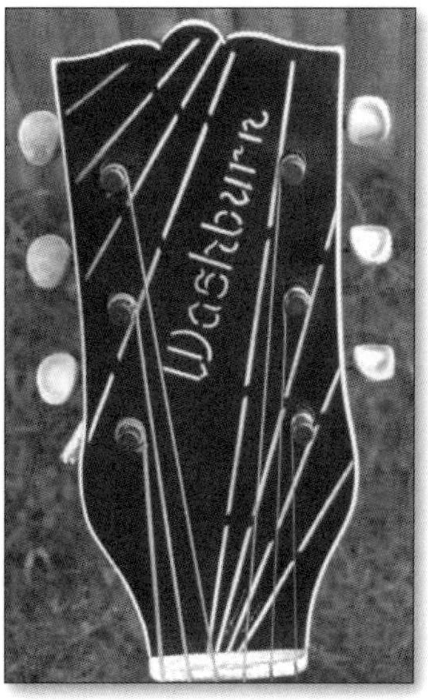

Regal-made Style 5240, SN 3329
(Duke Robillard)

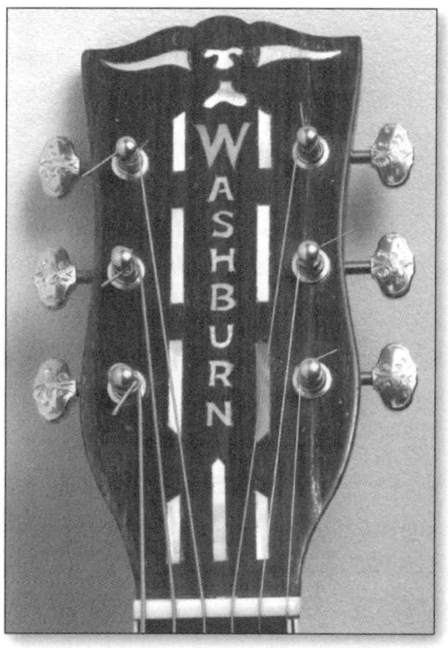

1938 Gibson-made Style 5249
(Solo Deluxe), non-original tuners
(Mike Rivamonte)

Washburn trademark, revived the 1928 headstock design in the 1990s in a slightly different form on a number of acoustic and electric guitar models.

The headstock of the rosewood-bodied top-of-the line Style 5257 ½ of 1935 was slightly wider than the standard shape used for the less expensive models. A unique feature of this sunburst-finished dreadnought was also that the Washburn name on its headstock was inlaid vertically in abalone between the tuners and embellished with deco pearl stripes. Around 1937 the cheaper Washburn guitar styles were fitted with a new black celluloid headstock overlay with the brand name diagonally engraved in white between radial white lines.

The Washburns of the late 1930s show inconsistencies in their headstock shapes. These can be attributed to tooling differences between the jigs used by Regal and Gibson for the manufacture of these guitars. Typically the headstock sides of Gibson-made Washburns have an outward taper towards the top and a more pronounced moustache shape with a smaller dome in the center. The Gibson-made Washburn headstocks look slightly wider than the Regal headstocks, which have straighter or inward tapered sides. Both the engraved diagonal lines and the Washburn logo on the celluloid headstock overlays are interrupted on almost all Regal models, and continuous on all but a few of the Gibsons. These differences are also noticeable in the 1939 Tonk Bros catalog, which evidently shows illustrations of both Regal and Gibson-made Washburn styles (see also the chapter 'number of frets').

The headstock slots on Washburn guitars had a rectangular top and bottom between 1887 and 1915, at which time a new guitar line was introduced on which the slots were rounded on both ends. This remained unchanged until 1935, when solid headstocks were introduced. Some of the earliest instruments -predating the 1887 guitar styles- also have rounded headstock slots. As with most of the instrument particulars discussed here with regard to Washburns, these guidelines do not apply equally to the other Lyon & Healy guitar lines that were manufactured at the time.

Number of frets

Almost all Washburn guitars made prior to 1930 have 18-fret necks. The only exceptions are the tenor guitars made before 1928 (17 or 19 frets), and the auditorium sized Styles 404 and 423 that sported 19-fret necks.[45] A very small number of surviving guitars dating around 1930 also have 19-fret necks. In addition, the 1930 Tonk Bros catalog pictured all guitar styles with 19-fret necks. It is likely that these 19-fret neck Washburns were made by J.R. Stewart and introduced during late 1929 or early 1930, just before the company went bankrupt and production went to Regal.

Early 1890s Style 404 with 19-fret fingerboard (Richard Ralls)

The start of the Regal era in May 1930 coincided with the introduction of a 20-fret neck on all guitar styles, which resulted in the soundhole being repositioned slightly closer towards the bridge. Visually this made the Washburn guitars look a little more like Martins, some of which already had 20-fret necks since around the turn of the 20th century.[46]

As with most transition period instruments some inconsistencies are noticeable around the start of the 1930s, e.g. 19-fret neck (J.R. Stewart) guitars with Regal era serial numbers. The explanation for these anomalies is that for many of the guitars made in the early 1930s leftover bodies and necks were used, purchased by Tonk Bros at the May 1930 receiver's sale following Stewart's bankruptcy.

The post 1935 flattop and archtop styles were also equipped with 20-fret necks. In the 1939 Tonk Bros catalog however Washburn guitars with both 19 and 20-fret necks were pictured. This was not due to inaccurate artist renditions of the pictured styles. Actual examples from this period have turned up with both 19 and 20-fret necks, even on the same styles! These 19-fret neck versions of flattop Styles 5240, 5241, 5244 and 5246 and archtop Styles 5242 and 5243 were made by Gibson, since their cosmetic features and number of frets correspond to similar models manufactured by Gibson and marketed under the budget Kalamazoo brand. For example, the Gibson-made Washburn archtop guitar styles also have much wider f-holes in comparison to those on the 20-fret Regal-made

45 It is assumed that the post 1915 guitars of this size also had a 19-fret neck, though no surviving examples were available to verify this.
46 The change to 20-fret necks on Martin styles was encouraged by William Foden, who had become an endorser of Martin guitars during the early 1900s.

models, which were equal in size to the f-holes on the Kalamazoo archtops of the time. This is not only evidenced by the 1939 catalog illustrations, but is also clearly noticeable on actual examples.

The more expensive and bigger sized Gibson-made Washburn flattop Style 5249 and the top of the line archtop Style 5248 had 20-fret necks. These were also a feature of a number of Gibson guitars of the late 1930s, such as the J-100 and J-200 jumbos and the dreadnought-sized J-55.[47] Gibson and Tonk likely decided that the costs of retooling necessary for exactly copying the Regal designs of the cheaper 20-fret neck Washburns were not worth the expense. By opting for 19-fret necks these styles could be adapted from existing Kalamazoo models with little modifications, particularly the headstock shape and neck inlays. While the visual differences between the Regal and Gibson-made Washburn archtops were not very obvious, Gibson's version of the flattop Style 5240 showed much less resemblance to the original design. Its typical body with the truncated upper bout was identical to Gibson's budget Kalamazoo KG-11 and Recording King Carson Robison models, but without body binding and with a differently shaped pickguard.[48] As a consequence of the 19-fret neck the soundhole was located much closer to the neck than on Regal's design, while the lower bout was three quarters of an inch narrower than the original.

At left: Regal-made Style 5240 (serial #3329), 20 frets, formerly owned by blues guitar great Duke Robillard. The bridge screws are original (Bernunzio). At center: Gibson-made Kalamazoo KG 11, late 1930s, 19 frets (Retrofret.com). At right: Gibson-made 19-fret Style 5240 (serial #4008)

Lyon & Healy HANDBOOK of Everything Known in Music

MANDOLINS, BANJOS and GUITARS

Gibson Guitars

L-5	Deluxe Master model, carved top and back; F-type sound holes	$275.00
Super 400	Latest Gibson creation—carved top and back, extra size, in handsome leather case	400.00
L-10	Professional model carved top and back—F sound holes	150.00
L-4	Carved top Grand Concert size; F hole	100.00
L-50	Carved top Grand Concert size; F hole	50.00
L-37	Carved top	37.50
L-00	Flat top	27.50
	Gibson Mandolins and Gibson Banjos	*$25 to $550*

Gibson Kalamazoo Guitars

KG11	Flat top	$12.50
KG21	Arched top	17.50
KG31	Arched top	25.00
	Mandolins	*$12.50 to $17.50*
	Banjos—tenor, plectrum, 5-string—or mandolin model	*$15.00*

Special Lyon & Healy Beginner's Guitar Outfit, including case and instruction book........$8.95

Martin Guitars

017	Concert size—all mahogany, flat top	$30.00
017H	Concert size Hawaiian style	30.00
018	Concert size, mahogany with spruce top	40.00
0021	Grand Concert size	60.00
00028	Flat-top Orchestra model, auditorium size	90.00
	Carved-top Martin Guitars from $40.00 to	250.00
	Martin Mandolins	$22.50 up
	Martin Ukulele	10.00 up
	Martin Tiple	25.00 up
	Washburn Guitars	$30.00 to $125.00
	Washburn Mandolins	20.00 to 135.00
	National All-metal Guitars	62.50
	Dobro Guitars—wood, equipped with metal amplifier	$27.50 to $45.00

1935 Lyon & Healy catalog page, listing the Kalamazoo KG-11 for $12.50. Style 5240, its close cousin, was introduced in 1937 - at a price of $17.50. The pictured guitar is a Gibson L-12

The Gibson-made Washburns may also be distinguished by the differently shaped headstock in comparison to their Regal-made counterparts (see 'headstock and neck design'). Apart from the aforementioned factory order number stamps there are other constructional or visual details that could help determine if a specific late 1930s Washburn guitar is 'Gibson-made', such as bracing and internal body construction. These features may be identifiable by Gibson vintage guitar experts upon close inspection of the respective instrument.

The guitars made by Gibson for Tonk Bros were not limited to Washburns. Some American Conservatory guitars from the late 1930s also display typical Gibson features, such as 19-fret necks, 'firestripe' pickguards and the typical 'open book' headstock. The Regal-made American Conservatory guitars always came with 20-fret necks.

47 The revamped 1941 version of the J-55 which came without the typical 'stairstep' headstock had a 19-fret neck.
48 The Carson Robison model was later renamed Recording King Model K. It was also available in a square-necked Hawaiian version with 12 frets to the body.

Tonk Bros. Co., Chicago

"WASHBURN"

GUITARS

"Junior" Model
No. 5240

"Classic Model"
No. 5241

"Collegian" Model
No. 5242

NO. 5240 WASHBURN "JUNIOR" MODEL GUITAR

Grand concert orchestra size, finished throughout in dark chocolate brown color, high-lighted back and top.

Back and sides are carefully selected **Honduras Mahogany** whereas the top is genuine **Eastern Spruce.**

Solid, dark oval **Rosewood fingerboard** with wide frets, joining the body at the 14th fret, with beautifully rounded edges.

The sound hole bound with white celluloid. Professional tortoise effect pick guard.

Black celluloid covered headpiece, fancily decorated. Reliable nickel plated non-slip patent heads.

Hand rubbed semi-satin finish throughout. Beautifully toned instrument.

Each **$17.50**

NO. 5241 WASHBURN "CLASSIC" MODEL GUITAR

Super Auditorium size. Flat top and back model. The top is made of carefully selected **Eastern Spruce,** and the back and rim are made of **Honduras Mahogany.**

Construction of the top and back is made especially to give a fine tone.

The instrument is equipped with a hard wood neck with a **Rosewood fingerboard** with pearl position dots, bound with cream celluloid.

The top edge of the body is also bound with cream celluloid as is the inside of the sound hole.

The neck joins at the 14th fret and is equipped with first class non-slip nickel plated patent pegs. The head has a very fancily decorated celluloid head piece.

Genuine Rosewood bridge with off-set saddle.

The instrument is finished natural. This new finish is very popular and is being used on a great many very high priced instruments.

Each **$22.50**

NO. 5242 WASHBURN "COLLEGIAN" MODEL GUITAR

Super Auditorium size.

The top is genuine **Eastern Spruce,** finely arched. The back is beautifully figured **Honduras Mahogany,** arched. Both edges are bound with cream celluloid.

The top has attractive hand-cut "f" sound holes and is equipped with raised professional model guard plate.

Hand shaped **Mahogany neck** with genuine, dark oval **Rosewood fingerboard,** joining the body at the 14th fret.

Black celluloid covered headpiece beautifully decorated.

Nickel plated non-slip patent heads.

Adjustable off-set Rosewood bridge. Nickel plated trapeze style tailpiece.

Finished throughout in a dark brown with top and back artistically highlighted in the center. Hand rubbed finish throughout. Marvelous tone.

Each **$25.00**

1939 Tonk Bros catalog page, showing Regal-made Styles 5240 and 5242 with 20-fret necks and a 19-fret neck Gibson-made Style 5241. Note also the differently shaped Regal and Gibson headstocks

Patent stamp

On guitars and ukuleles made between 1922 and 1928 a "Pat Apl'd For" stamp was sometimes impressed on the back or upper end of the headstock. The patent application relates to the white or black celluloid soundhole ring that was a feature of various Washburn guitar and ukulele styles of the 1920s. According to inventor Walter Kirk the purpose of this ring, or 'annulus' as it was called in the 1921 patent application, was to prevent splitting or warping of the wood surrounding the soundhole. A patent was awarded in 1925.[49] Unfortunately a fair amount of the two-part celluloid rings on guitars and ukuleles disintegrated or came loose over time, which imparted a somewhat cheap look to even the most expensive instruments.

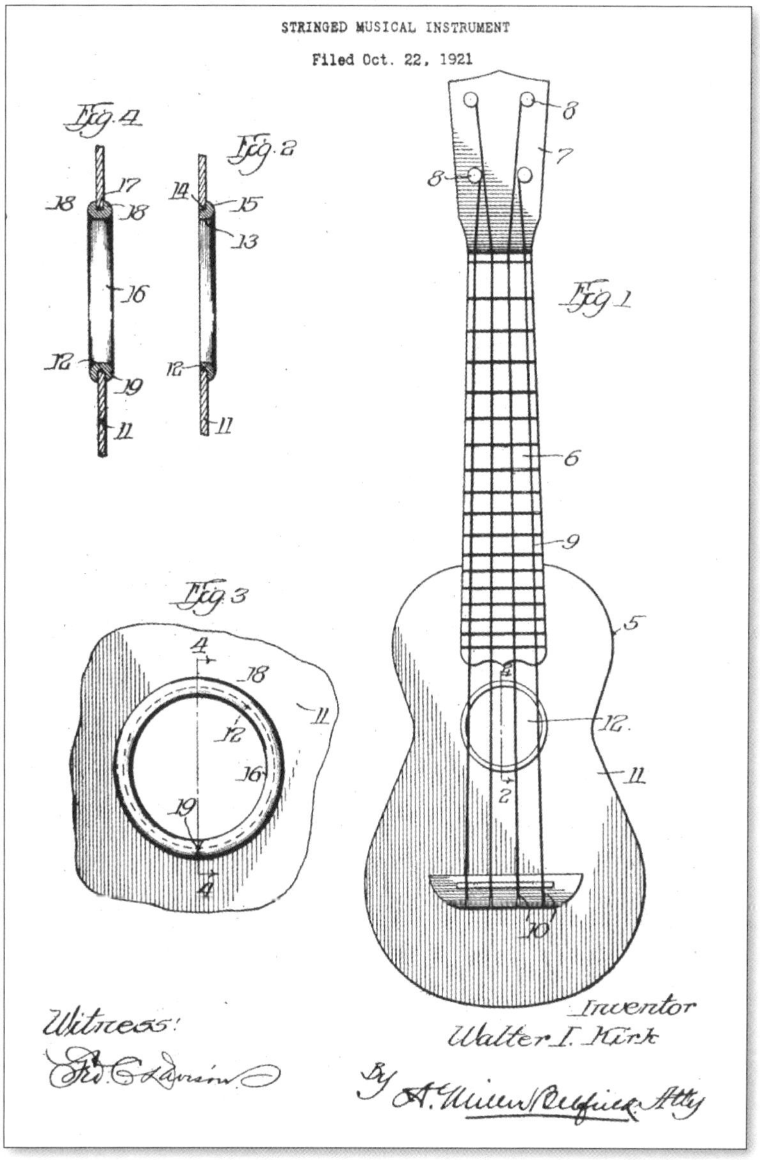

Patent drawing for Walter Kirk's invention of a celluloid soundhole ring. The patent was awarded four years after filing, which necessitated the "pat apld for' notice on many 1920s guitars and ukuleles

Metal Washburn / Lyon & Healy tag

Between around 1922 and 1930 a small oval metal tag with the words "Washburn / Lyon & Healy / Chicago, USA" was sometimes attached to the back of the headstock of guitars, mandolins, banjos and ukuleles. This tag does not necessarily mean that the respective instrument was made before the start of the Regal era, since it can also be found on some guitars made by Regal during the early 1930s. Either the tag could be an indication that the respective guitar was made of parts bought out of the Stewart bankruptcy, or Lyon & Healy continued to put the tag on Washburns that were ordered from Tonk Bros Co. and sold through the Lyon & Healy stores after 1930. Washburn guitars and mandolins were offered in the company's merchandise catalogs until at least 1935, and possibly thereafter as well.

Neck reinforcement

Late 1930s Tonk Bros catalogs mentioned for the first time that the necks of the more upscale Washburn guitars had a buried steel truss rod of the non-adjustable type. Starting in 1934/5 a seven-ply neck was introduced for the most expensive styles, which was changed to a five-ply neck around 1937. At least some –if not many- Washburn guitars from the 1890s and 1910s were factory equipped with a steel bar underneath the fingerboard that protruded into the top of the instrument.

Washburn / Lyon & Healy tag on an 1934 Style 5202 guitar. These tags can also be found on mandolins, banjos and ukuleles from the 1920s and early 1930s (Lowell Levinger)

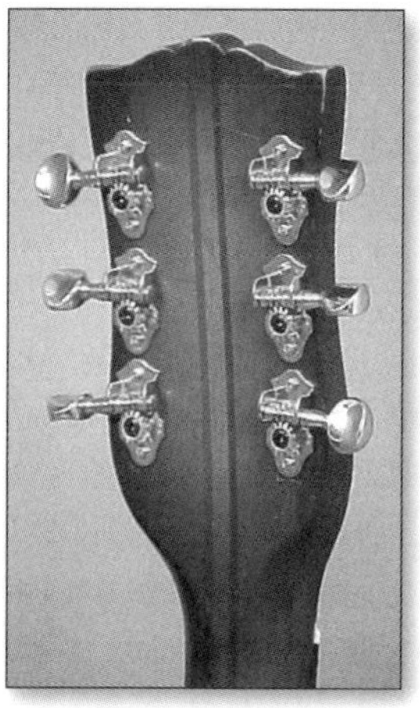

Headstock back of Gibson-made Style 5248, showing five-ply construction and non-original tuners (Elderly)

49 Patent number 1,559,108, which also shows in the patent drawing the 'smile' bridge that was first seen in another 1921 patent application filed by Kirk for a camp uke type instrument (Patent number 1,750,843, see 5.3.4).

Fingerboards

Ebony was used for the fingerboards for all Washburn guitars made between 1884 and 1915, with the exception of the solid pearl fingerboards that were featured on the top-of-the-line Styles 188, 175 and 3150. A rosewood fingerboard –mysteriously named 'rhodium wood' in the Lyon & Healy period catalogs- became a standard appointment on Style 1115, the cheapest model of the 1915 line. Engraved fingerboard inlays, which were a feature on many of the post 1896 guitars, were discontinued on the 1915 and later guitar styles. Washburn guitars did not have rectangular Martin-style bar frets except a few instruments manufactured during the early and late 1930s.

Engraved pearl fingerboard on a Style 175 (Gene McMillan)

Late 1920s 18-fret guitar with Washburn and J.R. Stewart stamps inside and no serial number, possibly a prototype. Note the snowflake inlays and different headstock shape (London Resonator Centre)

The fingerboards on the early Washburns made before 1889 did not have any position markers. In the 1889 and the 1892 catalogs the cheaper Washburns were shown with pearl dots at the 5th, 7th and 10th fret positions. On the 1896 model line as pictured in the catalogs the 10th fret position marker moved to the 9th position, but this change had occurred a few years earlier in the 50,000s – 60,000s serial number range.[50] For unknown reasons the 9th position marker moved back to the 10th position on the 1910-1915 models, then again to the 9th fret (1915-1922).

This brief change to the 10th fret position marker between 1910 and 1915 is intriguing. Both the 10th fret marker and the brown and beige marquetry styles used on the 1910-1915 Washburn guitars were typical features of a number of Regal instruments of the same period.[51] If these Washburns were actually Regal-made, then this would be an example of the temporary outsourcing by Lyon & Healy of instrument manufacturing activities prior to the completion of the new Fullerton factory in 1914. The start of this arrangement may have been after 1909, when the company launched a large-scale advertising campaign for the Lyon & Healy brand pianos. The intensive marketing efforts for these instruments were continued during the next years. The ensuing expansion of the piano manufacturing operations could have caused the company to outgrow the Union Park factory and resulted in the need to involve other makers for the manufacture of part of their instrument lines.

At least five variants of this one page ad appeared in 1909, illustrating Lyon & Healy's ambition to expand their piano manufacturing activities

On the new Styles A through E of 1922 the 9th fret marker moved once more to the 10th position. The 9th position marker was maintained only on the budget Styles F and G (1923-1925), which were both remnants of the 1915 line and were likely added to the catalog in order to find a use for leftover parts. The 10th fret marker was continued on the subsequent guitar styles of the 1920s. Around 1929 or 1930 –just before the start of the Regal era- this changed again (!), and until the Washburn instrument lines were discontinued the 9th position markers remained standard.[52]

50 The 1897 catalog picture of style 112 incorrectly shows a dot still located at the 10th position. This inaccuracy is fairly typical for many Washburn and Lyon & Healy catalogs. In spite of the reasonably detailed artist impressions of the featured instruments it is not uncommon to spot differences on actual production models, in particular with regard to neck and bridge inlays.

51 The brown/beige marquetry trimmings were also a feature of the 1910 Washburn mandolin line.

52 This haphazard choice for the 9th and 10th position markers does not correspond to the theory that the 9th position marker on late 19th century and early 20th century guitars would indicate a gut stringed, and the 10th position marker a steel stringed instrument *(Michael Wright, Connecting the Dots, Vintage Guitar Magazine, May 2001, p 42-51).*

Interestingly, all mandolin, ukulele and banjo styles made prior to 1940 including the Washburn tenor guitars have a position marker located at the 10th fret. The only exceptions are some of the five-string banjo styles made between 1913 until the early 1920s.

The most expensive guitar Styles 5202 and 5203 (1925-1935) and their larger sized variants originally had pearl dot fingerboard markers, which were later replaced by snowflake inlays. This change to snowflake inlays -and 9th fret position markers- likely occurred during the J.R. Stewart era around 1930, a few months before Regal took over production of the Washburn lines. A number of examined instruments support this theory. One of these is a unique 18-fret guitar carrying both Washburn and J.R. Stewart stamps inside with snowflake fingerboard inlays and a 9th position marker. This instrument may well have been a prototype in view of its many non-standard appointments, including a headstock shape not found on any other Washburn. In the 1930 Tonk Bros catalog Styles 5202 and 5203 were still pictured with snowflake inlays and a 19-fret neck. Since all Regal-made instruments sported 20-fret necks and Regal did not start making Washburns until later in 1930, it is likely that the pictured guitars still showed the styles as made by the J.R. Stewart Co.

2.4.2 Bridges

Standard and 'Durkee' bridge

The typical rectangular flattened pyramid bridge was a standard feature on all Washburn guitars until around 1922, with the exception of certain more expensive models made between 1889 and 1905 (Styles 106, 108, 109, 802, 804, 167, 188, 199) that were fitted with a luxurious variant of the 'Durkee bridge' with shell shaped ends. This unique bridge was named after its designer and Lyon & Healy foreman George B. Durkee, and was patented in 1887.[53] Its design resembles the 'wraparound' guitar bridge as used by Gibson on various electric models since the 1950s, whereby a string is introduced at the front of the bridge and passes back over it, except that in Durkee's design the strings were first wound around the bridge pins before passing over the saddle. According to the patent description the purpose of this design was to reduce string breakage caused by the steep angle of strings passing over a saddle

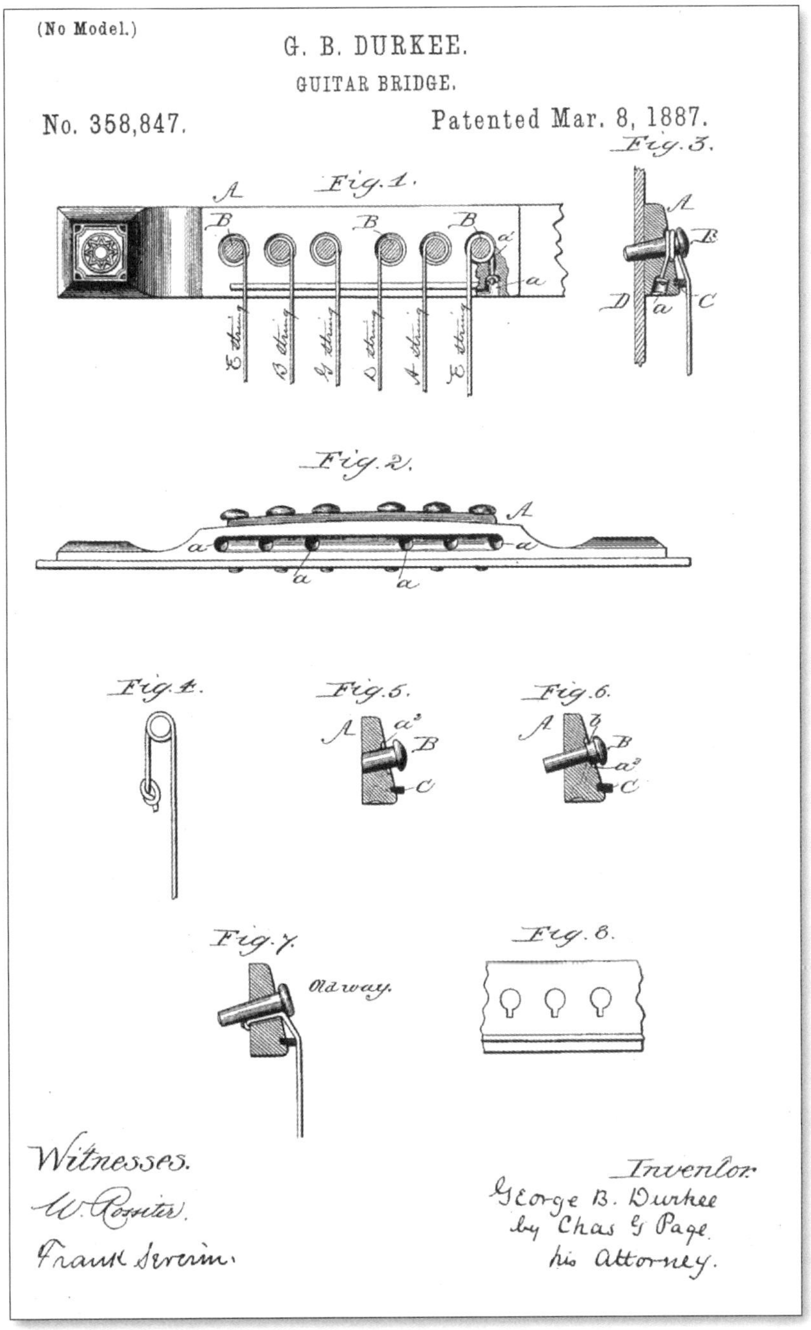

1887 patent drawing for the 'Durkee' bridge

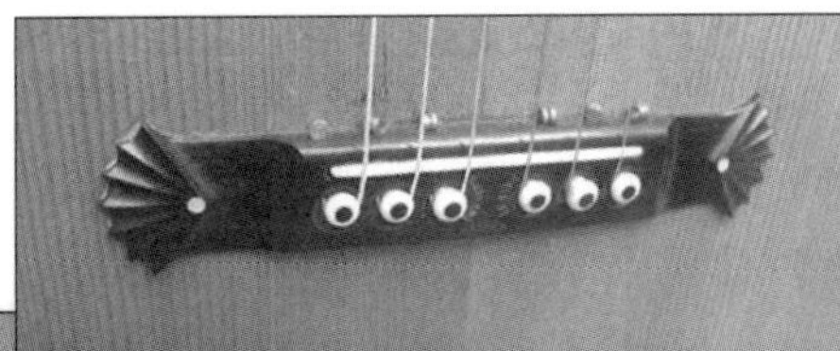
'Durkee' bridge, late 1890s.

Washburn 'flattened pyramid' bridge with engraved pear l inlays, late 1880s

53 Patent number 358,847. These bridges usually are stamped 'Durkee's patent'. It is likely that there was a license arrangement in place between the designer and Lyon & Healy, since the patent was not assigned to Lyon & Healy.

on a traditional pin bridge design. The Durkee bridges were discontinued on the 1905 model line. This change was probably necessitated by stability problems, since the Durkee bridge has been replaced on many surviving guitars from this period. The ultra fancy Style 3150 of 1912 reintroduced a bridge with shell shaped ends. The catalog description of this model no longer mentioned that the bridge was a 'Durkee', so it may have been a conventional design.

Bridges for all guitar styles were made of ebony until the new instrument line of 1915. Beginning with the guitars introduced in that year some of the cheapest styles made until WWII were equipped with rosewood bridges. A slant saddle did not replace the straight saddle on all guitar bridges until the introduction of the 1934/5 line.

Other Lyon & Healy guitars

Some of the cheaper Lyon & Healy-made guitars were available with a tailpiece and modified bridge in order to enable the use of steel strings (see also 2.4.1). These guitars were marketed under the Jupiter, Columbus, Marquette, Lakeside, Arion, American Conservatory and Lyon & Healy brand names.[54] The Marquette and Columbus brands were derived from the names of two of Patrick Healy's sons.

The 1896 Jupiter, Columbus and Marquette models were built for and factory shipped with steel strings. These guitars could either be ordered with a standard pin bridge or, for a quarter more, with a metal tailpiece. The slightly more expensive Lakeside and Arion models came standard with gut strings, but were also available strung with steel strings. The steel string versions were fitted with a stamped metal tailpiece with tapered sides shaped like a violin tailpiece, and a simplified flattened pyramid bridge made of ebony containing a bone saddle but no bridge pins or pin holes.[55] Relatively few of these cheaper Lyon & Healy guitars have stood the test of time. The same applies to the cheaper mandolin, banjo and ukulele lines made by Lyon & Healy. The company's most expensive guitars, marketed under the American Conservatory and Washburn brands, were until 1915 constructed exclusively for gut strings. Nonetheless these instruments were sometimes modified by their owners with a metal tailpiece.

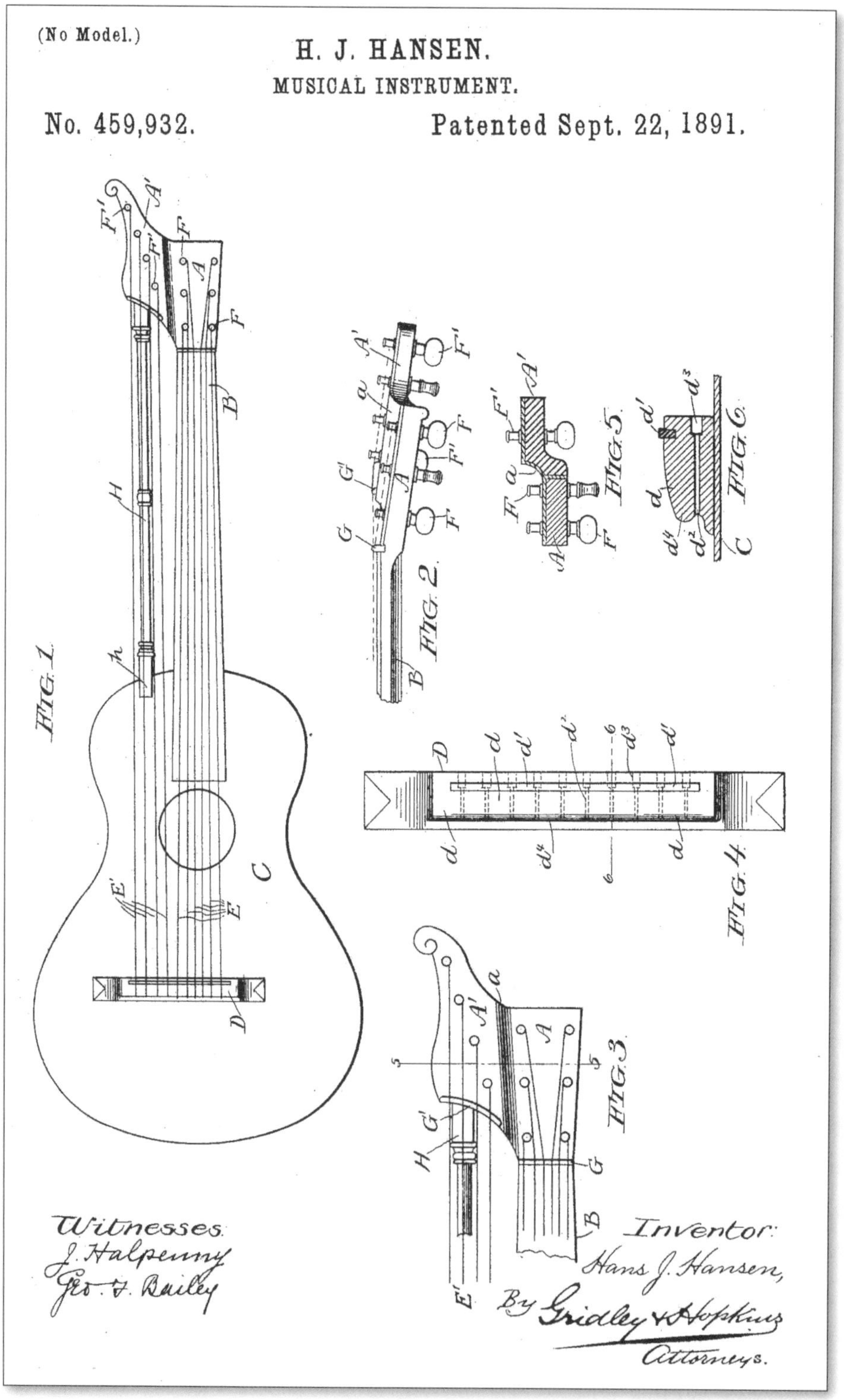

H.J. Hansen's design for a 'wraparound' guitar bridge

54 These brand names –introduced around the late 1880s and early 1890s- are listed here in the order of less to more expensive models. Jupiter' was used for the cheapest L&H made instruments, 'American Conservatory' (initially 'Conservatory') and 'Lyon & Healy' usually for the most expensive guitars after the Washburn line. Later L&H brand names for guitars also include College Line (1905-1908) and L.H. Leland (early 1910s, likely made by the Larson Bros). The name 'Arlington' is also listed in catalogs for guitars for a very brief period during the late 1890s.

55 Starting in the early 1900s Arion guitars were also available constructed for gut strings.

'Hansen' bridge

Hansen bridge on a Lyon & Healy Jupiter guitar, around 1900

Some of the Lyon & Healy Jupiter models had a unique 'Durkee' type bridge bearing a patent date of September 22, 1891. On these bridges the strings are introduced at the front like on Durkee's design, but there are no bridge pins or pin holes going through the top of the guitar. The bridge on these specific instruments is made of rosewood and slightly bigger and more solid in appearance than the Durkee bridge used on Washburn guitars. Since the Durkee bridge had already been patented in 1887, it is tempting to assume that the 1891 bridge represented a later modification of the original design in order to withstand the strain of steel strings. However, the bridge on the Jupiter guitars falls under a patent awarded to one H.J. Hansen, a Chicago resident, for his invention of a harp guitar equipped with this bridge. No connection with Lyon & Healy is apparent from the patent documentation.[56] At the time of its registration the patent had not been assigned to Lyon & Healy, and the harp guitar pictured in the patent documents does not look like anything that ever came out of the Lyon & Healy factories. It is somewhat ironic to see this interesting bridge that 'borrowed' so much of George Durkee's design end up on a Lyon & Healy guitar. The 'Hansen' bridge was also featured –but without the 1891 patent stamp- on a highly ornate custom made Washburn guitar ordered by Colonel John Hancock III, great grandson of U.S. founding father John Hancock and a prominent guitar collector. Could it be that Lyon & Healy threatened inventor Hansen with a patent infringement suit, whereupon parties struck a license deal permitting Lyon & Healy to use Hansen's design? No records have turned up to date to answer this question.

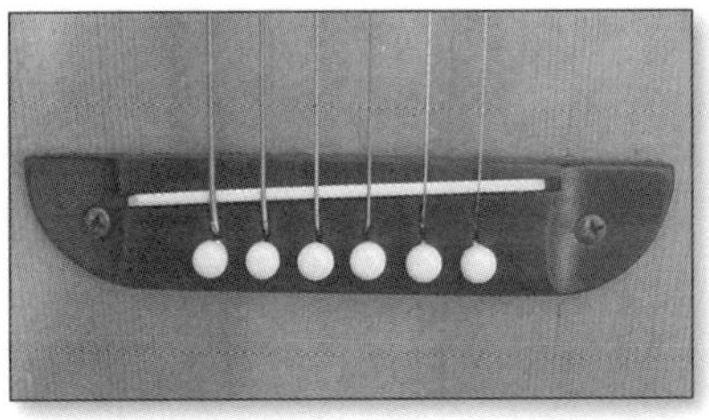

Many of the 'smile' bridges were secured with screws or rivets after the mid-1930s (Frank Ford)

'Smile' bridge

Beginning around 1922 with the introduction of the Models A through G, the elegantly styled ebony or rosewood 'smile' shaped bridges became standard on most guitars until WWII. Exceptions were Styles F and G (1923-1925) which retained the standard flattened pyramid bridge, the late 1930s styles 5240 ('Junior') and 5241 ('Classic') that came with a rectangular bridge, and the archtop guitars of the 1930s which were all equipped with a conventional bridge/tailpiece combination.[57] Unfortunately many 'smile' bridges started lifting or developed cracks and had to be replaced. The shortcomings of this design became more evident around 1935, when the larger guitar styles with their increased scale length and bigger string tension were introduced. By 1937 Regal was apparently aware of the problem. They opted for a simple solution by permanently bolting the bridges to the guitar tops with steel rivets or screws! Though the results were not esthetically pleasing, the method proved effective, as evidenced by many surviving guitars of this period.[58] Bridges with screws can also be found on other flattop guitars of the 1930s carrying the Regal brand, even on more expensive models.

Straight sided bridge on a 1937 Regal-made Style 5241 (Elderly)

56 Patent number 459,932.

57 Style 5270 (the Washburn Hawaiian Harp guitar), had a gondola shaped bridge, which was used also on the shrine guitars, tenor guitars and ukuleles.

58 Since many original bridges have been replaced, it is not certain if Gibson also bolted down the smile bridges on the Washburns made in their factory.

2.4.3 Body woods

Style 404 with typical shrunk binding around the edges of the fingerboard (Richard Ralls)

Until 1920 the backs and sides for all standard Washburn guitar styles were made of Brazilian rosewood. During the late 19th century and possibly shortly thereafter mahogany bodies were available as a special order, though surviving guitars from this period with this feature are very rare. In a rather strange advertising move, the 1889 Washburn catalog extensively praised mahogany as possessing superior characteristics for instrument building in comparison to rosewood, in spite of the fact that all of the listed guitar styles had rosewood bodies!

Style 2123 of 1920 became the first standard guitar model that was offered with a mahogany back and sides. However, the first mahogany Washburn was Style 1522, a Hawaiian guitar with a mahogany body and top that was introduced in 1915. After 1920 until WWII mahogany was used on the less expensive models, while rosewood was reserved for a few top-of-the-line styles. After 1935 the only rosewood guitars that were listed were Styles 5257 (Solo, renumbered 5246 around 1937), and 5257 ½ (Solo De Luxe, renumbered 5249 around 1937). The only Washburns with maple bodies were the archtop guitar styles 5258 and 5259 of the 1934/5 line.

The staple wood for all guitar and mandolin tops according to the Lyon & Healy and Washburn catalogs between 1905 and the mid 1930s was white spruce (picea glauca), to be distinguished from red or 'Adirondack' spruce (picea rubens) which Martin predominantly used until the 1940s.[59] The 1935 and later catalogs specify the wood used for the guitar tops as 'eastern spruce', a generic name used to designate either red or white spruce. A few models departed from the norm. Exceptions were the Hawaiian guitars (1915-1928), Style D (1923-1925) and the Shrine guitar (1927-1928), which all had mahogany or koa bodies and tops, and Style E (1923-1925) that was specified as having a 'Nyssawood' body and a two-ply laminated top.[60] Style E was also unique because all other Washburn guitars made prior to 1940 had solid tops.

Lyon & Healy started experimenting with laminated sides for guitar bodies as early as the 1880s, which is evidenced by a few surviving Washburns with three-ply sides that date back to the 1884-1887 period. The company apparently reserved this process for their most expensive guitars in order to add strength and prevent cracking. The instruments of the 1887 Washburn guitar line were redesigned with solid sides, though laminated sides would be reintroduced a few decades later. The first mention thereof in the company catalogs was made in relation to the Washburn guitars and ukulele models of the 1922 line, which were specified as having three-ply laminated sides.

Celluloid was used for the body, soundhole and neck bindings on all Washburns. As the older celluloid types unfortunately proved to be more prone to shrinking, the bindings on a fair amount of period instruments show gaps around the fingerboard edges, at the inside of the soundhole or at the lower body bout.

59 Catalogs prior to 1905 do not specify the type of spruce used.

60 'Nyssawood' is most likely pearwood. Other (later) surviving examples of Style E have a spruce/mahogany body. Although briefly catalogued, the all-pearwood models may never have been marketed.

2.4.4 Body sizes

Few of the Lyon & Healy and Tonk Bros catalogs contain any details regarding the advertised guitar sizes. The measurements listed below were therefore taken from surviving examples. Variations of up to ¼″ are not uncommon.

1884-1887

Size[61]	**lower bout**	**upper bout**	**depth lower bout**	**depth upper bout**	**body length**	**scale length**
Standard	12″	8″	3 ½″	3 3/8″	18″	24 ¼″
Concert	13 1/8″	9 3/8″	3 ¾″	3 5/8″	19″	24 ¾″
Grand Concert	13 ¾″	9 5/8″	3 ¾″	3 5/8″	19 ¼″	25″

The body shape of these early guitars differs from the post-1887 'new model' styles that were designed by George Durkee, and is characterized by a relatively smaller upper bout, a slightly narrower waist and a differently curved lower bout.

1887-1922

Size	**lower bout**	**upper bout**	**depth**[62] **lower bout**	**depth upper bout**	**body length**	**scale length**
¾	11 ¼″	7 ¾″	3 5/8″	3″	15 ½″	21 ¾″
1	12 ½″	8 ¾″	4 1/8″	3 ¼″	18″	24 ¼″
2 (Concert)	13 1/8″	9 ½″	4 1/8″	3 ½″	18 ½″	24 ¾″
3 (Grand Concert)	13 ¾″	9 ¾″	4 ¼″	3 ½″	19″	25″
4 (Auditorium)[63]	14 ½″	10 ¼″	4 ½″	3 ½″	19 ¼″	25 ½″
5 (Style 503)[64]	15″	10 ¾″	4 ½″	3 7/8″	20 ¾″	27″

1922-1935

Size	**lower bout**	**upper bout**	**depth lower bout**	**depth upper bout**	**body length**	**scale length**
Concert	13″	9 ½″	3 ¾″	3 ¼″	18 ½″	24 ¾″
Grand Concert	14 1/8″	10 ¼″	3 ¾″	3 ¼″	19 ¼″	25″
Auditorium	15 1/4″	11″	4 1/8″	3 ¼″	20″	25 3/8″
'Bell'	15 5/8″	N/A	3 ¾″	N/A	17 ¾″	24 ¾″

61 The sizes listed here correspond respectively with the 'Large', 'Concert' and 'Extra Large Concert' sizes in the 1884 catalog.
62 The lower and upper bout depth of the shallower post 1915 models are respectively 3 ¾″ and 3″ for all sizes.
63 The 1892 and 1896 catalogs specify the lower end depth as 4 5/8″ and 4 ¼″, respectively, and 10″ and 19 ½″ for the upper bout and body length measurements.
64 The 1889 catalog lists a 10 ½″ upper bout, 5″ lower bout and a 27 ½″ scale.

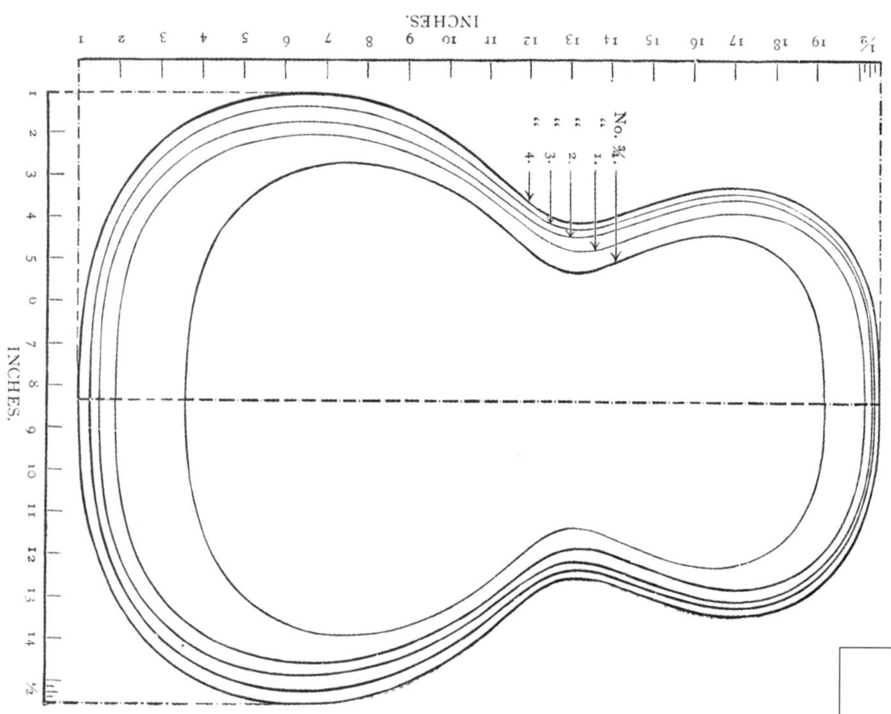

No. ¾. THREE-QUARTER SIZE.

Intended for the youth of either sex and having the smallest neck and shortest scale used in the Washburn Guitar. Also a favorite size for ladies who desire a small and light instrument for home use. The tone is exceedingly sweet and clear, though of course not so powerful as in the larger sizes.

No. 1. STANDARD SIZE.

This Guitar is somewhat larger than the usual Ladies' size, but of beautiful proportions and a very elegant model. It is the popular style; is a great favorite as a lady's instrument. The tone, though rich and mellow, possesses much volume and is quite powerful enough for all home purposes.

No. 2. CONCERT SIZE.

The favorite size for a gentleman's instrument or for concert purposes. The pattern is very graceful, and pronounced remarkably handsome by many well-known artists. The tone is rich and powerful.

No. 3. GRAND CONCERT SIZE.

A powerful instrument for stage and concert use. As its dimensions exceed those of the usual concert size, the tone is exceptionally strong and possesses a remarkable carrying power. This Guitar must surely please any purchaser who desires the most effective solo instrument now made.

No. 4. AUDITORIUM SIZE.

This is an extra large size Guitar and meets with hearty approval for use in Guitar, Banjo, or Mandolin Clubs, very useful for accompaniments, but perfectly appropriate as a solo instrument, if desired. It measures 14½ inches across the face at the bridge, 10 inches across the face above the sound-hole, and has a depth of 4⅝ inches at the lower end.

Washburn guitar sizes, 1896 catalog

Available Washburn body sizes in a 1889 catalog – the largest size, Auditorium, is not pictured

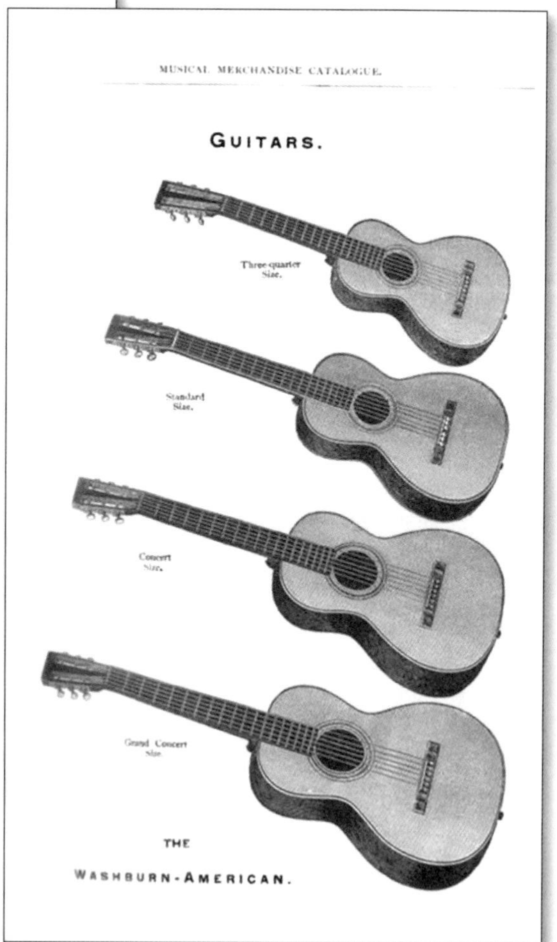

During this period there are more variations in body measurements and other features of individual instruments than prior to 1935.

Size	lower bout	upper bout	depth lower bout	depth upper bout	body length	scale length
Concert	13 ½″	10″	4″	3 ¼″	19″	24 ¾″
Grand Concert Orchestra	15 ½″	10″	3 ¾″	3 ¼″	19″	24 ¾″[65]
Full Auditorium	15 ¼″	11 ¼″	4″	3 ½″	19″	25 3/8″
Large Auditorium	15 ¼″	11 ½″	4 ½″	3 ¾″	19″	25 ¼″
Super Auditorium	15 ¾″	11 ¼″	3 ¾″	3 ¼″	19 ¾″	25 3/8″[66]
Large Super Auditorium	15 ¾″	11 ½″	4 ½″	3 ¾″	19″	25 ¼″
Extra Super Auditorium	16″	11 3/8″	4 ½″	4″	19 ¾″	25 ½″[67]
Extra Super Auditorium	16 ¾″	11 ½″	4″	4″	20″	25 ¾″[68]

The only guitar in the catalogs that was specified as having a Large Super Auditorium sized body was the top of the line Style 5249 (1937-1939), a 15 ¾″ wide dreadnought shaped instrument. The identical looking predecessor of Style 5249, Style 5257 ½ (1935-1937), also had a dreadnought body but came in the slightly smaller Full Auditorium size, with a 15 ¼″ lower bout.

Though they apparently were not catalogued, a few more Large Super Auditorium sized guitars were made during the late thirties. Some surviving variants of Styles 5246 and 5244 dating around 1937 also have 15 ¾″ typical dreadnought bodies with measurements that correspond to the Large Super Auditorium size. According to the Tonk Bros catalogs Style 5246 was only available in the (15 ¼″) Large Auditorium size, whose outline resembles a grand auditorium shaped body similar to Martin's OM and OOO size guitars. Style 5244 was listed in the 1937-9 catalogs as having an Extra Super Auditorium sized body. The catalog drawing of this model shows a narrow waisted jumbo sized instrument similar to the 16 7/8″ Gibson J-100 and J-200 models of the late thirties, but the Extra Super Auditorium variant of Style 5244 was actually smaller, having a 16″ lower bout.[69]

Most of the Styles 5244 that were reported have the 15 ¾″ dreadnought shaped body. It is likely that these were replaced by the larger bodied Extra Super Auditorium version during 1937. The only other Washburn that was advertised in this size was Style 5248 (1937-1939), an archtop guitar, but its measurements are not necessarily identical to those of the Extra Super Auditorium Style 5244! The Gibson-made version of Style 5248 has a 16″ wide body that was also used for most of the factory's Kalamazoo, Recording King and Cromwell brand archtop guitars, while the Regal-made Style 5248 measures 16 ¾″ across the lower bout. This all adds to the confusion surrounding the Washburn lines of the late 1930s.

The introduction of the 16″ and 16 ¾″ Washburn flattop and archtop styles in or before 1937 was not a 'first'. Gibson's prototype of the 16 7/8″ SJ-200 Super Jumbo, ordered by Hollywood cowboy star Ray "Crash" Corrigan, had seen the light in late 1935 or early 1936, and the SJ-200 became a regular production model in 1937.[70] The Gibson L-5 archtop changed to a 17″ body in 1934 and the company's Super 400 and Epiphone's Emperor model both debuted in the same year, respectively with 18″ and 18 ½″ bodies. The first Washburn dreadnought, Style 5257 ½, did not come on the market until 1935, four years after Martin had introduced their D-1 and D-2 models.[71] Tonk Bros did not pursue Lyon & Healy's tradition in the design and marketing of novel and experimental instruments, and opted to follow

65 These measurements are for the Regal-made version. The Gibson-made version has a 14 ¾″ lower bout, a body length of 17 ½″, a 4″ depth at the end pin and a 25″ scale.

66 For Super Auditorium sized archtops the upper bout, lower bout and lower bout depth are respectively 11 ½″, 16″ and 3 ¼″ (depth of sides only – these guitars have an arched back as well), with a 20″ body length.

67 Measurements for flattop guitar Style 5244, Regal-made version.

68 Measurements for Regal version of archtop guitar Style 5248. The uniform depth of the sides does not include the arched back. The Gibson-made version of Style 5248 has a 16″ body and a 24 ¾″ scale.

69 This measurement was taken from a Regal-made version of Style 5244. Until one of the Gibson-made 5244 jumbos turns up we won't know if there ever was such a thing as a 16 7/8″ 1930s Washburn flattop!

70 Hank Risan and Bianca Soros, the SJ-200: Uncovering the Origins of Gibson's Legendary Flat-Top Jumbo Guitar, Vintage Gallery, April 1995. The "Corrigan" J-200 predates fellow cowboy star Ray Whitley's famous J-200 by almost two years, but other sources dispute this.

71 A possibly unique 14-fret Gibson dreadnought debuted as early as 1929.

MUSICAL MERCHANDISE CATALOGUE. 29

HARP-GUITAR.

OUR OWN MANUFACTURE.

12 String Bass Guitar with Supplementary Aluminum Head Piece.

"THE AMERICAN CONSERVATORY" AUDITORIUM SIZE.

No.		Each.
1210.	12 Strings, Rosewood Back and Sides, Beautifully Hand Polished, Spruce Top, Fancy Colored Wood inlaying around Sound-hole and Edge, Top and Back Edges bound with White Celluloid, Fancy Colored Wood Stripe in Back, Mahogany Neck, Supplementary Aluminum Head Piece, Ebony Fingerboards with Pearl Position Dots, Ebony Bridge...........	$65 00

No. 1210.

American Conservatory Harp Guitar (1903 catalog)

Style 5249 (1939), Large Super Auditorium size. The waist of this Gibson-made guitar is narrower than the Regal-made Style 5246 pictured below (Mike Rivamonte)

1937 Style 5246, Large Super Auditorium size. This dreadnought-sized version was never catalogued. The standard size listed for Style 5246 was Large Auditorium (Frank Ford)

NO. 5244 WASHBURN "INSPIRATION" MODEL GUITAR

1939 catalog image of the Extra Super Auditorium sized Style 5244. These jumbo models are extremely rare. Have you got one?

Style 5241, Super Auditorium size, 20 frets (1937) – compare this to the 1939 Tonk Bros catalog picture of the 19-fret Gibson-made version on page 38 (Elderly)

emerging trends instead. Tonk's policy was understandable in view of the unstable economic conditions of the 1930s. Nonetheless, many fine sounding Washburns were made during this era.

Style 503

The 1889 catalog title "Contra Bass Guitar" for this 15" wide instrument was not that far from the truth –a minor third interval, to be exact.[72] Though Style 503 was a six string guitar with a 27" scale length and a fretted fingerboard suitable for chord playing, the lowest strings were most likely meant to be used for unison bass lines. The original catalog description stated that it was intended for accompaniment purposes and not well suited for 'solo use'. The catalog also mentioned that the guitar was equipped with "specially made strings", but these were not steel strings.[73] This would neither be likely in view of the firmly voiced objections raised by Lyon & Healy in the same catalog regarding the use of steel or 'wire' strings. The strings advertised by Lyon & Healy for a six string 'contra bass guitar' around 1900 were wound silk and steel strings (with wound violin strings being recommended for the two top strings), in contrast to the wound pure steel strings that were also offered at the time by the company for use with guitars.

Style 503, early 1890s (Retrofret.com)

Contrary to the standard guitar styles the neck of Style 503 joined the body between the 10th and 11th frets. In view of its G' C' F Bb D G tuning, Style 503 could be regarded as the world's first commercially marketed fretted 'bass' guitar.[74] Apparently this innovative instrument was too far ahead of its time and therefore failed to achieve commercial success. By 1892 it was no longer listed in the Washburn catalogs.

In 20th century Lyon & Healy catalogs, the term 'Contra Bass Guitar' was also used to indicate a twelve string guitar with two necks (see below). Similarly styled guitars had been known in Europe under this name since the mid 1800s, and are still made today by a few classical guitar makers.

Other Lyon & Healy guitars

Some models of the cheaper Lyon & Healy-made guitar lines were available in even larger sizes than the Washburn styles of the same period. The American Conservatory Style 1210 "12 String Bass Guitar with Supplementary Aluminum Head Piece" had two necks and was available before the 1920s initially in Auditorium size and later in Lyon & Healy's 'Large Auditorium' size –which according to the catalogs from the early 1900s implied a lower bout of 16 ¼" at a body length of 20 ½". It should be noted that the standard dimensions of the Large Auditorium size were changed after 1935, as shown above. The fretted neck was tuned in standard guitar tuning, while the sympathetic strings on the fretless neck were tuned F G A B C D.[75]

Twelve-string Washburn guitars were never catalogued. In an endorsement printed in the 1896 catalog Chicago guitarist Wayne Wadhams nonetheless sung praise to the virtues of his 12-string Washburn Contra Bass guitar. The likely explanation is found in an announcement by the manufacturers in the same catalog that for $25 extra an "attachment carrying six extra strings" –meaning a second fretless neck- could be added to the Washburn Auditorium sized guitars. The catalog also contains many photos of guitar and mandolin orchestras in which a few double necked guitars can be seen, but these are clearly not Washburns or Lyon & Healy-made guitars.

---

72 The double or contra bass standard tuning is E'A'D G, while G' is the lowest string of Style 503.

73 As stated in Teagle, p. 67.

74 Style 503 was *not* tuned from C' to C (as in Teagle, p. 67). The 1892 catalog description of Style 802 (a terz guitar) mentions that the A string of that guitar was tuned down to C, "just one octave above the tuning of the Washburn Contra Bass Guitar No. 513" (sic). Descriptions of string sets sold for the Contra Bass Guitar listed in turn of the century catalogs of Lyon & Healy also specify the G tuning.

75 Lyon & Healy catalog 1919, p. 70. A 1917 L&H catalog suggests Eb, D, C, B, Bb, A.

Lyon & Healy, Chicago

American Conservatory Harp Guitar

Style G 2210
G 3740

The body of the Lakeside Jumbo was identical in size to that of the American Conservory Style 2210 harp guitar (picture from 1917 catalog). Picture this body with one neck and the cosmetics of the guitar No. 740 on the right and you get the idea

36 LYON & HEALY, CHICAGO

L. & H. Guitars

"The Lakeside"—Standard Size

No. Each

725. Birch back and sides, rosewood finish, spruce top, broad fancy wood inlaying around sound-hole and edge, top and back edges bound with white celluloid, fancy stripe in back, body grained a rich rosewood and beautifully finished, neck mahogany finish, veneered head-piece, rosewood finger-board, pearl position dots, nickel plated patent head, tail-piece, nickel plated, strung with steel strings....................$14.38

720. Same description as No. 725, but has plain head-piece, lighter inlay, and ebonized finger-board........... 13.75

Jumbo Size

No. Each

740. Same description as No. 725, but extra large, with rosewood bridge. Length 20½ inches. Depth, 5¼ inches. Width across bridge 16¼ inches, with bridge and GUT strings............................$25.88

Mahogany Guitars

Standard Size

No. Each

965. Mahogany back and sides hand rubbed, spruce top, broad fancy colored wood inlaying around sound-hole and down center of back, top edge inlaid with fancy colored wood, and both edges bound with white celluloid, body finished a beautiful shade of mahogany, hand polished, neck mahogany finish, ebonized finger-board with pearl position dots, nickel-plated patent head and metal tail-piece, nickel-plated, strung with steel strings..$15.88

Standard Size

No. Each

966. Beautiful figured mahogany back and sides, hand polished, broad fancy corded colored wood inlaying around sound-hole and edge, top and back edges bound with white celluloid, broad fancy corded stripe in back, mahogany neck, rosewood veneered head-piece, finger-board and head-piece bound with celluloid, pearl position dots, ebony bridge.................................. 18.00

Standard Size

No. Each

970. Dark mahogany finish back and sides, hand polished, spruce top, fancy colored wood inlaying around sound-hole and edges and down center of back, top and back edges bound with celluloid, ebonized finger-board with pearl position dots, brass patent heads, ebonized bridge..$16.25

Standard Size

No. Each

980. Beautiful figured dark mahogany back and sides, hand polished, broad fancy wood inlaying around sound-hole and edge, top and back edges bound with white celluloid, broad fancy corded stripe in black, mahogany neck, rosewood veneered head-piece, ebony finger-board bound with celluloid, and pearl position dots, nickel plated patent head, ebony bridge, strung with GUT strings..........................$22.25

No. 740 No. 965

1919 catalog page with a description of th Lakeside Jumbo guitar

The Lakeside Jumbo – the original 'dreadnought'?

The intriguing birch bodied Lyon & Healy Lakeside Style 2740 of 1912, later renamed Style 740, has been claimed to be the first 'real' dreadnought sized guitar ever made.[76] It came in 'Jumbo Size', which had identical dimensions as the pre-1935 Large Auditorium size (lower bout 16 ¼", upper bout 12", depth at lower bout 5 ¼", while the body length was respectively specified as 20 ¼", 20 3/8" and 20 ½" in different period catalogs). The measurements of the Lakeside Jumbo are remarkably close to those of the typical dreadnought guitars that rose to prominence during the 1930s. The 1919 Lyon & Healy catalog contains a picture of Style 740 –a handsome instrument with a bound body and neck, marquetry inlaid sides and soundhole, and pearl figures inlaid in the fingerboard. Unfortunately the catalog picture does not reflect the guitar's actual size, as it is identical to another picture in the same catalog of the smaller sized (12 ½") Lakeside Style 847. A further clue as to how this important guitar really looked is provided by the 1917 catalog picture of the American Conservatory Harp Guitar (Style 2210), which according to the catalogs had identical body dimensions as Style 740 but sported two six string necks, one with and one without frets. The body of Style 2210 looks like a cross between the later classic Martin dreadnought design and a grand auditorium sized instrument, due to its narrower waist and more rounded shoulders.[77]

This Hawaiian outfit has a good reason to be jolly – those two necks are attached to the first dreadnought-sized guitar body (Jim Garber)

The Lakeside Jumbo was originally introduced as the "Lakeside Bass Guitar" in 1912 –four years before the first Martin-made dreadnoughts were offered under the Ditson brand- and came with steel strings. It was listed in the catalogs until the mid 1920s. In 1918 it was no longer referred to as a "bass" guitar, and the 1919 catalog indicated that it was shipped with gut strings instead of the steel strings which were originally specified for this model. This could mean that the instrument, which was probably ladder braced like almost all of the less expensive larger sized Lyon & Healy guitars, did not hold up well under the pressure of steel strings. It could also explain why no surviving examples of the Lakeside Jumbo have surfaced yet –though this seems to be a matter of time.

Lakeside Bass Guitar

Jumbo Size

Style G 2740

SIZE — Length of body, 20⅜ inches; width at upper end, 12 inches; width at lower end, 16¼ inches; total length, 39½ inches.

Rosewood finished birch back and sides. Spruce top. Highly polished.

Broad, fancy wood inlaying around top edge, soundhole and down center of back.

Top and back edges bound with white celluloid.

Neck, mahogany finish, with veneered headpiece.

Rosewood fingerboard with pearl position dots.

Nickel plated patent head with white celluloid buttons.

Strung with best steel strings.

Rosewood bridge with bone saddle and ebony bridge pins with pearl dot.

A very handsome instrument, possessing a powerful tone and great carrying quality. Indispensable to the up-to-date mandolin and guitar club.

1917

76 *Teagle*, p. 73.

77 Style 2210 was listed in the post 1918 catalogs as Style 1210 and had a rosewood body like most of the American Conservatory instruments. The same model was also available with a rosewood finished birch body under the Lakeside brand, initially named the Lakeside Harp Guitar (Style 3740), and after 1918 renamed as 'Lakeside Bass Guitar' (sic), Style 1740.

The College Line Style 2089, aptly nicknamed 'Monster Bass Guitar', was pictured in a few Lyon & Healy catalogs in the 1910s and had even bigger body dimensions: a lower bout of 22 ¼", body length of 20 ¾", body depth of 5" and a scale length of 25 3/8" characterized this huge guitar, introduced according to the makers "to satisfy the fast growing demand for a giant size instrument"(!). The rosewood bodied ladder braced behemoth was available on a made-to-order basis only. Style 2090 was a twelve-string harp guitar version with an additional fretless neck. Small quantities of both styles were actually made, and a few surviving examples have been offered for sale in recent years. After the College Line brand was retired by Lyon & Healy, the Monster Bass Guitar remained in the catalogs until the late 1910s under the American Conservatory brand.

The Cincinnati Glee and Mandolin Club, around 1895. On the left is a huge Washburn guitar, possibly a prop. Did they ban women?

A photograph from the 1896 Washburn souvenir catalog shows a guitar and mandolin orchestra grouped around an enormous Washburn guitar that looks to be the size of a double bass! The large 'Washburn Guitars - Best in the World' label stuck on the lower bout of this instrument adds to the impression that it was constructed for publicity purposes only and not meant to be played. Even if its strings could be tuned to pitch, playing the guitar would be next to impossible as the player would have to be standing up and try to find his way on a gargantuan fretted neck much too wide for mere mortals. However, it cannot be ruled out that this guitar was intended as a real instrument. Another period photograph shows vaudeville banjoist Tom Cleary with a similarly proportioned Washburn banjo, which he was known to use at concerts. Both instruments were never listed in period Lyon & Healy catalogs.

> August 17, 1903.
>
> **A NOVEL "SOLO" GUITAR.**
>
> Demain Wood, of Rochester, exhibited to a few musicians who happened into the Chase & Smith Co's store the other day what is undoubtedly the most remarkable instrument ever seen in this city. For twenty years he has spent his leisure moments perfecting inventions o make his guitar a solo instrument. By the use of three sets of bass strings, a bellows and mouth blow pipe, and other extremely clever mechanical devices, Mr. Wood was enabled to give a fine entertainment..
>
> Mr. Wood started with a full-size Washburn guitar. He fitted it out with three sets of strings for playing accompaniments, carrying the melody on the solo string. All sorts of mechanical devices were on the guitar to enable one pair of hands to operate it. He stopped the frets of the solo string with a tube, which he operated with his mouth. To this tube was also attached a blowpipe, which worked a small bellows at the head of the guitar. This was a part of a device for giving the tremolo effect (by tightening and loosening the strings) so sought by violin players.
>
> Mr. Wood has the contrivance so arranged that by touching buttons, little rods would rise from the frets and stop the strings on any note the operator desired. A sliding bar also carried a stop used in stopping the frets.

It seems hard to believe, but Professor DeMain Wood's customized 'solo guitar' once began life as an Auditorium sized Washburn. In 2004 the sorry remains of this instrument turned up on eBay, together with its original custom made coffin case (Michael Holmes, Publisher, Mugwumps online)

Washburn endorser Tom Cleary (pictured left) with the 'Monster Banjo' (Ron Middlebrook)

College Line Style 2089, around 1910. The inflated version of the Washburn Style 134 guitar (1896-1905) (Gil Southworth, Southworth Guitars)

College Line Style 2090 (the Randy Hall family, Warren, OH)

1917 catalog picture of the Monster Bass guitar. The caption incorrectly lists the model number as G2740, which stood for the Lakeside Bass guitar, a/k/a the Lakeside Jumbo

2.4.5 Bracing

Until the early 1920s the tops of almost all Washburn guitars were ladder braced. This may be partly explained by the fact that all standard Washburn styles until 1915 were solely constructed for the use of gut strings, even though certain models of the cheaper Lyon & Healy guitar lines were made for steel strings as early as 1896.

In the 1889 Washburn catalog the manufacturers recommended the use of gut and silk wound strings under all circumstances. Charles N. Post, the author of the 1889 and later Washburn catalogs, explained this as follows: "the efforts of the manufacturer are earnestly directed toward the production of a rich, mellow and sympathetic tone, and in order to accomplish this result (the guitars) use a sensitively constructed sounding-board and a delicately graduated frame, which are not made to withstand the strain of the wire strings." Interestingly, this text was used almost literally in the guitar section of the 1894-1897 Sears Roebuck catalogs, which in its turn was copied word for word from the same section of an 1890s catalog of competitor Montgomery Ward's! The text also warned buyers that the use of steel strings on Washburn guitars would invalidate the factory warranty. Both Sears and Ward's sold Washburns and also a number of cheaper Lyon & Healy-made guitars during the 1890s, which explains the use by both mail order giants of Lyon & Healy's catalog text in their own sales catalogs.

Even though Lyon & Healy did not champion the use of steel strings for their premium guitars, Washburn guitars constructed to take steel strings –which implied that they were equipped with X-braced and/or steel bar reinforced necks- were available on special order as far back as 1889.

Many of the larger sized pre-1915 Washburns that were examined have X-bracing. Since this feature was found on almost all of the size 3 and 4 guitars, X-bracing may well have been a standard appointment on these models, and available as custom order on the smaller sized guitars in case the customer preferred to use steel strings. The largest Washburn guitar made before 1930, Style 503 of 1889, also had X-bracing.

Though ladder bracing remained standard until the early 1920s before being replaced by X-bracing on most guitars with the introduction of the Styles A-G,[78] the Lyon & Healy catalogs indicated that the Washburn guitar styles made between 1915 and the launch of Styles A-G were constructed for the use of either gut or steel strings. In spite of this statement period catalogs again warned prospective buyers that the factory warranty would not be upheld in case steel strings were used, and specified that all guitars were shipped from the factory with "best quality gut strings and silk wound bass strings". The only exception was Style 2123 of 1920, which was the first Washburn standard guitar model shipped with steel strings. Style 1522, the first Washburn Hawaiian guitar, may have been factory set up with steel strings since its introduction in 1915.[79]

The top and back braces on the pre-1915 guitars vary in form and materials. Some instruments have straight braces that are tapered at the ends, similar to the current most widely used type of guitar braces, while others have arched braces that are shaped as half of an oval from one end to another. Usually the braces on guitars from this period were made of spruce, but very early guitars with cedar or mahogany braces have also been found. Most of the earlier styles were characterized by five lateral back braces that crossed the center strip, which changed to four braces in the early 1890s. Both single and double X-bracing patterns can be found on the larger Washburn guitars made after 1935.

It is not unusual to find penciled dates, initials, inspection or style stamps and names on the top and back braces or at the underside of Washburn guitar tops, which may provide additional clues for dating purposes.

Lyon & Healy and Tonk Bros apparently were not convinced about the tonal advantages of scalloped bracing as this was never a standard feature on prewar Washburn guitars, including the Regal and Gibson-made examples. The only exceptions are a few of the earliest guitars made before 1889.[80] The last of the ladder braced Washburn flattops was Style 5240 (1937-1940).[81]

78 A number of surviving post 1922 guitars does not have X-bracing. Styles F and G (1923-1925) were based on the previous (1915) model line and therefore probably had ladder braced tops.

79 Between 1917 and 1919 Style 1522 was catalogued as the 'Washburn Hawaiian Steel Guitar', and the 1919 catalog stated that it came with steel strings.

80 There are reports about 1930s Washburns with very lightly scalloped braces. Whether these are original is uncertain.

81 Surviving examples of Style 5241 have been found with ladder bracing and with X-bracing.

Style 8, 1884-7
(Gary Hughes)

Style 6,
1884-7,
version with solid
headstock and
friction tuners
(Carmel Music Co.)

Style 1, 1884-7 (Eltjo Haselhoff)

2.5 Guitar styles 1883-1940

Washburn guitar styles 1883/4-1887

The 1884 Lyon & Healy Musical Merchandise catalog contained one page devoted to the new Washburn guitar line that consisted of eight models. The unnamed guitar pictured on this page has a double bound body with a herringbone pattern around its soundhole and body perimeter, an oversized Washburn logo stamp inside, a Martin style pyramid bridge, a 20-fret neck, no fingerboard inlays and a square slotted headstock. Only the last two features seem to be consistent with early Washburns that were examined. Some of the early Washburn guitars (probably dating before 1887) have a solid headstock with mechanical friction peg tuners or round topped headstock slots. An 1885 company catalog titled 'Musical Holiday Goods' mentions six Washburn guitar styles priced between $20 and $75, but pictures or a description of these guitars were not provided.

(The top material for all guitars listed below is spruce, and all headstocks are of the slotted type unless indicated otherwise. 'b/s' stands for 'back and sides', 'fb' for 'fingerboard')

Size	Large	Concert	Extra Large Concert	
	1			rosewood b/s, mahogany neck, 18-fret ebony fb without position markers, ebony flattened pyramid bridge, no binding on top, back and neck, colored rings around s/h, inlaid backstrip
	2			rosewood b/s, mahogany neck, 18-fret ebony fb without position markers, ebony flattened pyramid bridge, colored rings around s/h and top edge, unbound back and fingerboard, inlaid backstrip
	3			rosewood b/s, mahogany neck, 18-fret ebony fb without position markers, ebony flattened pyramid bridge, s/h and edges bound w marquetry patterns, fancy inlaid backstrip
	4			as Style 3, but with celluloid bound body
		5		rosewood b/s, mahogany neck, 18-fret ebony fb without position markers, ebony flattened pyramid bridge, celluloid inlays around s/h and top, fancy inlaid backstrip
		6		as Style 5, but with celluloid bound top and back
			7	same appointments as Style 5
			8	same appointments as Style 6

WASHBURN GUITAR.

STYLES 101¾ TO 301.

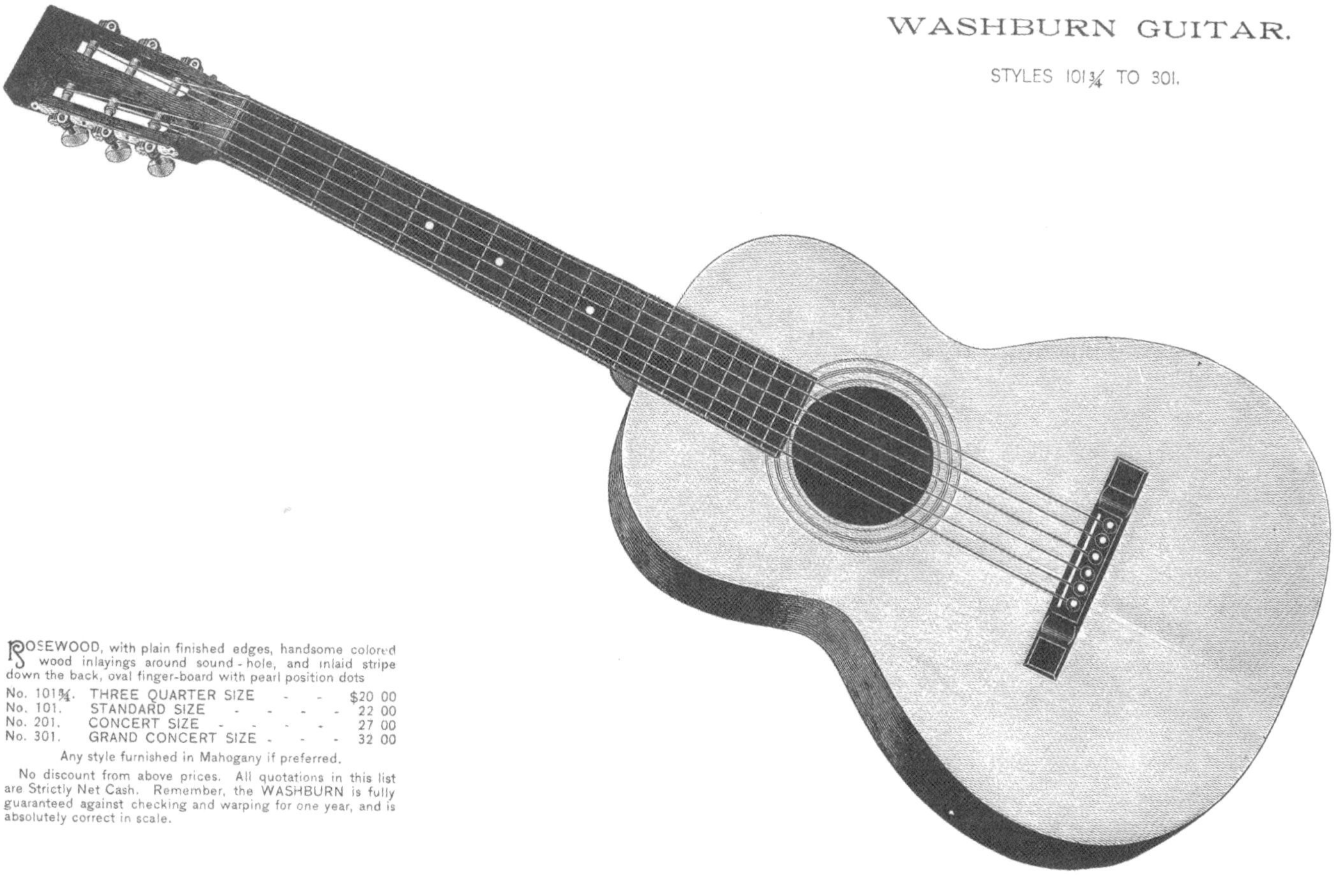

ROSEWOOD, with plain finished edges, handsome colored wood inlayings around sound-hole, and inlaid stripe down the back, oval finger-board with pearl position dots

No. 101¾.	THREE QUARTER SIZE - -	$20 00
No. 101.	STANDARD SIZE - - - -	22 00
No. 201.	CONCERT SIZE - - - -	27 00
No. 301.	GRAND CONCERT SIZE - - -	32 00

Any style furnished in Mahogany if preferred.

No discount from above prices. All quotations in this list are Strictly Net Cash. Remember, the WASHBURN is fully guaranteed against checking and warping for one year, and is absolutely correct in scale.

Style 301 (1889)

WASHBURN GUITAR.

STYLES 102¾ TO 402.

ROSEWOOD, with neatly inlaid edges, beautifully colored wood inlayings around sound-hole, and a handsome stripe of inlaying down the back. Oval Ebony finger board with pearl position dots

No 102¾.	THREE QUARTER SIZE - -	$24 00
No. 102	STANDARD SIZE - - - -	26 00
No. 202.	CONCERT SIZE - - - -	32 00
No. 302.	GRAND CONCERT SIZE - - -	37 00
No. 402.	AUDITORIUM SIZE - - -	45 00

To insure perfection throughout, the makers of the Washburn instruments manufacture all the machine heads used thereon.

No discount from above prices. All quotations in this list are strictly Net Cash.

Style 302 (1889)

Washburn guitar styles 1887-1889

For all guitars made between 1887 and 1925 size 1 equals 'Standard Size', size 2 'Concert Size', size 3 'Grand Concert Size', and size 4 'Auditorium Size'.

Size ¾	1	2	3	
101 3/4	101	201	301	rosewood b/s, cedar or mahogany neck, 18-fret ebony fb without position markers, ebony flattened pyramid bridge, no binding on top, back and fingerboard, colored rings around s/h, inlaid backstrip
102 3/4	102	202	302	rosewood b/s, cedar or mahogany neck, 18-fret ebony fb without position markers, ebony flattened pyramid bridge, no binding on top, back and fingerboard, colored rings around s/h and top edge, fancy inlaid backstrip
	103	203	303	rosewood b/s, cedar or mahogany neck, 18-fret ebony fb without position markers, ebony flattened pyramid bridge, s/h bound w colored wood and celluloid, top edge bound w celluloid, fancy inlaid backstrip
	104	204	304	rosewood b/s, cedar or mahogany neck, inlaid headstock, 18-fret ebony fb without position markers, ebony flattened pyramid bridge, s/h bound w colored wood and celluloid, top and back bound w celluloid and colored marquetry pattern, fancy inlaid backstrip

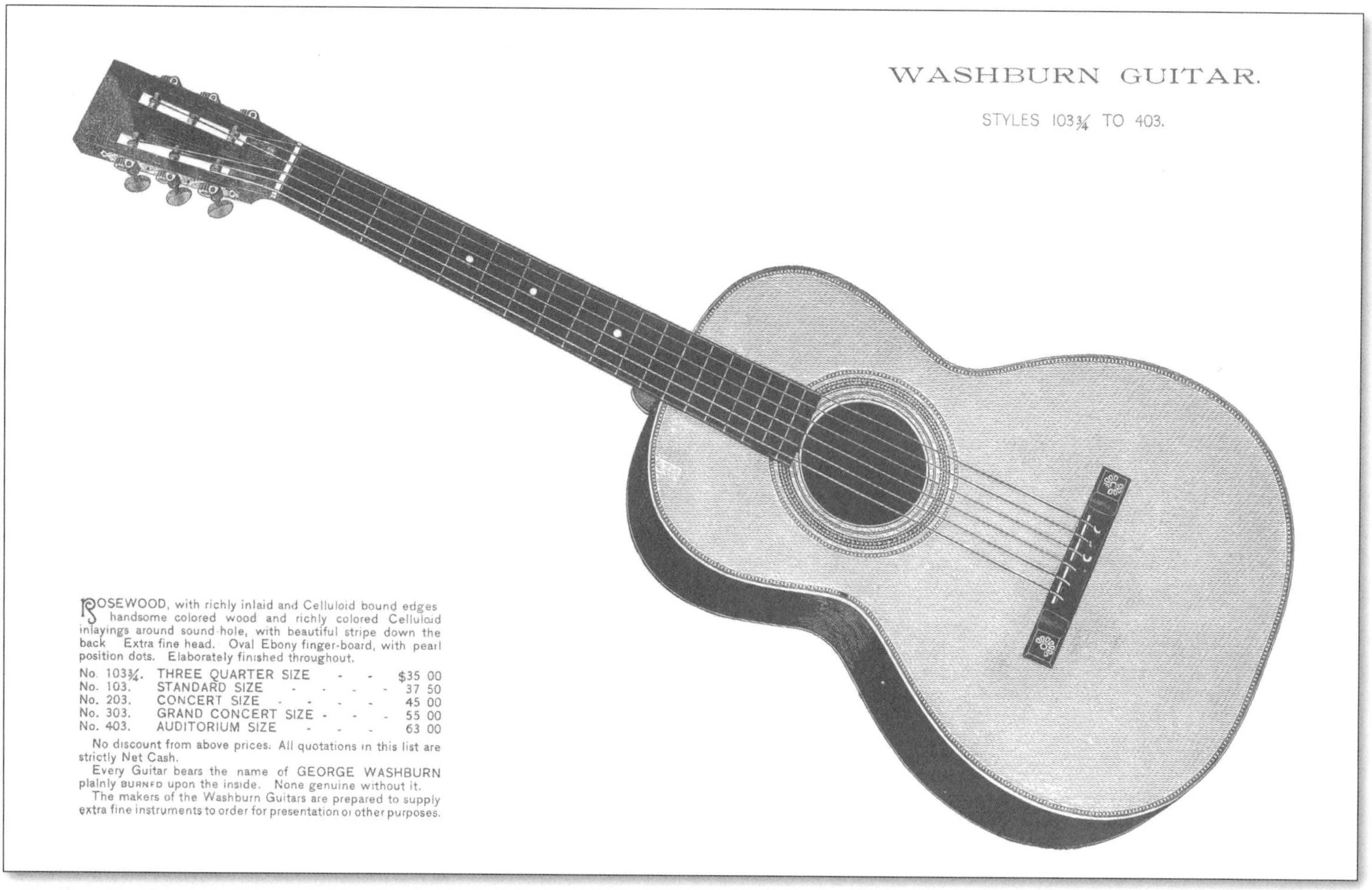

WASHBURN GUITAR.

STYLES 103¾ TO 403.

ROSEWOOD, with richly inlaid and Celluloid bound edges handsome colored wood and richly colored Celluloid inlayings around sound-hole, with beautiful stripe down the back Extra fine head. Oval Ebony finger-board, with pearl position dots. Elaborately finished throughout.

No. 103¾.	THREE QUARTER SIZE - -	$35 00
No. 103.	STANDARD SIZE - - - -	37 50
No. 203.	CONCERT SIZE - - - - -	45 00
No. 303.	GRAND CONCERT SIZE - - -	55 00
No. 403.	AUDITORIUM SIZE - - -	63 00

No discount from above prices. All quotations in this list are strictly Net Cash.

Every Guitar bears the name of GEORGE WASHBURN plainly BURNED upon the inside. None genuine without it.

The makers of the Washburn Guitars are prepared to supply extra fine instruments to order for presentation or other purposes.

Style 303 (1889)

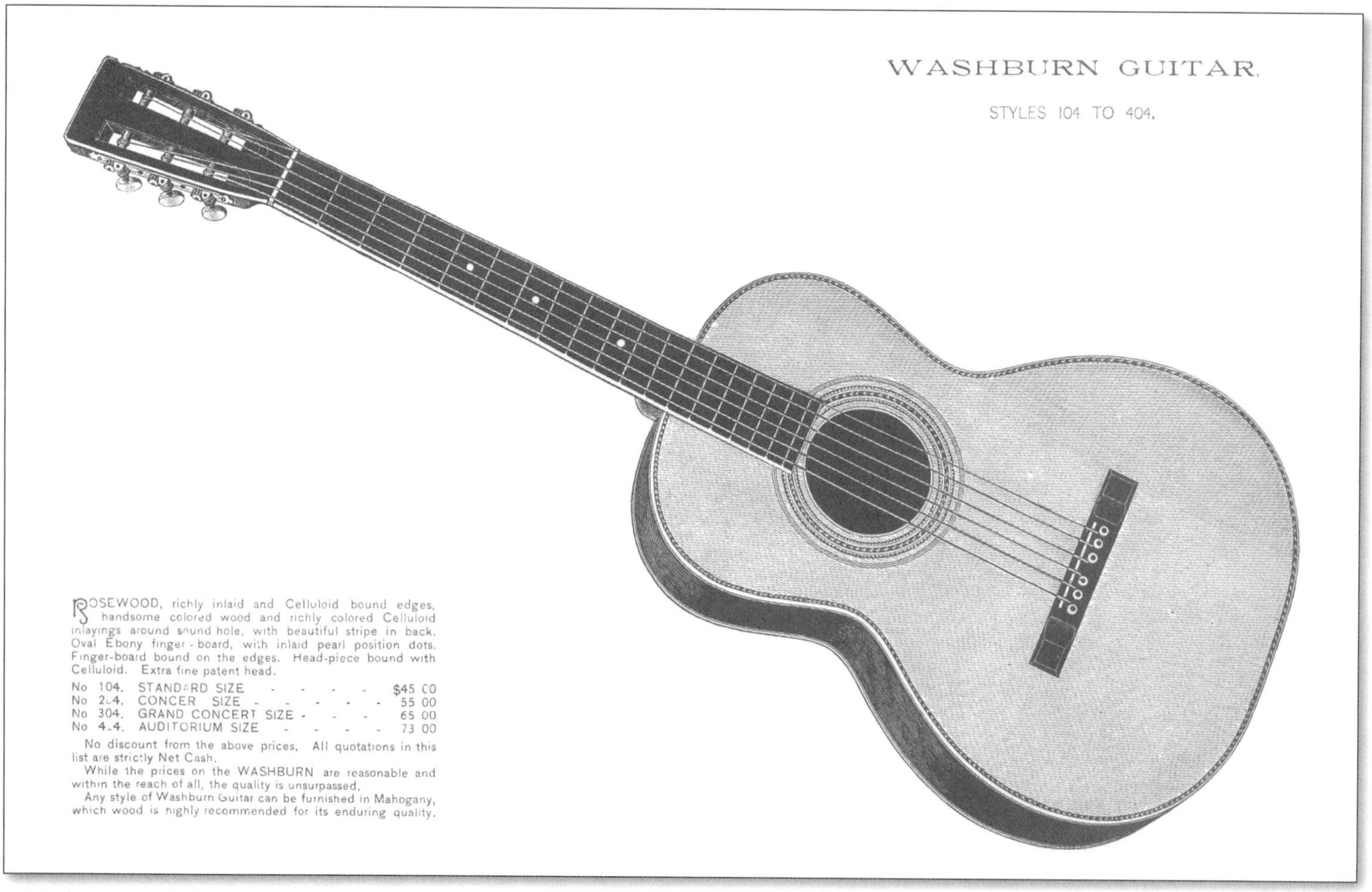

WASHBURN GUITAR.

STYLES 104 TO 404.

ROSEWOOD, richly inlaid and Celluloid bound edges, handsome colored wood and richly colored Celluloid inlayings around sound hole, with beautiful stripe in back. Oval Ebony finger-board, with inlaid pearl position dots. Finger-board bound on the edges. Head-piece bound with Celluloid. Extra fine patent head.

No 104.	STANDARD SIZE - - - - -	$45 00
No 204.	CONCER SIZE - - - - - -	55 00
No 304.	GRAND CONCERT SIZE - - - -	65 00
No 404.	AUDITORIUM SIZE - - - - -	73 00

No discount from the above prices. All quotations in this list are strictly Net Cash.

While the prices on the WASHBURN are reasonable and within the reach of all, the quality is unsurpassed.

Any style of Washburn Guitar can be furnished in Mahogany, which wood is highly recommended for its enduring quality.

Style 304 (1889)

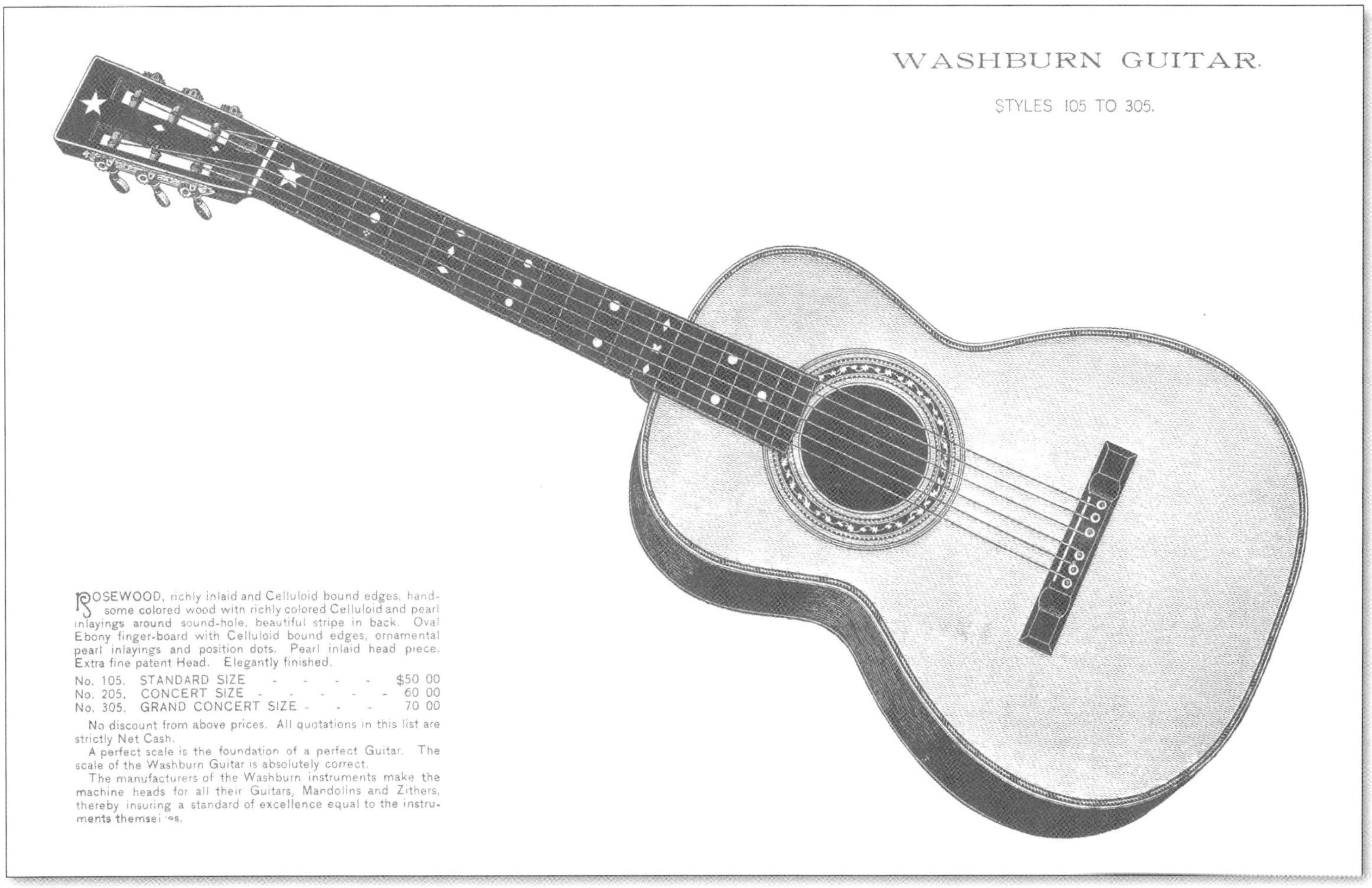

WASHBURN GUITAR.

STYLES 105 TO 305.

ROSEWOOD, richly inlaid and Celluloid bound edges, handsome colored wood with richly colored Celluloid and pearl inlayings around sound-hole, beautiful stripe in back. Oval Ebony finger-board with Celluloid bound edges, ornamental pearl inlayings and position dots. Pearl inlaid head piece. Extra fine patent Head. Elegantly finished.

No. 105.	STANDARD SIZE - - - - -	$50 00
No. 205.	CONCERT SIZE - - - - - -	60 00
No. 305.	GRAND CONCERT SIZE - - -	70 00

No discount from above prices. All quotations in this list are strictly Net Cash.

A perfect scale is the foundation of a perfect Guitar. The scale of the Washburn Guitar is absolutely correct.

The manufacturers of the Washburn instruments make the machine heads for all their Guitars, Mandolins and Zithers, thereby insuring a standard of excellence equal to the instruments themselves.

Style 305 (1889)

WASHBURN GUITAR.

STYLES 106 TO 306.

ROSEWOOD, very elaborate inlayings around sound hole, top elegantly inlaid around the edges, two Celluloid inlaid stripes in sides, beautifully inlaid stripes around the back and through the center, edges all Celluloid bound. Oval Ebony finger-board bound and richly inlaid with pearl; in all representing the most artistic, yet richest display of ornamentation, of any style quoted.

No. 106.	STANDARD SIZE - - - - -	$55 00
No. 206.	CONCERT SIZE - - - - - -	65 00
No. 306.	GRAND CONCERT SIZE - - -	75 00

No discount from above prices. All quotations in this list are strictly Net Cash

Read the articles on pages 3, 4 and 5, as they are interesting to any one contemplating the purchase of an instrument

Style 306 (1889)

WASHBURN GUITAR.

STYLES 108 TO 308.

ROSEWOOD, very elaborately inlaid around sound-hole, and edges of top, with pearl, richly colored woods and Celluloid top, Celluloid inlaid stripes in sides, beautifully inlaid stripes around the back and through the center,. edges all Celluloid bound Oval ebony finger board, bound and richly inlaid with pearl. Extra fine machine head. Altogether the most gorgeous instrument yet offered.

No 108.	STANDARD SIZE - - - - -	$80 00
No. 208.	CONCERT SIZE - - - - - -	90 00
No 308.	GRAND CONCERT SIZE - - -	100 00

No discount from above prices. All quotations in this list are strictly Net Cash.

Instruments inlaid with Special Designs, Monograms, or Sketched Figures of any nature can be supplied to order.

Style 308 (1889)

WASHBURN GUITAR.

STYLE 503.

CONTRA BASS GUITAR.

INTENDED ESPECIALLY FOR ACCOMPANIMENTS.

Measurements.—Across body back of bridge, 15 inches; across body above sound-hole, 10½ inches; depth of body at lower end, 5 inches; length of scale, 27½ inches.

No. 503. ROSEWOOD, with richly inlaid and white Celluloid bound edges, handsome colored wood and richly colored Celluloid inlayings around sound-hole, beautiful inlaid stripe in back. Extra fine machine head. Oval ebony finger-board, finely finished throughout, - - - - - - $75.00

No discount from above prices. All quotations in this list are strictly Net Cash

The Contra Bass Guitar is the largest instrument of the kind attempted. It is strung with specially made strings, and in tone quite harp-like. It is intended for use in clubs for accompaniments, and is too large for successful solo use.

Style 309 (1889)

Washburn guitar styles 1889-1892

Size ¾	1	2	3	4	
101 3/4	101	201	301		rosewood b/s and headstock overlay, cedar neck, 18-fret ebony fb w three pearl dots at frets 5, 7 and 10, black heelcap, ebony flattened pyramid bridge, black bridge pins w pearl dots, ebony nut, no binding on top, back and neck, white/black/red rings around s/h, inlaid backstrip w rope marquetry pattern
102 3/4	102	202	302	402	rosewood b/s and headstock overlay, cedar neck, 18-fret ebony fb w three pearl dots at frets 5, 7 and 10, ebony flattened pyramid bridge, black bridge pins w pearl dots, ebony nut, top bound w white celluloid and colored lines, rings around s/h, inlaid backstrip w rope marquetry pattern
103 3/4	103	203	303	403	rosewood b/s and headstock overlay, cedar neck w volute, 18-fret ebony fb w three pearl dots at frets 5, 7 and 10, ebony flattened pyramid bridge w chrysanthemum inlays, white bridge pins w black or abalone dots, bone nut, top bound w white celluloid and checkerboard pattern, s/h bound w white celluloid, herringbone pattern and checkerboard rings, back bound w white celluloid, inlaid backstrip
	104	204	304	404	rosewood b/s, rosewood headstock overlay, cedar neck w volute, 18-fret (404: 19-fret) ebony fb w three pearl dots at frets 5, 7 and 10, headstock and fingerboard bound w white celluloid, ebony Durkee bridge w flattened pyramid ends, white bridge pins w black or abalone dots, bone nut, top bound w white celluloid and herringbone pattern, s/h bound w white celluloid, herringbone pattern and rings, back bound w white celluloid, inlaid herringbone backstrip
	105	205	305		rosewood b/s, ebony headstock overlay, cedar neck w volute, 18-fret ebony fb w pearl inlays at frets 1, 3, 5, 7, 10, 12, 15 and 17, star shaped inlay on headstock, headstock and fingerboard bound w white celluloid, ebony Durkee bridge w flattened pyramid ends, white bridge pins w black or abalone dots, bone nut, top bound w white celluloid and marquetry pattern, s/h bound w white celluloid, checkerboard pattern and rings plus inlaid pearl leaf shaped figures, back bound w white celluloid, inlaid backstrip

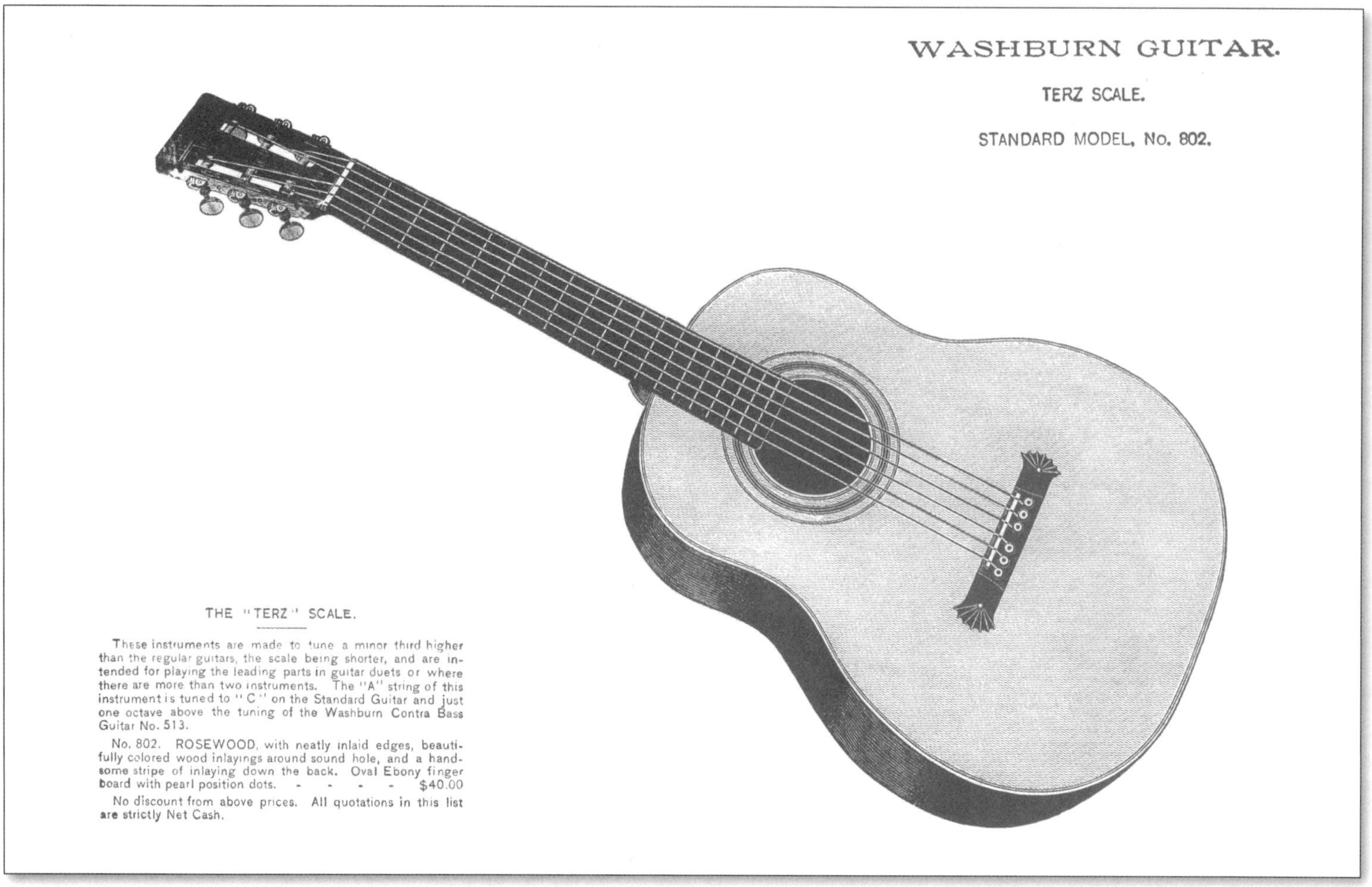

WASHBURN GUITAR.

TERZ SCALE.

STANDARD MODEL, No. 802.

THE "TERZ" SCALE.

These instruments are made to tune a minor third higher than the regular guitars, the scale being shorter, and are intended for playing the leading parts in guitar duets or where there are more than two instruments. The "A" string of this instrument is tuned to "C" on the Standard Guitar and just one octave above the tuning of the Washburn Contra Bass Guitar No. 513.

No. 802. ROSEWOOD, with neatly inlaid edges, beautifully colored wood inlayings around sound hole, and a handsome stripe of inlaying down the back. Oval Ebony finger board with pearl position dots. - - - - $40.00

No discount from above prices. All quotations in this list are strictly Net Cash.

Style 802 (1892)

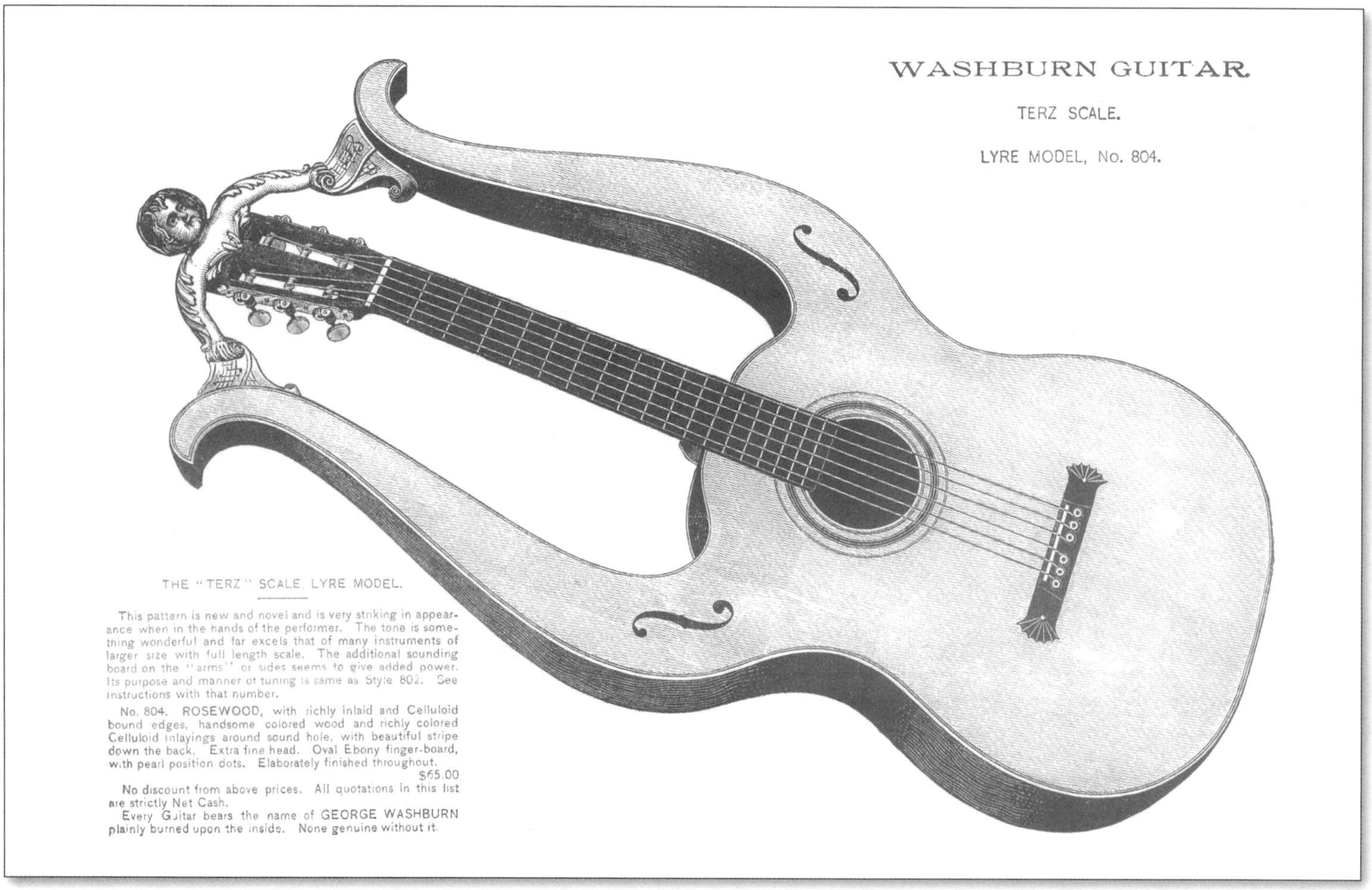

WASHBURN GUITAR.

TERZ SCALE.

LYRE MODEL, No. 804.

THE "TERZ" SCALE, LYRE MODEL.

This pattern is new and novel and is very striking in appearance when in the hands of the performer. The tone is something wonderful and far excels that of many instruments of larger size with full length scale. The additional sounding board on the "arms" or sides seems to give added power. Its purpose and manner of tuning is same as Style 802. See instructions with that number.

No. 804. ROSEWOOD, with richly inlaid and Celluloid bound edges, handsome colored wood and richly colored Celluloid inlayings around sound hole, with beautiful stripe down the back. Extra fine head. Oval Ebony finger-board, with pearl position dots. Elaborately finished throughout. $65.00

No discount from above prices. All quotations in this list are strictly Net Cash.

Every Guitar bears the name of GEORGE WASHBURN plainly burned upon the inside. None genuine without it.

Style 804 (1892)

Size ¾	1	2	3	4	
	106	206	306		rosewood b/s, ebony headstock overlay, cedar neck w volute and white celluloid heelcap, 18-fret ebony fb w pearl inlays at frets 1, 3, 5, 7, 10, 12, 15 and 17, pearl arrow shaped inlays on headstock, headstock and fingerboard bound w white celluloid, ebony Durkee bridge w shell shaped ends and pearl dots, white bridge pins w black or abalone dots, bone nut, top bound w white celluloid and herringbone/ checkerboard pattern, s/h bound w white celluloid, checkerboard pattern and ring pattern, back bound w white celluloid and marquetry, inlaid sides, inlaid backstrip
	108	208	308		rosewood b/s, ebony headstock overlay, cedar neck w volute, 18-fret ebony fb w pearl inlays at frets 1, 3, 5, 7, 10, 12, 15 and 17, pearl wave shaped inlay on headstock, headstock and fingerboard bound w white celluloid, ebony Durkee bridge w shell shaped ends and pearl dots, white bridge pins w black or abalone dots, bone nut, top and soundhole bound w white celluloid and herringbone/ checkerboard pattern plus inlaid pearl leaf shaped figures, lyre inlaid on bottom of lower bout, back bound w white celluloid and marquetry, inlaid backstrip
					503 ('Contra Bass Guitar') 15″ body, 27″scale (1st string tuned down to G), neck joins body between 10th and 11th fret, rosewood b/s and headstock overlay, cedar neck, 18-fret ebony fb* w three pearl dots at frets 5, 7 and 10, headstock and fingerboard bound w white celluloid, ebony flattened pyramid bridge, black bridge pins w pearl dots, bone nut, top bound w white celluloid and herringbone pattern, s/h bound w white celluloid, herringbone and checkerboard pattern, back bound w white celluloid and marquetry, inlaid backstrip

* The 1889 catalog drawing of Style 503 shows a 17-fret fingerboard without any position markers, and specifies a 27 ½″ scale.

Washburn Guitar.

Styles 111 and 211.

T. W. REAMER.
(TEACHER, SEATTLE, WASH.)
"The Washburn Guitars are perfection. I use and recommend them in preference to any others."

KATHLEEN S. BLISS.
(TEACHER, ROCHESTER, N. Y.)
"I have used the Washburn Guitars on the Pacific coast and in this city, and find them equal to both climates. The tone mellow, clear and powerful, they give perfect satisfaction at all times."

DESCRIPTION.

ROSEWOOD, with inlaid and celluloid-bound top edge; three colored wood stripes inlaid around sound-hole; inlaid stripe down the back; cedar-neck; fine quality ebony finger-board, with pearl position marks; ebony bridge; all French polished; good quality patent head, bronze-plated.

No. 111.—Standard size,	$15.00
No. 211.—Concert size,	18.00

No discount from above prices.

To insure perfection throughout, the manufacturers of the WASHBURN make EVERY PART of the instrument, including the machine head, inlay, plating, etc.

27

Style 211 (1896)

Washburn Guitar.

Styles 112 to 312.

MISS SYRENA GRAHAM.
(TEACHER GUITAR, MANDOLIN AND BANJO, OIL CITY, PENN.)
"After much experience with the various so-called first-class instruments, I unhesitatingly pronounce the Washburns the best. Absolutely correct scale, superior tone, and artistic in finish and workmanship."

MARIO ANCONA.
(ABBEY & GRAU GRAND OPERA CO.)
"I am more than pleased with the Mandolin made for me. * * * You are fairly entitled to the credit of making the best Mandolin in the World."

DESCRIPTION.

ROSEWOOD, with fancy wood inlaid and celluloid-bound top edge; three fancy wood inlaid circles around sound-hole; inlaid stripe down the back, cedar neck, fine quality ebony finger-board, with pearl inlaid position marks; ebony bridge; French polished; good quality patent head, fancy bronzed.

No. 112.—Standard size,	$18.00
No. 212.—Concert size,	21.00
No. 312.—Grand Concert size,	24.00

No discount from above prices.

WASHBURN instruments are all fully guaranteed, but should be purchased through regular sources. See full explanation on page 3.

29

Style 212 (1896)

Washburn guitar styles 1892-1896

Size ¾	1	2	3	4	
101 3/4	101	201	301		as Style 101 (1889)
102 3/4	102	202	302	402	as Style 102 (1889)
103 3/4	103	203	303	403	as Style 103 (1889)
	104	204	304	404	as Style 104 (1889)
	105	205	305		as Style 105 (1889)
	106	206	306		as Style 106 (1889)
	108	208	308		as Style 108 (1889)
	109	209	309		rosewood b/s, ebony headstock overlay, cedar neck w volute, 18-fret ebony fb w elongated engraved pearl flowerpot and vine inlays, leaf shaped inlays on headstock, headstock and fingerboard bound w white celluloid, ebony Durkee bridge w shell shaped ends, pearl dots and inlaid white strips, white bridge pins w black or abalone dots, bone nut, top and soundhole bound w white celluloid and elaborate marquetry/pearl pattern, pearl inlaid stripes on sides, back bound w white celluloid and marquetry, inlaid backstrip
					802* ('Terz Scale, Standard Model', tuned a minor third higher than a standard guitar), rosewood b/s and headstock overlay, cedar neck, plain 18-fret ebony fb, ebony Durkee bridge w shell shaped ends and pearl dots, white bridge pins w black or abalone dots, bone nut, top bound w white celluloid and colored lines, rings around s/h, inlaid backstrip
					804 ('Terz Scale, Lyre Model', tuned a minor third higher than a standard guitar), lyre shaped body w central soundhole and inverted f-holes on top**, rosewood b/s and headstock overlay, steel cherub figure on top of headstock, cedar neck, plain 18-fret ebony fb, ebony Durkee bridge w shell shaped ends and pearl dots, white bridge pins w black or abalone dots, bone nut, top bound w white celluloid and colored lines, rings around s/h, inlaid backstrip

* In the description of Style 802 in the 1892 Washburn catalog reference is made to the Contra Bass Guitar No. *513* (sic) but there is no picture or description of this instrument in said catalog, which is why it is not listed here as a standard model

** Some Lyre terz guitars were made without f-holes and with dot fingerboard position markers at frets 5, 7, 9 or 10

Washburn Guitar.

Styles 123¾ to 423.

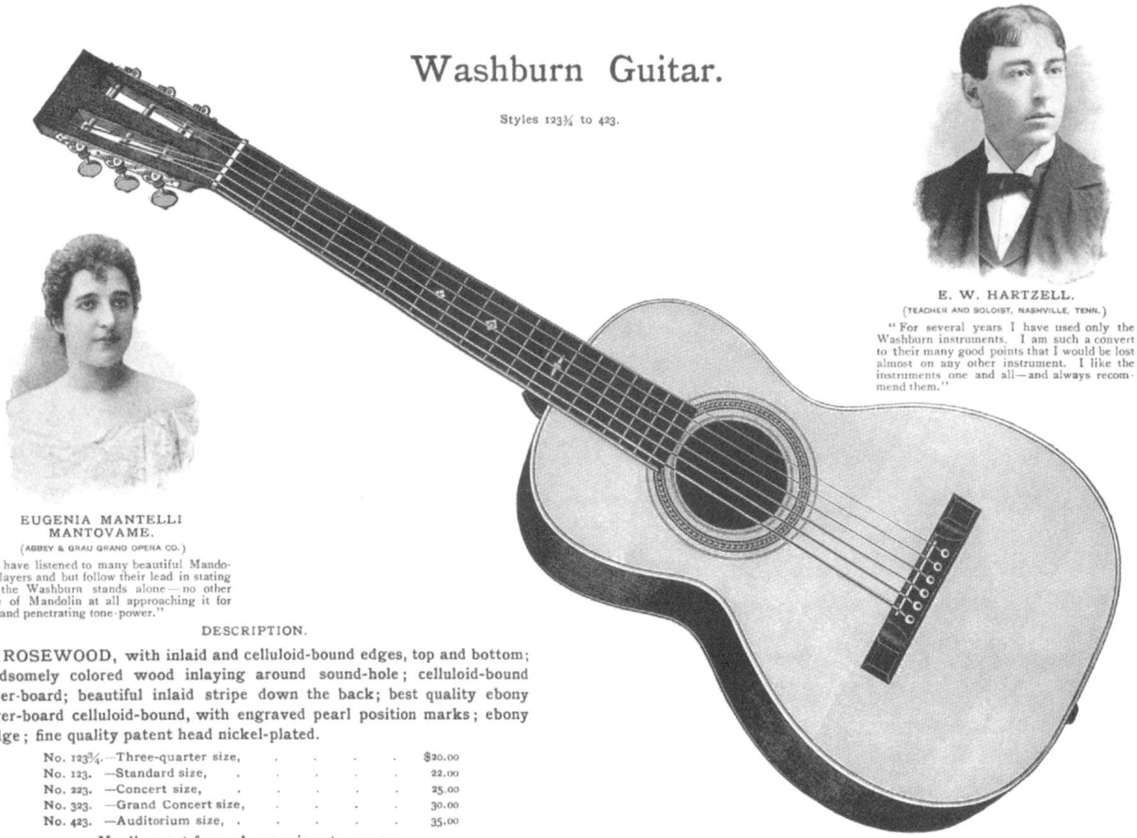

E. W. HARTZELL.

(TEACHER AND SOLOIST, NASHVILLE, TENN.)

"For several years I have used only the Washburn instruments. I am such a convert to their many good points that I would be lost almost on any other instrument. I like the instruments one and all—and always recommend them."

EUGENIA MANTELLI MANTOVAME.

(ABBEY & GRAU GRAND OPERA CO.)

"I have listened to many beautiful Mandolin players and but follow their lead in stating that the Washburn stands alone—no other make of Mandolin at all approaching it for pure and penetrating tone-power."

DESCRIPTION.

ROSEWOOD, with inlaid and celluloid-bound edges, top and bottom; handsomely colored wood inlaying around sound-hole; celluloid-bound finger-board; beautiful inlaid stripe down the back; best quality ebony finger-board celluloid-bound, with engraved pearl position marks; ebony bridge; fine quality patent head nickel-plated.

No. 123¾.	—Three-quarter size,	$20.00
No. 123.	—Standard size,	22.00
No. 223.	—Concert size,	25.00
No. 323.	—Grand Concert size,	30.00
No. 423.	—Auditorium size,	35.00

No discount from above prices to anyone.

Remember that the prices for WASHBURN instruments are the same everywhere throughout the United States.

31

Style 223 (1896)

Washburn Guitar.

Styles 134 to 334.

CHAS. E. SCHARF.

(GUITAR SOLOIST, BALTIMORE, MD.)

"I consider the Washburn Guitars to be the best instruments ever made. Have used them for years for solo work, both in public and private, and found their acoustic properties to be perfect."

MRS. FRANK JAMES SQUIRES.

(GUITAR TEACHER, MEDINA, N. Y.)

"For ease in playing, volume of tone, mellowness in quality, absolute perfection in scale, graceful model, exquisite finish, and faultless workmanship, the Washburn Guitars lead them ail."

DESCRIPTION.

ROSEWOOD, with fancy wood inlaid and celluloid-bound top and bottom edges; beautiful fancy colored woods and celluloid inlaid around sound-hole; rich inlaid stripe down the back; cedar neck, selected ebony finger-board, celluloid-bound with neatly engraved pearl position marks; ebony bridge, pearl inlaid on ends; finely French polished; fine quality patent head nickel-plated.

No. 134.	—Standard size,	$30.00
No. 234.	—Concert size,	35.00
No. 334.	—Grand Concert size,	40.00

No discount from above prices.

The strong testimonials presented in this catalogue from scores of well known professional people cannot be duplicated by other makers.

33

Style 234 (1896)

Size ¾	1	2	3	4	
	111	211			rosewood b/s and headstock overlay, cedar neck, 18-fret ebony fb w three pearl dots at frets 5, 7 and 9, black heelcap, ebony flattened pyramid bridge, black bridge pins w pearl dots, ebony nut, top bound w white celluloid and colored lines, rings around s/h, back bound w white celluloid, inlaid backstrip w rope pattern
	112	212	312		rosewood b/s and headstock overlay, cedar neck, 18-fret ebony fb w three pearl dots at frets 5, 7 and 9, ebony flattened pyramid bridge, black bridge pins w pearl dots, ebony nut, top bound w white celluloid and rope pattern, rings and rope pattern around s/h, inlaid backstrip
123 3/4	123	223	323	423	rosewood b/s and headstock overlay, cedar neck, 18-fret (423: 19-fret) ebony fb w three pearl engraved inlays at frets 7, 9 and 12, fingerboard bound w white celluloid, ebony flattened pyramid bridge, white bridge pins w abalone dots, bone nut, top bound w white celluloid and colored lines, herringbone pattern and rings and around s/h, inlaid backstrip (three colored lines)
	134	234	334		rosewood b/s and headstock overlay, cedar neck w volute, 18-fret ebony fb w four pearl engraved inlays at frets 5, 7, 9 and 12, fingerboard bound w white celluloid, ebony flattened pyramid bridge w chrysanthemum inlays, white bridge pins w abalone dots, bone nut, top bound w white celluloid and herringbone pattern, s/h bound w white celluloid, herringbone/checkerboard pattern and white/red/black rings, inlaid backstrip
	145	245	345		rosewood b/s and ebony headstock overlay, cedar neck w volute, 18-fret ebony fb bound w white celluloid w four pearl engraved inlays at frets 5, 7, 9 and 12, pearl snowflake shaped inlay on headstock, headstock and fingerboard bound w white celluloid, ebony Durkee bridge w flattened pyramid ends and chrysanthemum inlays, white bridge pins w abalone dots, bone nut, top bound w white celluloid and marquetry, s/h bound w white celluloid, checkerboard pattern and rings plus inlaid pearl leaf shaped figures, back bound w white celluloid, inlaid backstrip w marquetry pattern

Washburn Guitar.

Styles 145 to 345.

MRS. J. H. TOMPKINS.

(TEACHER OF GUITAR, RICHMOND, VA.)

"After using the Washburn Guitars and Mandolins for ten years, I can truly say they are faultless."

PROF. EDWARD TOUGAS.

(TEACHER AND SOLOIST, ALBANY, N. Y.)

"I consider the Washburn Mandolin superior to all others. Perfect in workmanship and finish, and playing with ease in all the positions, it combines wonderful sweetness and brilliancy of tone. Please add my endorsement to your long list of testimonials."

DESCRIPTION.

ROSEWOOD, with variegated wood inlaid and celluloid-bound top and bottom edges; beautifully inlaid with pearl around sound-hole; rich inlaid stripe in the back; cedar neck; selected ebony finger-board with finely engraved pearl position marks; finger-board and head-piece bound with celluloid; head-piece inlaid with pearl; Durkee's patent, ebony bridge inlaid with pearl on ends; finely French polished; fine quality patent head nickel-plated.

No. 145.—Standard size, ... $40.00
*No. 245.—Concert size, ... 45.00
*No. 345.—Grand Concert size, ... 50.00

No discount from above prices.

*These styles require a few days time to supply after order is received.

The makers of the WASHBURN instruments are prepared to supply special made instruments for presentation, to order upon short notice.

35

Style 245 (1896)

Washburn Guitar.

Styles 156 to 356.

W. W. PERRY.

(TEACHER OF MANDOLIN AND BANJO, TOLEDO, O.)

"I use and endorse the Washburn instruments. I consider them unequaled in all points of excellence."

MISS LUTIE RIGGS.

(TEACHER MANDOLIN AND GUITAR, COLORADO SPRINGS, COLO.)

"I use and recommend the Washburn Guitars and Mandolins, because I believe them to be the best. Beautiful finish, exquisite tone, and perfect scales are their principal points of excellence."

DESCRIPTION.

ROSEWOOD, with elaborate design of colored wood, inlaid and celluloid-bound top and bottom edge; rich pearl inlay beautifully engraved around sound-hole; wide inlaid stripe down the back; cedar neck, with fine quality ebony finger-board, containing eight rich pearl ornamentations handsomely engraved as position marks; finger-board and head-piece celluloid-bound; head-piece inlaid with pearl; ebony bridge; Durkee's patent; pearl ornaments inlaid on ends; finely French polished; best quality patent heads nickel-plated.

No. 156.—Standard size, ... $50.00
*No. 256.—Concert size, ... 55.00
*No. 356.—Grand Concert size, ... 60.00

No discount from above prices.

*These styles require a few days time to supply after order is received.

Every WASHBURN instrument contains, besides the brand plainly burned upon the inside, a guaranty label, with consecutive number. Look for it.

37

Style 256 (1896)

Washburn guitar styles 1896-1905 (coninued)

Size ¾	1	2	3	4	
	156	256	356		rosewood b/s and ebony headstock overlay, cedar neck w volute, 18-fret ebony fb bound w white celluloid w eight pearl engraved inlays at frets 1, 3, 5, 7, 9, 12, 15 and 17, pearl snowflake shaped inlay on headstock, headstock and fingerboard bound w white celluloid, ebony Durkee bridge w flattened pyramid ends and chrysanthemum inlays, white bridge pins w abalone dots, bone nut, top bound w white celluloid and marquetry, s/h bound w broad engraved pearl ring and checkerboard pattern, back bound w white celluloid, inlaid backstrip
	167	267	367		rosewood b/s and ebony headstock overlay, cedar neck w volute, 18-fret ebony fb bound w white celluloid w eight pearl engraved inlays at frets 1, 3, 5, 7, 9, 12, 15 and 17, pearl snowflake shaped inlay on headstock, pearl tuner buttons, headstock and fingerboard bound w white celluloid, ebony Durkee bridge w shell shaped ends and dot inlays, white bridge pins w abalone dots, bone nut, top bound w white celluloid and marquetry, s/h bound w pearl rings and marquetry pattern, back and sides bound w white celluloid, inlaid backstrip
	188	288	388		rosewood b/s and ebony headstock overlay, cedar neck w volute, 18-fret solid pearl fb bound w celluloid w engravings at frets 1, 3, 5, 7, 9, 12, 15 and 17, snowflake shaped pearl inlay on headstock, pearl tuner buttons, headstock and fingerboard bound w white celluloid, ebony Durkee bridge w shell shaped ends and dot inlays, white bridge pins w black dots, bone nut, top bound w white/red celluloid, checkerboard pattern and abalone/pearl inlay, s/h bound w white celluloid, abalone/pearl and white/black/red rings and checkerboard pattern, two double white/red/white lines inlaid on sides, back bound w white celluloid and checkerboard pattern, inlaid Martin Style 45 marquetry backstrip, black end piece bound w white/black lines and checkerboard pattern
	199	299	399		as Style 109 (1892)

Washburn Guitar.

Styles 167 to 367.

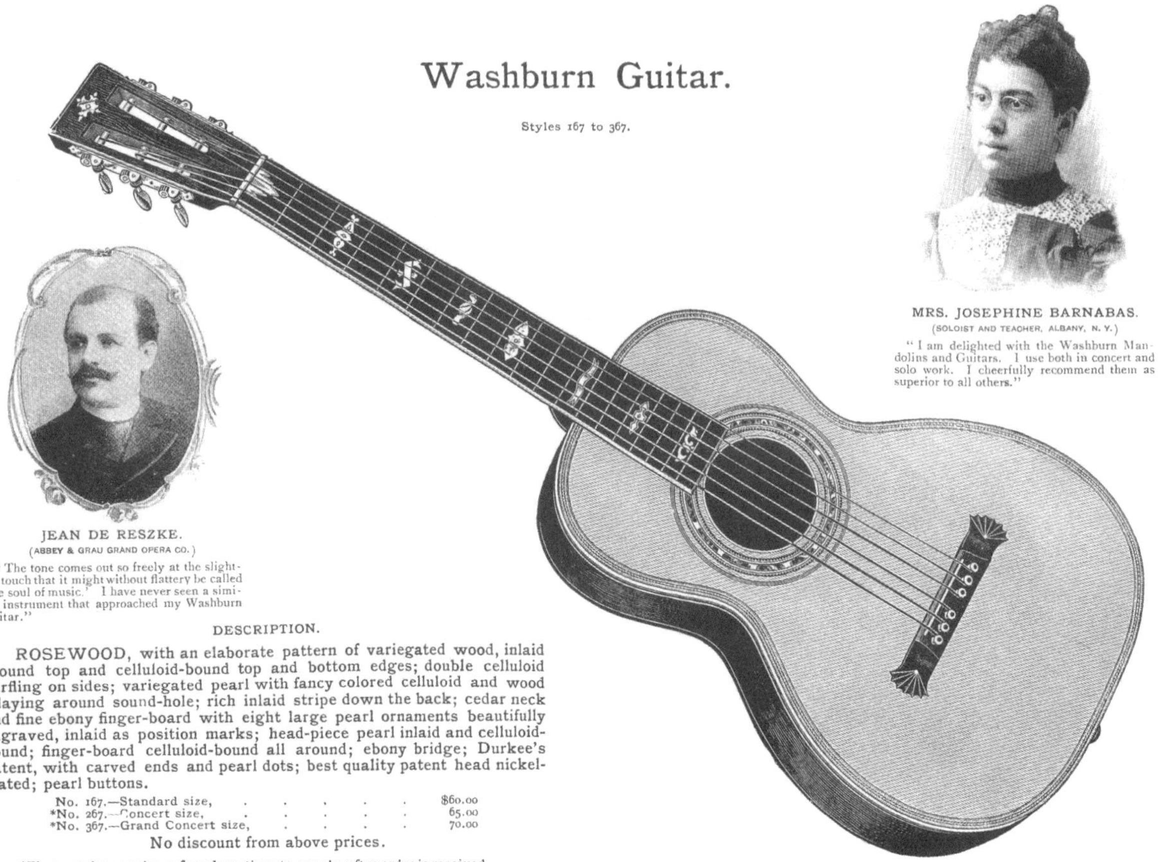

MRS. JOSEPHINE BARNABAS.

(SOLOIST AND TEACHER, ALBANY, N. Y.)

"I am delighted with the Washburn Mandolins and Guitars. I use both in concert and solo work. I cheerfully recommend them as superior to all others."

JEAN DE RESZKE.

(ABBEY & GRAU GRAND OPERA CO.)

"The tone comes out so freely at the slightest touch that it might without flattery be called 'the soul of music.' I have never seen a similar instrument that approached my Washburn Guitar."

DESCRIPTION.

ROSEWOOD, with an elaborate pattern of variegated wood, inlaid around top and celluloid-bound top and bottom edges; double celluloid purfling on sides; variegated pearl with fancy colored celluloid and wood inlaying around sound-hole; rich inlaid stripe down the back; cedar neck and fine ebony finger-board with eight large pearl ornaments beautifully engraved, inlaid as position marks; head-piece pearl inlaid and celluloid-bound; finger-board celluloid-bound all around; ebony bridge; Durkee's patent, with carved ends and pearl dots; best quality patent head nickel-plated; pearl buttons.

No. 167.—Standard size,	$60.00
*No. 267.—Concert size,	65.00
*No. 367.—Grand Concert size,	70.00

No discount from above prices.

*These styles require a few days time to supply after order is received.

The WASHBURN instruments contain invariably true scales, all perfect and all alike. No other makers achieve such uniformity or perfection.

39

Style 267 (1896)

Style 267 (Laguitare.com)

Washburn Guitar.

Styles 188 to 388.

CHAS. H. LEWIS.
(TEACHER, CINCINNATI, O.)
"The Washburn instruments are perfectly true in scale, durable in workmanship and finish, and possess the most powerful, yet sweet and mellow tone of any like instruments I know."

H. A. WEBBER.
(SOLOIST AND TEACHER, PORTLAND, ORE.)
"I have used the Washburn instruments for six years, and can highly recommend them. My Washburn Guitar is especially a source of delight to me, and I could not be induced to part with it."

DESCRIPTION.

ROSEWOOD, with a very rich variegated pearl and celluloid pattern of inlay around top; celluloid-bound top and bottom edges; double celluloid purfling on the sides; variegated pearl with fancy colored wood and celluloid inlaying around sound-hole; rich inlaid stripe in back; solid Sidney pearl finger-board; beautifully engraved position marks of contrasting pearl; head-piece inlaid with pearl and celluloid bound; celluloid-bound finger-board; Durkee's patent bridge with carved ends, inlaid with pearl; finely French polished; extra fine patent heads; silver-plated, with pearl buttons.

*No. 188.—Standard size, ... $80.00
*No. 288.—Concert size, ... 85.00
*No. 388.—Grand Concert size, ... 90.00

No discount from above prices.

*These styles require a few days time to supply after order is received.

To insure a positive standard of excellence the makers of the WASHBURN instruments make all the component parts, including the patent heads.

41

Style 288 (1896)

Washburn Guitar.

Styles 199 to 399.

J. HENRY ROBSON.
(THE FAVORITE CHICAGO GUITARIST.)
"The Washburn Guitar has been my standard for the past ten years. No other Guitar approaches it in my estimation. I am thoroughly familiar with their construction and know that they are made upon honor. It's a pleasure to recommend them."

SENOR JULIAN K. MUNOZ.
(DIRECTOR LOUISVILLE MANDOLIN AND GUITAR CLUB, LOUISVILLE, KY.)
"I have used the Washburn Guitars for past five years, both for solo work and as contra bass with club, and they have proved thoroughly satisfactory in every case. I unhesitatingly pronounce them the King of Guitars."

DESCRIPTION.

ROSEWOOD, richly inlaid around sound-hole and edges of top with variegated colored woods and mother of pearl; pearl inlaid stripes in sides; beautifully inlaid stripes around the back and down the centre; celluloid-bound edges; oval ebony finger-board, bound and most elaborately inlaid with pearl in handsome pattern; extra fine machine head; the richest Washburn Guitar yet offered.

*No. 199.—Standard size, ... $125.00
*No. 299.—Concert size, ... 135.00
*No. 399.—Grand Concert size, ... 145.00

No discount from above prices.

*These styles require a few days time to supply after order is received.

An enormous stock of completed Washburns may always be seen in the drying rooms. Unseasoned Washburn instruments are never marketed.

43

Style 299 (1896)

Style 125 (1905)

Style 115 (1905)

Style 135 (1905)

Size ¾	1	2	3	4	
	115*	217	320		rosewood b/s, ebony headstock overlay, mahogany neck w ebony heelcap, 18-fret ebony fb w three pearl dots at frets 5, 7 and 9, ebony flattened pyramid bridge, bone bridge pins, ebony nut, top bound w white celluloid and rope pattern, s/h inlaid w white celluloid and three sets of white/black/red colored rings, back bound w white celluloid, inlaid backstrip, bone end pin
¾ 24	125	227	330	435	rosewood b/s, ebony headstock overlay, mahogany neck, 18-fret (435: 19-fret) ebony fb w five engraved pearl inlays at frets 1, 5, 7, 9 and 12, fingerboard bound w white celluloid, ebony flattened pyramid bridge, bone bridge pins, bone nut, top bound w white celluloid and red/white/blue herringbone pattern, s/h inlaid w white celluloid and red/white/blue herringbone pattern and rings, back bound w white celluloid, inlaid red/white/blue herringbone backstrip, bone end pin
	135	237	340		rosewood b/s, ebony headstock overlay, mahogany neck w volute, 18-fret ebony fb w eight engraved pearl inlays at frets 1, 3, 5, 7, 9, 12, 15 and 17, headstock and fingerboard bound w white celluloid, snowflake shaped inlay on headstock, ebony flattened pyramid bridge w pearl inlays, ivory bridge pins, ivory nut, top bound w white celluloid, pearl ring, herringbone marquetry pattern, s/h inlaid w white celluloid and herringbone pattern and white/black/red rings, back and heelcap bound w white celluloid, inlaid herringbone backstrip, bone end pin
	150	252	355		rosewood b/s, ebony headstock overlay, mahogany neck w volute, 18-fret ebony fb w elaborate engraved pearl/metal vine inlays over entire length, headstock and fingerboard bound w white celluloid, snowflake shaped inlay on headstock, ebony flattened pyramid bridge w pearl inlays, ivory bridge pins, ivory nut, top bound w white celluloid and elaborate marquetry pattern, s/h inlaid w white celluloid, pearl ring and marquetry patterns, back bound w white celluloid, inlaid herringbone backstrip and edges, bone end pin

BACK AND FRONT VIEWS OF NOS. 150–252–355.

Style 150 (1907)

BACK AND FRONT VIEWS OF NOS. 115–217–320.

Style 115 (1911)

Washburn guitar styles 1905-1910 (continued)

Size ¾	1	2	3	4	
	175	277	380		rosewood b/s, ebony headstock overlay, mahogany neck w volute, 18-fret solid pearl fb w engraved inlays, headstock and fingerboard bound w white celluloid, pearl figures inlaid on headstock, pearl tuner buttons, ebony flattened pyramid bridge w pearl inlays, ivory bridge pins, ivory nut, top bound w pearl, white celluloid and marquetry pattern, s/h inlaid w pearl, white celluloid and marquetry pattern, back bound w white celluloid, inlaid pearl and marquetry backstrip and marquetry inlaid at edges, bone end pin

* In many Lyon & Healy/Washburn catalogs published between 1905 and the early 1920s the style numbers of catalogued instruments and other musical items have a 'G' prefix. This is a reference to Lyon & Healy's Department G, which was responsible for all retail activities

Washburn guitar styles 1910-1915

Size	1	2	3	4	
	115	217	320		as Style 115 (1905), except w brown/white/beige trapezoid marquetry, back of neck finished black, dots at frets 5, 7 and 10
	122	225	330	435	as Style 125 (1905), except w brown/white/beige marquetry, inlays at frets 1, 5, 7, 10 and 12
	132	235	340		as Style 135 (1905), except w brown/white/beige marquetry, inlays at frets 1, 3, 5, 7, 9, 12, 15 and 17 (no pearl ring)
	150	252	355		as Style 150 (1905), except w bone nut/bridge pins, brown/beige/red marquetry patterns inlaid around s/h (no pearl ring), top and back
	175	277	380		as Style 175 (1905), except w bone nut/bridge pins
			3150		(introduced 1912) rosewood b/s, ebony headstock overlay, mahogany neck w volute, 18-fret solid pearl fb w inlaid pearl vine motifs, headstock and fingerboard bound w pearl, pearl torch shaped figure inlaid on headstock, pearl tuner buttons, ebony bridge w shell shaped ends, pearl bridge pins, pearl nut, top and back bound w double lines of pearl, s/h inlaid w four pearl rings, white celluloid and marquetry pattern, back bound w white celluloid, inlaid three line pearl backstrip, pearl end pin

Style 125 (1911)

Back and Front Views of Nos. 225–435.

Back and Front Views of No. 235.

Style 135 (1911)

Back and Front Views of Nos. 150–252–355.

Style 150 (1911)

Washburn guitar styles 1915-1920

Size	1	2	3	4	
	1115/1118*	1222	1324		rosewood b/s, rhodium headstock overlay, mahogany neck, 18-fret rhodium fb w four pearl dots at frets 5, 7, 9 and 12**, ebony flattened pyramid bridge w bone or black pearl dotted bridge pins, top bound w black/white celluloid, s/h bound w three groups of rings of black and white celluloid, unbound back, inlaid backstrip, bone nut
	1124*	1228	1330	1435	rosewood b/s, rhodium headstock overlay, mahogany neck, 18-fret (1435: 19-fret) ebony fb w four pearl dots at frets 5, 7, 9 and 12** bound w faint line of white celluloid, ebony flattened pyramid bridge, top bound w black/white celluloid, s/h bound w three groups of rings of black and white celluloid, back bound w black and white celluloid, inlaid backstrip, bone nut
	1136	1240	1345		rosewood b/s, rhodium headstock overlay, mahogany neck, 18-fret ebony fb w six pearl dots and snowflakes at frets 1, 5, 7, 9, 12 (2)**, bound w faint line of white celluloid, ebony flattened pyramid bridge w ebony bridge pins, top bound w black/white celluloid, s/h bound w three groups of rings of black and white marquetry, back bound w black and white celluloid, inlaid marquetry backstrip, bone nut, ebony heelcap w white celluloid binding
	1148	1254	1360		rosewood b/s, ebony headstock overlay bound w white celluloid and pearl snowflake inlays, mahogany neck w volute, 18-fret ebony fb w pearl snowflakes inlaid at frets 1, 3, 5, 7, 9, 12, 15**, bound w faint line of white celluloid, ebony flattened pyramid bridge w pearl snowflake inlays and pearl saddle, ebony bridge pins w pearl inlay, top bound w black/white celluloid, s/h bound w four groups of rings of black and white herringbone marquetry, back bound w black and white celluloid, inlaid black and white herringbone marquetry backstrip, pearl nut, ebony heelcap w white celluloid binding, engraved tuners w pearl buttons, pearl end pin
		1522***			Hawaiian steel guitar, flamed mahogany b/s, mahogany top, rosewood headstock overlay, mahogany neck, 18-fret ebony fingerboard bound w faint line of white celluloid w four pearl dots at frets 5, 7, 9, 12**, ebony bridge w black bridge pins w pearl dots, top, back and s/h bound w black and white celluloid, inlaid backstrip, bone nut

Style 175 (1911)

Back and Front Views of Nos. 175-277-380.

Back and Front Views of No. 3150.

Style 3150 (1912)

No. 1522

Style 1522 (1919)

Washburn guitar styles 1915-1920 (continued)

* The last two digits of the style numbers between 1905 and 1922 reflect the actual retail prices of the respective models in Chicago at the time. As prices in general were very volatile between 1915 and the early 1920s, the style numbers on the labels of Washburn instruments were often changed during this period and thus may deviate from the catalog numbers indicated above (e.g. 1120 for a Style 1118, 3130 for a Style 3136, 2125 for a Style 2128, etc. Style 1115 was renumbered to 1118 around 1917

** Although the catalog pictures show dots or inlays for most styles positioned at the 10th fret, on all 1915-1920 models these are located at the 9th fret except for guitars in the 36,800-37,800 serial number range. The Style 1115 guitars in this range also have three instead of four fingerboard dots

*** A 1917 catalog lists a similar looking guitar as Style 1524 with a koa top, back and sides. In 1919 this guitar is again listed as a mahogany-bodied Style 1522

Washburn guitar styles 1920-1922

Size ¾	**1**	**2**	**3**	**4**	
3136*	2123				mahogany b/s, rosewood headstock overlay, cedar neck, 18-fret ebonized fb w four pearl dots at frets 5, 7, 9 and 12**, ebonized flattened pyramid bridge, top and back bound w black/white celluloid, s/h bound w black and white celluloid in ring pattern, back bound w black celluloid, inlaid backstrip, bone nut
	2128	2231	2333		as Style 1115/1118 (1915)
	2135	2238	2342	2444	as Style 1124 (1915)
3148	2146	2250	2354		as Style 1136 (1915)
	2165	2270	2375		as Style 1148 (1915)
		2535			as Style 1522 (1915)

* See note * for the 1915-1920 styles

** The catalog pictures show dots or inlays for most styles positioned at the 10th fret, but on all 1920-1922 models reported to date these are located at the 9th fret

Washburn Guitars

No. 1124

No.		Price
1118.	Standard size; rosewood back and sides; selected spruce top; top edge bound with black celluloid and inlaid with three line black and white wood stripe inlaying; sound-hole bound with black celluloid and inlaid with three rings of black and white wood; ebony bridge with bone saddle; ebony bridge pins and end pin; top edge of side inlaid with faint line of white celluloid; inlaid strip in center of back; mahogany neck; rhodium headpiece; rhodium wood fingerboard inlaid with four pearl position dots; Liberty silver frets; bone nut; highest grade nickel-plated patent heads	$27.00
1222.	Same as above—Concert size	33.00
1325.	Same as above—Grand Concert size	37.50
1124.	Standard size/ same as No. 1118 but with both top and back edges bound with black celluloid; top edge ornamented with one faint line of white celluloid next to black celluloid edge and inlaid with three strips of black and white wood inlaying; top and back edge of sides inlaid with faint line of white celluloid; ebony fingerboard bound with black celluloid, with faint line of white celluloid inlaying	36.00
1228.	Same as above—Concert size	42.00
1330.	Same as above—Grand Concert size	45.00
1435.	Same as above—Auditorium size	52.50

The guitars described above are constructed for the use of either steel or gut strings

No.		Price
1136.	Standard size; selected handsomely figured rosewood back and sides; choicest selected well-seasoned white spruce top, highly finished; top back edges bound with black celluloid; both top and back edges of sides inlaid with a faint line of white celluloid, top ornamented with a faint line of white celluloid next to black celluloid edge, and inlaid with black and white marquetry; sound-hole bound with black celluloid and inlaid with three rings of black and white marquetry; ebony bridge, and bridge pins; back edge inlaid with faint line of white celluloid; fancy wood marquetry strips in center of back; mahogany neck; rhodium wood headpiece; ebony fingerboard inlaid with six fancy pearl position dots on side; edge of fingerboard bound with black celluloid with faint line of white celluloid inlaying; Liberty silver frets; bone nut; ebony heel with faint line of white celluloid inlaying; highest grade nickel-plated engraved patent heads	54.00
1240.	Same as above—Concert size	60.00
1345.	Same as above—Grand Concert size	67.50

No.		Price
1148.	Standard size, carefully selected, handsomely figured rosewood back and sides; choicest selected white spruce top, highly finished; top and back edges bound with black celluloid with faint line of white celluloid; sound-hole bound with black celluloid, inlaid with four rings of black and white marquetry; ebony bridge inlaid with handsome pearl ornament; pearl saddle; rich mother-of-pearl bridge pins; pearl head end pin; top and back edge of sides inlaid with faint line of white celluloid; top edge inlaid with two rows of artistic marquetry of black and white; back edge inlaid with faint line of white celluloid; strip of two rows of black and white marquetry inlaid in center of back; mahogany neck of special design; ebony headpiece bound with black celluloid with faint line of white celluloid, and inlaid with three pearl ornaments; ebony fingerboard inlaid with fourteen fancy pearl position ornaments on top, and five inlaid position dots on the side; edge of fingerboard bound with black celluloid with faint line of white celluloid; Liberty silver frets; pearl nut; nickel-plated engraved patent heads with pearl buttons; ebony heel trimmed with faint line of white celluloid inlaying	$72.00
1254.	Same as above—Concert size	81.00
1360.	Same as above—Grand Concert size	90.00

The Washburn guaranty does not cover the instruments described on this page when steel strings are used.

No. 1148

Styles 1124 and 1148 (1919)

Washburn guitar styles 1922-1925

Size	Standard	Grand Concert	
	G	(introduced around 1923)	mahogany b/s, no headstock overlay, cedar neck, 18-fret rosewood fingerboard w three pearl dots at frets 5, 7, 9 or 10, rosewood flattened pyramid bridge, top, back and heelcap bound w black celluloid, three sets of rings inlaid around soundhole, black tuner buttons, inlaid black backstrip
	F	(introduced around 1923)	mahogany b/s, rosewood headstock overlay, cedar neck, 18-fret ebonized rosewood fingerboard w three pearl dots at frets 5, 7, 9 or 10, ebonized rosewood flattened pyramid bridge, top, back and soundhole bound w black and white celluloid, three sets of rings inlaid around soundhole, inlaid black and white backstrip
	E**	E*	mahogany or 'nyssawood' (pearwood) three-ply b/s, no headstock overlay, spruce or pearwood two-ply laminated top, black tuner buttons, mahogany or cedar neck w black heelcap, 18-fret rosewood fb w four pearl dots at frets 5, 7, 10 and 12, rosewood 'smile' bridge w white bridge pins, ebony nut, top (sometimes also back) bound w black and white celluloid, s/h bound w raised black celluloid ring, black backstrip, bone nut, rosewood end pin, black tuner buttons
	D**	D*	mahogany b/s, no headstock overlay, mahogany or spruce top, top/soundhole bound w white celluloid, cedar neck w black or white heelcap, 18-fret rosewood fb w four pearl dots at frets 5, 7, 10 and 12, ebony nut, mahogany 'smile' bridge w white bridge pins and ebony or bone saddle, black tuner buttons, one piece back w no backstrip, ivory end pin
	C	C*	flamed mahogany b/s, two-ply back, three-ply laminated sides, 18-fret ebony fb w four pearl dots at frets 5, 7, 10 and 12 bound w black celluloid, cedar neck w black heelcap, ebony 'smile' bridge w ebony saddle and white bridge pins, top back and s/h bound w black celluloid, black tuner buttons, inlaid black backstrip, white end pin***
	B	B*	three-ply laminated rosewood sides, two-ply rosewood back, mahogany neck w white/black heelcap, vulcanized fiber headstock overlay bound w white celluloid, 18-fret ebony fb w four pearl dots at frets 5, 7, 10 and 12 bound w white celluloid, ebony 'smile' bridge w white ivory bridge pins and bone saddle, bone nut, top and back bound w white/black celluloid, s/h bound w raised white celluloid ring, inlaid backstrip, ivory end pin

WASHBURN GUITARS

1923-24 Series

STYLE F

In the past we have received many, many requests from Musicians for Washburn Guitars at a low price.

They realized, of course, that such instruments would have to be built along very economical lines, eliminating all embellishments characteristic of Washburn instruments.

The demand became so insistent that we have incorporated in our 1923-24 Series, two new models, Styles F and G.

These instruments, as you will readily perceive, are finely built and carry the World-famous Washburn Guarantee. We also guarantee that the wonderful tone of these instruments will agreeably surprise the purchaser. Remember—these instruments are not CHEAP—they simply represent Washburn quality of workmanship throughout with the exception of costly selected woods and ultra-smart trimmings.

STYLE F

Regulation Standard Model: Dull oil finish, selected mahogany back and sides, inlaid stripe in back, spruce top, sound hole with bound edge and inlaying as shown in illustration, both top and back edges bound with black fibre—the top edge binding is flanked by a strip of white and black, Spanish cedar neck, ebonized finger-board, 3 pearl position dots, bone nut, rosewood veneered headpiece, good quality nickel-plated patent heads, ebonized bridge, strung with steel strings. Each..**$25.00**

STYLE G

Style G is practically the same in design as Style F, with the exception that the black trimming around the edges and top is not flanked by the white strip. The materials used are the same as those in style F but it has less inlaying around top edges, has mahogany finish neck and lacks some of the niceties of detail in Style F—hence the difference in price. It is undoubtedly the best value in an inexpensive guitar on the market today and possesses a splendid tone. Each **$20.00**

Styles F, G (1923)

Washburn guitar styles 1922-1925 (continued)

Size	Standard	Grand Concert	
	A	A*	three-ply laminated rosewood sides, two-ply rosewood back, vulcanized fiber headstock overlay w hand carved flower figure, headstock bound w white celluloid, nickel plated gears w black tuner buttons, mahogany neck w volute and white/black celluloid heelcap, 18-fret ebony fb w four pearl dots at frets 5, 7, 10 and 12, ebony 'smile' bridge w ivory bridge pins and bone saddle, bone nut, top w gold leaf type appliqué, top and back bound w white and black celluloid, s/h bound w raised white celluloid ring, inlaid backstrip, ivory end pin, bone nut

* Grand Concert size available only on special order

** Surviving examples of Style E have either a pearwood body and spruce top or a spruce/mahogany body, with the latter version apparently succeeding the pearwood model. The 1923/4 catalog states 'nyssawood' (pearwood) for both body and top, but it is doubtful if guitars with these specifications were actually produced. The same applies to Style D, which was listed as having a mahogany body and top, but only guitars with spruce tops have been reported to date

*** A few Styles C have been reported with herringbone body trim and three rings around the soundhole instead of the celluloid ring and other non-standard specs. These may have been constructed with leftover parts

WASHBURN GUITARS

1923-24 Series

Style C

Style D

Style E

STYLE C—Standard Size

A full sized instrument with 24-inch scale. The sides are of 3-ply and the back of 2-ply selected Brown Mahogany rubbed to a dull finish and very attractive in appearance.

The Neck is of Natural finish Cedar.

The Top is of fine selected Spruce providing a rich sonorous tone. The Top and Back edges are inlaid with Black Celluloid. Raised Black Celluloid trim around Sound Hole. Black stripe down center of Back. L. & H. Improved Bridge with Ebony Saddle. Ebony covered Heel. White Bridge Pins. White End Pin.

Convex Ebony Fingerboard, improved type, bound with Black Celluloid, Pearl position dots. Bone String Nut. Nickel Plated Patent Heads with Black Buttons.

This instrument is strung with the highest quality Gut and silvered wire wound strings................**$60.00**

Can be furnished in Grand Concert Size on Special Order.

STYLE D—Standard Size

This is a handsome Model of standard size—it has a 24-inch scale. Back, Top and Sides are of a fine selected Brown Mahogany, dull rubbed by hand to a splendid finish.

The Neck is of the best grade of Cedar, natural finish.

The Top is nicely bound in solid White Celluloid affording a splendid contrast to the Brown body. The Heel is covered with white celluloid also. The Sound Hole is bound with White Celluloid, raised Bridge Pins and End Pin of Ivory. Improved Mahogany Bridge with Ebony Saddle.

Convex, Rosewood Fingerboard with 17 Nickel Silver frets. 4 Pearl position dots. Highest grade Nickel Plated Patent Heads with black composition buttons. Strung with finest quality gut and silvered wire wound strings. Reinforced internally throughout....................**$40.00**

Can be furnished in Grand Concert Size on Special Order.

STYLE E—Standard Size

A standard size instrument of selected Nyssawood, chosen because of its beautiful grain—24-inch scale. Three-ply Nyssawood Sides, 2-ply Nyssawood Back and Top. The Top edge inlaid with Black Celluloid. Raised Black Celluloid trim around Sound Hole. Hand rubbed to a fine dull finish. The Neck is of Cedar, natural finish.

Flat Rosewood Fingerboard with German Silver Frets and Bone String Nut. L. & H. Improved Rosewood Bridge with Bone Saddle, Rosewood End Pin. Nickel Plated Patent Heads with Black Buttons. Strung with High grade Gut and Silvered wire wound strings................**$35.00**

Can be furnished in Grand Concert Size on Special Order.

Styles C, D, E (1923)

WASHBURN BANJOS, MANDOLINS, GUITARS, UKULELES 9

WASHBURN GUITARS

1923-24 Series

The Guitar is, preeminently, an instrument for the home. It is complete in itself, supplying its own melody and accompaniment. Its soft, round, beautiful tone harmonizes perfectly with any other instrument, and as an accompaniment to the human voice it has no superior. In the college mandolin and glee clubs it is simply indispensable.

Throughout the Continent of Europe, particularly in Italy, Spain, and Portugal, the Guitar has been for centuries the favorite instrument of all, regardless of station. In Mexico and South America it is found in almost every home.

Some of the world's famous musicians (notably Berlioz and Paganini) were Guitarists, and many splendid compositions by other celebrities testify to their regard for its wonderfully pleasing musical qualities.

We take pardonable pride in offering the 1923-24 Series Washburn Guitars. To improve upon a line firmly established as the World's best was no easy task. But improvements have been made and all styles, in model, workmanship, materials, tonal qualities and beauty of finish again will take the indisputable lead among the fine Guitars of the day.

Style A

Style A. Standard Size. Can be furnished in Grand Concert size on special order. 24¾ inch scale.

A wonderful model with Sides of 3 ply and Back of 2 ply beautiful grained Rosewood, hand rubbed and polished. The Top is of even grained carefully selected thoroughly seasoned Spruce conducive to splendid tonal qualities.

The Top is ornamented with one faint line of white celluloid next to Black celluloid and followed by another white strip. Bottom and Back edges of sides ornamented in same way. Black and Gold stripe down center of back. The Top is daintily decorated with Golden Leaf flowery design. The Sound Hole is bound with Raised White Celluloid binding. Heel is covered with White Celluloid. Ebony Bridge with White Bone Saddle. White Ivory Bridge and End Pins.

The Neck is of Mahogany with inlaid Vulcanized Fibre headplate artistically hand carved—resembles Pearl inlay. Ebony Oval Top Fingerboard bound with White Celluloid. 3 position dots on side. 4 Pearl position dots on top. German Silver frets. Bone String Nut. Highest grade Nickel Plated Patent heads, with Black Composition Buttons Strung with finest quality gut and Silver wound strings. Each................................**$127.00**

Style B

Style B. Standard Size. Can be furnished in Grand Concert size on special order. 24¾ inch scale.

A handsome model with Back and Sides constructed of choice 3 ply Rosewood, hand rubbed to a beautiful finish. The Top is of even grained Spruce of highest quality which assures a splendid quality of Tone.

The Top edge is ornamented with one Black strip of celluloid followed by White strips. Bottom and Back edges of sides ornamented with Celluloid inlay—white, black and white. Gold stripe down center of back.

The Sound Hole is bound with raised white celluloid binding. The Heel is covered with white celluloid bound with strip of black.

L. & H. Improved Ebony Bridge with White Bone Saddle. White Ivory End and Bridge Pins.

The Neck is of Mahogany with Inlaid Vulcanized Fibre headplate bound with White Celluloid. Ebony Oval Top Fingerboard with White Celluloid binding. 3 position dots on side. 4 Pearl dots on top.

L. & H. Patent Head with Black Buttons. The finish of the Neck and Body is Natural finish, dull hand rubbed. Strung with highest grade gut and silver wound strings. Each **$92.00**

Styles A, B (1923)

Style A, 1922 (Frank Ford)

Style 5200 (1925)

Style 5201 (1925)

Style 5202 (1925)

Style 5265 (1925)

Size	Concert	Grand Concert	
	5200	5235 (Inspiration)	three-ply mahogany sides, two piece mahogany back, rosewood headstock overlay, black tuner buttons, whitewood neck w rosewood heelcap (straight sided headstock changed to 'sailor's cap headstock' around 1926-7), 18-fret ebonized rosewood fb w four pearl dots at frets 5, 7, 10 and 12, ebony nut, ebonized rosewood 'smile' bridge w bone saddle and ebonized bridge pins, s/h bound w black and white celluloid (three sets of rings), top bound w black and white celluloid, back bound w black celluloid, inlaid backstrip, ebonized end pin
	5201	5236 (Classic)	three-ply mahogany sides, two piece mahogany back, mahogany headstock overlay, black tuner buttons, cedar neck w black celluloid heelcap (straight sided headstock changed to 'sailor's cap headstock' around 1926-7), 18-fret rosewood fb w four pearl dots at frets 5, 7, 10 and 12, rosewood 'smile' bridge w bone saddle and white celluloid bridge pins, bone nut, top and back bound w black and white celluloid, s/h bound w raised black celluloid ring, inlaid backstrip, white celluloid end pin
	5202	5237 (Aristocrat)	as Style B (1922), straight sided headstock changed to 'sailor's cap headstock' around 1926-7, 18-fret ebony fingerboard bound w black celluloid, top bound w black and white celluloid, s/h bound w three sets of black/white rings, back bound w white celluloid, inlaid backstrip, black heelcap, white celluloid bridge pins and end pin
	5203	5238 (DeLuxe)	as Style A (1922), straight sided headstock changed to 'sailor's cap headstock' around 1926-7, three-ply laminated rosewood sides, two piece rosewood back, ebony headstock overlay w pearl flower inlay, gold plated tuners w pearl buttons, white celluloid bridge pins and end pin
5260/5273 (Hawaiian harp guitar)			flamed koa b/s, large bell shaped body, rosewood headstock overlay w diamond shaped inlay, neck joins body at 3rd fret, pointed headstock, white celluloid bound rosewood fingerboard w pearl dots at frets 5, 7, 10, 12 and 15, soundhole, top and back bound w black/green celluloid, ebony 'gondola' shaped bridge, white bridge pins, bone nut

144 LYON & HEALY, CHICAGO

The WASHBURN "DELUXE" Guitar

Made in the Lyon & Healy Factory

Style 5203 (1925)

Size	Concert	Grand Concert	
5265 (Tenor guitar)			mahogany b/s, pear shaped body, mahogany neck, 17-fret ebony fingerboard bound w white celluloid w pearl inlays at frets 1, 5, 7, 10 and 12, solid headstock w pointed end, four mechanical friction pegs w white tuner buttons, ebony heelcap, soundhole, top and back bound w black and white celluloid, bridge w ebony top, nickel plated oval 'ashtray' tailpiece, inlaid backstrip, bone nut
5270 (Bell guitar)			as Style 5271 (1925), but with mahogany body, 18-fret rosewood fingerboard, bridge and headstock overlay, celluloid tuner buttons, black celluloid body binding
5271 (Bell guitar)			bell shaped rosewood body, three piece mahogany neck w ebony center strip and pointed headstock w ebony overlay inlaid w pearl square, 18-fret ebony fingerboard bound w white celluloid w four pearl dots at frets 5, 7, 10, 12, bone nut, gold plated engraved tuners w pearl buttons, top and back bound w black and white celluloid, s/h bound w raised celluloid ring, factory strung w gold plated strings, white celluloid heelcap, inlaid backstrip
Shrine guitar and tenor guitar (1927-8)			mahogany b/s, mahogany neck w 18 (guitar) or 19 (tenor guitar) frets, balalaika-shaped body, rosewood fingerboard w green celluloid dots at frets 5, 7, 10, 12, headstock, body top, back, heelcap and s/h bound w green celluloid, rosewood gondola shaped bridge, ukulele-shaped pointed headstock, four string neck w solid headstock (tenor guitar), six string neck w slotted headstock (guitar)

Style 5260/5273 (Dana Erlandson)

The
WASHBURN "BELL"
Guitar

Made in the Lyon & Healy Factory

Style 5270 (1925)

*Washburn guitar styles 1928-1934/5**

Size	Concert	Grand Concert	Auditorium	
	5200	5235 (Inspiration)		as Style 5200 (1925), but with mahogany neck, single dome headstock (all around 1928), four pearl dots at frets 5, 7, 9, 12, one set of rings around soundhole, 19-fret neck (all around 1929-30), 20-fret neck (around 1930)
	5201	5236 (Classic)		as Style 5201 (1925), but with single dome headstock (around 1928), four pearl dots at frets 5, 7, 9, 12, 19-fret neck (all around 1929-30), 20-fret neck (around 1930)
	5202	5237 (Aristocrat)	5239	(5239 added around 1930 or earlier) as Style 5202 (1925), but with single dome headstock w "Washburn" inlaid in pearl (around 1928), snowflakes at frets 5, 7, 9, 12 and 16, 19-fret neck (all around 1929-30), 20-fret neck (around 1930)
	5203	5238 (DeLuxe)	5234	(5234 added around 1930 or earlier) as Style 5203 (1925), but with single dome headstock w "Washburn" inlaid in pearl (around 1928), snowflakes at frets 3, 5, 7, 9, 12 and 16, smile bridge w inlaid snowflakes, three sets of rings around s/h, 19-fret neck (all around 1929-30), 20-fret neck (around 1930). Around 1934 or earlier: herringbone marquetry inlaid around top, s/h and in backstrip
			5250**	(Archtop, added early 1930s) Mahogany b/s, arched back, rosewood headstock overlay w "Washburn" inlaid in pearl, natural finished carved top w round soundhole, seven-ply neck w 14 frets to the body (4-ply mahogany, 3 rosewood), 20-fret ebony fingerboard w four dots at frets 5, 7, 9, 12, ebony bridge w bone saddle, nickel plated tailpiece, soundhole, top and back bound w black celluloid, black fiber guard plate
5225, 5226 (Tenor guitar)				mahogany b/s (rosewood on 5226), guitar shaped body, mahogany neck, 20-fret ebony fingerboard w pearl dots/snowflakes, solid headstock w pointed ukulele shape and rosewood headstock overlay ("Washburn" inlaid in pearl on 5226), four mechanical friction pegs w white tuner buttons, ebony heelcap, soundhole, top, and back bound w black and white celluloid (herringbone marquetry around soundhole and top on 5226), ebony smile bridge w white celluloid bridge pins, inlaid backstrip, bone nut

* Two surviving 19-fret converted Hawaiian guitars with 5242 and 5246 style stamps from this period have been reported that were not listed in company catalogs. Style 5242 has a double bound koa body and top and a bound fingerboard with dot inlays, Style 5246 has a spruce top, a double bound rosewood body and abalone trim around the body perimeter and soundhole, and a bound fingerboard with snowflake inlays

** One Style 5250 tenor guitar has been reported with a 21-fret neck

Style 5200, 19 frets (1930)

Style 5236, early 1930s (Folkway Music, Canada)

Style 5201 (1930)

Style 5202 (1930)

Style 5203 (1930)

Style 5225 (1930)

Style 5226 (1930)

2.5.1 Guitar Styles 1934/5-1940 - Flattop Guitars

Washburn flattop guitar styles 1934/5-1937

Size	Concert	Large Auditorium	
	5200 (Inspiration)		mahogany b/s, rosewood headstock overlay w "Washburn" inlaid in pearl, mahogany neck joining body at 12th fret, 20-fret ebony fb w four pearl dots at frets 5, 7, 9 and 12, ebony 'smile' bridge w white celluloid bridge pins and bone (straight or slant) saddle, bone nut, top, back and s/h bound w black celluloid, black celluloid removable pickguard
	5206 (Classic)		mahogany b/s, solid headstock, rosewood headstock overlay w "Washburn" inlaid in pearl, mahogany neck joining body at 14th fret w black heelcap, 20-fret ebony fb w four pearl dots at frets 5, 7, 9 and 12, ebony 'smile' bridge w white celluloid bridge pins and bone (slant) saddle, bone nut, top, back and s/h bound w white celluloid, black celluloid removable pickguard, top and back finished in brown sunburst, inlaid white backstrip
		5256/7 (Solo)	mahogany b/s (rosewood on 5257), solid headstock, rosewood headstock overlay w "Washburn" inlaid in pearl, seven-ply mahogany neck joining body at 14th fret, 20-fret ebony fb w four pearl dots at frets 5, 7, 9 and 12, ebony 'smile' bridge w white celluloid bridge pins and bone (slant) saddle, bone nut, top, back and s/h bound w white/black celluloid lines (back single white bound), fixed tortoise celluloid pickguard, five-ply black/white inlaid backstrip
(around 1936)		5257 1/2 (Solo Deluxe)	rosewood b/s, solid headstock, rosewood headstock overlay w "Washburn" inlaid vertically in pearl w deco pearl lines, mahogany brown sunburst finished seven-ply neck joining body at 14th fret w white heelcap, 20-fret ebony fb bound w white/black celluloid w six pearl blocks at frets 3, 5, 7, 9, 12 and 15, ebony 'smile' bridge w white celluloid bridge pins and bone (slant) saddle, bone nut, top, back and s/h bound w white/black celluloid lines, top finished in brown sunburst, gold plated tuners
5227 (Tenor guitar)			mahogany b/s, solid headstock, rosewood headstock overlay w "Washburn" inlaid in pearl, brown sunburst finished mahogany neck joining body at 14th fret w white heelcap, 20-fret ebony fb w snowflake inlays at frets 3, 5, 7, 10, 12 and 15, ebony 'smile' bridge w white celluloid bridge pins and bone (straight) saddle, bone nut, top, back and s/h bound w white/black celluloid lines, top and back finished in brown sunburst, four planetary gear tuners w white celluloid buttons

Style 5227 (1935) (Lowell Levinger, Players Vintage Instruments)

Style 5206 (1935)

Style 5257 (1935)

Style 5200 (1935)

Style 5256 (1935)

Washburn flattop guitar styles 1937-1939

Size					
Grand Concert Orchestra	**Large Auditorium**	**Super Auditorium**	**Large Super Auditorium**	**Extra Super Auditorium**	
5240 (Junior)*					mahogany b/s, solid headstock, celluloid headstock overlay w engraved "Washburn" name and radial lines, neck joining body at 14th fret, 19 or 20-fret* rosewood fb w five pearl dots at frets 5, 7, 9 and 12 (two dots), rosewood rectangular bridge w white celluloid bridge pins and bone (slant) saddle, bone nut, unbound top and back, s/h bound w white/black celluloid lines or w white celluloid ring, fixed tortoise celluloid pickguard, white celluloid heelcap, brown sunburst finish
		5241 (Classic)**			mahogany b/s, solid headstock, celluloid headstock overlay w engraved "Washburn" name and radial lines, mahogany neck joining body at 14th fret, 19 or 20-fret* rosewood fb bound w white celluloid w five pearl dots at frets 5, 7, 9 and 12 (two dots), rectangular bridge w white celluloid bridge pins and bone (slant) saddle, bone nut, top, back and s/h bound w white/black celluloid lines, white celluloid heelcap, fixed tortoise celluloid pickguard, natural finish
				5244 (Inspiration)	mahogany b/s, dreadnought or jumbo shaped body***, solid headstock, rosewood headstock overlay w "Washburn" inlaid in pearl, mahogany seven-ply neck joining body at 14th fret, 19 or 20-fret* ebony fb w four pearl dots at frets 5, 7, 9 and 12, ebony rectangular bridge w white celluloid bridge pins and bone (slant) saddle, bone nut, top and s/h bound w white/black celluloid lines, s/h inlaid w black and white herringbone marquetry pattern, back bound w white celluloid, fixed tortoise celluloid pickguard, brown sunburst finish, inlaid backstrip, heelcap bound w white celluloid

Style 5240 (1937)

Style 5244 (1937)

Style 5246 (1937)

Style 5249 (1937). The picture is incorrect, as it is identical to the 1935 catalog picture of the smaller Full Auditorium sized Style 5257 ½

Style 5246, Large Auditorium version (Fred Oster/Vintage Instruments)

Style 5246, dreadnought version (Large Super Auditorium size) (Frank Ford)

Washburn flattop guitar styles 1937-1939 (continued)

Grand Concert Orchestra	Large Auditorium	Super Auditorium	Large Super Auditorium	Extra Super Auditorium	
	5246 (Solo, formerly 5257)				as Style 5257 (1934/5), changed during 1937 from Large Auditorium size to Large Super Auditorium dreadnought shaped body***, rosewood headstock overlay w "Washburn" inlaid in pearl, also made w celluloid headstock overlay w engraved "Washburn" name and radial lines, herringbone or colored marquetry inlay around soundhole, seven-ply mahogany neck joining body at 14th fret, 19 or 20-fret* ebony fb w four pearl dots at frets 5, 7, 9 and 12, ebony 'smile' bridge w white celluloid bridge pins and bone (slant) saddle, bone nut, top, back and s/h bound w white/ black celluloid lines (back single white bound, natural or sunburst finished top, one piece back or two piece back w inlaid backstrip, individual nickel plated tuners or three on a strip tuners on versions with the celluloid overlay headstock
			5249 (Solo Deluxe, formerly 5257 1/2)		as Style 5257 ½ (1936), but with Large Super Auditorium body

* The 19-fret versions are made by Gibson, the 20-fret models by Regal

** Style 5241 was not listed in the 1937 catalog. The serial numbers of a number of surviving instruments indicate nonetheless that it was introduced in this year

*** Though not specified in the catalogs, Styles 5244 and 5246 were available in the dreadnought-shaped Large Super Auditorium size (see 2.4.4)

Style 5250 (1935)

Style 5241 (1939), Gibson version with 19 frets

Style 5255 (1935)

Washburn flattop guitar styles 1939-1940

Grand Concert Orchestra	Large Auditorium	Super Auditorium	Large Super Auditorium	Extra Super Auditorium	
5240					as Style 5240 (1937)*
		5241 (Classic)			as Style 5241 (1937)*
				5244 (Inspiration)	as Style 5244 (1937), but with five-ply neck w non adjustable truss rod
	5246				as Style 5246 (1937), but with five-ply neck w non adjustable truss rod
			5249 (Solo Deluxe)		as Style 5257 ½ (1936), but with larger sized body and five-ply maple/ mahogany neck w steel truss rod

* See Flattop Guitar Styles 1937-1939, note *

2.5.2 Guitar Styles 1935-1940 - Archtop guitars

Washburn archtop guitar styles 1935-1937

Size	Full Auditorium	
	5250 (Collegian)	as Style 5250 (1930)
	5255 (Superb)	mahogany b/s, arched (pressed) back, solid headstock, rosewood headstock overlay w "Washburn" inlaid in pearl, brown sunburst finished carved top w round soundhole, seven-ply neck (4-ply mahogany, 3 rosewood) w 14 frets to the body, 20-fret ebony fingerboard w four dots at frets 5, 7, 9, 12, ebony bridge w bone saddle, nickel plated tailpiece, soundhole, top and back bound w white celluloid, black celluloid bound guard plate
	5258 (De Luxe)	maple b/s, arched (pressed) flamed maple back, solid headstock, rosewood headstock overlay w "Washburn" inlaid in pearl, brown sunburst finished carved top w low positioned f-holes, seven-ply neck w 14 frets to the body (4-ply mahogany, 3 rosewood), 20-fret ebony fingerboard w four dots at frets 5, 7, 9, 12, ebony bridge, nickel plated tailpiece, top and back bound w white celluloid, tortoise celluloid guard plate bound w white celluloid, individual nickel plated metal tuners

Style 5258 (1935)

Style 5259 (1935)

Washburn archtop guitar styles 1935-1937 (continued)

Size	Full Auditorium	
	5259 (Super De Luxe)	flamed maple b/s, carved top and back, solid headstock, rosewood headstock overlay w "Washburn" inlaid in pearl, brown sunburst finished top w oval soundhole, seven-ply neck w 14 frets to the body (4-ply mahogany, 3 rosewood), 20-fret ebony fingerboard w six pearl triple slant bar position markers at frets 3, 5, 7, 9, 12 and 15, on snowflakes and star-shaped inlays at frets 1, 3, 5, 7, 12 and 15, adjustable ebony bridge, gold plated tailpiece, top and back bound w white celluloid, tortoise celluloid guard plate bound w white celluloid, individual gold plated metal tuners

Washburn archtop guitar styles 1937-1939

Size	Super Auditorium	Extra Super Auditorium	
	5242 (Collegian)		mahogany b/s, arched (pressed) back, solid headstock w celluloid headstock overlay w engraved "Washburn" name and radial lines, brown sunburst finished laminated top w split or 'standard' f-holes, mahogany neck w 14 frets to the body, 19 or 20-fret* rosewood fingerboard w four pearl dots at frets 5, 7, 9, 12, rosewood bridge, nickel plated tailpiece, top and back bound w white celluloid, tortoise celluloid guard plate
		5248 (Superb)	mahogany b/s, arched (pressed) back, solid headstock w "Washburn" inlaid in pearl, six individual nickel plated tuners, brown sunburst finished carved top w f-holes, mahogany laminated neck w 14 frets to the body, 20-fret ebony fingerboard w six pearl triple slant bar position markers at frets 3, 5, 7, 9, 12 and 15, adjustable ebony bridge, nickel plated tailpiece, top and back bound w white celluloid, raised guard plate bound w white celluloid**

* The 19-fret versions are made by Gibson, the 20-fret models by Regal

** The 16" body versions with checkerboard top and pickguard trim are Gibson-made, the 16 ¾" wide guitars with a single-ply white top and pickguard binding are made by Regal

Regal-made Style 5248, 1939, 16 3/4″ body (Leyton Collins)

Style 5248, Regal version (1937)

Style 5242 (1937)

Style 5248, 16″ body Gibson-made (Elderly)

Style 5243, Gibson version (1939)

Style 5248, Gibson version (1939)

Headstock of Gibson-made Style 5248 (Elderly)

Washburn archtop guitar styles 1939-1940

Size	Super Auditorium	Extra Super Auditorium	
	5242 (Collegian)		as Style 5242 (1937)*, but top w 'standard' (not split) f-holes*
	5243 (Aristocrat)		mahogany b/s, arched (pressed) back, solid headstock w celluloid headstock overlay w engraved "Washburn" name and radial lines, brown sunburst finished carved top w f-holes, mahogany neck w 14 frets to the body, 19 or 20-fret* ebony fingerboard w six position markers at frets 3, 5, 7, 9, 12 and 15, adjustable rosewood bridge, nickel plated tailpiece, top and back bound w white celluloid, tortoise celluloid guard plate bound w white celluloid
	5248 (Superb)		as Style 5248 (1937), but with maple pressed back and sides, 20-fret five-ply maple/mahogany laminated neck w buried truss rod, adjustable rosewood bridge**

* The 19-fret versions are made by Gibson, the 20-fret models by Regal

** The 16″ body versions with checkerboard top and pickguard trim are Gibson-made, the 16 ¾″ wide guitars with a single-ply white celluloid top and pickguard binding were made by Regal

CHICAGO

June 16, 1926

Red Path Bureau
Kimball Bldg.
City

Gentlemen:

We find upon examining your Harp Guitar which was left with us for repairs, that to repair sides by reinforcing from the inside, straighten and repair back and top, fit celluloid plate in top where worn, adjust fingerboard, refinish and restring will cost $ 24.75.

If a new fingerboard is wanted, there would be an extra charge of $ 7.50 as we do not carry this particular pattern in stock and it would have to be made up special.

Please let us know if we shall start repairing as per the estimate above and just what you want done in regard to the fingerboard.

Kindly use the enclosed envelope for your reply

Yours truly,
LYON & HEALY INC.
BY L. E. Johnson
L. E. JOHNSON

MA

Two 1926 letters from Lyon & Healy to a customer regarding the repair of a harp guitar

ESTABLISHED 1864 TELEPHONE WABASH 7900

Lyon & Healy
INC.
Everything Known in Music
WABASH AVE. AT JACKSON BLVD.
CHICAGO

October 7, 1926

Redpath Bureau
Kimball Bldg.
Chicago, Illinois

Gentlemen:

We are again writing you in regards to the Harp Guitar we have in our shop for repair. Please let us know what disposition you wish us to make of your Instrument. Kindly let us know if the estimate of $24.75 is unsatisfactory so that we may return your Instrument not repaired, no charge.

An early reply will be greatly appreciated. We are enclosing an envelope for your convenience.

Yours truly,
LYON & HEALY, INC.
BY L. E. Johnson
L. E. JOHNSON

LS
ENC.

CHAPTER THREE

Mandolins

Noman Blake with Lyon & Healy Style B Mandolin (Norman and Nancy Blake)

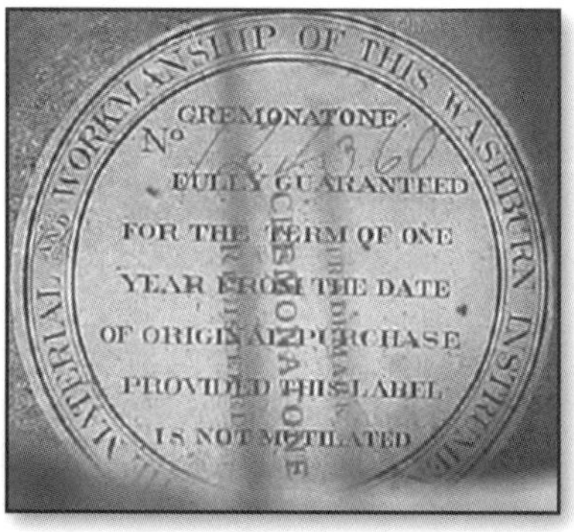

1896-1905

1896-1900

1900-1905

1905-6 (Lodestar Express)

1906 - the 'P.J. Healy commemorative label'

1906/7-1915

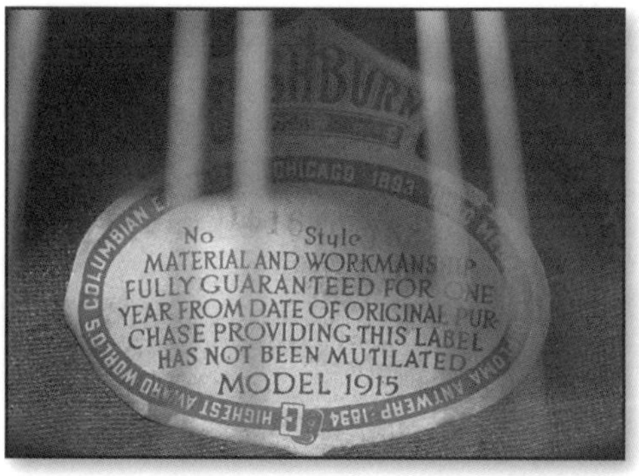

1915-1922 (Paul Gregory)

1923-4

1925

George W. Lyon 'mandloin' (1890s)

Lyon & Healy, 1917

American Conservatory

Lyon & Healy

L.H. Leland

American Conservatory

3.1 Dating of Washburn mandolins

Follow the steps described under “Dating of Washburn guitars”.

3.2 Mandolin labels and stamps

3.2.1 Mandolin labels

Mid to late 1896 until 1905:
Small round white paper warranty label with black lettering, stating “Cremonatone / No. ___ / the material and workmanship of this Washburn instrument / fully guaranteed for the term of one year from the date of original purchase provided this label is not mutilated” with a red ink stamp “Crematone, Registered Trademark”, serial number of instrument is handwritten on label.

Mid to late 1896 until 1900:
Larger oval label, copper/gold with black lettering, stating “The New Washburn 1897 Model / Highest award at World’s Columbian Exposition, Chicago 1893 / Gold Medal and Diploma of Honor, Antwerp 1894”.

1900 until 1905:
Oval label, copper/gold with black lettering, stating “The New Washburn / Latest Model / Highest award at World’s Columbian Exposition, Chicago 1893 / Gold Medal and Diploma of Honor, Antwerp, 1894”.

1905 until 1915:
White, black and red label stating “The Washburn / Best in The World / No. ___ / Highest award at World’s Columbian Exposition, Chicago 1893, Gold Medal and Diploma of Honor, Antwerp 1894 / The material and workmanship of this Washburn instrument, fully guaranteed for the term of one year from date of original purchase provided this label is not mutilated”. Serial number is handwritten on label. Between 1905 and 1907 ‘Cremonatone Registered Trademark’ is also printed in red at the bottom of the label.

1915 until 1923:
Oval label, crown shaped at top (white, black and red) stating “No. __ Style __ / Material and workmanship fully guaranteed for one year from date of original purchase providing this label has not been mutilated / model 1915 / Highest award World’s Columbian Exposition Chicago - 1893 - Gold Medal and Diploma Antwerp - 1894”, number and style designations are ink stamped or handwritten on label.

Around 1917 (Lyon & Healy brand mandolins only):
White/beige oval label w text “Lyon & Healy / Chicago / Makers of highest grade musical instruments / Sold under our unlimited guarantee / No. __ Style __”, number and style designations are handwritten on label.

1917 until 1923 (Lyon & Healy mandolin styles A-C only):
Gold/yellow large oval label stating “Made and Guaranteed by Lyon & Healy / World’s largest music house / Chicago, USA” , number and style designations are handwritten on label.

Approx. 1923 until 1925:
Oval white, black and red label, crown shaped at top, stating “No. __ Style __ / Material and workmanship fully guaranteed for one year from date of original purchase providing this label has not been mutilated / Model 1923-24”, number and style designations are ink stamped or handwritten on label.

1922 until 1928:
Oval light yellow label stating “Made and guaranteed by / (Lyon & Healy signature logo) / Worlds largest music house / Chicago, USA / WASHBURN / No ___ Style” ___, number and style designations are handwritten on label.

1934/5 until 1940:
Oval white/light yellow label stating “Genuine Washburn, Style No.___ Serial No.___ / Made of choicest materials by workmen of exceptional skill, knowledge and experience / Tonk Bros. Co. Chicago / Exclusive Distributors” (changed to “Exclusive Wholesale Distributors” around 1936).

3.2.2 Mandolin stamps

1885-1922:
Branded Washburn logo stamp inside instrument picturing a belt encircling a guitar with name "George Washburn" on belt.

1892-1896/7:
Branded stamp inside instrument stating "NEW MODEL."

After 1928/9 (some mandolin styles):
Impressed stamp on back of headstock stating "WASHBURN."

1928/9-1934/5, and during late 1930s:
Branded stamp inside instrument stating "genuine / WASHBURN / Tonk Bros. Co. / Chicago / sole distributors."

Late 1880s - single cross brace

1892 - double cross brace

1892 - example without a cross brace

1896 - note neck block logo, truss rod (Bill Bussmann)

1896 - serial number stamped on headstock (Richard Myers / photo Dan'l Terry)

1905 - style number stamp

1928-9

1928-9 Tonk Bros. stamp

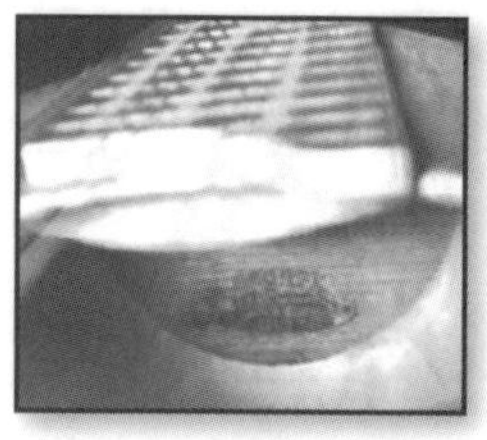

1905 - logo stamp

3.3 General appointments

1887-1896-7:

Starting around 1889 consecutive serial numbers starting at 1 are ink stamped on the neck block or on the top brace in front of the soundhole and on some instruments also on the end block. Some of the earlier instruments do not have a stamped serial number. Around mid 1896 numbers are in the mid 50,000s up to the early 60,000s range. All instruments are of the bowlback type, have 17 frets and black mushroom shaped pickguards (Styles 71, 72) or crown shaped pickguards (all other styles), and do not have any labels. Ribs are usually cross-braced on the inside with an oval wooden centerpiece on which the Washburn logo depicting a guitar is branded. Between 1892 and 1896-7 the words "new model" are also branded on the oval centerpiece.

1896-7-1905:

All instruments are of the bowlback type. The cross bracing method (1889) is abandoned in favor of the traditional paper gluing of the inside ribs. A large oval label stating "The New Washburn 1897 Model" (around 1900 in the 113,000-114,000s number range replaced by a label stating "The New Washburn. Latest Model") is glued inside the instrument. Numbering continues from the 50-60,000s (1896-7) up to the mid 190,000s (around start of 1905), numbers are ink stamped on the neck block and handwritten on a small round warranty label inside the instrument. Style and serial numbers are usually also stamped in the upper end of the headstock. All styles receive a slightly bigger cloud shaped tortoise celluloid pickguard with a small point at the sides. Between 1898-9 and 1901 all styles except 115 and 118 are redesigned with a 20-fret fingerboard that extends partly over the soundhole.

1896 - The "Pet Sounds" Ad

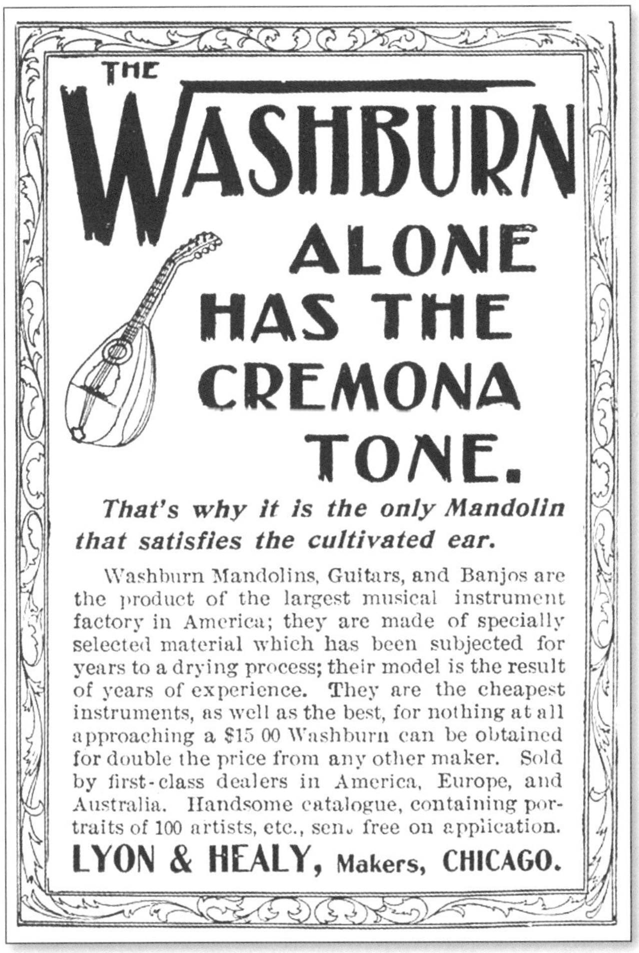

1898 ad. Cremonatone was a registered trademark of Lyon & Healy, used for Washburn mandolins and Lyon & Healy violins

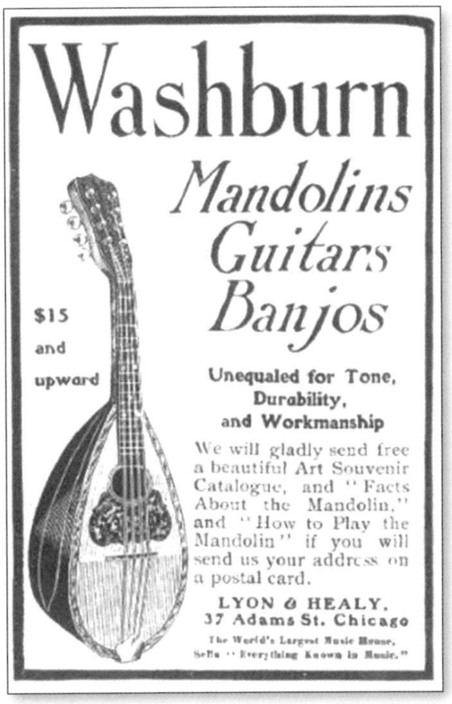

1904

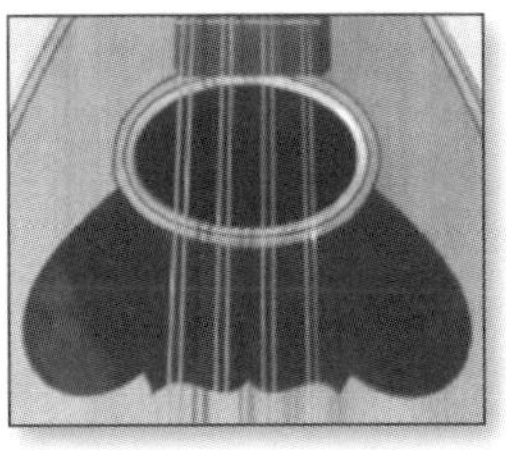

'Mushroom' pickguard on a Style 71 mandolin

'Crown' pickguard. The mandolin is a Style 73 (Elderly)

'Cloud' pickguard on a Style 250 mandolin

1905-1915:
All instruments are of the bowlback type. Serial numbers continue from the mid 190,000s up to the high 220,000s and are handwritten on a white, black and red label inside the instrument stating "The Washburn, Best in The World", and are usually also ink stamped on the neck block. Mandolins made between late 1905 and 1907 often have a black ring surrounding the label instead of the customary red ring, likely to commemorate the death of company founder and president Patrick J. Healy. Around 1907 numbering starts again with 1 up to the 8,000s (around 1910) and continues into the 19,000s (1915), serial numbers up to the 17,000s are usually preceded by "A or A-". Around the start of the 17,000s number range the A-prefix is dropped and a grey cloth lining replaces the light colored paper lining inside the bowl. All styles have an extension fingerboard with 20 frets. The small warranty label (1896-1905) is discontinued.

1915–1922:
Flatback models are introduced alongside the bowlback styles. Numbering continues up from the 19,000s to the 23,000s, serial numbers are ink stamped together with a style number on a white, black and red Washburn label stating "1915 model" inside the instrument. The bowlback styles have an inside lining of dark grey cloth. The Lyon & Healy Styles A-C (carved top/back) styles introduced in 1917 have a serial number sequence separate from the Washburn mandolins until 1925.

1922-1928:
All bowlback mandolin styles are discontinued in August 1924. Serial numbers are handwritten on an oval white/yellow/black label inside the instrument stating "Made and guaranteed by", a Lyon & Healy signature logo, "Worlds largest music house", "Chicago USA", "WASHBURN", "No" (indicating serial #) and "Style" (indicating model designation). Starting in 1925 the mandolin styles are identified by a four digit number starting with 52XX.[82] From 1922 to 1926-7 batch numbers are sometimes stamped on the neck block. After 1926-7 batch numbers are stamped in the headstock back, running into the high 14,000s around 1928-9. No serial numbers are stamped on instruments between mid 1926 and 1930.[83]

Between 1923 and 1924/5 some mandolins can also be found with a white, black and red Washburn label inside the instrument stating '1923-24 model', oval shaped with a crown on top, with inked serial numbers in the 24,000-27,000 range. In or before 1921 the scale length of the Lyon & Healy A, B and C Styles is decreased from 13 ¾" to 13", the body style for Style A instruments changes to an asymmetrical outline (with the exception of Style A mandolas and mandocellos, which keep their symmetrical two-point body) and the 'stairstep' headstock shape for Styles B and C is changed. Around 1922-3 the A, B and C style mandolins receive a Washburn label and are no longer catalogued under the Lyon & Healy brand name. After 1925 the former Styles A and C (renumbered as Styles 5283 and 5282) are serial numbered in the same sequence as the other Washburn mandolin models. Style B is discontinued in or prior to 1925.

1928-1935:
All mandolins no longer have a label but are branded on the center strip "Genuine WASHBURN Tonk Bros. Co. Chicago Sole Distributors. Usually the style number (52XX) is printed on the neck block, and serial numbers are not stamped on the instruments.

1935-1940:
Mandolins share their serial numbering sequence with guitars.[84] Serial numbers start again at 1 up to the low 7,000s and are ink stamped or typewritten on an oval white/light yellow label stating "Genuine Washburn, Style No.___ Serial No.___, made of choicest materials by workmen of exceptional skill, knowledge and experience, Tonk Bros. Co. Chicago, Exclusive (with "Wholesale" added after 1936) Distributors", instruments are also branded on the center strip "Genuine WASHBURN Tonk Bros. Co. Chicago Sole Distributors".

82 The exceptions are the carved top and back Washburn mandola (Style 5300) and matching mandocello (Style 5310).
83 See 2.3.
84 The shared numbering with guitars may have started already in 1930. Not enough surviving mandolins were reported to verify this.

3.4 Construction / general remarks

Early variants of the mandolin were known in Europe since the 15th century. The 'modern' bowlback mandolin, whose design was perfected by the Vinaccia family of Naples, Italy, became popular in Western Europe during the 18th century and was featured in works of classical composers such as Vivaldi and Mozart, but it was a virtually unknown instrument in late 19th century America.

On New Year's Day of 1880 a group of touring musicians from Spain performed their first concert in New York City's Booths Theater. They called themselves the Figaro Spanish Students, an English translation of their original name, Estudiantina Figaroa, and performed in traditional student attire consisting of dark uniforms with short cloaks. Twelve of its members played the bandurria, a small guitar-like instrument with twelve strings tuned in pairs and a flat top and back. The band also featured six guitars, a violin and a violoncello. The sweet sound of these instruments playing together in arrangements of classical music and Spanish folk music pieces caused a sensation. When the group returned to Europe in March, a host of copycat bands immediately sprung up that started imitating their act and billing themselves as the 'Spanish Students'. The most successful of these groups was led by Carlo Curti, a prominent New York violinist, and consisted mostly of Italian immigrants who played bowlback mandolins instead of bandurrias. For a few years they toured the country with great success and helped spark the 'mandolin craze' that swept the nation and would continue into the next decades. Mandolin orchestras were formed everywhere in the United States and thousands started to play the mandolin. As the instruments available during the early 1880s were mostly imports from Italy, Spain and Germany, domestic manufacturers soon entered the field. Lyon & Healy claimed in its sales literature to be the first American maker of mandolins, and hired many Italian and Spanish immigrant workmen to meet with the explosive demand for good inexpensive instruments. During the peak years of the mandolin craze the company made around 20,000 bowlback mandolins per year, ranging from simple student models that could be had for a few dollars to

The 1896 Washburn catalog contained many endorsements by artists and mandolin orchestras. Jeannie Durkee (pictured upper right) was the daughter of L&H superintendent George Durkee. Around 1900 she became an endorser of the guitars made by the May Flower company, another Chicago manufacturer. Lyon & Healy would acquire the trademarks and distribution rights for this brand in 1912

Another band of fake Spaniards, this time from Utah (1896 catalog)

LYON & HEALY, CHICAGO. 273

THE L. H. LELAND MANDO FAMILY.

SHOWING RELATIVE SIZES.

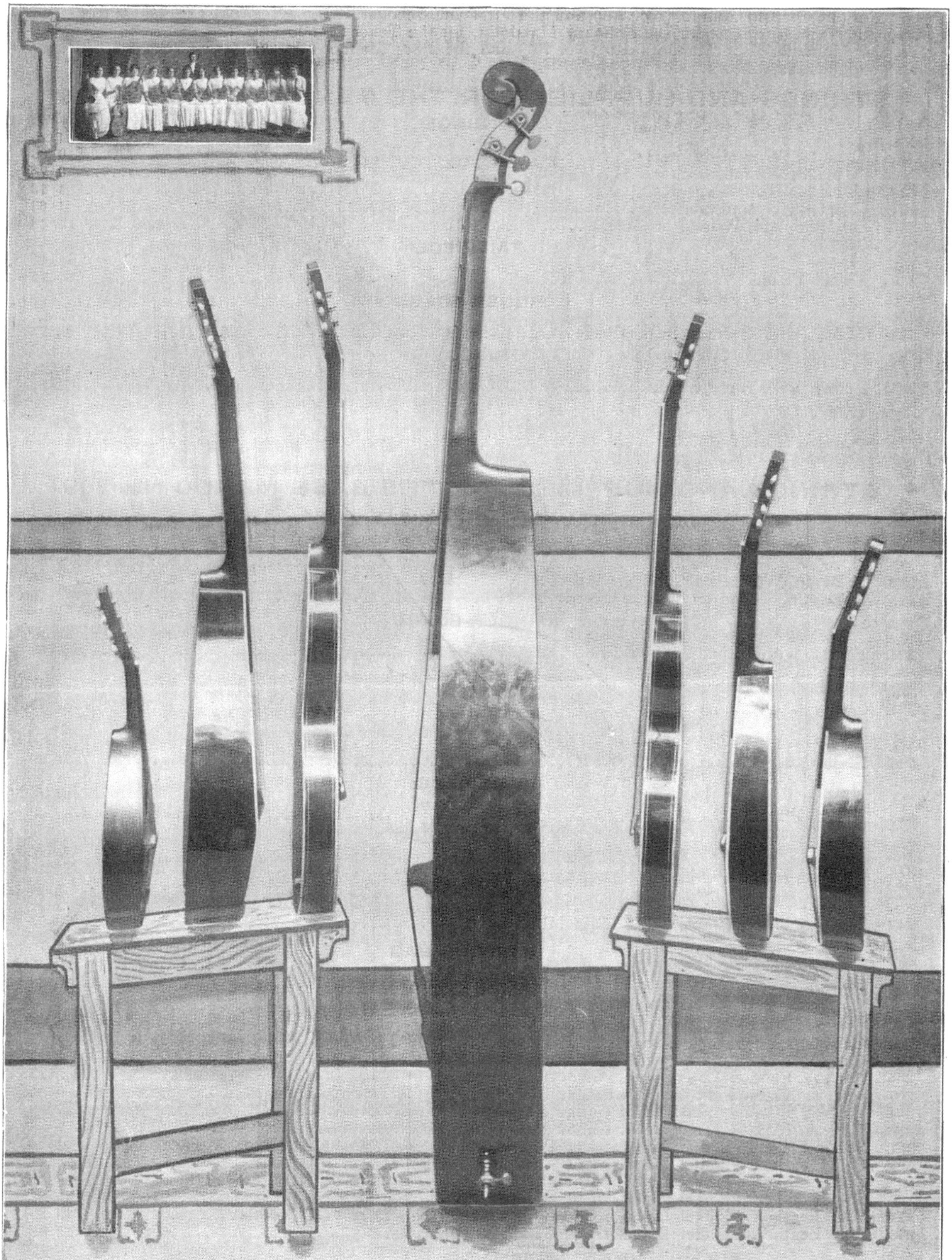

Side view of the L.H. Leland family, consisting of four mandolin type instruments, two guitars and a mando bass (Jim Garber)

highly ornate and expensive styles adorned with different varieties of pearl.

The first known catalog showing the Washburn mandolin line dates back to 1889, but production started a few years earlier. Lyon & Healy ads from 1887 already mention Washburn "mandolines", which was changed to 'mandolins' in an ad from 1888. New or revised lines were launched in 1892, 1896-7, 1905, 1910, 1915, 1920, 1922, 1925 and 1935.

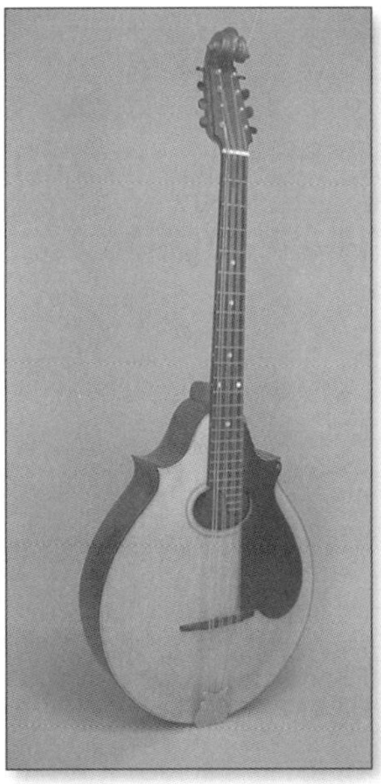

Lyon & Healy Mandocello, around 1920 (Frank Ford)

The first Washburn mandola, intended to be tuned either one fifth or an octave below standard tuning, was introduced in 1892. A mandocello was not offered by Lyon & Healy until around 1911, when the short-lived L.H. Leland line made its appearance in the company's catalogs. This also included a standard and short scale mandolin, a mandola and a huge 'mando bass', plus two novel guitar models with very shallow bodies that were forbearers of the 'thinline' electric guitars introduced in the 1950s. It is almost certain that the Larson Bros of Chicago were the manufacturers of the L.H. Leland line, which was meant to provide a complete program of instruments for use by guitar and mandolin orchestras.[85] Lyon & Healy were apparently determined to compete with their fast growing rival Gibson, who had been very successful in convincing many of these orchestras of the superiority of their products. But Lyon & Healy's efforts to reclaim this territory came much too late. The company also left the task to promote the Leland line mostly to the dealers, who were not up to compete against the aggressive and costly marketing campaigns employed by Gibson, and the entire line was discontinued by the mid 1910s. The only Washburn mandocello, catalogued between the early 1920s and 1928, was identical to the Lyon & Healy Style A mandocello introduced around 1917, the sole difference being the 'Washburn' label.

L.H. Leland guitar – the first 'thinline'? (Tony Klassen)

Other mandolin family instruments that were made in the Lyon & Healy factories between the 1890s and the 1920s include the mandolinetto, a small eight-stringed guitar shaped instrument with an 8" lower bout and an identical tuning and scale length as a standard mandolin, and twelve-string bowlback mandolins. Both variants were not marketed under the Washburn brand.

(1903)

J.R. Stewart and Gibson-made mandolins

By the end of the 1920s production figures for Washburn mandolins dropped steeply. Washburn mandolins were listed in the Tonk Bros catalogs throughout the 1930s, but surviving instruments from this era are very rare. Though Gibson also made small numbers of flatback Styles 5280 and 5281 between 1938 and 1940[86], actual examples have not turned up on the instrument market in recent years. For that reason no guidelines can be given for distinguishing Gibson from Regal-made mandolins, or even J.R. Stewart from Lyon & Healy-made instruments.

85 In the 1890s Lyon & Healy marketed a piano under the name "Leland by Washburn Piano Co.". The L.H. Leland brand was recently revived for a budget line of acoustic guitars made in the Far East.
86 See 2.4 for sources. Gibson likely never made the carved-back Style 5283.

L. & H. Mandolins

12 STRING MANDOLINS

The "Lakeside"

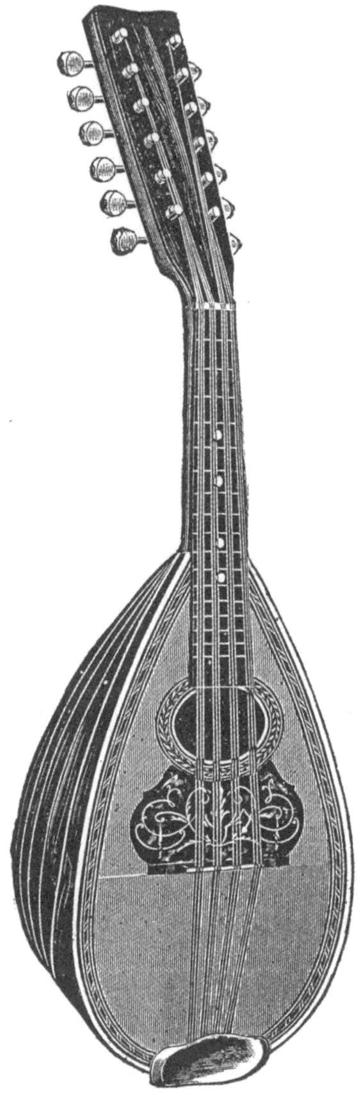

No. 1603

No.

1502. 12 strings, 18 ribs of solid mahogany with black inlaying between, extended rosewood apron, high varnish finish, broad fancy colored wood inlaying around sound-hole and edge, celluloid bound, spruce top, mahogany finish neck, rosewood fingerboard and tortoise celluloid guard plate, pearl position dots, our own nickel-plated patent head, nickel-plated shell pattern tailpiece .... Each $13.75

The "American Conservatory"

No.

1603. 12 strings, 28 ribs of rosewood, white inlay between, hand polished, broad fancy colored corded inlaying around sound-hole and edge, celluloid bound edge and apron, tortoise celluloid guard plate handsomely white inlaid, mahogany neck, rosewood veneered headpiece, ebony fingerboard, pearl position marks, our own nickel-plated patent head, nickel-plated combined wrist rest and tailpiece................ Each $20.63

12-String Mandolin Cases

No. Each

18. Canvas (to fit our Nos. 1502 and 1603—12-string mandolins), flannel lined, with patent fastenings, superior model and quality.................... $ 3.53
19. Leather, hand sewed, flannel lined, black color (to fit our Nos. 1502 and 1603—12-string mandolins).. 24.75

To insure a right fit, give measurement of instruments, if known, when ordering

Guitar-Mandolins

A mandolin with a guitar-shaped body. It has a fingerboard same as on a mandolin and is played in same manner; possesses a sweet, clear tone, and with its neat appearance and absolutely correct scale, has won public favor.

No. 91

The "American Conservatory"

No. Each

81. Beautiful imitation rosewood back and sides, hand polished, spruce top, celluloid guard plate, inlaid edge and sound-hole, imitation mahogany neck, rosewood fingerboard with pearl position marks, our own make machine head, nickel covered shell pattern tailpiece.. $10.38
91. Genuine rosewood back and sides, hand polished, fancy strip inlaid in back, back edge bound with white celluloid, front edge bound with celluloid and fancy colored wood, spruce top, celluloid guard plate, inlaid sound-hole, mahogany neck, ebony fingerboard, pearl position marks, our own make machine head, nickel covered shell pattern tailpiece.. 14.13

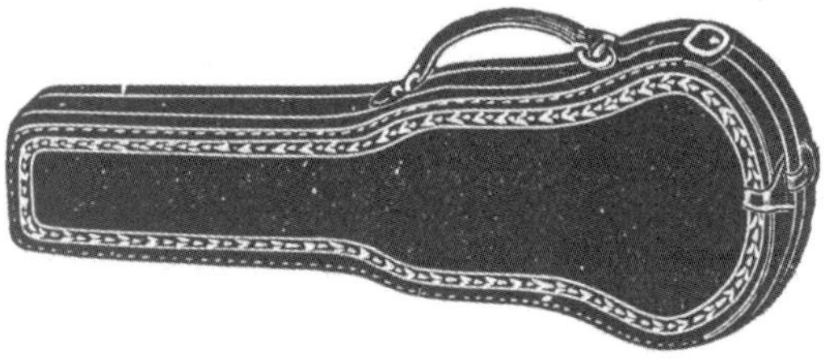

No. 14

Guitar-Mandolin Cases

Each

12. Canvas, flannel lined, opening at end, superior model and quality .... $ 3.38
14. Leather, hand sewed, embossed, black.................... 21.13

(1919)

Early Endorsers: Samuel Siegel and Valentine Abt

Around the turn of the 20th century just about anyone seemed good enough in the eyes of Lyon & Healy to be recruited as endorser of the Washburn instrument lines. Amidst the many obscure players who sung praise to the Washburns in period catalogs –mostly teachers and opera singers- a few famous virtuosos stood out. Samuel Siegel, one of the early Washburn endorsers of the late 1890s, was considered by many as the best mandolin player in America. He was born in 1875 in Des Moines, Iowa, and became one of the first mandolinists to advance from the vaudeville circuit –where most players performed at the time- to the classical music scene. He was signed in 1900 to Emile Berliner's Gramophone Company and made several solo recordings during the following years, mostly of original compositions. This was a relatively new approach as most of the musical pieces performed by mandolinists at the time were transcribed from the violin, which shared its G D A E tuning with the mandolin. Around 1901 Siegel also appeared in ads as endorser of Regal mandolins, in spite of his claim printed in Lyon & Healy catalogs until the 1910s that "we use and endorse Washburn instruments exclusively". Besides his career as a concert performer Siegel was also an active mandolin teacher. In 1919 he was granted a patent for a toy metallophone intended to accelerate the musical education of children. Siegel died in 1948, by which time the mandolin craze of the early 1900s had long been forgotten. The mandolin would never regain the huge popularity of its heyday, but again attained prominence through a new country music style pioneered by another world-class virtuoso, Bill Monroe.

SAMUEL SIEGEL.
(SIEGEL CONCERT CO.)
"We use and indorse Washburn instruments exclusively. I have played a Washburn Mandolin for years. Consider it the best made."

(1896 catalog)

1902 concert poster announcing a performance by Samuel Siegel

Siegel had declared that the fact that he had started out on mandolin instead of violin gave him a better right-hand technique "than some great players". This likely was a stab at another renowned mandolin soloist and Washburn endorser, Valentine Abt (1873-1942), who originally had studied the violin. Like Siegel, Abt composed many pieces for solo mandolin and also recorded for the Victor Talking Machine Company. Before he started endorsing the Washburn mandolins, Abt had played an innovative aluminum bodied bowlback design made by the Aluminum Musical Instrument Company and patented by Neil Merrill in the late 1890s. He was also a proficient harp player, and was pictured in an ad campaign promoting the Larson Bros-made Dyer Symphony harp guitars. Around 1908 Abt formed the first American classical mandolin quartet, which featured two mandolins, a mandola and a mandocello. A few years later he started to endorse the instruments of the Boston based Vega Company, and an "Abt model" mandolin was marketed briefly. A 1937 article stated "...those fortunate enough to have attended a recital by Andres Segovia or William Foden on the guitar; Giuseppe Pettine or the late Valentine Abt on the mandolin; Alfred Farland or Frederic Bacon on the banjo, will look back on that occasion as a never to be forgotten event of their musical experience".[87] This certainly was a testament to the stature of Abt as one of the foremost musicians of his time -though he was still very much alive in 1937!

(1901)

Recently a biography of Abt was published, written by Dr. John L. Abt, a great-grandson of the artist.[88][89]

87 George C. Krick, *Fun with Fretted Instruments, Etude magazine, November 1937* p. 756.
88 The Biography of Valentine Abt: Mandolin and Harp Virtuoso, Composer and Teacher. 1873-1942.
89 Details of the described artists careers are partly derived from Paul Sparks, *The Classical Mandolin*, Oxford University Press (1995) p. 124-129.

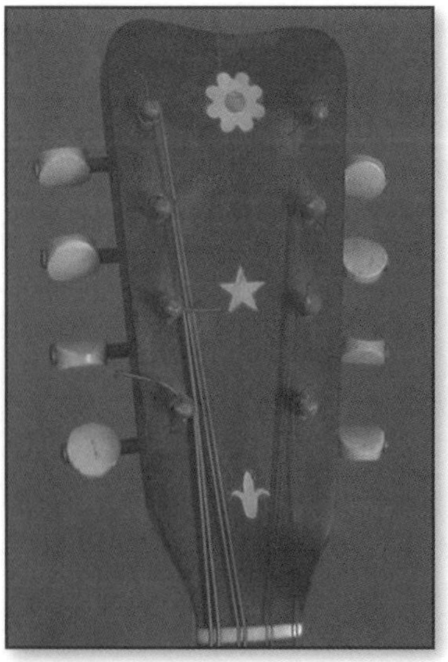

1889 - Style 73 (Elderly)

1889 - pictured is a 1892 Style 80 (Richard Myers)

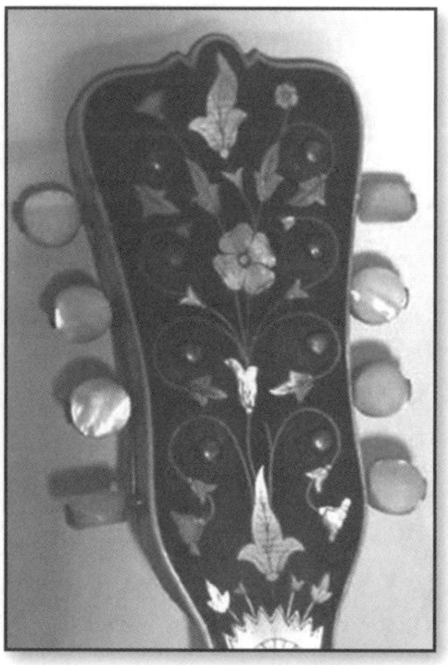

1896 - Style 1125 (Richard Myers)

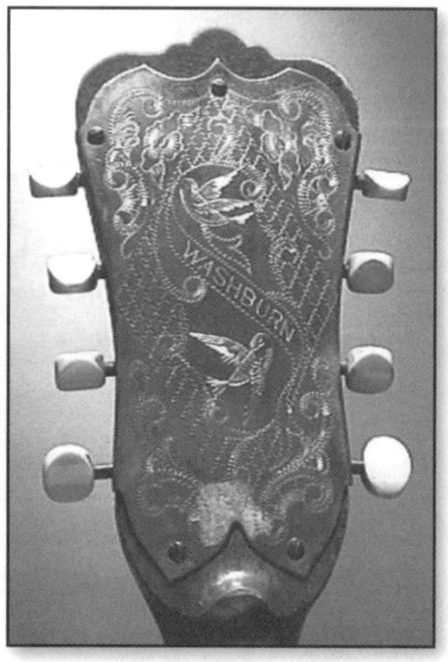

1905 - engraved headstock cover (Style 235)

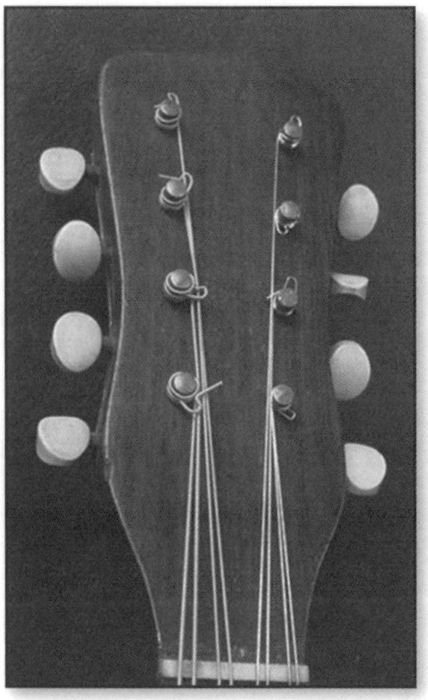

1915

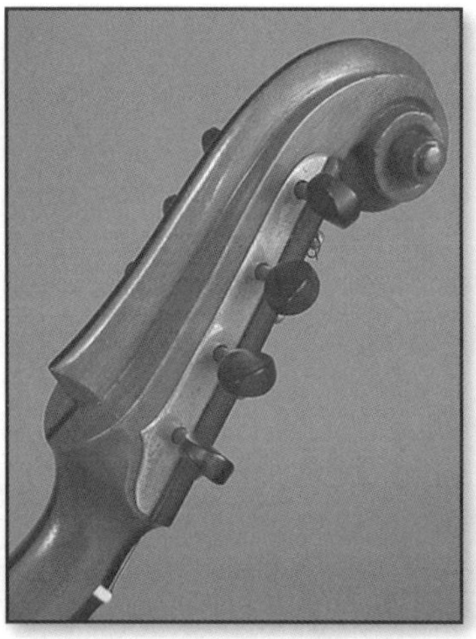

Two views of the Lyon & Healy Style A (1917) headstock. Both the scroll and the top loaded tuner arrangement were derived from a patented design by John Brandt. The far right picture shows the headstock of a late 1890s Brandt bowlback mandolin (Frank Ford/ Ron LaPoff, Lark Street Music)

1925

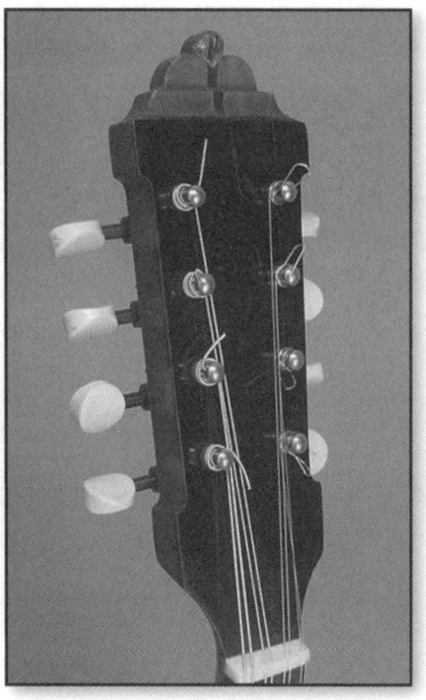

1917 - 'stairstep' headstock of Lyon & Healy Styles B and C (Frank Ford)

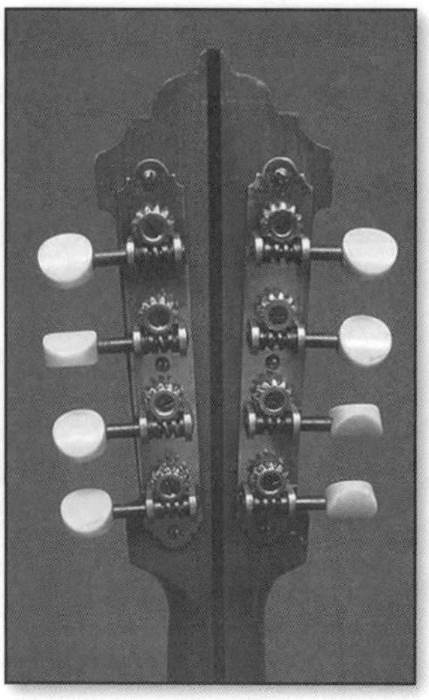

1917 (Elderly)

1920-1 - 'deco' headstock (Frank Ford)

3.4.1 Necks, headstocks, fingerboards

Necks

Cedar necks characterized practically all of the earlier Washburn mandolin styles until these were replaced by mahogany necks in 1905. Most mandolins had a steel reinforcement rod running the length of the fingerboard that was buried in the neck and part of the instrument's top. The 1917 Lyon & Healy Styles A-C (and the later versions of these instruments) came with a specially designed mahogany neck, reinforced by a center piece of 'vulcanized fibre' flanked by two wedge shaped strips of maple. The only Washburn mandolin styles fitted with a maple neck were the top of the line bowlback Styles 85, 175 and 1125.

Headstock shape

The 1889 mandolin models up to Style 74 had a rather plain headstock design with rounded corners and an inward curved top, which was used on the cheaper models until 1896. The more expensive styles of the 1889 catalog were characterized by a different headstock, also with rounded corners but with three small domes in the middle at the upper end. This represented the classic headstock shape used for most Washburn bowlbacks until these styles were dropped from the catalog in August 1924. A third, simpler design was introduced in 1915 for the cheapest bowlback and all flatback styles, outward tapered towards the top with a small point at the top end. It was slightly modified in 1925 to a narrower outline with sharper corners and straight sides. Style A sported the distinctive large 'scroll' headstock throughout its entire production period, while Styles B and C –which like Style A had been introduced in 1917 under the Lyon & Healy name- originally had a pointed 'stairstep' headstock that was changed in the early 1920s to an elaborate mustache shaped outline with a scroll figure carved in relief, also known among collectors as the 'deco' headstock. The last incarnation of Style C had a simpler, straight sided headstock with a small point at the top.

1892 (Elderly)

American Conservatory

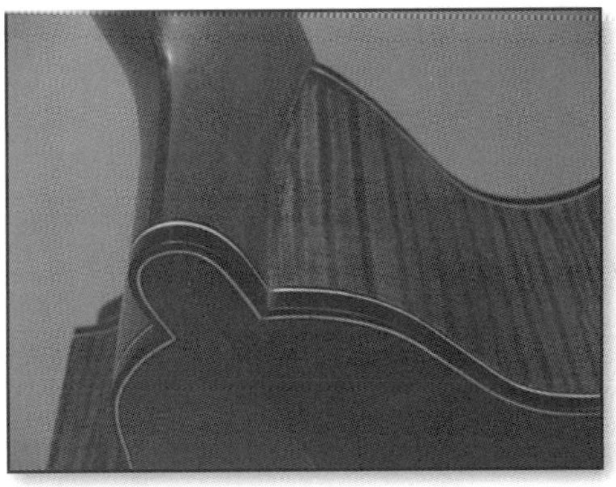

Style A (Frank Ford)

1892 - the Aerosmith signature model! (Elderly)

1905 - Style 275

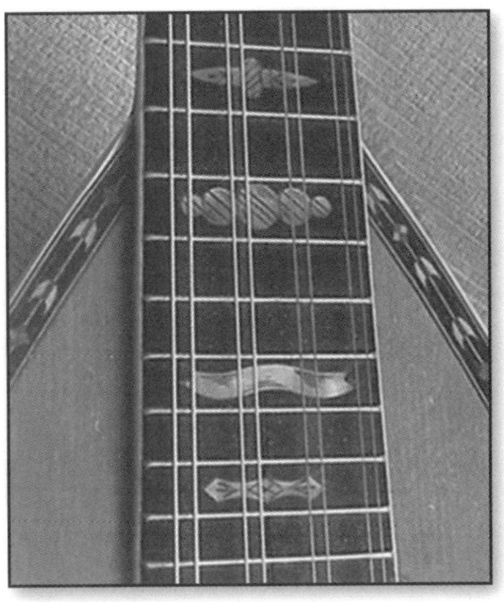

1910 - Style 235

Lyon & Healy Style A mandolin (early 1920s) with asymmetrical body points, 13″ scale. This model has a rare 27-fret neck – one fret is missing (Frank Ford)

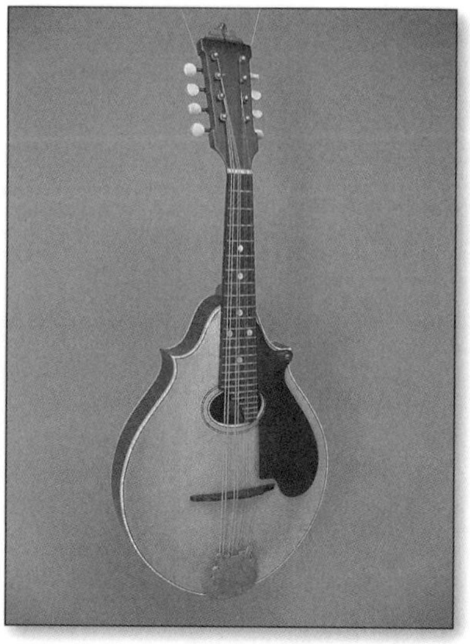

Style B mandolin, early 1920s. The change from the 'stairstep' (pictured here) to the 'deco headstock' happened before the decrease of the scale length from 13 ¾″ to 13″ – this is the shorter scale version. Note the cutout in the pickguard (Frank Ford)

Style C mandolin, late 1910s. The tailpiece is not original (Frank Ford)

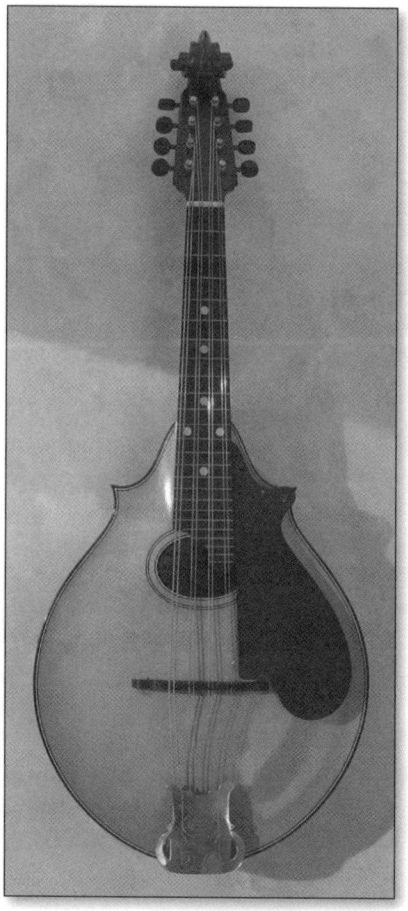

1917 Lyon & Healy Style A mandolin, first version with symmetrical body points and 13 ¾″ scale (Kieron Seamons)

The Joseph & Frazier Orchestra might have also called themselves 'The Rich Dudes'. Besides four Washburn banjos and four top-of-the-line 'Bell guitars, there are also four Style A mandolins in the picture, and the gentleman at the right is resting his hand on what could be a Style A Mandocello – no wonder they were Washburn endorsers! (1925 catalog picture) (Brian Lydford)

1918 ad showing Bernardo de Pace (1886-1966), a/k/a the Wizard of the Mandolin, a world famous virtuoso at the time, holding an early A Style mandolin with symmetrical body points

The scroll headstock of Style A with its top loaded tuner arrangement was not an original Lyon & Healy design. It was created and patented in 1898 by John Brandt, one of the many smaller instrument manufacturers in Chicago that were eventually acquired by Lyon & Healy.[90] Many surviving mandolins and mandolas made by Brandt have this scroll headstock.

Fingerboards

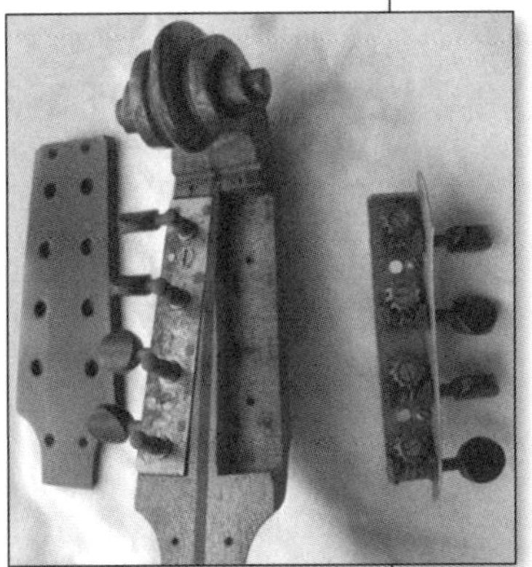

Headstock of Style A mandolin w disassembled tuners (Kieron Seamons)

Until around the turn of the 20th century all Washburn mandolins had a 17-fret fingerboard. The 1905 Washburn catalog showed an extension fingerboard with 20 frets as a new feature on all styles, but it actually had been introduced a few years earlier on the pre-1905 model line. For Style 1125 this happened around 1898-9, for the other styles except 115 and 118 probably around 1901, shortly after the introduction of a new label inside the instruments that stated 'the Latest Model' (see 3.2.1). For some reason the new extension fingerboard was not pictured in the catalogs prior to 1905, which continued to show the lithographed catalog images of the instruments that were first published in 1896.

Shortly after the introduction of the 1922 model line a 21-fret extension fingerboard became standard for Washburn flatback mandolins.[91] The last styles introduced in 1935 went back to 20 frets. An exception were Styles A (renamed 5283 around 1925), B and C (renamed 'Aristocrat' around 1925), which came since their introduction in 1917 with a 24-fret extension fingerboard. Style A was also available for a number of years with a 27-fret fingerboard.

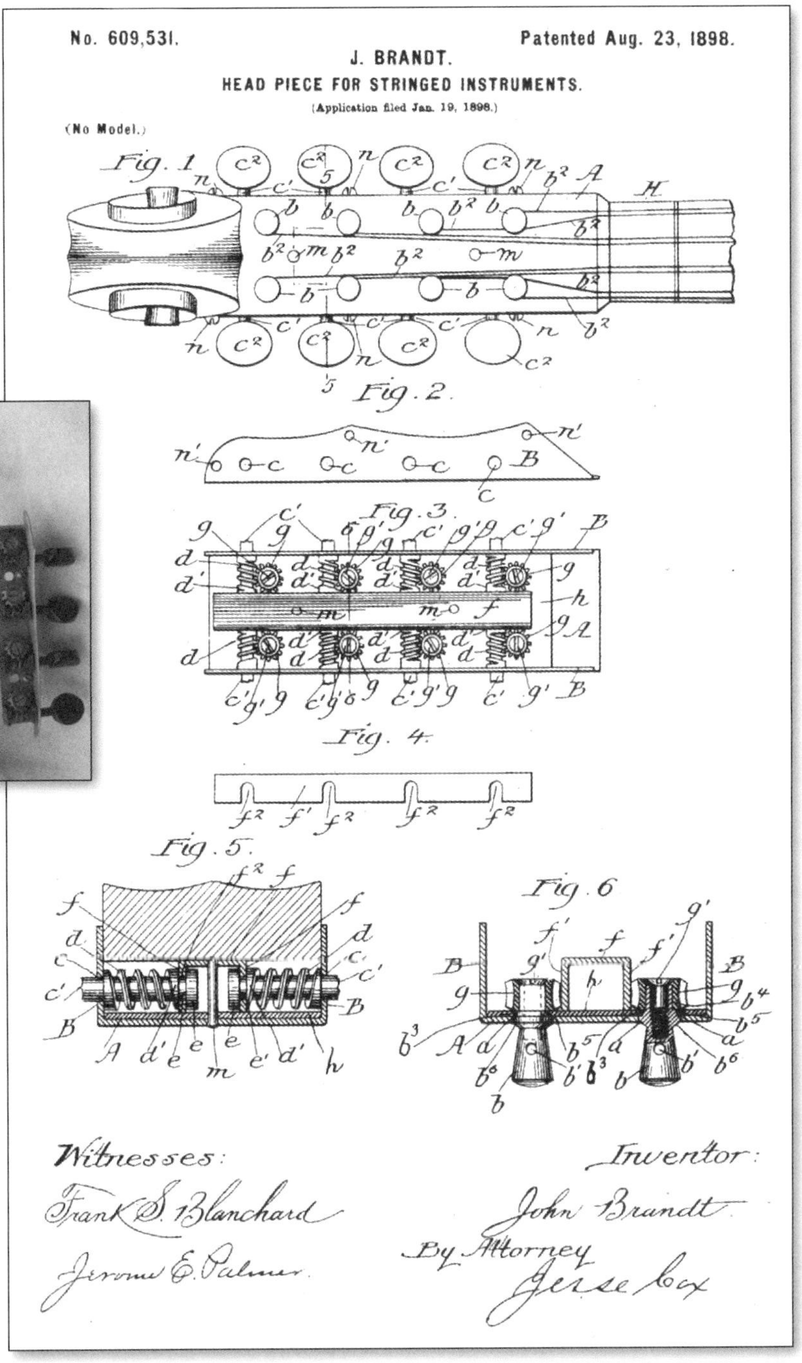

1898 patent drawing for John Brandt's invention of the top loaded tuning machines, used by designer Walter Kirk for the 1917 Lyon & Healy Style A mandolin

All mandolins of the 1889 line –including the very ornate Style 80– had unbound fingerboards. Of the 1892 models only the revised Style 80 and the newly introduced Style 85 were designed with bound fingerboards. As manufacturing costs for the Washburn instrument lines steadily decreased between the early 1890s until around 1910, which was also evidenced by lower catalog prices on the more ornate models, most 1896 mandolin styles and all models between 1905 and 1915 were equipped with a bound fingerboard. Engraved pearl fingerboard inlays were typical of many mandolin styles catalogued between 1892 and 1915. After 1922 all styles came with fingerboards that had pearl dots as position markers. The construction of the solid pearl fingerboards that were featured on the most expensive bowlback styles before 1915 was slightly different from the standard method as these were not glued directly to the neck, but on a thin layer of spruce that was backed by another thin layer of ebony or ebonized wood.[92]

90 Patent number 609,531.

91 Surviving examples froma the 1922-1925 period of the same styles have 20 or 21-fret fingerboards.

92 This laminated construction is visible at the end but not at the sides of the neck (information courtesy of Neil Russell).

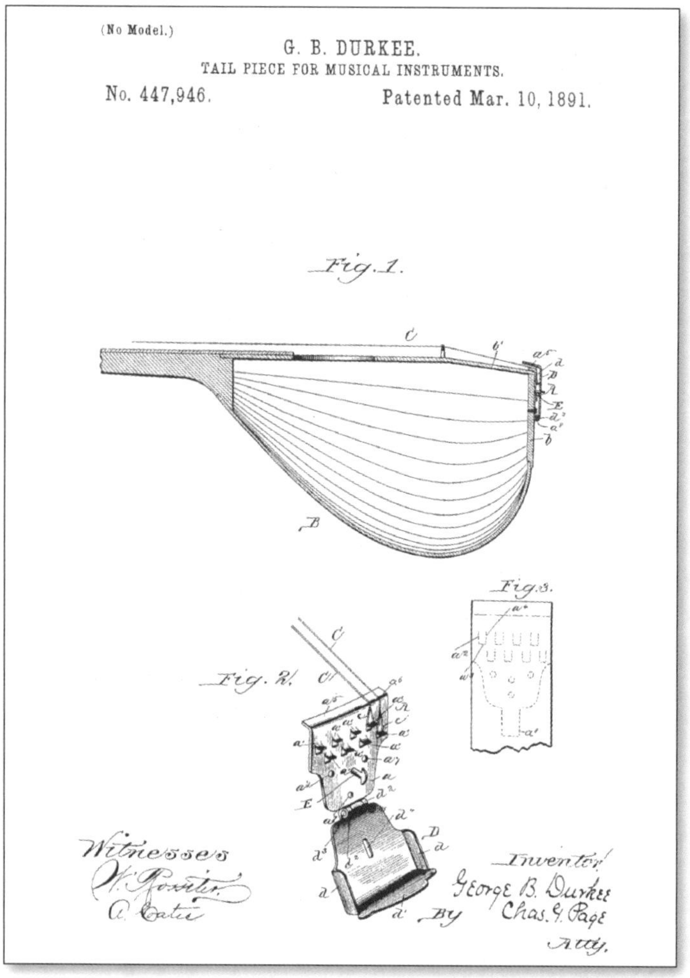

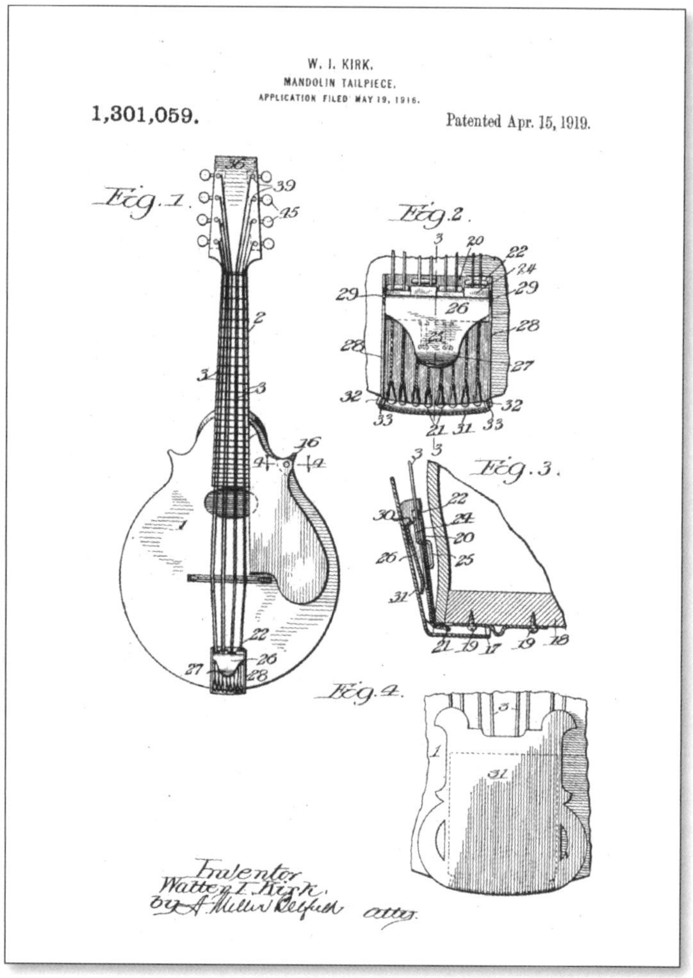

Mandolin tailpiece with hinged cover by George Durkee

1919 patent drawing

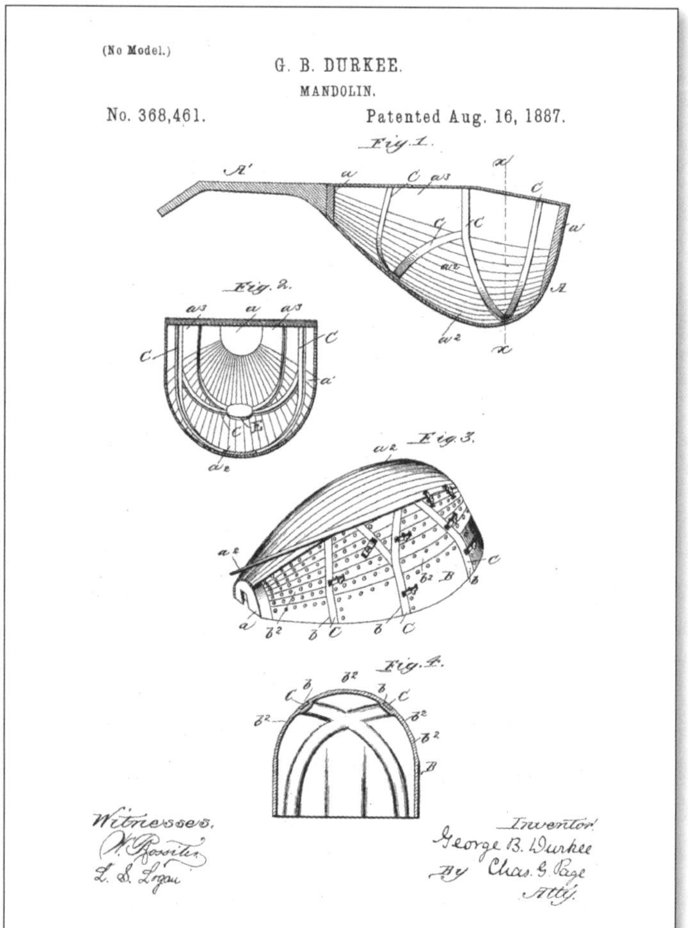

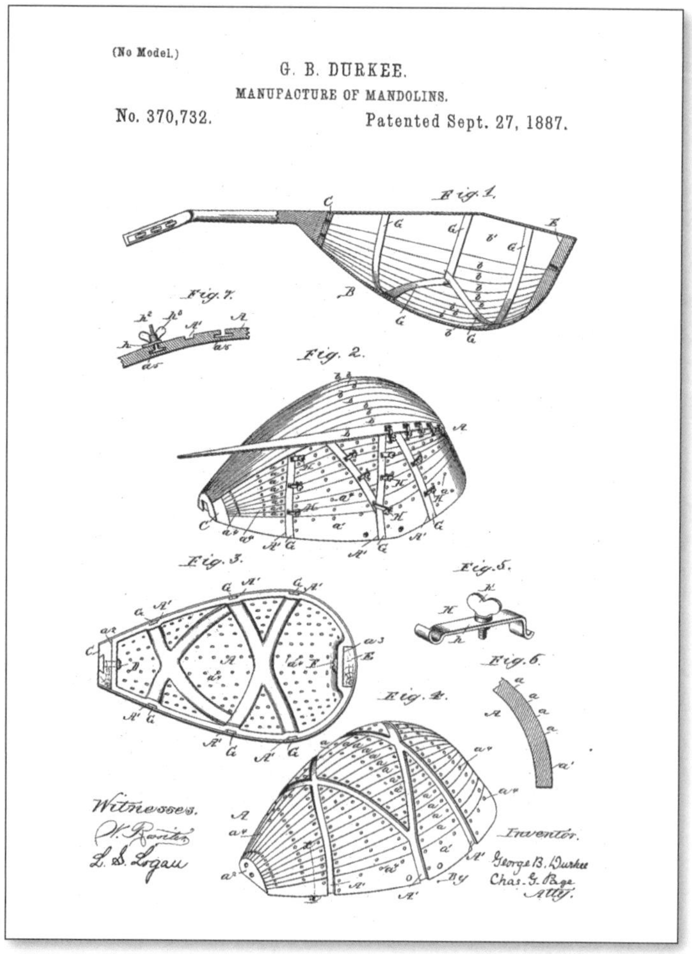

Patent drawings for the cross bracing of body ribs. The right picture shows the jig used for this method and the hooks for fixing the glued ribs

Scale length

The Lyon & Healy Styles A-C of 1917 constituted with their 13 ¾″ scale length a departure from the original 13″ scale used on the standard sized bowlback and flatback mandolins. Around 1921 the scale length of Styles A-C was reduced to 13″. This also resulted in the necks of these styles joining the body at the 9th fret (previously between frets 10 and 11). This change certainly affected tone and playability of the instruments, but did not result in a diminished appeal for these styles from mandolin players. The standard 13″ scale length of the 1925 mandolin line was changed again to 14″ on the two cheapest styles (5280 and 5281) of the last pre-WWII mandolin line introduced in 1935.

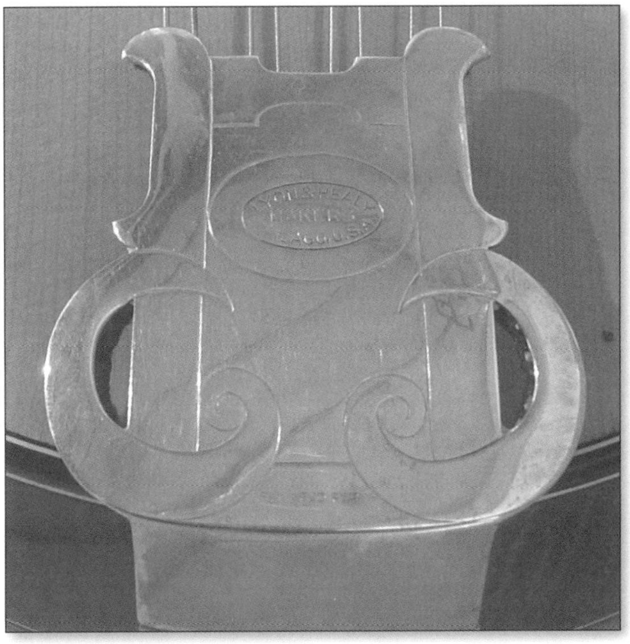

Very rare earlier style tailpiece on Style A mandolin, 1917 (Kieron Seamons)

3.4.2 Tailpieces

Only Styles 71 and 72 of the earliest (1889) mandolin line did not have the hinged crown shaped tailpiece cover –designed by George Durkee and patented on March 4, 1891- that would become a standard feature on all Washburn mandolins for the next decades.[93] Before 1896-7 the higher end styles came with serrated tailpiece covers (with four small ear-like forms cut out on top). After 1896 all styles received a closed cover with hinges, which was replaced by a slide-on cover around 1915.

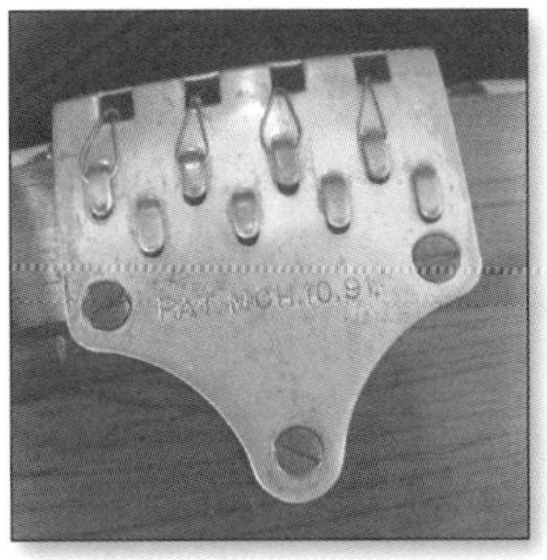

1891 patent stamp on Lyon & Healy mandolin

Engraved tailpiece, Style 250 mandolin

The 1917 Lyon & Healy Style A-C mandolins were fitted with a newly designed tailpiece with a larger lyre shaped cover that allowed for preset overtones for the string vibrations behind the bridge. It received a patent on April 15, 1919.[94] The patent documents state Walter Kirk as inventor and Lyon & Healy as assignee. The tailpiece cover was stamped "Lyon & Healy", which remained unchanged after these mandolin styles were revised and renamed "Washburn" around 1922. The last examples of Style A (renamed Style 5283 in the mid 1920s) made by Regal during the late 1930s were still equipped with the Lyon & Healy stamped tailpiece, though the company had ceased manufacturing these instruments in 1928.[95] The lyre shape was much reminiscent of tailpieces found on older bowlback instruments, most notably those made by New York mandolin maker Angelo Mannello (1858-1922). A few of the very first Style A –and possibly also Style B and C- mandolins came with a differently shaped tailpiece cover, which also can be seen on the 1916 patent drawing. In addition, a 'Pat Apld For' notice was sometimes stamped into the tailpiece cover on the early models.

'Durkee' tailpiece with serrated cover (pre 1892)

Walter Kirk's lyre tailpiece as used on Lyon & Healy Styles A-C (Frank Ford)

3.4.3 Body styles

The Washburn bowlback or 'tater bug' mandolin styles were made between the late 1880s and August 1924. Prior to 1896 most styles had a body consisting of alternating maple and rosewood ribs, while the most expensive models –Style 80 of the 1889 line and Styles 78, 80 and 85 of 1892- had rosewood bodies. All models of the 1896 line had rosewood ribs[96]. Another important change from the earlier styles was that the cross bracing of the inside ribs –a patent-

93 Patent number 447,946. The March '91 patent date was stamped on these tailpieces for some time. Some of the cheaper L&H mandolins came with a Durkee tailpiece that had a shell shaped cover.

94 Patent number 1,301,059.

95 Only one Style A with a Tonk Bros label has been reported, which could imply that during the 1930s remaining inventory was sold by Tonk and that Regal did not manufacture any new instruments of these models.

96 The older styles 071 and 71 with mixed maple and rosewood ribs remained briefly available after the introduction of the 1897 line and were renamed as Styles 115 and 118, respectively. Later versions of Style 115 and 118 had rosewood ribs.

Pullout metal knee rest on a Style B mandolin (Frank Ford)

Style 235 with rosewood ribs. The beige/brown side marquetry is typical for the post 1910 models

Mixed rosewood and maple ribs as used on many early mandolins (pre-1896)

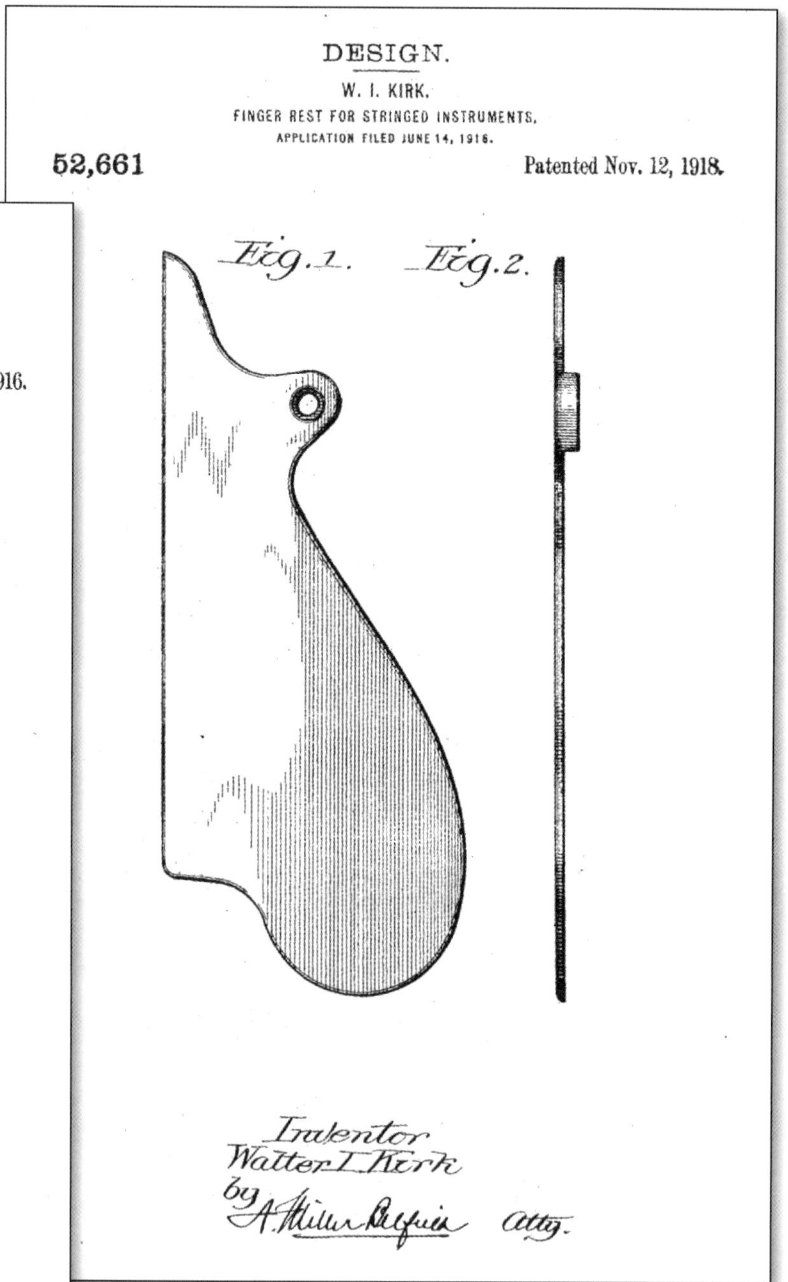

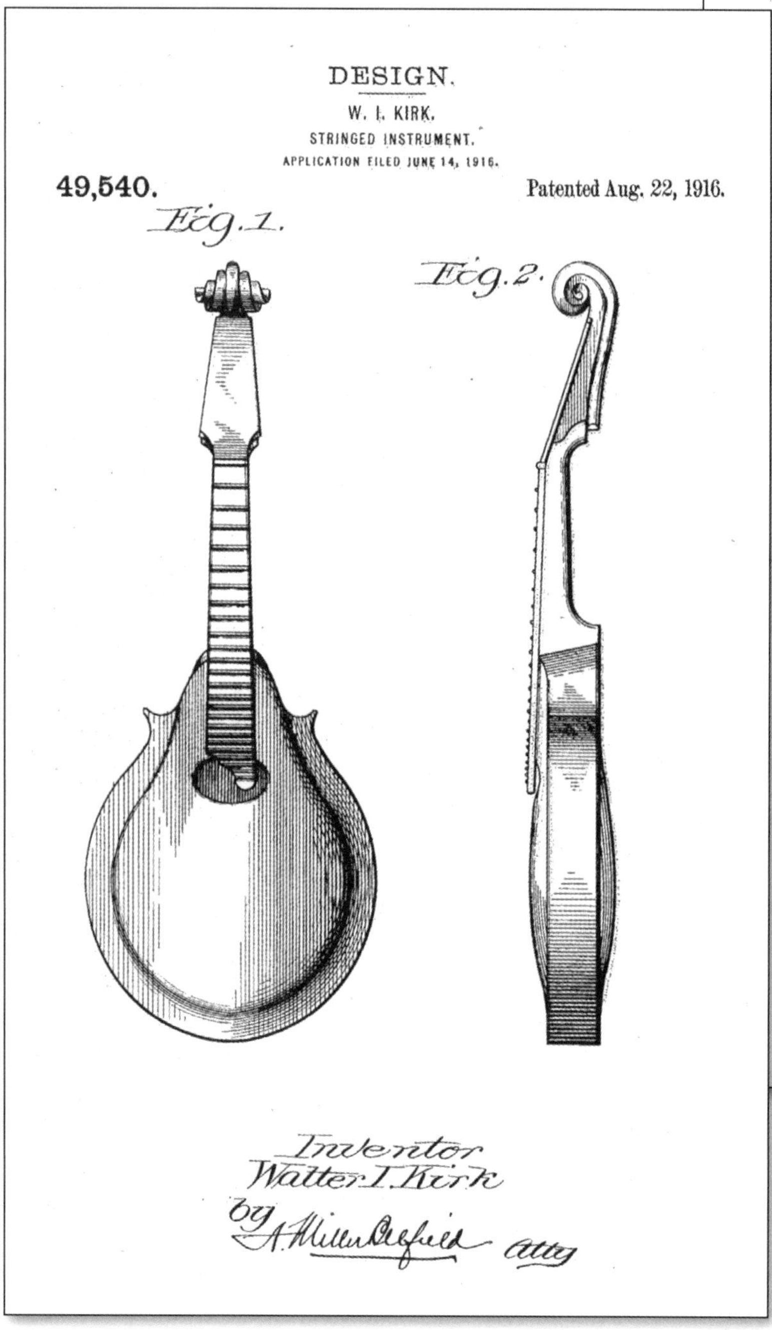

Design patents for the Style A mandolin. The pickguard shown here does not have the soundhole cutout of the later Styles A and B guards

ed invention of George Durkee that aimed to increase the resonant properties of bowlback bodies- was dropped in 1896 and replaced by the conventional method of gluing of a paper lining to the ribs. It is likely that this was a move not induced by cost saving motives alone. Since relatively fewer of the cross-braced mandolins seem to have survived in comparison to the later more traditional designs, constructional problems may have been the main reason for this change. A contributing factor may have been stability issues caused by the mix of rosewood and maple ribs used on most of the pre-1896 styles. The construction of the cross braced instruments was also very cumbersome as all individual ribs had to be secured in various places by tiny metal hooks after they had been glued together. The light colored paper lining of the post 1896 models was replaced by a dark grey cloth lining on the 1915 and later bowlback styles.

The first flatback mandolin styles were introduced in 1915, initially with pear shaped rosewood bodies containing two small symmetrical body points. As instrument retail prices rose sharply after the start of WWI the cheaper mahogany bodied Style 2424 was introduced around 1920, which had a pear shaped body without the body points. After 1925 this body style was used for all models until 1940, with the exception of the two pointed body of Style 5283 that was identical to the former Style A. Body woods used for the post 1920 lines were mostly mahogany and rosewood (the latter being discontinued on the 1935 styles). The only maple bodied Washburn mandolins were Styles A (Style 5283 after 1925), B and C (renamed 'Aristocrat'), the short-lived Style D (1922-1925) and Style 5281 of 1935.

In many ways Styles A-C were a breed apart from the other Lyon & Healy mandolin styles. They had carved tops and backs, specially designed reinforced necks, different ornamental headstock shapes, detachable pickguards and maple bodies. Styles A and B were also fitted between 1917 and the mid 1920s with a pullout metal knee rest, with the exception of some of the earliest models. Lyon & Healy were justifiably proud of these mandolins created by their chief designer Walter Kirk. Three patent applications were filed in May and June 1916: one regarding the tailpiece,[97] a second for the design of Style A with the symmetrical pointed body –around 1921 changed to an asymmetrical two point shape- and the scroll headstock, and a third for the shape of the detachable vulcanized fiber pickguard of Styles A and B. The last two design patents were awarded respectively on August 22, 1916 and November 12, 1918.[98] The 11.12.1918 patent notice was impressed for a number of years on the pickguards of most A, B and C style mandolins – even though the Style C pickguard had a different shape than the patented design! On some of the earlier Style A-C mandolins 'Pat Apld For' can be found stamped in the pickguard. The shape of the pickguards on Style A and B mandolins was later slightly revised with a cutout around the soundhole. This change occurred for the Style A instruments at the time the asymmetrical body outline was introduced, for Style B mandolins a few years earlier. All Style C mandolins had a straight sided pickguard without the cutout during their entire production period.

PRICE LIST

to Catalog of

Mandos, Mandolins, Mandolas, Mandocellos

All Prices are F. O. B. Chicago

Page	Catalog Number	CONTENTS	Price
7	Style A	Lyon & Healy Own Make Mandolin	**$100.00**
9	Style B	Lyon & Healy Own Make Mandolin	**75.00**
11	Style C	Lyon & Healy Own Make Mandolin	**65.00**
13	G-2683	Washburn Mandolin	**83.00**
13	G-2662	Washburn Mandolin	**62.00**
15	G-2643	Washburn Mandolin	**43.00**
15	G-2632	Washburn Mandolin	**32.00**
15	G-2627	Washburn Mandolin	**27.00**
17	*G-2442	Washburn Flat Back Mandolin	**36.00**
17	†G-2434	Washburn Flat Back Mandolin	**28.00**
19	‡G-2424	Washburn Flat Back Mandolin	**20.00**
21	Style AA	Martin Mandolin	**24.00**
23	Style BB	Martin Mandolin	**36.00**
25	Style CC	Martin Mandolin	**60.00**
27	G-208	Vega Mandolin	**40.00**
29	G-2	Vega Mandolin	**57.50**
31	G-201	Vega Lute Mandolin	**30.00**
31	G-203	Vega Lute Mandolin	**57.50**
33	G-2604	American Conservatory Mandolin	**15.00**
35	G-2603	American Conservatory Mandolin	**14.00**
37	G-2601	American Conservatory Mandolin	**13.00**
39	G-2503	Lakeside Mandolin	**12.00**
39	G-2502	Lakeside Mandolin	**9.50**
39	G-2501	Jupiter Mandolin	**8.50**
41	G-2400	American Style Mando	**12.00**
41	G-2350	American Style Mando	**10.00**
41	G-2325	American Style Mando	**8.00**
43	Style A	Lyon & Healy Own Make Mandola	**125.00**
45	**G-1642	Washburn Flat Back Mandola	**38.00**
47	Style A	Lyon & Healy Own Make Mandocello	**150.00**

*Number changed to G2436
†Number changed to G2428
‡Number changed to G2420
**Number changed to G1638

LYON & HEALY

October, 1921 **CHICAGO**

L64446 9-21

Price list from October 1921. Martin and Vega mandolins were also offered by Lyon & Healy at the time. The price you had to pay for Martin's pearl inlaid Style CC flatback mandolin did not quite get you a L&H Style C (Richard Myers)

97 See 3.4.2.
98 Patent numbers D49,540 and D 52,661.

WASHBURN MANDOLIN.

STYLE 71.

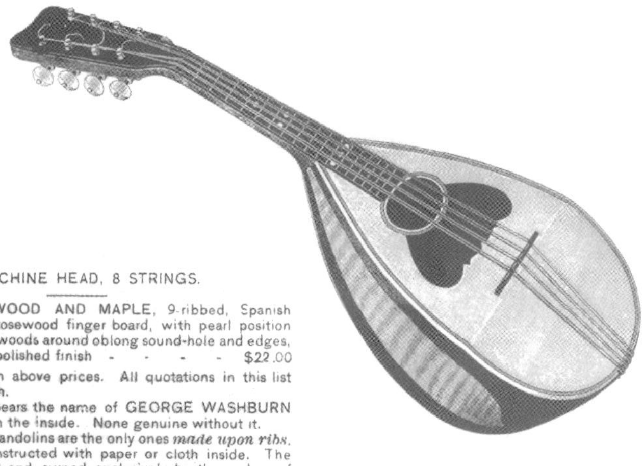

MACHINE HEAD, 8 STRINGS.

No. 71. ROSEWOOD AND MAPLE, 9-ribbed, Spanish cedar neck, oval Rosewood finger board, with pearl position dots, inlaid colored woods around oblong sound-hole and edges, inlaid guard plate, polished finish - - - - - $22.00

No discount from above prices. All quotations in this list are strictly Net Cash.

Every Mandolin bears the name of GEORGE WASHBURN plainly BURNED upon the inside. None genuine without it.

The Washburn Mandolins are the only ones *made upon ribs*. All others being constructed with paper or cloth inside. The process is patented and owned exclusively by the makers of the Washburn.

Style 71 (1889)

WASHBURN MANDOLIN

STYLE 72.

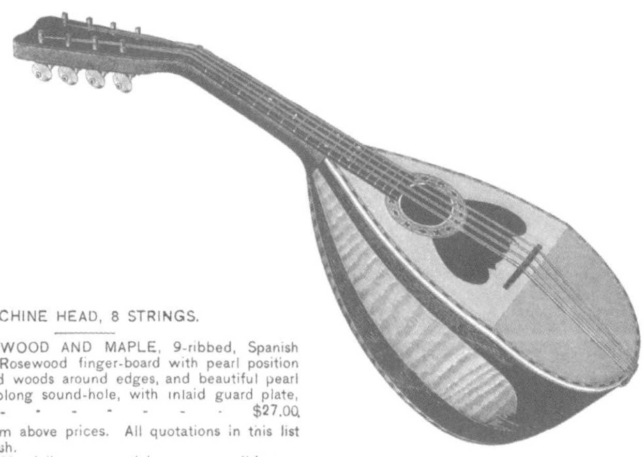

MACHINE HEAD, 8 STRINGS.

No. 72. ROSEWOOD AND MAPLE, 9-ribbed, Spanish cedar neck, oval Rosewood finger-board with pearl position dots, inlaid colored woods around edges, and beautiful pearl inlaying around oblong sound-hole, with inlaid guard plate, polished finish, - - - - - - - - $27.00

No discount from above prices. All quotations in this list are strictly Net Cash.

The Washburn Mandolins are used by many well-known clubs and give wonderful satisfaction for stage purposes. Their carrying power and volume are unsurpassed.

Style 71 (1889)

WASHBURN MANDOLIN.

STYLE 73

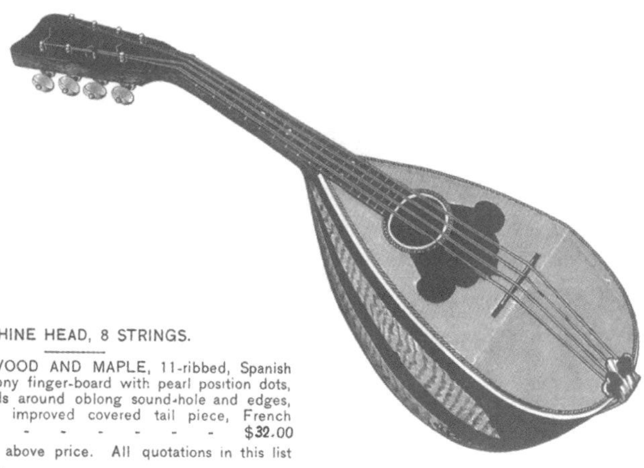

MACHINE HEAD, 8 STRINGS.

No. 73. ROSEWOOD AND MAPLE, 11-ribbed, Spanish cedar neck, oval ebony finger-board with pearl position dots, inlaid colored woods around oblong sound-hole and edges, inlaid guard plate, improved covered tail piece, French polished, - - - - - - - - - - $32.00

No discount from above price. All quotations in this list are strictly Net Cash.

A perfect scale. Strings carefully adjusted and close to the finger board, a full, rich and mellow tone are important points always found in a WASHBURN.

Style 73 (1889)

3.5 Mandolin styles 1887-1940

(all styles prior to 1915 are of the 'bowl back' type, all mandolin tops are made of spruce and have an oval soundhole)

No catalog information was available regarding the pre-1889 mandolin styles. Washburn mandolins were advertised already in 1887, and it is likely that these early instruments were identical to some or all of the styles listed in the 1889 catalog.

Washburn mandolin styles 1889-1892

standard size	
71	9 rosewood/maple ribs, Spanish cedar neck, 17-fret rosewood fingerboard with pearl dots/squares at frets 5, 7, 10 and 12, headstock w rosewood overlay, top and s/h bound with white celluloid and colored lines, black mushroom shaped pickguard, no tailpiece cover
72	9 rosewood/maple ribs, Spanish cedar neck, 17-fret rosewood fingerboard with seven pearl dots/squares at frets 5, 7, 10 (2) and 12 (3), headstock w rosewood overlay, top bound w white celluloid and checkerboard marquetry, s/h bound w white celluloid and pearl engraved ring, black mushroom shaped pickguard, no tailpiece cover
73	11 rosewood/maple ribs, Spanish cedar neck, 17 fret ebony fingerboard with pearl dots/squares at frets 5, 7, 10 and 12, headstock w ebony overlay, top bound w white celluloid and rope marquetry, s/h bound w white celluloid and herringbone pattern, crown shaped pickguard, crown shaped tailpiece cover
74	11 rosewood/maple ribs, Spanish cedar neck, 17-fret ebony fingerboard with pearl dots/squares at frets 3, 5, 7, 10 and 12, headstock w ebony overlay, top bound w whi te celluloid and rope marquetry, s/h bound w white celluloid and engraved pearl ring, crown shaped pickguard, crown shaped tailpiece cover
75	17 rosewood/maple ribs, Spanish cedar neck, 17-fret ebony fingerboard with pearl dots/squares at frets 3, 5, 7, 10 and 12, headstock w ebony overlay and engraved plates on top of headstock surrounding tuner posts, top bound w white celluloid and rope marquetry, s/h bound w white celluloid and herringbone pattern, crown shaped pickguard, serrated crown shaped tailpiece cover

WASHBURN MANDOLIN.

STYLE 74

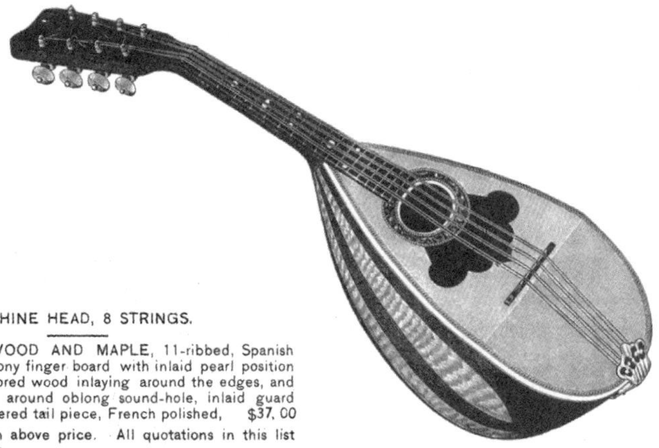

MACHINE HEAD, 8 STRINGS.

No. 74. ROSEWOOD AND MAPLE, 11-ribbed, Spanish cedar neck, oval ebony finger board with inlaid pearl position dots, handsome colored wood inlaying around the edges, and rich pearl inlaying around oblong sound-hole, inlaid guard plate, improved covered tail piece, French polished, $37.00

No discount from above price. All quotations in this list are strictly Net Cash.

Every Mandolin bears the name of GEORGE WASHBURN plainly BURNED upon the inside. None genuine without it.

Style 74 (1889)

WASHBURN MANDOLIN.

STYLE 75

FINELY ENGRAVED MACHINE HEAD, 8 STRINGS.

No. 75. ROSEWOOD AND MAPLE, 17-ribbed Spanish cedar neck, oval ebony finger-board with richly inlaid position ornaments, elegant inlaying around oblong sound-hole and guard plate, also around edges, inlaid guard plate, colored wood inlaying between ribs, handsomely plated improved covered tail piece, elegantly French polished, - $40.00

No discount from the above price. All quotations in this list are strictly Net Cash.

While the prices for the WASHBURN are reasonable and within the reach of all, the quality is unsurpassed

Style 75 (1889)

WASHBURN MANDOLIN.

STYLE 76.

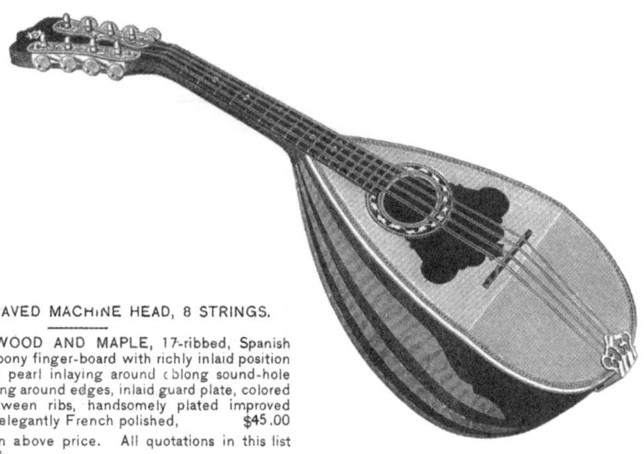

FINELY ENGRAVED MACHINE HEAD, 8 STRINGS.

No 76. ROSEWOOD AND MAPLE, 17-ribbed, Spanish cedar neck, oval ebony finger-board with richly inlaid position ornaments, elegant pearl inlaying around oblong sound-hole and elaborate inlaying around edges, inlaid guard plate, colored wood inlaying between ribs, handsomely plated improved covered tail piece, elegantly French polished, $45.00

No discount from above price. All quotations in this list are strictly Net Cash.

The manufacturers make all the machine heads used upon their instruments to insure perfection in every feature.

Style 76 (1889)

Washburn mandolin styles 1889-1892 (continued)

standard size	
76	17 rosewood/maple ribs, Spanish cedar neck, 17-fret ebony fingerboard with pearl dots/squares at frets 3, 5, 7, 10 and 12, headstock w ebony overlay, chrysanthemum pearl inlay and engraved plates on top of headstock surrounding tuner posts, top bound w white celluloid and herringbone pattern, s/h bound w white celluloid and pearl ring w leaf shaped and checkerboard pattern, crown shaped pickguard, serrated crown shaped tailpiece cover
80	35 rosewood ribs, Spanish cedar neck, 17-fret ebony fingerboard with pearl inlays at frets 3, 5, 7, 10 and 12, headstock w ebony overlay, chrysanthemum pearl inlay and engraved plates on top of headstock surrounding tuner posts, top bound w white celluloid and herringbone pattern, s/h bound w white celluloid and pearl ring w leaf shaped and checkerboard pattern, crown shaped pickguard w star, square and cloud shaped inlays, serrated engraved crown shaped tailpiece cover

Washburn mandolin styles 1892 1896

small size*	standard size*	mandola	
071	71		as Style 71 (1889), but with nickel plated crown shaped tailpiece cover
072	72		as Style 72 (1889), but with nickel plated crown shaped tailpiece cover and ebony fingerboard
073	73		as Style 73 (1889), but top bound with white celluloid and herringbone pattern
074	74		as Style 74 (1889), but top bound with white celluloid and herringbone pattern, s/h bound w white celluloid and pearl ring w inlaid or engraved triangular shapes, pearl chrysanthemum inlay on headstock, engraved nickel plated tailpiece cover
075	75		as Style 75 (1889), but s/h bound with white celluloid and herringbone pattern, tuner plates mounted on sides of headstock, engraved silver plated tailpiece cover, pearl inlay on headstock, engraved silver plated tailpiece cover
076	76		as Style 76 (1889), but top bound with white celluloid and two layers of checkerboard marquetry, s/h bound w white celluloid and pearl ring w inlaid or engraved triangular shapes, tuner plates mounted on sides of headstock, engraved silver plated tailpiece cover, pearl inlay on headstock

WASHBURN MANDOLIN.

STYLE 80.

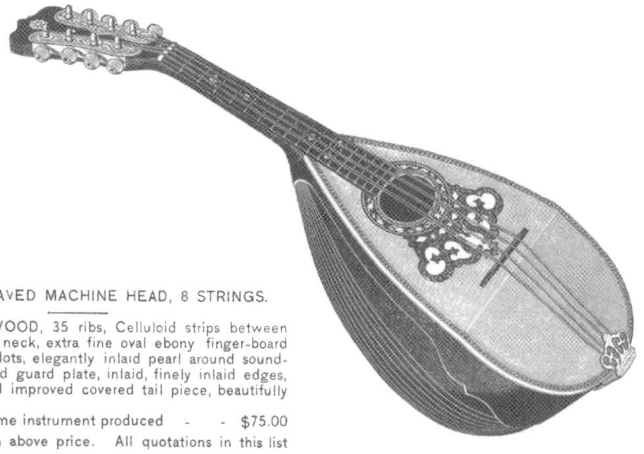

FINELY ENGRAVED MACHINE HEAD, 8 STRINGS.

No 80. ROSEWOOD, 35 ribs, Celluloid strips between ribs, Spanish cedar neck, extra fine oval ebony finger-board with pearl position dots, elegantly inlaid pearl around sound-hole, fancy Celluloid guard plate, inlaid, finely inlaid edges, engraved and plated improved covered tail piece, beautifully French polished.

The most handsome instrument produced - - $75.00

No discount from above price. All quotations in this list are strictly Net Cash.

A perfect scale is the foundation of a perfect instrument. The scale of the Washburn Instruments is absolutely correct.

Style 80 (1889)

WASHBURN MANDOLIN.

STYLE 71.

NEW MODEL—1892.

NICKEL-PLATED MACHINE HEAD, 8 STRINGS.

No 71. ROSEWOOD AND MAPLE, 9-ribbed, Spanish cedar neck, oval Rosewood finger-board, with pearl position dots, inlaid colored woods around sound-hole and edges, inlaid Celluloid guard plate, finely polished finish, patent Crown tail-piece nickel-plated.

- - - - - - - - - - - - - $22 00

No. 071. Same as No. 71. Smaller model, - 22 00

No Discount from above prices. All quotations in this list are strictly Net Cash.

Every Mandolin bears the name of GEORGE WASHBURN plainly BURNED upon the inside. None genuine without it.

The Washburn Mandolins are the only ones *made upon ribs*, all others being constructed with paper or cloth inside. The process is patented and owned exclusively by the makers of the Washburn.

Style 71 (1892)

WASHBURN MANDOLIN

STYLE 72.

NEW MODEL—1892.

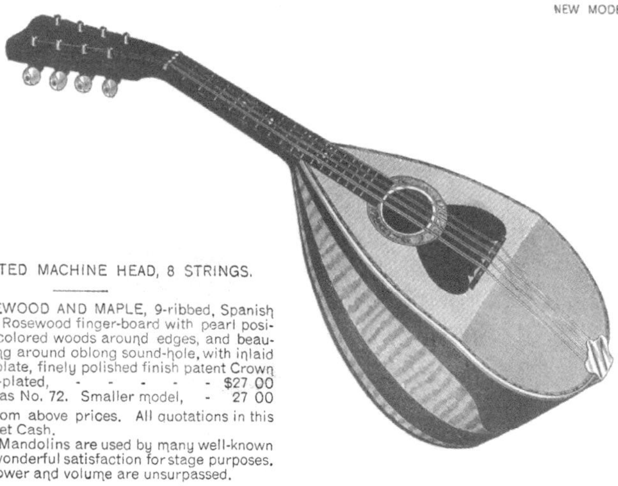

NICKEL-PLATED MACHINE HEAD, 8 STRINGS.

No. 72. ROSEWOOD AND MAPLE, 9-ribbed, Spanish cedar neck, oval Rosewood finger-board with pearl position dots, inlaid colored woods around edges, and beautiful pearl inlaying around oblong sound-hole, with inlaid Celluloid guard-plate, finely polished finish patent Crown tail-piece, nickel-plated, - - - - - - $27 00

No. 072. Same as No. 72. Smaller model, - 27 00

No discount from above prices. All quotations in this list are strictly Net Cash.

The Washburn Mandolins are used by many well-known clubs and give wonderful satisfaction for stage purposes. Their carrying power and volume are unsurpassed.

Style 72 (1892)

Washburn mandolin styles 1892-1896 (continued)

small size*	standard size*	mandola	
078	78		17 rosewood ribs, Spanish cedar neck, 17-fret ebony fingerboard with pearl inlays at frets 1, 3, 5, 7, 10 and 12, headstock w ebony overlay and pearl inlay, tuner plates mounted on sides of headstock, top bound with white celluloid and two layers of checkerboard marquetry, s/h bound w white celluloid and pearl ring w inlaid or engraved triangular shapes, crown shaped tortoise pickguard, bridge w two inlaid pearl dots, crown shaped silver plated engraved tailpiece cover
080	80		36 rosewood ribs, Spanish cedar neck, 17-fret ebony fingerboard bound w white celluloid with vine pearl inlays over entire length and inlaid water bird, headstock w ebony overlay and vine and snowflake inlays, tuner plates mounted on sides of headstock, top bound with white celluloid and multiple layers of checkerboard marquetry, s/h bound w white celluloid and pearl ring w inlaid or engraved triangular shapes, crown shaped pickguard w star, square and cloud shaped inlays, bridge w two inlaid pearl dots, crown shaped engraved silver plated tailpiece cover
085	85		36 rosewood ribs w inlaid metal strips, curly maple neck, pearl bound apron, 17-fret ebony fingerboard bound w white celluloid with vine pearl inlays over entire length, headstock w ebony overlay and vine inlays, gold plated engraved tuner plates mounted on sides of headstock, top bound with white celluloid and multiple layers of checkerboard marquetry, s/h bound w white celluloid and pearl ring w inlaid or engraved triangular shapes, crown shaped pickguard w star, square and cloud shaped inlays, bridge w two inlaid pearl dots, crown shaped engraved gold plated tailpiece cover
		89	Mandola, appointments identical to Style 74 (1892) but with 19 rosewood/maple ribs

* the bodies of the small sized bodied mandolins measure approximately 7 ½″ wide and 5 ¾″ deep, the larger (standard) instruments made between 1889 and 1896 are 8 3/8″ wide and 6 1/2″ deep and the mandolas are 10″ wide and 8″ deep (all measurements for pre 1889 styles only)

WASHBURN MANDOLIN.

STYLE 73.

NEW MODEL—1892.

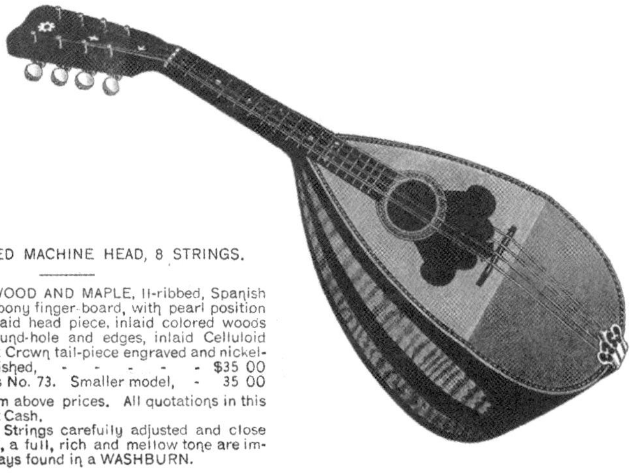

NICKEL-PLATED MACHINE HEAD, 8 STRINGS.

No. 73. ROSEWOOD AND MAPLE, 11-ribbed, Spanish cedar neck, oval ebony finger-board, with pearl position dots and pearl inlaid head piece, inlaid colored woods around oblong sound-hole and edges, inlaid Celluloid guard plate, patent Crown tail-piece engraved and nickel-plated, French polished, - - - - - $35 00
No. 073. Same as No. 73. Smaller model, - 35 00

No discount from above prices. All quotations in this list are strictly Net Cash.

A perfect scale. Strings carefully adjusted and close to the finger-board, a full, rich and mellow tone are important points always found in a WASHBURN.

Style 73 (1892)

WASHBURN MANDOLIN.

STYLE 74.

NEW MODEL—1892.

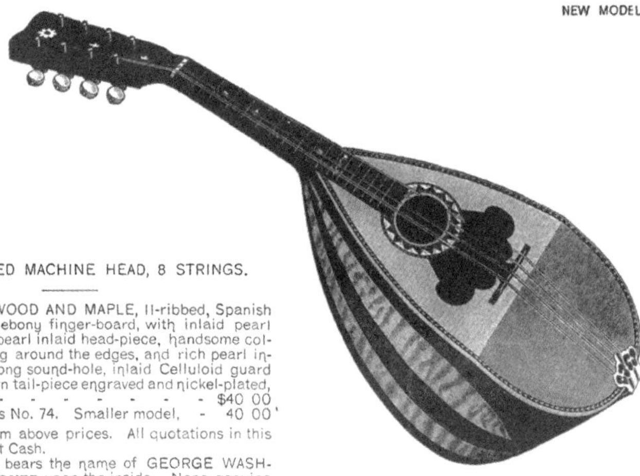

NICKEL-PLATED MACHINE HEAD, 8 STRINGS.

No. 74. ROSEWOOD AND MAPLE, 11-ribbed, Spanish cedar neck, oval ebony finger-board, with inlaid pearl position dots and pearl inlaid head-piece, handsome colored wood inlaying around the edges, and rich pearl inlaying around oblong sound-hole, inlaid Celluloid guard plate, patent Crown tail-piece engraved and nickel-plated, French polished, - - - - - - - $40 00
No. 074. Same as No. 74. Smaller model, - 40 00

No discount from above prices. All quotations in this list are strictly Net Cash.

Every Mandolin bears the name of GEORGE WASHBURN plainly BURNED upon the inside. None genuine without it.

Style 74 (1892)

WASHBURN MANDOLIN

STYLE 75.

NEW MODEL—1892.

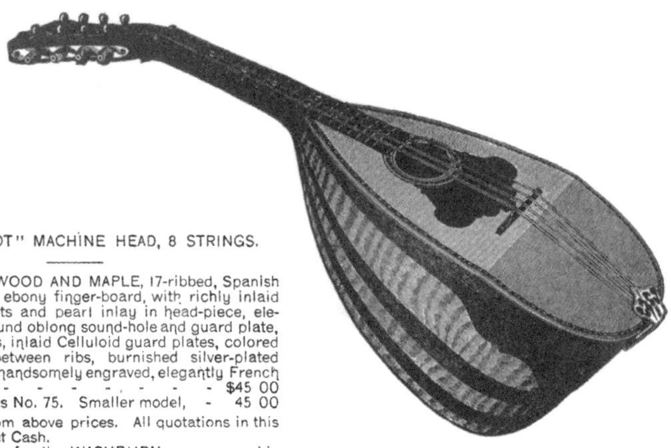

NEW "MASCOT" MACHINE HEAD, 8 STRINGS.

No. 75. ROSEWOOD AND MAPLE, 17-ribbed, Spanish cedar neck, oval ebony finger-board, with richly inlaid position ornaments and pearl inlay in head-piece, elegant inlaying around oblong sound-hole and guard plate, also around edges, inlaid Celluloid guard plates, colored wood inlaying between ribs, burnished silver-plated Crown tail-piece, handsomely engraved, elegantly French polished, - - - - - - - - - - $45 00
No. 075. Same as No. 75. Smaller model, - 45 00

No discount from above prices. All quotations in this list are strictly Net Cash.

While the prices for the WASHBURN are reasonable and within the reach of all, the quality is unsurpassed.

Style 75 (1892)

WASHBURN MANDOLIN.

STYLE 76.

NEW MODEL—1892.

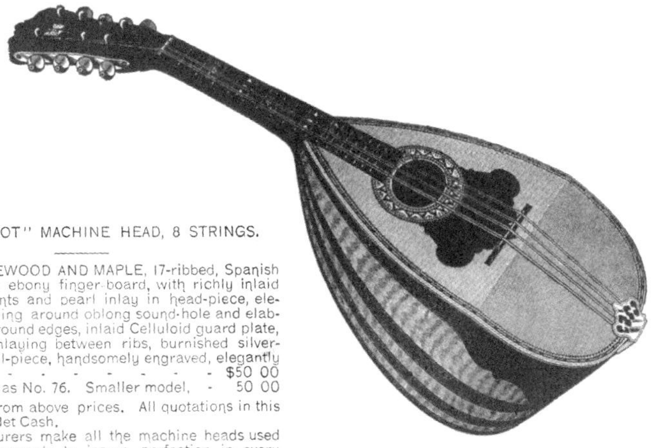

NEW "MASCOT" MACHINE HEAD, 8 STRINGS.

No. 76. ROSEWOOD AND MAPLE, 17-ribbed, Spanish cedar neck, oval ebony finger-board, with richly inlaid position ornaments and pearl inlay in head-piece, elegant pearl inlaying around oblong sound-hole and elaborate inlaying around edges, inlaid Celluloid guard plate, colored wood inlaying between ribs, burnished silver-plated Crown tail-piece, handsomely engraved, elegantly French polished, - - - - - - - $50 00
No. 076. Same as No. 76. Smaller model, - 50 00

No discount from above prices. All quotations in this list are strictly Net Cash.

The manufacturers make all the machine heads used upon their instruments to insure perfection in every feature.

Style 76 (1892)

WASHBURN MANDOLIN.

STYLE 78.

NEW MODEL—1892.

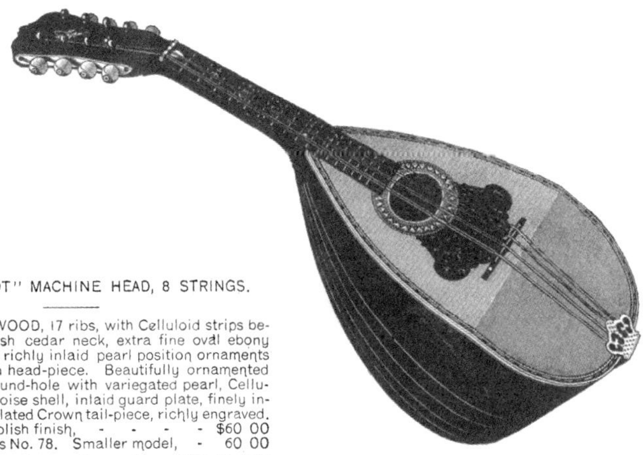

NEW "MASCOT" MACHINE HEAD, 8 STRINGS.

No. 78. ROSEWOOD, 17 ribs, with Celluloid strips between ribs, Spanish cedar neck, extra fine oval ebony finger-board, with richly inlaid pearl position ornaments and pearl figure in head-piece. Beautifully ornamented around oblong sound-hole with variegated pearl, Celluloid, imitation tortoise shell, inlaid guard plate, finely inlaid edges, silver-plated Crown tail-piece, richly engraved. Elegant French polish finish, - - - - $60 00
No 078. Same as No. 78. Smaller model, - 60 00

No discount from above prices. All quotations in this list are strictly Net Cash.

Style 78 (1892)

WASHBURN MANDOLIN.

STYLE 80.

NEW MODEL—1892.

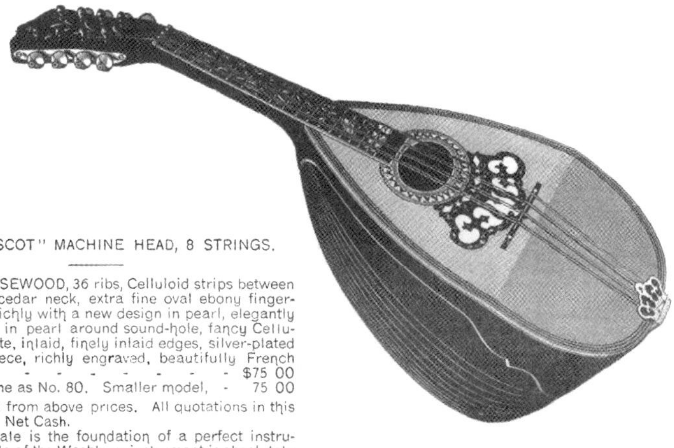

NEW "MASCOT" MACHINE HEAD, 8 STRINGS.

No. 80. ROSEWOOD, 36 ribs, Celluloid strips between ribs, Spanish cedar neck, extra fine oval ebony finger-board, inlaid richly with a new design in pearl, elegantly inlaid pattern in pearl around sound-hole, fancy Celluloid guard plate, inlaid, finely inlaid edges, silver-plated Crown tail-piece, richly engraved, beautifully French polished, - - - - - - - - - $75 00
No. 080. Same as No. 80. Smaller model, - 75 00

No Discount from above prices. All quotations in this list are strictly Net Cash.

A perfect scale is the foundation of a perfect instrument. The scale of the Washburn instrument is absolutely correct.

Style 80 (1892)

WASHBURN MANDOLIN

STYLE 85.

NEW MODEL—1892.

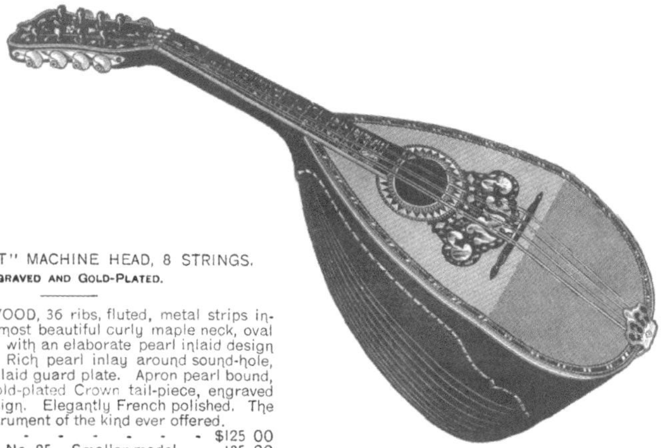

NEW "MASCOT" MACHINE HEAD, 8 STRINGS.
ENGRAVED AND GOLD-PLATED.

No. 85. ROSEWOOD, 36 ribs, fluted, metal strips inlaid between ribs, most beautiful curly maple neck, oval ebony finger-board with an elaborate pearl inlaid design and pearl bound. Rich pearl inlay around sound-hole, beautifully pearl inlaid guard plate. Apron pearl bound, and engraved. Gold-plated Crown tail-piece, engraved with landscape design. Elegantly French polished. The most gorgeous instrument of the kind ever offered. - - - - - - - - - - - $125 00

No. 085. Same as No. 85. Smaller model, - 125 00

No discount from above prices. All quotations in this list are strictly Net Cash.

Style 85 (1892)

WASHBURN MANDOLA.

STYLE 89.

NEW MODEL—1892.

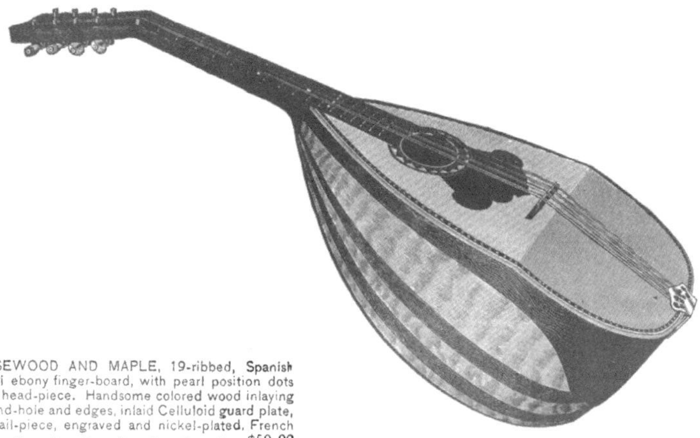

No. 89. ROSEWOOD AND MAPLE, 19-ribbed, Spanish cedar neck, oval ebony finger-board, with pearl position dots and pearl inlaid head-piece. Handsome colored wood inlaying around oval sound-hole and edges, inlaid Celluloid guard plate, patent Crown tail-piece, engraved and nickel-plated. French polished, - - - - - - - - - $50 00

No discount from above price. All quotations in this list are strictly Net Cash.

Style 89 (1892)

No. 115.

Style 115 (1903)

Washburn mandolin styles 1896-1905

standard size*	mandola*	
115**		9 rosewood ribs, cedar neck, 17-fret unbound ebony fingerboard with four pearl dots at frets 5, 7, 10 and 12, headstock w rosewood overlay, top and s/h bound w white celluloid and white/red/black lines, cloud shaped tortoise pickguard, crown shaped tailpiece cover
118**		11 rosewood ribs, cedar neck, 17-fret unbound ebony fingerboard with six pearl dots at frets 5, 7 (two), 10 and 12 (two), rosewood headstock overlay, s/h bound w white celluloid and white/red/black lines, top bound w white celluloid and colored marquetry pattern, cloud shaped tortoise pickguard, crown shaped tailpiece cover
122		15 rosewood ribs, cedar neck, 17-fret ebony fingerboard bound w white celluloid with four pearl engraved inlays at frets 5, 7, 10 and 12 (20-fret extension fingerboard around 1901), headstock w ebony overlay and engraved metal back plate, top bound w white celluloid and rope pattern, s/h bound w white celluloid and colored split herringbone pattern w red center strip, cloud shaped tortoise pickguard, crown shaped tailpiece cover
130		19 rosewood ribs, cedar neck, 17-fret ebony fingerboard bound w white celluloid with five pearl engraved inlays at frets 1, 5, 7, 10 and 12 (20-fret extension fingerboard around 1901), headstock w ebony overlay, top bound w white celluloid and herringbone/checkerboard pattern w green lines, s/h bound w white celluloid and herringbone/checkerboard pattern w red lines, cloud shaped tortoise pickguard, crown shaped tailpiece cover
140		23 rosewood ribs, cedar neck, 17-fret ebony fingerboard bound w white celluloid with six pearl engraved inlays at frets 1, 3, 5, 7, 10 and 12 (20-fret extension fingerboard around 1901), headstock w ebony overlay, top bound w white celluloid and marquetry, s/h bound w pearl ring and checkerboard marquetry, cloud shaped tortoise pickguard, crown shaped tailpiece cover

New Washburn Mandolin.

1897 MODEL.

Style 122.

EDOUARD DE RESZKE.
(ABBEY & GRAU GRAND OPERA CO.)

"It is with pleasure that I add my mite of praise to the volumes that have already been written in favor of the Washburn instruments. My own has the sweetest tone imaginable and yet it surpasses in power any guitar I have ever heard played."

W. O. BARNWELL.
(TEACHER AND SOLOIST, ATLANTA, GA.)

"The Washburn Mandolin, which I have been using for over a year, has proven most satisfactory. Its tone is rich and powerful, scale true, and in all, a magnificent instrument."

DESCRIPTION.

The Washburn Special Patent Head with Etched and Nickel-plated Covering; 8 Strings.

No. 122—ROSEWOOD, 15 ribs, white celluloid inlaid between each rib; cedar neck, ebony veneered head-piece; ebony finger-board, celluloid-bound with four engraved pearl inlaid position marks; fancy inlaid woods and celluloid around sound-hole and edge; inlaid tortoise celluloid guard-plate; finely polished, tastefully etched crown tail-piece, nickel-plated, ... $22.00

No discount from above price.

If the Washburn factory were not the largest in the world Washburn instruments could not be sold for present prices.

Style 122 (1896)

New Washburn Mandolin.

1897 MODEL.

Style 130.

LILLIAN NORDICA.
(ABBEY & GRAU GRAND OPERA CO.)

"The Washburn Banjo which I obtained of you last season has given me great pleasure, and proved wonderfully satisfactory in every respect. The tone is particularly attractive; my Washburn is very easy to play, and the workmanship is exquisite."

H. SCOVEL BRICKEL.
(CURRY CONSERVATORY OF MUSIC, PITTSBURGH, PENN.)

"Having used Washburn Mandolins and Guitars for several years, I desire to say that they fully meet the demands of all artistic work. I consider them without an equal and can conscientiously recommend them."

DESCRIPTION.

The Washburn Special Patent Head with Etched and Nickel-plated Covering; 8 Strings.

No. 130—ROSEWOOD, 19 ribs, white celluloid inlaid between each rib, cedar neck; ebony veneered head-piece; ebony finger-board, celluloid-bound with five engraved pearl inlaid position marks; fancy inlaid woods and celluloid around sound-hole and edge; inlaid tortoise celluloid guard-plate; finely polished, tastefully etched and nickel-plated crown tail-piece, ... $30.00

No discount from above price.

The finish of the Washburn instruments is the despair of other makers; the processes used are peculiar to the Washburn.

13

Style 130 (1896)

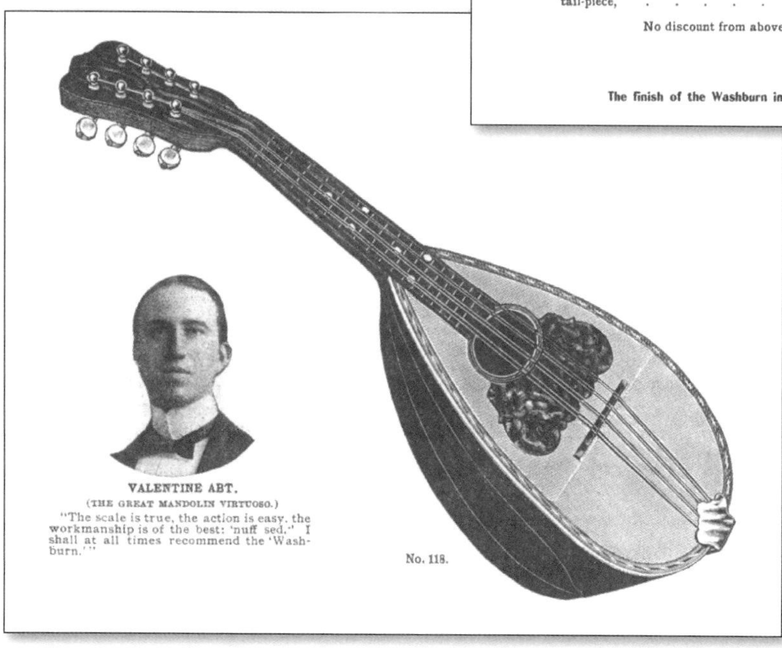
VALENTINE ABT.
(THE GREAT MANDOLIN VIRTUOSO.)

"The scale is true, the action is easy, the workmanship is of the best: 'nuff sed.' I shall at all times recommend the 'Washburn.'"

No. 118.

Style 118 (1903)

Washburn mandolin styles 1896-1905 (continued)

standard size*	mandola*	
150		28 rosewood ribs, cedar neck, 17-fret ebony fingerboard bound w white celluloid with eight pearl engraved inlays at frets 1, 3, 5, 7, 10 and 12, 15 and 17 (20-fret extension fingerboard around 1901), headstock w ebony overlay and snowflake inlay, top bound w white celluloid and marquetry, s/h bound w engraved pearl ring and checkerboard marquetry, cloud shaped tortoise pickguard w engraved pearl mandolin/bugle/sheet music ornament, engraved crown shaped nickel plated tailpiece cover
160		34 rosewood ribs, cedar neck, 17-fret ebony fingerboard bound w white celluloid with eight pearl engraved inlays at frets 1, 3, 5, 7, 10 and 12, 15 and 17 (20-fret extension fingerboard around 1901), headstock w ebony overlay and three inlaid pearl snowflakes, top bound w white celluloid and marquetry, s/h bound w white celluloid, broad pearl ring and checkerboard marquetry, top bound w marquetry patterns, outer top border bound w checkerboard pearl/ebony pattern, cloud shaped tortoise pickguard w no inlays, engraved crown shaped nickel plated tailpiece cover
175		36 rosewood ribs, 17-fret engraved pearl fingerboard bound w white celluloid (20-fret extension fingerboard around 1901), figured maple neck w volute, headstock w ebony overlay and pearl snowflake inlays, top and s/h bound w white celluloid, checkerboard marquetry and pearl center line, cloud shaped tortoise pickguard w pearl vine inlay, engraved crown shaped nickel plated tailpiece cover, pearl tuner buttons
1125		42 rosewood ribs w inlaid metal strips, 17-fret engraved pearl fingerboard bound w white celluloid (20-fret extension fingerboard around 1898-9), maple neck w volute, headstock bound w white celluloid w ebony overlay and pearl vine/flower inlays, engraved gold plated cover on back of headstock, top and s/h bound w white celluloid, checkerboard marquetry and pearl center line, outer top border bound w checkerboard pearl/ebony pattern, s/h bound w engraved pearl ring and checkerboard marquetry, cloud shaped tortoise pickguard w pearl butterfly inlay, engraved crown shaped gold plated tailpiece cover, pearl nut, pearl bound apron, pearl tuner buttons

New Washburn Mandolin.

1897 MODEL.

Style 140.

JOHN J. EBERHARDT.

(TEACHER AND DIRECTOR, SPRINGFIELD, MASS.)

"I have used the Washburn Mandolins for nearly eight years, and have no fear of making a testimonial too decided. They possess all the points of excellence that can be expected or found in a perfect instrument."

G. CAMPANARI.

(ABBEY & GRAU GRAND OPERA CO.)

"Could I purchase another Washburn Mandolin from you exactly like the one sent me last week? It has the most delightful tone imaginable and I am more than delighted with it."

DESCRIPTION.

The Washburn Special Patent Head with Etched and Nickel-plated covering; 8 Strings.

No. 140—ROSEWOOD, 23 ribs, white celluloid inlaid between each rib; ebony veneered head-piece, ebony finger-board, celluloid bound with six engraved pearl inlaid position marks; variegated pearl inlaid around sound hole; fancy wood and celluloid around edge; inlaid tortoise celluloid guard-plate; finely polished, nicely etched and nickel-plated crown tail-piece, $40.00

No discount from above price.

The matchless workmanship to be found in all Washburns comes only from long experience of the workman, and cannot be imitated.

15

Style 140 (1896)

New Washburn Mandolin.

1897 MODEL.

Style 150.

EMMA CALVÉ.

(ABBEY & GRAU GRAND OPERA CO.)

"I have never, in all my travels, found anything that seemed to me as near perfection in the way of a Mandolin as the Washburn."

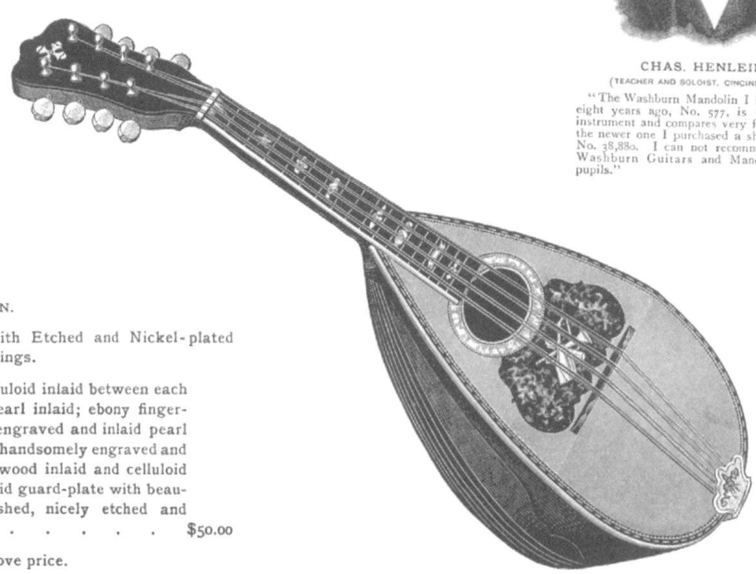

CHAS. HENLEIN.

(TEACHER AND SOLOIST, CINCINNATI, O.)

"The Washburn Mandolin I bought of you eight years ago, No. 577, is yet a perfect instrument and compares very favorably with the newer one I purchased a short time ago, No. 38,880. I can not recommend any but Washburn Guitars and Mandolins to my pupils."

DESCRIPTION.

The Washburn Special Patent Head with Etched and Nickel-plated Covering; 8 Strings.

No. 150—ROSEWOOD, 28 ribs, white celluloid inlaid between each rib; ebony veneered head-piece pearl inlaid; ebony finger-board celluloid bound, with eight engraved and inlaid pearl position marks; rich Sidney pearl, handsomely engraved and inlaid around sound-hole; fancy wood inlaid and celluloid bound edges; inlaid tortoise celluloid guard-plate with beautiful pearl ornament; finely polished, nicely etched and nickel-plated crown tail-piece, ... $50.00

No discount from above price.

An ivory or pearl plate bearing the purchaser's initials or monogram can be let into any finger-board at $2.50 extra, net.

17

Style 150 (1896)

standard size*	mandola*	
	225	11 rosewood ribs, cedar neck, 17-fret unbound ebony fingerboard with pearl dots, top and s/h bound w white celluloid and rings, cloud shaped tortoise pickguard, crown shaped tailpiece cover
	235	17 rosewood ribs, cedar neck, 17-fret unbound ebony fingerboard bound w white celluloid with pearl engraved inlays, top bound w white celluloid and rope marquetry pattern, s/h bound w white celluloid and herringbone marquetry pattern, cloud shaped tortoise pickguard, engraved crown shaped nickel plated tailpiece cover

* The standard size models have a bowl that is 7 3/8″ wide and 5 ½″ deep, the mandolas are 9 ½″ wide and 7″ deep

** The earliest catalogued versions of Styles 115 and 118 (1896) were identical to respectively Styles 071 and 71 of the 1892 mandolin line, likely to use up remaining inventory and parts. The last batches of these older style mandolins had 15 ribs instead of 9. The rosewood bodied Styles 115 and 118 started to appear around the turn of the 20th century

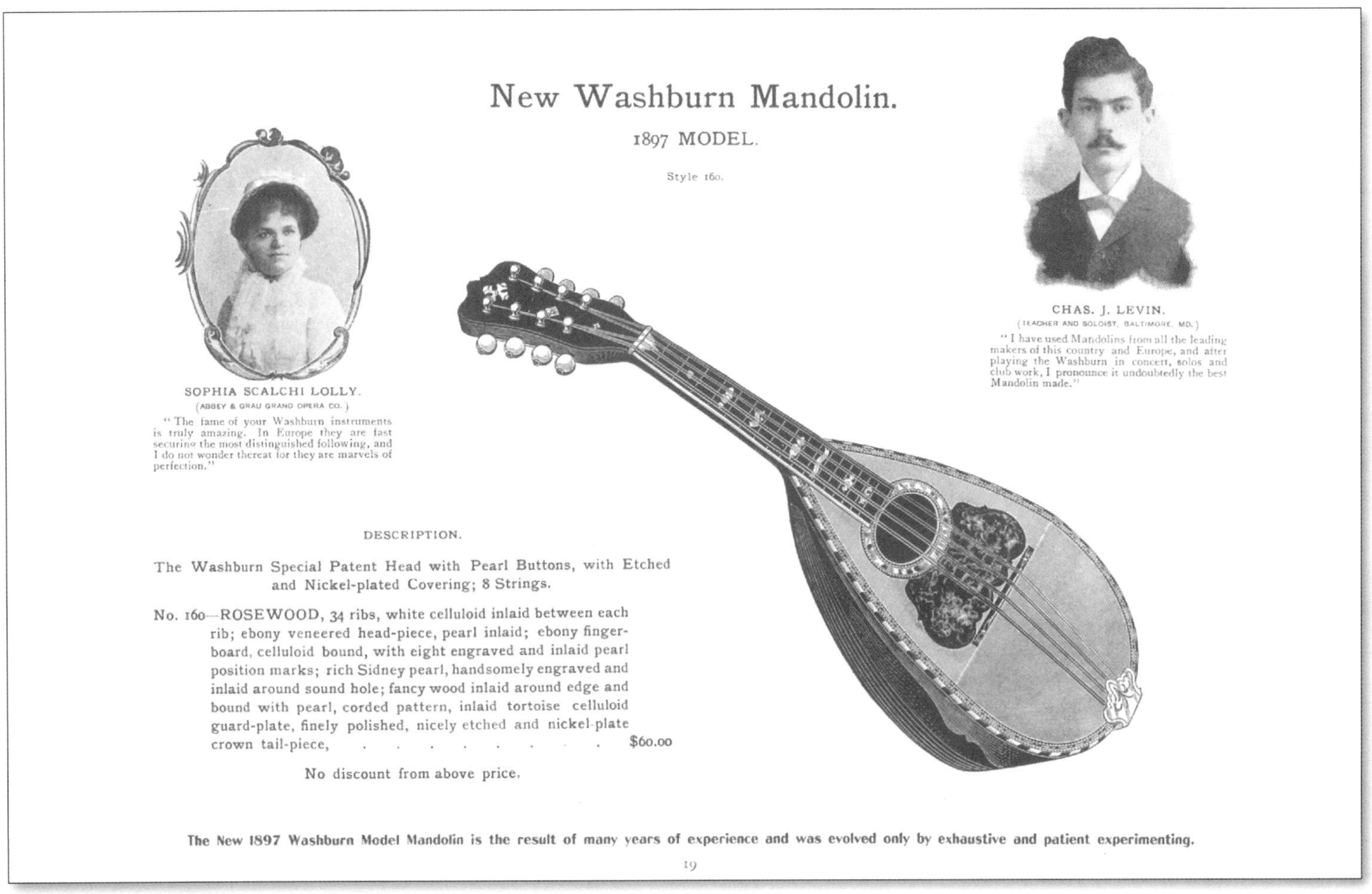
New Washburn Mandolin.

1897 MODEL.

Style 160.

SOPHIA SCALCHI LOLLY.
(ABBEY & GRAU GRAND OPERA CO.)
"The fame of your Washburn instruments is truly amazing. In Europe they are fast securing the most distinguished following, and I do not wonder thereat for they are marvels of perfection."

CHAS. J. LEVIN.
(TEACHER AND SOLOIST, BALTIMORE, MD.)
"I have used Mandolins from all the leading makers of this country and Europe, and after playing the Washburn in concert, solos and club work, I pronounce it undoubtedly the best Mandolin made."

DESCRIPTION.

The Washburn Special Patent Head with Pearl Buttons, with Etched and Nickel-plated Covering; 8 Strings.

No. 160—ROSEWOOD, 34 ribs, white celluloid inlaid between each rib; ebony veneered head-piece, pearl inlaid; ebony finger-board, celluloid bound, with eight engraved and inlaid pearl position marks; rich Sidney pearl, handsomely engraved and inlaid around sound hole; fancy wood inlaid around edge and bound with pearl, corded pattern, inlaid tortoise celluloid guard-plate, finely polished, nicely etched and nickel-plate crown tail-piece, ... $60.00

No discount from above price.

The New 1897 Washburn Model Mandolin is the result of many years of experience and was evolved only by exhaustive and patient experimenting.

19

Style 160 (1896)

New Washburn Mandolin.

1897 MODEL.

Style 175.

SIG. E. BEVIGNANI.

(MUSICAL DIRECTOR METROPOLITAN OPERA CO., NEW YORK, AND HER MAJESTY'S OPERA, LONDON.)

"The Washburn Mandolin purchased of you has proven such a source of pleasure that I am now desirous of adding a Banjo to my collection of instruments. Send me one of these handsome Washburns without delay."

MISS EMMA SCHUBERT.

(302 SOUTH 13TH STREET, PHILADELPHIA, PA.)

"It gives me much pleasure to recommend your Washburn Guitars for their clear full tone. I find them especially good for concert and club work."

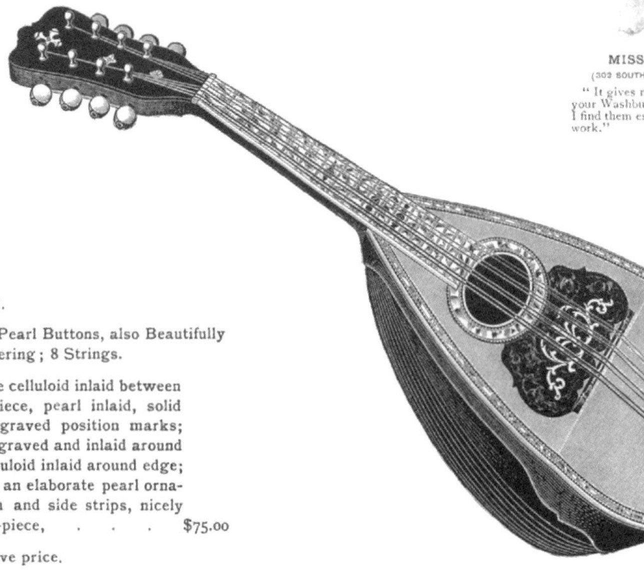

DESCRIPTION.

The Washburn Special Patent Head with Pearl Buttons, also Beautifully Etched and Silver-plated Covering; 8 Strings.

No. 175—ROSEWOOD, 36 ribs, with white celluloid inlaid between each rib; ebony veneered head-piece, pearl inlaid, solid pearl finger-board with richly engraved position marks; rich gold-fish pearl handsomely engraved and inlaid around sound-hole; beautiful pearl and celluloid inlaid around edge; tortoise celluloid guard-plate with an elaborate pearl ornament inlaid; celluloid-bound apron and side strips, nicely etched and silver-plated crown tail-piece, ... $75.00

No discount from above price.

The Washburn Mandolins are further in advance of all competition to-day than ever before; they form a class by themselves.

21

Style 175 (1896)

New Washburn Mandolin.

1897 MODEL.

Style 1125.

"CORINNE."

(JENNIE KIMBALL OPERA COMIQUE CO.)

"The Washburn Mandolin is perfectly exquisite. The tone sweet and powerful. The finish all that could be desired."

R. E. WELLS.

(TEACHER AND SOLOIST, NEW ORLEANS, LA.)

"No other instruments compare with the Washburn. I have used and recommended them for years and believe thoroughly that no others made are their equal in any respect."

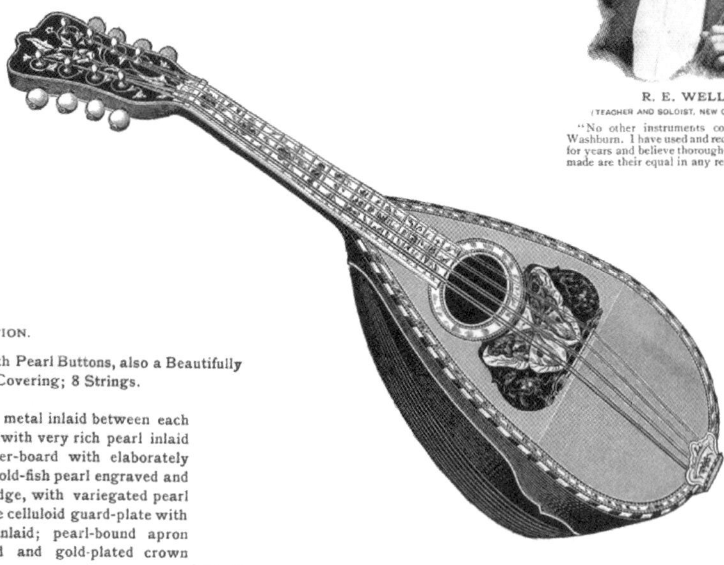

DESCRIPTION.

The Washburn Special Patent Head with Pearl Buttons, also a Beautifully Etched and Gold-plated Covering; 8 Strings.

No. 1125—ROSEWOOD, 42 fluted ribs, metal inlaid between each rib; ebony veneered head-piece with very rich pearl inlaid vines; solid Sidney pearl finger-board with elaborately engraved position marks; rich gold-fish pearl engraved and inlaid around sound hole and edge, with variegated pearl cording around the edge; tortoise celluloid guard-plate with a variegated pearl butterfly inlaid; pearl-bound apron and side strips; richly etched and gold-plated crown tail-piece, ... $125.00

No discount from above price.

The tone of the Washburn instruments, being of extraordinary richness and depth, makes them without a rival for out-door playing.

23

Style 1125 (1896)

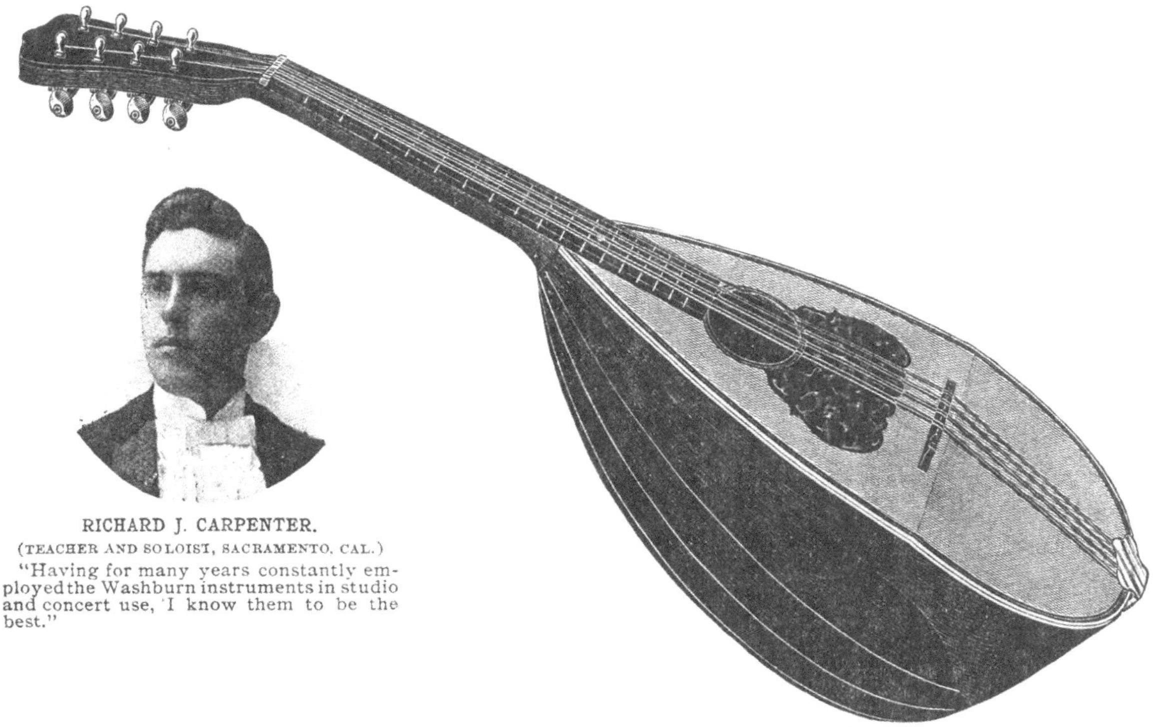

RICHARD J. CARPENTER.
(TEACHER AND SOLOIST, SACRAMENTO, CAL.)
"Having for many years constantly employed the Washburn instruments in studio and concert use, I know them to be the best."

No. 225.

No.		Each.
225.	11 Rosewood Ribs, Hand Polished, White Inlay between, Spanish Cedar Neck, Ebony Finger Board, and Veneered Head Piece, Pearl Position Dots, Inlaid and Celluloid Bound Sound-Hole and Edges, Tortoise Celluloid Guard Plate, Crown Tail-Piece, Nickel-Plated Patent Head...........	$37 50

Style 225 (1903)

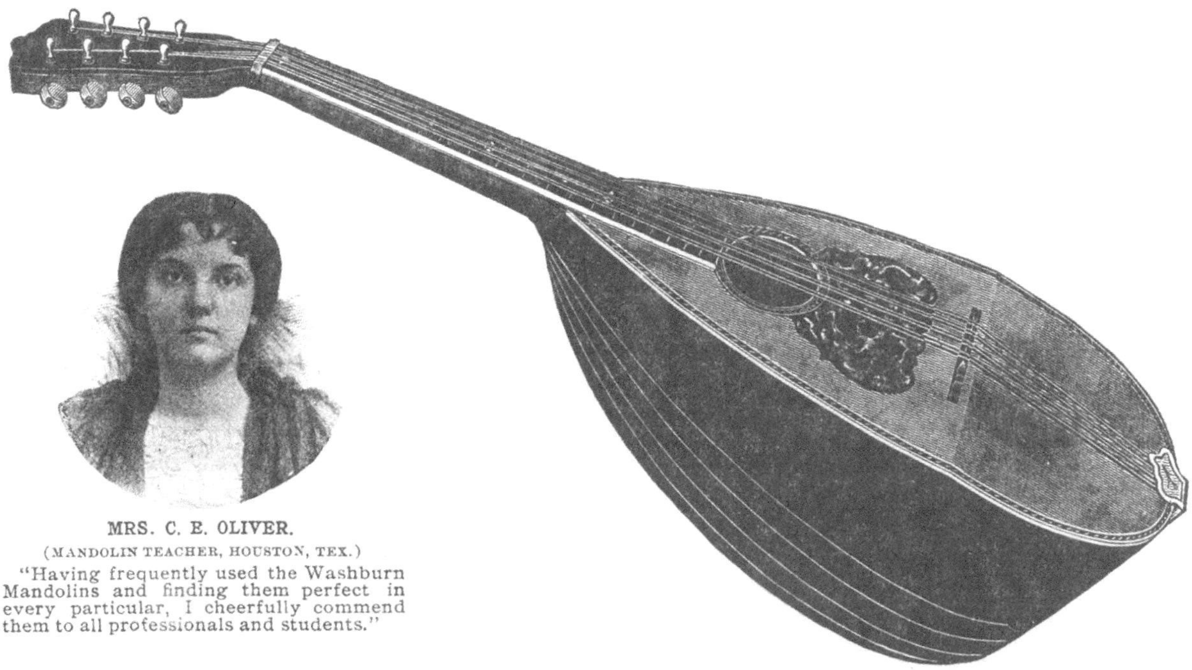

MRS. C. E. OLIVER.
(MANDOLIN TEACHER, HOUSTON, TEX.)
"Having frequently used the Washburn Mandolins and finding them perfect in every particular, I cheerfully commend them to all professionals and students."

No. 235.

No.		Each.
235.	17 Rosewood Ribs, Finely Polished, White Inlaying between Ribs, Spanish Cedar Neck, Celluloid Bound, Ebony Finger Board, Ebony Veneered Head Piece, Fine Engraved Position Marks, Variegated Wood Inlaid and Celluloid Bound Sound-Hole and Edges, Tortoise Celluloid Guard Plate, Hand Polished, Washburn Special Patent Head and Crown Tail-Piece, Handsomely Engraved and Nickel-Plated..	$51 25

Style 235 (1903)

Style 215 (1905)

Style 225 (1905)

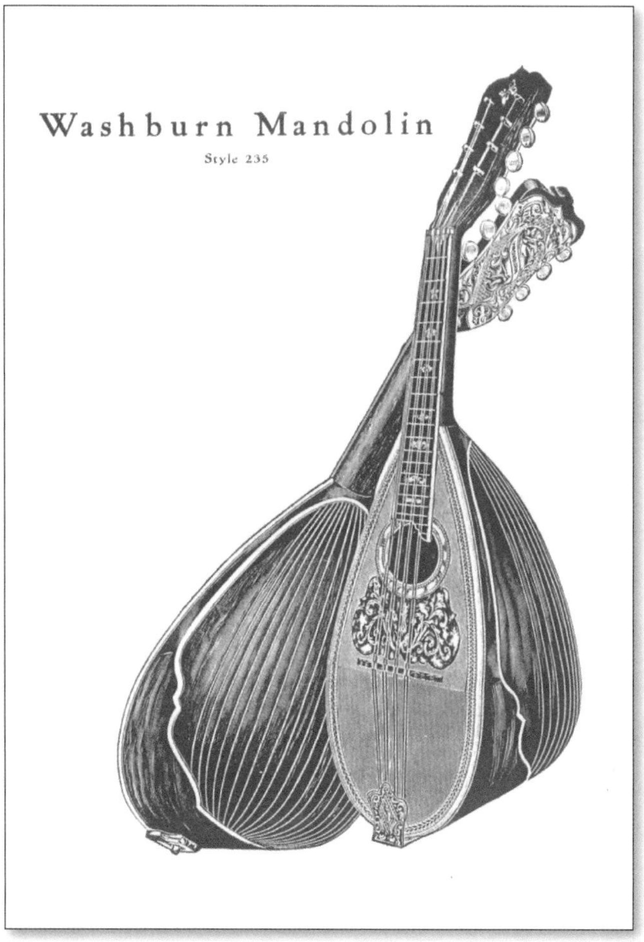

Style 235 (1905)

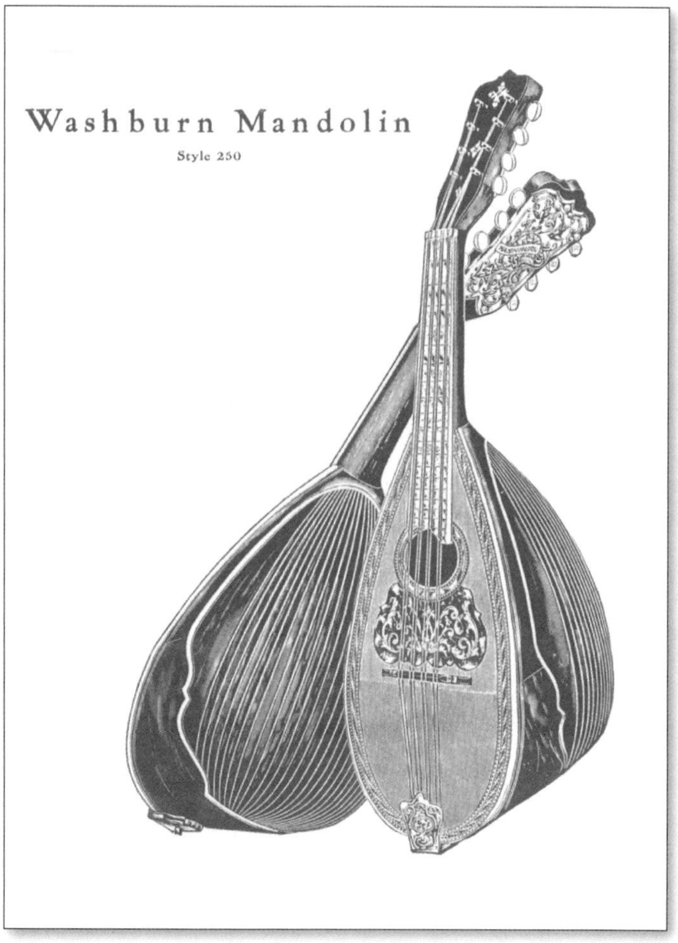

Style 250 (1905)

standard size	mandola	
215*		15 rosewood ribs, mahogany neck, 20-fret ebony fingerboard bound w white celluloid with four pearl dots at frets 5, 7, 10 and 12, headstock w ebony overlay (no metal back plate), top bound w white celluloid and rope pattern, s/h bound w white celluloid and black/red/white colored lines, ebony bridge, cloud shaped tortoise pickguard, crown shaped tailpiece cover, bone nut
220**		15 rosewood ribs, mahogany neck, 20-fret ebony fingerboard bound w white celluloid with four pearl engraved inlays at frets 5, 7, 10 and 12, headstock w ebony overlay and engraved metal back plate, top bound w white celluloid and black/red/beige marquetry/checkerboard pattern, s/h bound w white celluloid and black/red/white colored lines, ebony bridge, cloud shaped tortoise pickguard, crown shaped tailpiece cover, bone nut
225		21 rosewood ribs, mahogany neck, 20-fret ebony fingerboard bound w white celluloid with five engraved pearl inlays at frets 1, 5, 7, 10 and 12, headstock w ebony overlay and engraved metal back plate, top bound w white celluloid and split herringbone pattern, s/h bound w white celluloid and split herringbone pattern, ebony bridge, cloud shaped tortoise pickguard w pearl vine inlay, crown shaped engraved nickel plated tailpiece cover, bone nut
235		28 rosewood ribs, mahogany neck w volute, 20-fret ebony fingerboard bound w white celluloid with eight engraved pearl inlays at frets 1, 3, 5, 7, 10, 12, 15 and 18, headstock w ebony overlay w pearl snowflake inlay and engraved metal back plate, top bound w white celluloid and split herringbone pattern, s/h bound w white celluloid, pearl ring and checkerboard pattern, ebony bridge, cloud shaped tortoise pickguard w pearl vine inlay, crown shaped engraved nickel plated tailpiece cover, bone nut

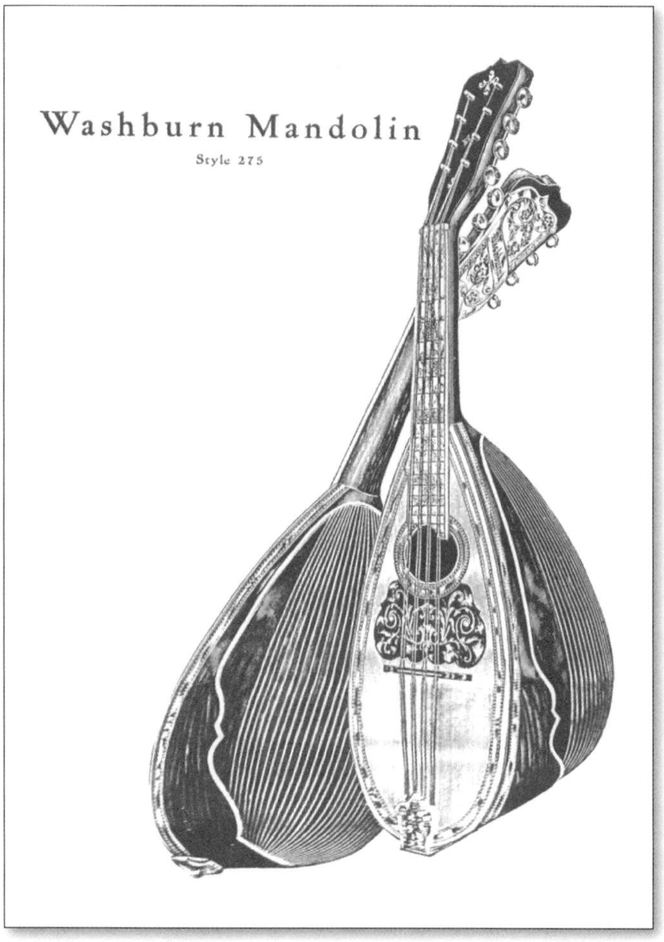

Style 275 (1905)

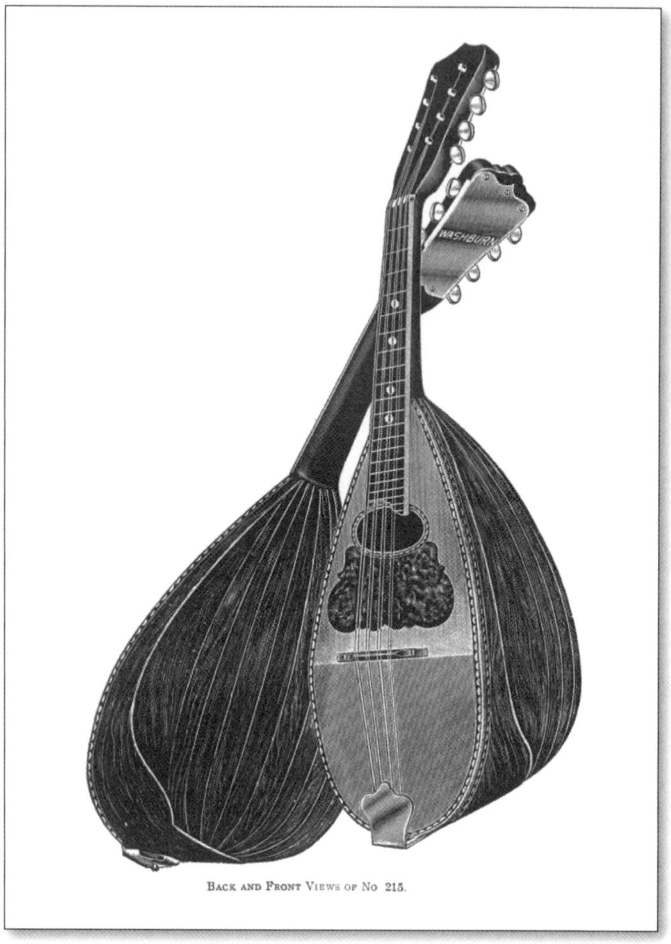

Style 215 (1912)

Style 220 (1912)

Style 225 (1912)

Washburn mandolin styles 1905-1910 (continued)

standard size	mandola	
250		36 rosewood ribs, mahogany neck, 20-fret pearl engraved fingerboard bound w white celluloid, headstock w ebony overlay w pearl snowflake inlays and engraved metal back plate, top bound w white celluloid and broad marquetry/checkerboard pattern, s/h bound w white celluloid, pearl ring and checkerboard pattern, sides bound w black/white/red lines, ebony bridge, cloud shaped tortoise pickguard w pearl vine inlay, crown shaped engraved nickel plated tailpiece cover, bone nut
275		44 rosewood ribs, mahogany neck, 20-fret pearl engraved fingerboard bound w white celluloid, headstock w ebony overlay w pearl snowflake inlays and engraved silver plated metal back plate, top bound w white celluloid, pearl ring and checkerboard pattern, s/h bound w white celluloid, pearl ring and checkerboard pattern, sides bound w pearl and colored marquetry, ebony bridge, cloud shaped tortoise pickguard w pearl vine inlay, crown shaped engraved silver plated tailpiece cover, pearl nut
	225	11 rosewood ribs, mahogany neck, 17-fret unbound ebony fingerboard with pearl dots, top and s/h bound w white celluloid and variegated wood, ebony veneered head piece, ebony bridge, bone nut, cloud shaped tortoise pickguard, nickel plated crown shaped tailpiece cover

* In many Lyon & Healy/Washburn catalogs published between 1905 and the early 1920s the style numbers of catalogued instruments and other musical items have a 'G' prefix. This is a reference to Lyon & Healy's Department G, which was responsible for all retail activities

** Style 220 was not listed in the 1905 Washburn catalog but became available shortly after 1905

Washburn mandolin styles 1910-1915

standard size	mandola	
215		as Style 215 (1905), but with engraved metal headstock back plate and brown/beige wave shaped marquetry on top, s/h and sides*
220		as Style 220 (1905), but with brown/beige wave shaped/checkerboard marquetry on top, s/h and sides
225		as Style 225 (1905), but with brown/beige wave shaped/checkerboard marquetry on top, s/h and sides
235		s Style 235 (1905), but with flower shaped marquetry around s/h, top and on sides

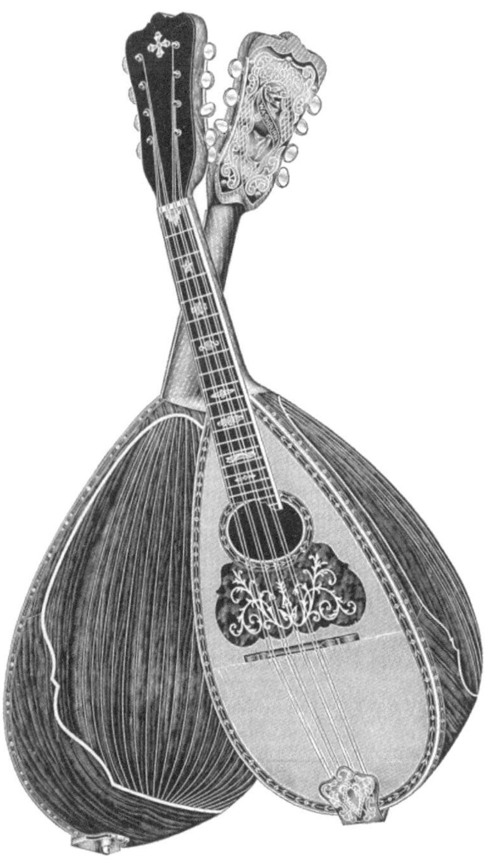

BACK AND FRONT VIEWS OF No. 235.

Style 235 (1912)

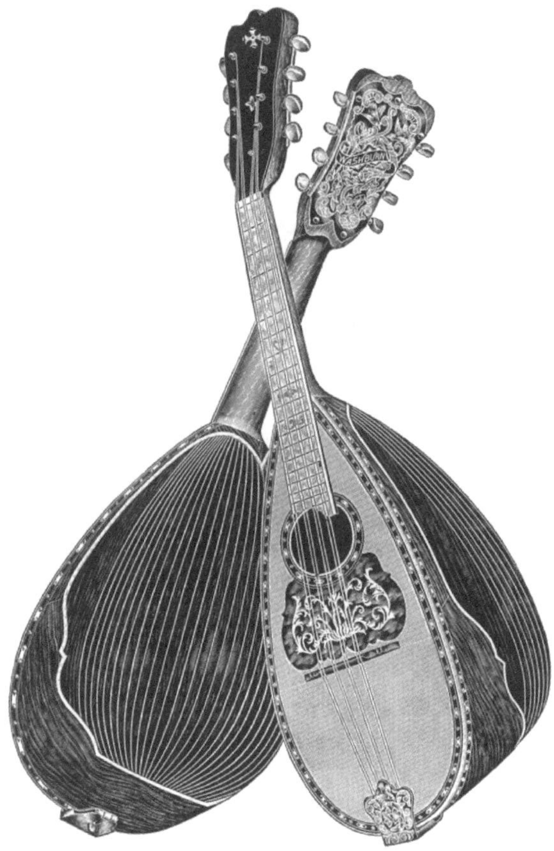

BACK AND FRONT VIEWS OF No. 250.

Style 250 (1912)

BACK AND FRONT VIEWS OF No. 275.

Style 275 (1912)

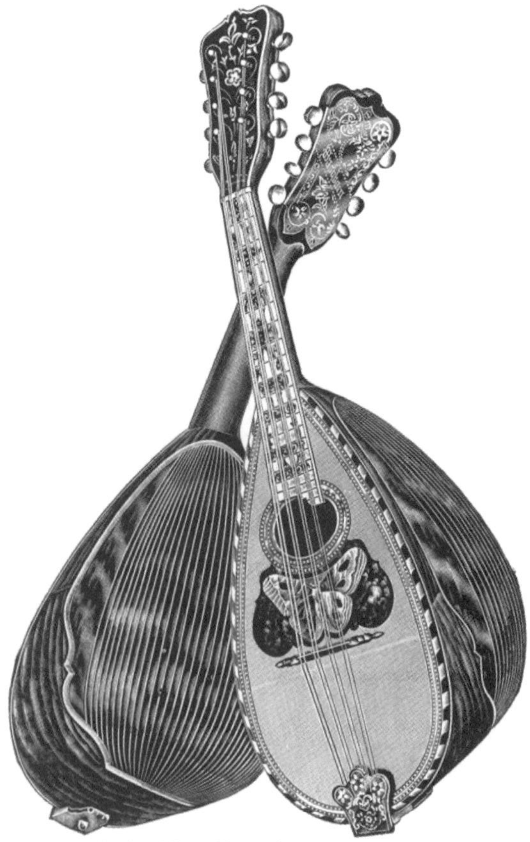

Back and Front Views of No. 1125.

Style 1125 (1912)

Washburn mandolin styles 1910-1915 (continued)

standard size	mandola	
250		as Style 250 (1905), but with different marquetry pattern, also inlaid in sides, headstock with rosewood or ebony overlay
275		as Style 275 (1905)
1125		as Style 1125 (1896), but with 20-fret extension fingerboard
	225	as Style 225 (1905)

* Around 1914 replaced again by a rope marquetry pattern, slightly smaller than on the 1905-1910 models

Washburn mandolin styles 1915-1920

standard size	mandola	
1422		rosewood b/s, mahogany neck, flatback design w pear shaped body w two symmetrical body points, 20-fret ebony fingerboard w four pearl dots at frets 5, 7, 10, 12, headstock w rosewood overlay and metal back plate, top, back and s/h bound w black/white celluloid, compensated ebony bridge w bone saddle, wing shaped tortoise pickguard, crown shaped nickel plated tailpiece cover, ebony heelcap, bone nut
1430		rosewood b/s, mahogany neck, flatback design w pear shaped body w two symmetrical body points, 20-fret ebony fingerboard w black/white celluloid edge w ten pearl dots, headstock w rosewood overlay, pearl inlay and engraved metal back plate, back bound w black/white celluloid, top and s/h bound w black/white celluloid and marquetry pattern, compensated ebony bridge w bone saddle, wing shaped tortoise pickguard, crown shaped nickel plated tailpiece cover, ebony heelcap, bone nut
	1638	rosewood b/s, mahogany neck, flatback mandola w pear shaped body, 18 fret ebony fingerboard w six pearl dots/snowflakes at frets 1, 5, 7, 10 and 12 (two), headstock w ebony overlay and engraved metal back plate, top, s/h bound w black/white celluloid and checkerboard marquetry pattern, back bound w black/white celluloid, ebony bridge, cloud shaped tortoise pickguard w copper and pearl inlaid floral pattern, crown shaped nickel plated engraved tailpiece cover, bone nut

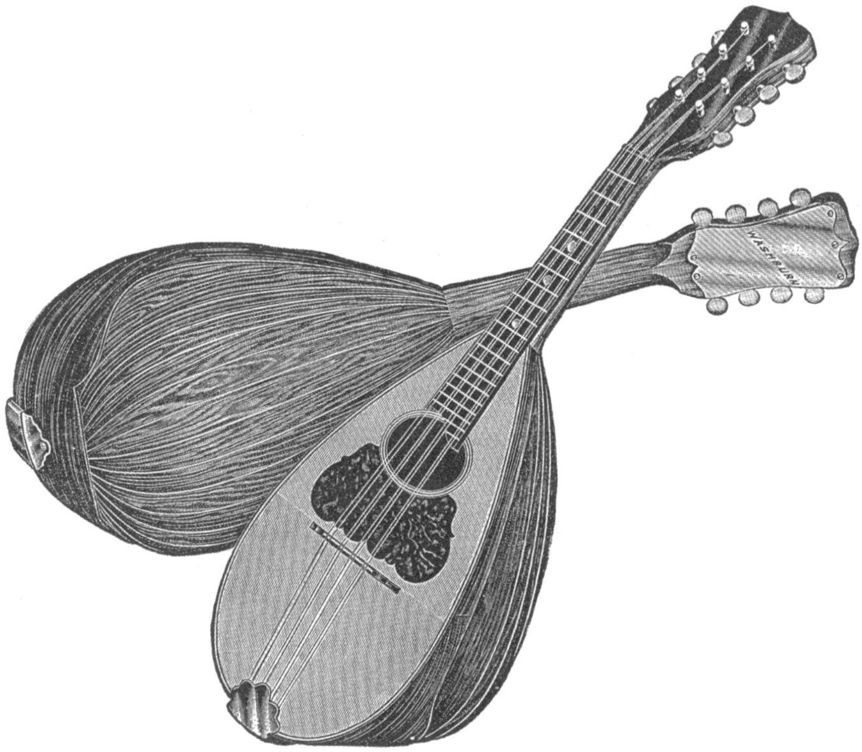

No. 1618

Style 1618 (1919)

No. 1642

Style 1642 (1920)

No. 1648

Style 1648 (1919)

standard size	**mandola**	
1615 (renamed 1618 in 1917)		15 rosewood ribs, mahogany neck, bowlback design, 20-fret rhodium fingerboard bound w white celluloid w three pearl dots at frets 5, 7 and 10, headstock w rosewood overlay and engraved metal silver plated back plate, top and s/h bound w black and white celluloid lines, ebony bridge w bone saddle, cloud shaped tortoise pickguard, crown shaped silver plated tailpiece cover, bone nut
1620 (1624 after 1917)		15 rosewood ribs, mahogany neck, bowlback design, 20-fret ebony fingerboard bound w black and white celluloid w four inlaid pearl dots at frets 5, 7, 10 and 12, headstock w ebony overlay and engraved metal silver plated back plate, top and s/h bound w black and white celluloid lines, ebony bridge w bone saddle, cloud shaped tortoise pickguard, crown shaped silver plated tailpiece cover, bone nut
1630 (1636 after 1917)		21 rosewood ribs, mahogany neck, bowlback design, 20-fret ebony fingerboard bound w black and white celluloid w inlaid pearl snowflakes at frets 1, 5, 7, 10 and 12, headstock w ebony overlay and engraved metal silver plated back plate, top and s/h bound w black and white celluloid lines, ebony bridge w bone saddle, cloud shaped tortoise pickguard w pearl vine leaves inlay, crown shaped silver plated tailpiece cover, bone nut
1648 (introduced 1917 or earlier)		28 rosewood ribs, mahogany neck, bowlback design, 20-fret ebony fingerboard bound w black and white celluloid w inlaid pearl snowflakes at frets 1, 3, 5, 7, 10, 12 and 15, headstock w ebony overlay, pearl inlay and engraved metal silver plated back plate, top and s/h bound w black and white celluloid herringbone pattern, ebony bridge w bone saddle, cloud shaped tortoise pickguard w pearl vine leaves inlay, crown shaped silver plated tailpiece cover, pearl nut
1660 (introduced 1917 or earlier)		36 rosewood ribs, mahogany neck, bowlback design, 20-fret ebony fingerboard bound w black and white celluloid w eleven pearl snowflakes inlaid at frets 1, 3, 5 (2), 7, 10 (2), 12, 15 (2) and 17, headstock w ebony overlay, pearl inlay and engraved metal silver plated back plate, top and s/h bound w pearl and white celluloid, ebony bridge w bone saddle, cloud shaped tortoise pickguard w pearl inlay, crown shaped silver plated tailpiece cover, pearl nut and tuner buttons

Style 1642 (1921)

44 LYON & HEALY, CHICAGO

WASHBURN FLAT BACK
MANDOLA

STYLE NO. G 1642

10 LYON & HEALY, CHICAGO

LYON & HEALY OWN MAKE
MANDOLIN

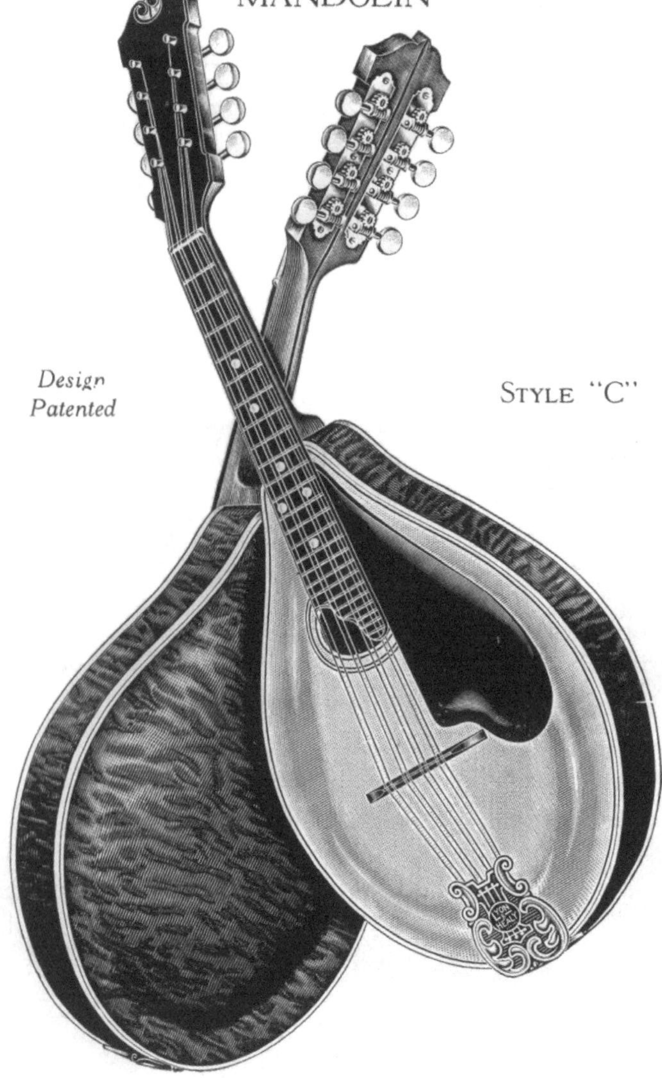

Design Patented

STYLE "C"

Style C (1921)

*Washburn mandolin styles 1920-1922**

standard size	mandola	
2424 (renamed 2420 in mid-1921)	mahogany b/s, mahogany neck, flatback design w pear shaped body, 20-fret rosewood fingerboard w three pearl dots at frets 5, 7, 10, headstock w rosewood overlay, back bound w black celluloid, top and s/h bound w black/white celluloid, compensated ebony bridge, wing shaped tortoise pickguard, crown shaped nickel plated tailpiece cover, bone nut	
2434 (2428 after mid-1921)		as Style 1422 (1917)
2442 (2436 after mid-1921)		as Style 1430 (1917)
	1642 (1638 after mid-1921)	rosewood b/s, mahogany neck, flatback mandola w pear shaped body, 18-fret rosewood fingerboard w four pearl dots at frets 5, 7, 10 and 12, headstock w rosewood overlay and metal back plate, top, s/h and back bound w black/white celluloid, compensated ebony bridge, wing shaped tortoise pickguard, crown shaped nickel plated tailpiece cover, bone nut
2627		as Style 1615 (1915)
2632		as Style 1620 (1915)
2643		as Style 1630 (1915)
2662		as Style 1648 (1917)
2683		as Style 1660 (1917)

* Lyon & Healy mandolins Styles A, B and C (with respective catalog style numbers 1100, 1075 and 1065) plus a Style A mandola (1125) and mandocello (1150) were introduced in 1917 and renamed 'Washburn' in the early 1920s

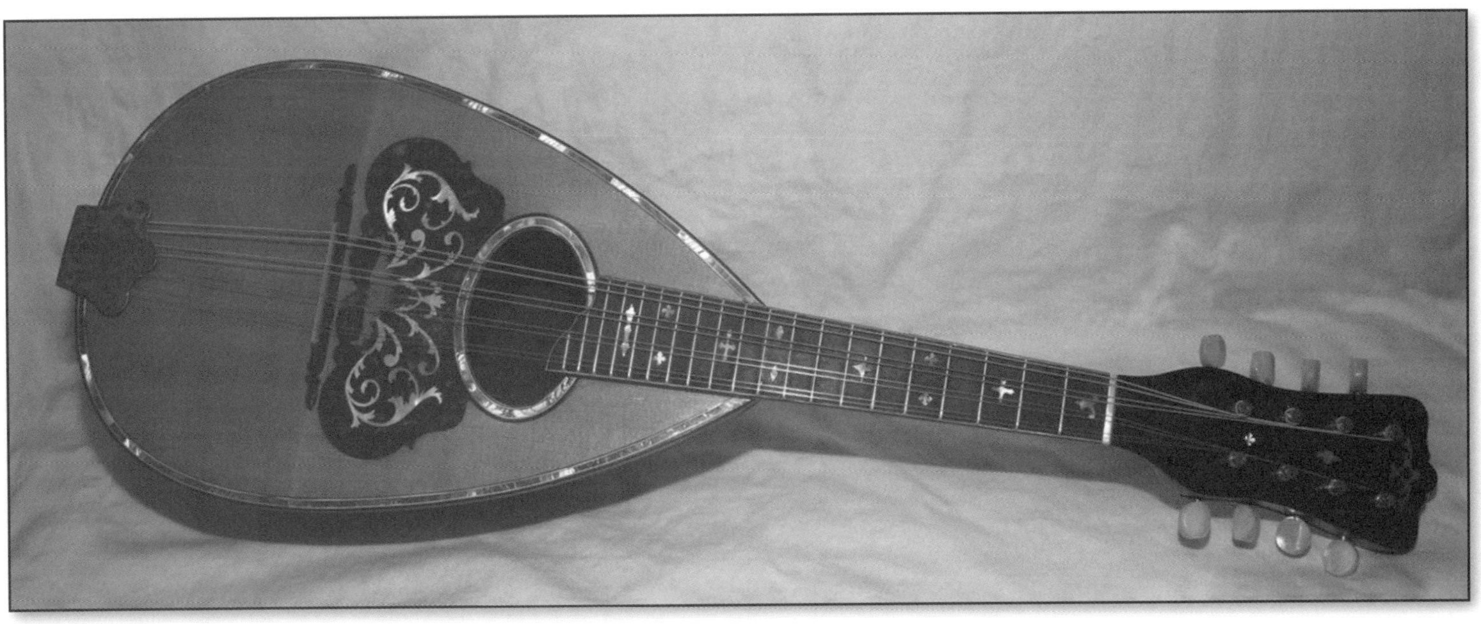

Style 2683, early 1920s (Bob Fairbanks)

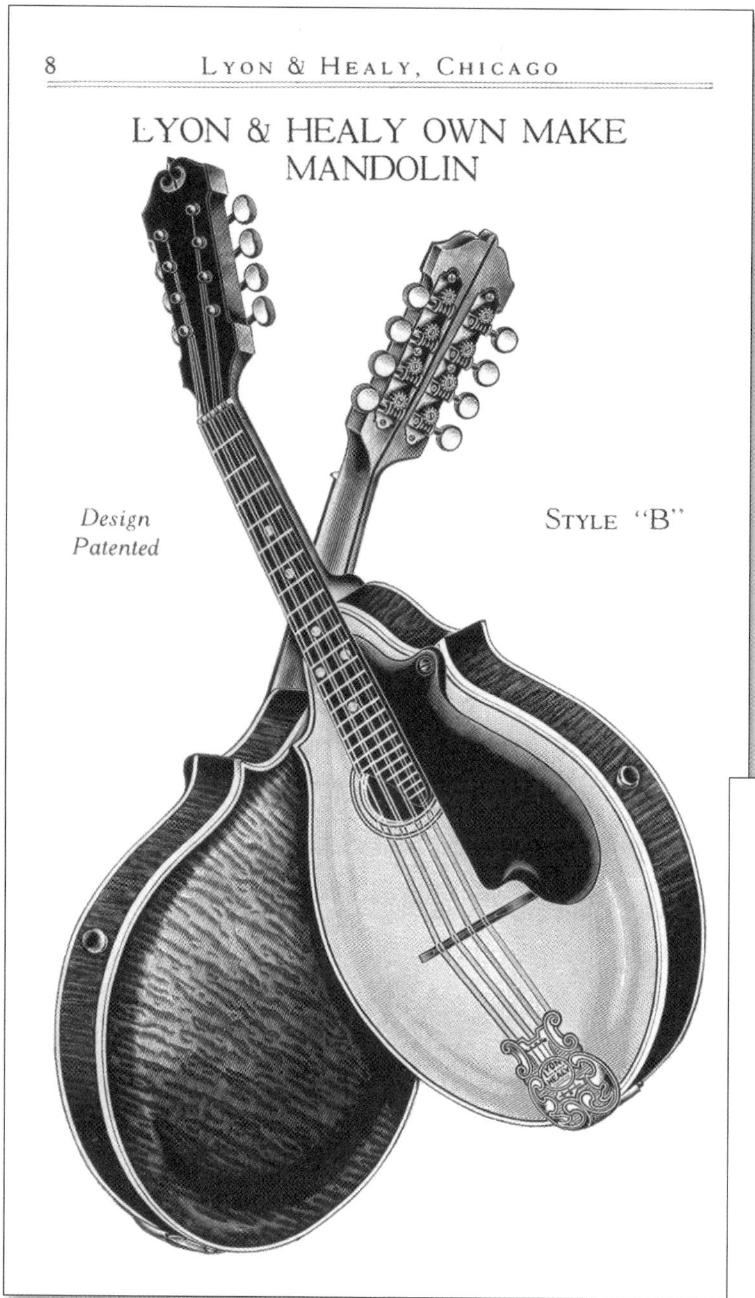
8 LYON & HEALY, CHICAGO

LYON & HEALY OWN MAKE
MANDOLIN

Design Patented

STYLE "B"

Style B (1921)

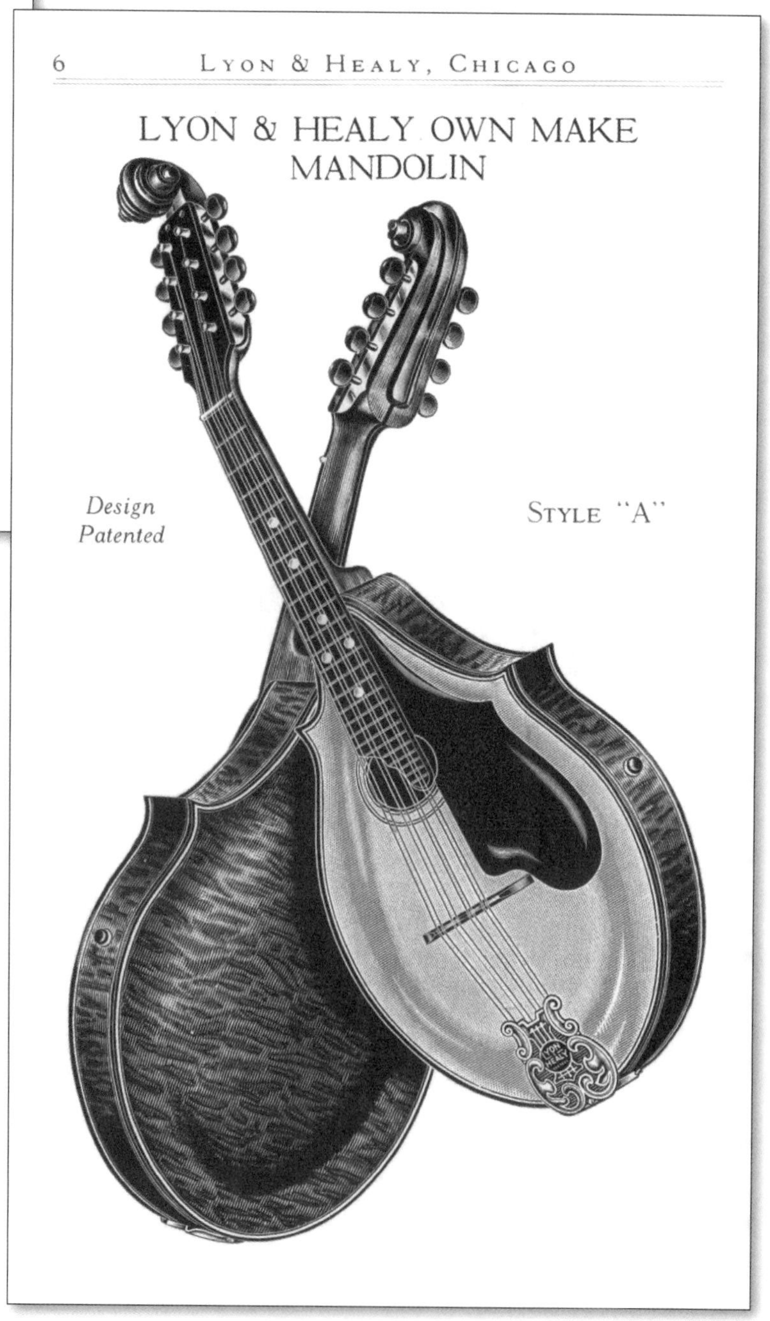
6 LYON & HEALY, CHICAGO

LYON & HEALY OWN MAKE
MANDOLIN

Design Patented

STYLE "A"

Style A (1921)

42 LYON & HEALY, CHICAGO

LYON & HEALY OWN MAKE
MANDOLA

Design
Patented

STYLE "A"

Style A Mandola (1921)

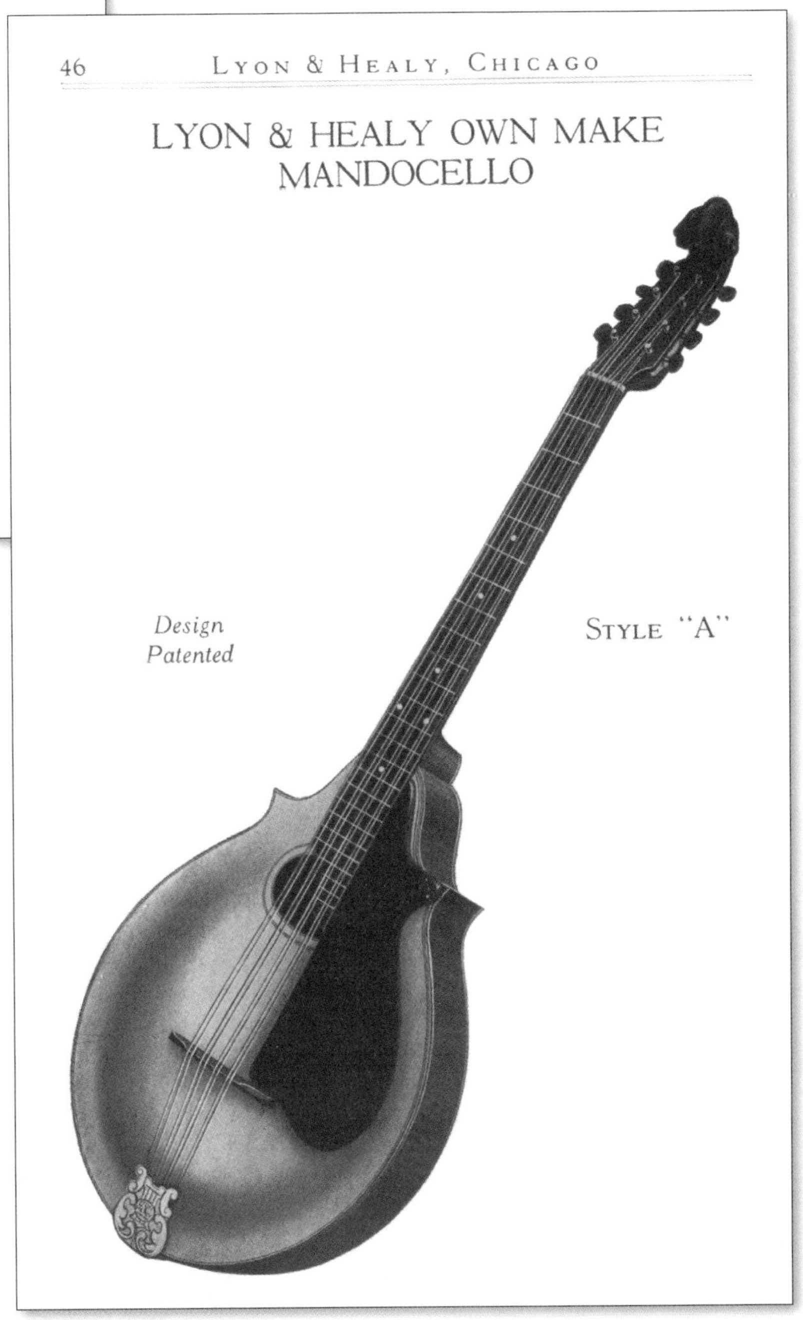

46 LYON & HEALY, CHICAGO

LYON & HEALY OWN MAKE
MANDOCELLO

Design
Patented

STYLE "A"

Style A Mandocello (1921)

18 LYON & HEALY, CHICAGO

WASHBURN FLAT BACK MANDOLINS

STYLE NO. G 2424

Style 2424 (1921)

16 LYON & HEALY, CHICAGO

WASHBURN FLAT BACK MANDOLINS

STYLE NOS. G 2434 AND G 2442

Style 2442 (1921)

Washburn mandolin styles 1922-1925

standard size	mandola	mandocello	
G*			mahogany b/s, mahogany finished neck, flatback design w pear shaped body, 20 or 21-fret ebonized rosewood fingerboard w five pearl dots at frets 5, 7, 10 and 12 (two dots) or three dots at frets 5, 7, 10, headstock w rosewood or ebony overlay, top and back bound w black celluloid, s/h bound w black/white celluloid lines, ebony compensating bridge, wing shaped tortoise pickguard, crown shaped nickel plated tailpiece cover, bone nut
F**			mahogany b/s, mahogany neck, flatback design w pear shaped body w two symmetrical body points, 20-fret ebony fingerboard w four pearl dots at frets 5, 7, 10 and 12 , headstock w rosewood or ebonized rosewood overlay, top and back bound w black celluloid, s/h bound w black/white celluloid lines, ebony compensating bridge, wing shaped tortoise pickguard, crown shaped nickel plated tailpiece cover, bone nut
E***			rosewood b/s, mahogany neck, flatback design w pear shaped body, 21-fret ebonized rosewood fingerboard bound w white celluloid w five pearl dots at frets 5, 7, 10 and 12 (two dots), headstock w rosewood or ebony overlay, top, back and s/h bound w black/white celluloid lines, ebony bridge, wing shaped tortoise pickguard, crown shaped nickel plated tailpiece cover, white celluloid heel-cap, inlaid backstrip, bone nut
D			flatback design w pear shaped body, three-ply maple sides****, figured maple back, 21-fret ebony fingerboard bound w white celluloid w five pearl dots at frets 5, 7, 10 and 12 (two dots), headstock w ebonized overlay, top, back and s/h bound w black/white celluloid lines, ebony bridge, wing shaped tortoise pickguard, crown shaped nickel plated tailpiece cover, bone nut

Style F

STYLE F. Selected Mahogany Back, Sides and Neck, dull finish. Fine Spruce Top. Both Top and Back Edges bound with black binding. Sound hole Celluloid bound and inlaid with four strips of black and white Purfling. Tortoise Celluloid Guard Plate, Ebony Extension Fingerboard, 4 inlaid Pearl position Dots, Bone Nut, Rosewood Veneered Headpiece. Ebony Compensating Bridge, mortised in and Covered Patent Head, Nickel plated Slide Tailpiece, Back plate Engraved "Washburn." Each **$25.00**

STYLE G. Selected Mahogany Back and Sides, dull finish. Fine Spruce Top. Mahogany finished Neck. Ebonized Extension Fingerboard. 3 Pearl position Dots. Top and Back edges bound with Black binding. Sound Hole surrounded by 4 stripe inlay of Black and White purfling. Celluloid Tortoise Guard Plate. Bone Nut. Ebony Compensating Bridge. Nickel Plated Slide Covered Tailpiece. Nickel Plated mortised covered patent heads. Nickel Plated Back plate engraved "Washburn." Strung with finest strings. Each........**$20.00**

Style G

Styles F, G (1923)

Style E

Style E (1923)

Style D

Style D (1923)

Style C

Style C w straight sided headstock (1923)

standard size	mandola	mandocello	
C			figured maple b/s, 13″ scale mahogany neck w vulcanized fiber reinforcement (13 ¾″ scale prior to 1921), carved back/top design w pear shaped body, 24-fret ebony fingerboard bound w black celluloid w six pearl dots at frets 5, 7, 10, 12 (two dots) and 15, moustache shaped headstock w ebonized overlay (prior to 1921 'deco' headstock w scroll carved in relief, preceded by stairstep shaped headstock), back bound w white celluloid, top and s/h bound w black/white celluloid lines, compensated ebony bridge, wing shaped tortoise pickguard, lyre shaped nickel silver plated tailpiece cover, bone nut, detachable black vulcanized fiber guard plate, black celluloid tuner buttons
B			figured maple b/s, 13″ scale mahogany neck w maple and vulcanized fiber reinforcement (13 ¾″ scale prior to 1921), carved back/top design w pear shaped body w two symmetrical points, 24-fret ebony fingerboard bound w black celluloid w six pearl dots at frets 5, 7, 10, 12 (two dots) and 15, moustache shaped 'deco' headstock w ebony overlay and scroll carved in relief (stairstep shaped headstock prior to early 1920s), back bound w white celluloid, top and s/h bound w black/white celluloid lines, compensated ebony bridge, lyre shaped nickel silver plated tailpiece cover, bone nut, detachable black fiber guard plate, black celluloid tuner buttons
A			figured maple b/s, 13″ scale mahogany neck w maple and vulcanized fiber reinforcement (13 ¾″ scale prior to 1921), carved back/top design w pear shaped body w two asymmetrical points (symmetrical points prior to early 1920s), 24-fret or 27-fret ebony fingerboard bound w black celluloid w six pearl dots at frets 5, 7, 10, 12 (two dots) and 15, headstock w carved scroll, top, back and s/h bound w black/white celluloid lines, compensated ebony bridge, lyre shaped nickel silver plated tailpiece cover, bone nut, detachable black vulcanized fiber guard plate, hard black rubber headstock top plate, black celluloid tuner buttons
	A		Mandola, appointments as Style A mandolin (1922) but with 15 ¾″ scale
		A	Mandocello, appointments as Style A mandolin (1922) but with 26″ scale
2615			as Style 1618 (1917), but with 16 ribs, ebonized fingerboard, black pickguard, top bound w black celluloid

WASHBURN MANDOLINS

1923-24 Series

STYLE B. 13 in. SCALE

The Top is carved from selected ¾" fine grain quartered sawed old Spruce and is scientifically graduated in thickness just like a fine Violin.

Body same as that of Style A except that points are even. No scroll head.

The Sides are of fine Curly Maple and the Back is carved from ¾" solid figured maple. Sides and Back in Walnut, Satin hand rubbed finish.

The Top and Back Edge of body inlaid with Black and White Celluloid.

The Neck is of Mahogany, Natural color finish, reinforced through center with strip of Vulcanized Fibre. Headpiece is Veneered and artistically Hand carved.

The Sound Hole bound with Black and White Celluloid.

The Fingerboard is of genuine Ebony, bound with Black Celluloid. Pearl position dots on top and celluloid dots on side. 24 Nickel Silver Frets. Ebony Bridge with Bone String Nut.

Other improvements are the L. & H. Patent Machine Heads, Vulcanized Fibre Guard Plate, Tail Piece, artistically decorated with Nickel Silver Cover. The finest quality strings are used.

Each $92.00

Style C

STYLE C. 13 in. SCALE

The Top is carved from selected ¾" fine grain quarter sawed old Spruce and is scientifically graduated in thickness, just like a fine Violin.

The sides are of fine Curly Maple and the Back is carved from ¾" solid figured Maple. Sides and Back in Walnut, Satin hand rubbed finish.

The Top edge of Body inlaid with Black and White Celluloid. The Back edge of Body is bound with white celluloid.

The Neck is of Mahogany, Natural color finish, reinforced through center with strip of Vulcanized Fibre. Headpiece is Veneered and artistically Hand carved.

The Sound Hole bound with Black and White Celluloid.

The Fingerboard is of genuine Ebony, bound with Black Celluloid. Pearl position dots on top and celluloid dots on side. 24 Nickel Silver Frets. Ebony Bridge with Bone String Nut.

Other improvements are the L. & H. Patent Machine Heads, Vulcanized Fibre Guard Plate, Tail Piece, artistically decorated with Nickel Silver Cover. The finest quality strings are used.

Each $60.00

Style D

STYLE D. 13 in. SCALE

The Top is of fine grain Spruce. Figured Maple Back and 3 ply Shell, Walnut Color. Top and Back Edge of Body inlaid with Black and White Celluloid.

The Sound Hole is bound with Black and White Celluloid.

Mahogany Neck, Ebonized Veneered Headpiece. Genuine Ebony Fingerboard, bound with White Celluloid. Pearl position dots on top, celluloid dots on side. 21 Liberty Silver frets.

Genuine Ebony Frets, Bone String Nut. Inlaid Tortoise Shell Celluloid Guard Plate. Nickel Plated Machine heads. Nickel plated Brass Tail Piece and cover. Finest quality steel strings used.

The instrument is hand rubbed to a fine dull finish.

Each $40.00

STYLE E

Beautiful selected Rosewood Back and Sides. Hand polished. Top is of finest quality selected Spruce. Both Top and Back edges are bound with White Celluloid—marquetry inlaying in upper edge of Top and around Sound Hole. Fingerboard and head bound with White Celluloid. Rosewood veneered head. Back Plate on Head nicely engraved. Tortoise celluloid Guard Plate. Mahogany Neck with ebony topped Heel. Ebony extension fingerboard, 20 Nickel Silver Frets, 4 Pearl Position Dots, Bone Nut, White Position dots on side also. Ebony Compensating Bridge. Full covered Patent Heads and Nickel Plated Covered Tailpiece. Strung with Fine Quality Strings.

Each $30.00

Style E

Styles C, D, E (1923)

Washburn mandolin styles 1922-1925 (continued)

standard size	mandola	mandocello	
2620			as Style 1618 (1917), but with ebony fingerboard
2625			as Style 1624 (1917), but with rosewood or ebonized headstock overlay
2635			as Style 1636 (1917)
2650			as Style 1648 (1917)
2675			as Style 1660 (1917)

* The earlier models had slightly simpler appointments (20 frets, three fingerboard dots, rosewood headstock veneer) and a differently shaped, larger headstock with tapered sides that was replaced by a narrower headstock with straight sides, and an ebony or ebonized overlay. These also had a slightly larger pickguard that almost touches the bridge

** The remarks made under * may also apply to this model, but this could not be verified

*** The actual 1923/4 catalog model has a symmetrical two point rosewood body, bound fingerboard and headstock, ebony heelcap and 20 frets. All Styles E that were examined however conform to the specifications listed above. As with Styles F and G, the pear shaped body Style E may have replaced the original model shortly after its introduction

**** The sole Style D that was reported had a rosewood body

Washburn mandolin styles 1925 1928

standard size	mandola	mandocello	
5280 (Inspiration)			as Style G (1922), but with 21-fret ebonized rosewood fingerboard w five pearl dots at frets 5, 7, 10 and 12 (two dots) bound w white celluloid, top bound w black and white celluloid
5281 (Classic)			as Style E (1922)
5282 (Aristocrat)			as Style C (1922)
5283 (DeLuxe)			as Style A (1922)
	5300		as Style A mandola (1922)
		5310	as Style A mandocello (1922)
'Shrine' mandolin (not catalogued)			(introduced 1927/8, discontinued in or before 1929) triangular mahogany body, spruce top, 21-fret ebony extension fingerboard w five pearl dots at frets 5, 7, 10 and 12 (2), headstock w inlaid green ivorine square, ebony bridge, top, back, headstock and s/h bound w green celluloid, white tuner buttons

WASHBURN MANDOLINS

"Classic" Model

Many an artist whose heart is set on the best mandolin obtainable must, for a while at least, content himself with an inexpensive instrument. In doing so his choice is one that is made considerately. This is why this WASHBURN is so highly received by him. It gives him the best design and workmanship obtainable and a tone of great richness and power.

Specifications

Body—Fine grained spruce top, natural color; figured rosewood back and 3-ply continuous sides; top and back edges of body inlaid with black and white celluloid; oval soundhole bound with white and black celluloid.

Neck—Thirteen-inch scale; polished mahogany neck and ebonized head plate; ebonized fingerboard bound with white celluloid; 5 pearl position dots; 21 nickel silver frets; ebony bridge and polished bone fingerboard nut; inlaid tortoise shell celluloid guard plate.

Trimmings—Nickel-plated patent heads; nickel-plated brass tailpiece with slide. Finest quality strings.

No. **5281** .... *Each $40.00*

"Inspiration" Model

Now even the beginner need not play on an inferior instrument. The WASHBURN *"Inspiration" Model* is made by the same workmen and under the same rigorous supervision as the other styles. It has been produced in a successful endeavor to give the musician a fine mandolin at small cost. It has a tone of a very fine musical quality.

Specifications

Body—Fine spruce top, natural color; selected mahogany back and 3-ply continuous sides; top edge of body inlaid with black and white purfling; top and back edge bound with black celluloid; soundhole encircled with white and black celluloid.
Neck—Thirteen-inch scale, polished mahogany neck; ebonized fingerboard with 4 pearl position dots and 21 nickel silver frets; ebony bridge and bone fingerboard nut; inlaid tortoise shell celluloid guard plate.
Trimmings—Nickel-plated brass patent heads; nickel-plated brass tailpiece with slide cover.
No. **5280** .... *Each $20.00*

Cases

Black seal grain Keratol covered 3-ply wood body; side opening; steel valance; nickel-plated brass trimmings, lock and clasps; leather handle; compartment for accessories.

No.		*Each*
6212	Flannel lined	*$ 9.00*
6214	Velvet lined	*10.75*
6216	Silk plush lined	*15.00*

Style 5280, 5281 (1925)

The WASHBURN "ARISTOCRAT" Mandolin

Made in the Lyon & Healy Factory

Though there is only one standard of WASHBURN quality, tastes vary. This style has been designed for the artist who looks to his mandolin primarily for tone and durability. Not that he is unresponsive to physical beauty for this style which is very popular with both the professional and amateur musician presents a design of grace and exquisite finish, but with less ornate treatment than the WASHBURN *"De Luxe."*

Specifications

Body—Top carved from ¾-inch fine grain spruce, natural color; graduated in thickness; golden brown curly maple sides; carved golden brown figured maple back; top edge of body inlaid with white and black fiberoid; back edge with ivory celluloid; oval soundhole bound with black and white fiberoid. Hand rubbed satin finish.

Neck—Thirteen-inch scale; mahogany neck reinforced with vulcanized fibre; ebonized headpiece; ebony extension fingerboard bound with black celluloid; 6 pearl position dots; 24 nickel silver frets; ebony bridge and polished bone fingerboard nut.

Trimmings—WASHBURN patent heads with black celluloid buttons; patent vulcanized fibre guard plate; patent tailpiece with artistic nickel silver cover.

Case—Black seal grain Keratol covered three-ply wood body; side opening; silk plush lined; nickel-plated brass trimmings, lock and clasps; steel valance; two compartments for accessories; leather handle.

No. **5282** *Complete with case* *$90.00*

Style 5282 (1925)

Tonk Bros. Co., Chicago

"WASHBURN" MANDOLINS

Washburn Mandolins are known the world over, for many years, for their beautiful design, exquisite finish and marvelous tone. No expense has been spared to perfect these instruments in every respect.

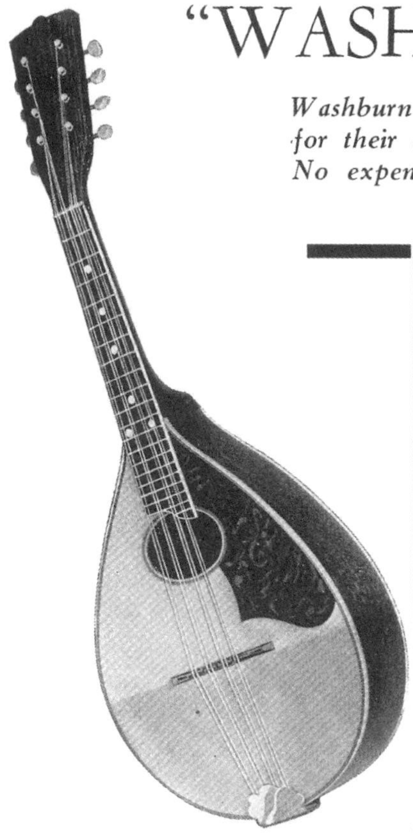

No. 5280

No. 5281

No. 5280 Handsome model body, made of first **choice mahogany** and best **Eastern spruce top.** The neck is also best seasoned mahogany, finished in its natural brown mahogany color, but the top is finished in its natural white color. Hand rubbed, and semi-satin finish throughout. Top and back edge, as well as sound hole and fingerboard, are bound with white celluloid. Top edge and sound hole inlaid with black and white strips. Genuine ebony, **full 14 inch scale extension fingerboard,** with German silver frets, correctly adjusted. Fine nickel-plated fancy patent heads. Compensating ebony bridge. Large tortoise color inlaid pick-guard. A truly remarkable instrument. Suitable for the advanced player.

Each **$22.50**

No. 5281 New type "WASHBURN". **Body designed especially for tone. Made of figured maple** and with a fine selected Eastern spruce top. The neck is maple reinforced through center with mahogany strip to avoid warping. Top and back edge, as well as sound hole, are inlaid with black and white strips and bound with fine Ivorine. The **fingerboard is genuine ebony, full 14 inch scale.** It is bound with celluloid and has five pearl position dots and position markers on the side. Entire instrument is finished in dark brown color, artistically hi-lighted in the center. Hand rubbed, and beautifully finished throughout in semi-gloss. Best grade nickel-plated patent heads. Headpiece inlaid with pearl.

Each **$35.00**

"DELUXE" MODEL

No. 5283 Undoubtedly one of the finest Mandolins made to-day. Suitable for the most exacting Professional. The **top is carved** out of best selected tone spruce. The **back is carved** out of figured maple. Both are graduated to perfection. **The neck** is genuine mahogany reinforced, and **has a hand carved scroll head.** The fingerboard is fine black ebony, extension type with 24 nickel-silver frets and six pearl position dots. Top and back edges, as well as sound hole, inlaid with black and white fiberoid. Marvelous hand finish throughout, highly polished. Especially made and improved patent heads, covered with black head plate. Fine professional black fibre guard-plate. Reliable tailpiece with artistic nickel-silver cover. The tone is exquisite. Fine 3-ply veneer keratol covered **case,** with silk plush lining **is included** in the price of the instrument.

Complete outfit **$135.00**

No. 5283—Front View

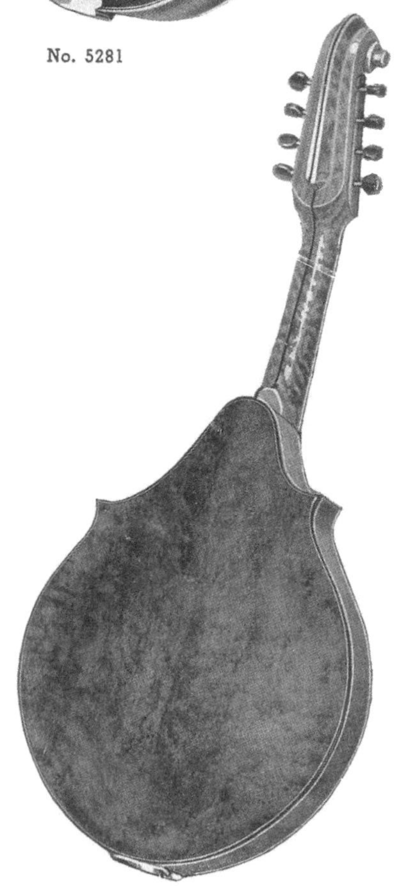

No. 5283—Back View

For NATIONAL amplifying and Electric Mandolins, see pages 106 and 109.

Mandolin line, 1939

Washburn mandolin styles 1928-1935

standard size

5280 (Inspiration)	as Style 5280 (1925)
5281 (Classic)	as Style E (1922)
5282 (Aristocrat)	as Style C (1922)
5283 (DeLuxe)	as Style A (1922)

Washburn mandolin styles 1935-1940

standard size

5280	mahogany b/s, 14" scale mahogany neck, flatback design w pear shaped body, 20-fret ebony fingerboard bound w white celluloid w six pearl dots at frets 3, 5, 7, 10 and 12 (two dots), headstock w rosewood overlay w "Washburn" inlaid in pearl, back bound w white celluloid, top and s/h bound w black/white celluloid lines, compensated ebony bridge, wing shaped tortoise pickguard, crown shaped nickel plated tailpiece cover, bone nut
5281	figured maple b/s, 14" scale maple neck, flatback design w pear shaped body, 20-fret ebony fingerboard bound w white celluloid w six pearl dots at frets 3, 5, 7, 10 and 12 (two dots), headstock w rosewood overlay w "Washburn" inlaid in pearl, top, back and s/h bound w black/white celluloid lines, compensated ebony bridge, wing shaped tortoise pickguard, crown shaped nickel plated tailpiece cover, bone nut, brown sunburst finish
5283 (DeLuxe)	as Style A (1922)

CHAPTER FOUR

Banjos

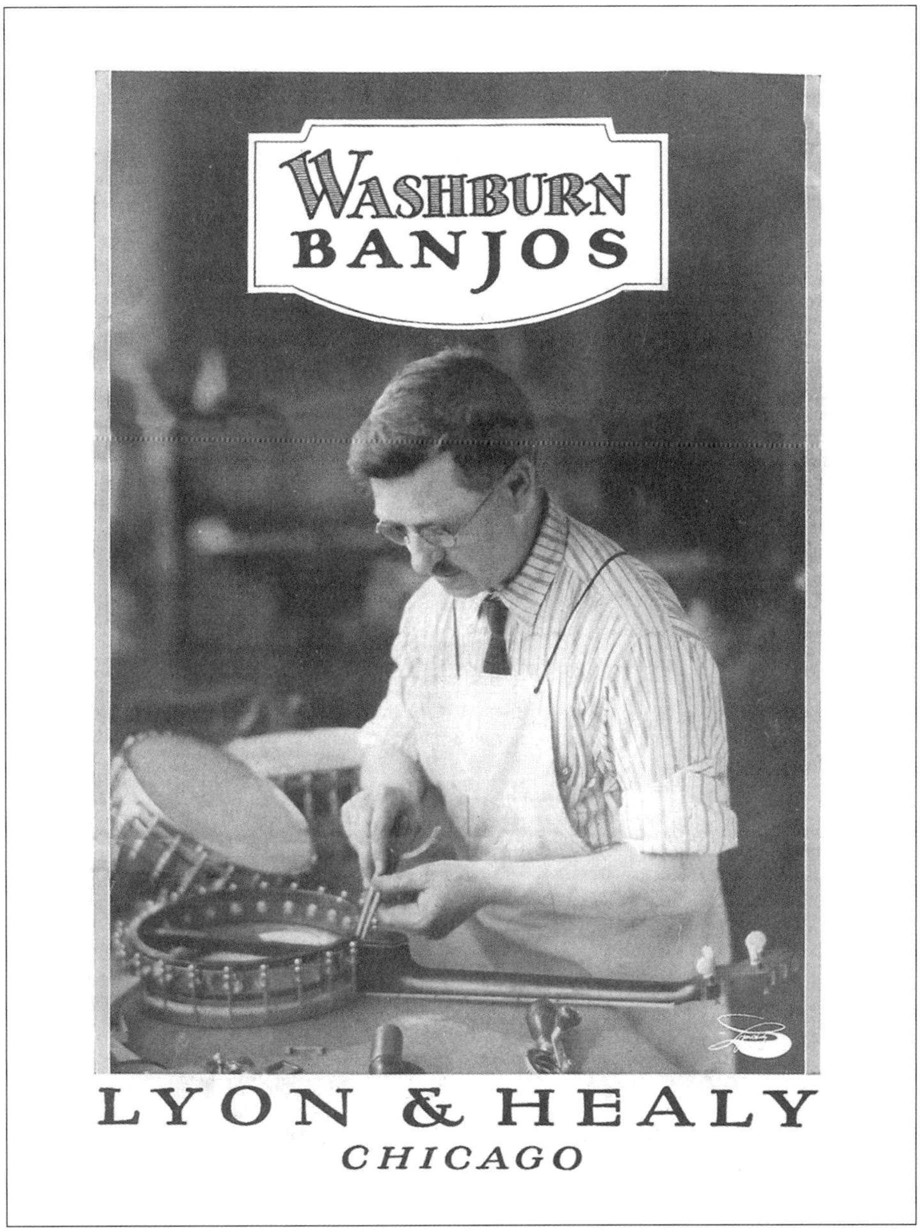

Washburn banjo catalog, mid-1920s (Brian Lydford)

4.1 Dating of Washburn banjos

Washburn banjos can be dated in most cases by the numbers stamped on the dowel stick. Dating is relatively easy because the banjos were only renumbered once during their production period (around 1923). During the late 1920s the serial numbers on the dowel stick were replaced by batch numbers, with the serial number no longer being stamped on the instruments. After checking the dowel stick number(s), compare the features of the respective instrument to those described under 'General appointments', 'Construction / general remarks' and, lastly, to the style descriptions provided hereunder. The Washburn banjos occasionally did not get a serial number or received only a stamped style number. These instruments must therefore be dated based strictly on their features. The banjo ukuleles were classified by Lyon & Healy as ukuleles, which is why the Washburn banjo ukuleles are listed in the Ukulele chapter.

4.2 General appointments

1892-1923:
Consecutive serial numbers starting at 1 up to 9,900s, impressed in the dowel stick together with Washburn a logo picturing a belt encircling a guitar. Some of the earliest banjos did not get a stamped serial number. Around 1913 new styles with an improved tone ring on spikes ('patent truss') are added to the line (starting around serial #3,000); on these newer styles a Washburn logo picturing a banjo encircled by a belt plus the words 'improved' and sometimes another set of digits (e.g. '1913' or '1570', in most cases indicating the style number) are impressed in the dowel stick. The traditional banjo styles retain the stamped Washburn guitar logo. After the mid 1910s banjos do not have a stamped serial number but only a style number impressed in the dowel stick. Starting around 1920 instruments again have both style and serial numbers stamped into the dowel stick.

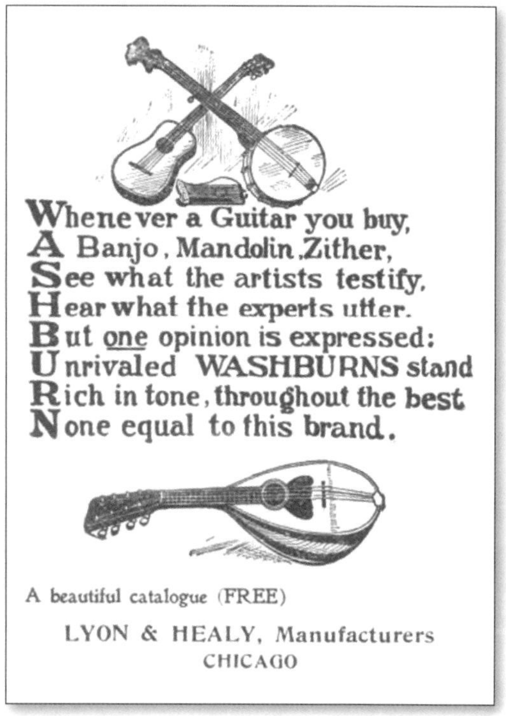

1898

Post 1923:
All banjo styles except Styles D and E sport the 'donut' style tone ring. Consecutive numbers start again with 1 (1923) into the low 4,000s (around 1925), impressed in the dowel stick together with the words 'Washburn' and 'Style' followed by a letter indicating the model (on the Style A and B banjos that were shipped without a dowel stick the serial number and style designation are stamped inside the shell). The branded Washburn belt logo (1892-1923) is discontinued. Banjos with a dowel stick sometimes have a batch number stamped inside the shell.

1925-1930:
Styles are indicated by four digit numbers beginning with 51, stamped in the dowel stick together with the instrument's serial number and the word 'Washburn'. Numbering continues from the low 4,000s (around 1925) up to the mid 7,000s (around 1926-7). After mid 1926 only the style and batch numbers are stamped in the dowel stick (high 8,000s up to 14,000s). Whether any Washburn banjos were made after 1930 is doubtful in view of the lack of surviving instruments from this period.

By the time of this 1904 ad only three 'Washburn babies' were left, named Major, Minor and Little Pick. Other period ads showed them being lost in the woods while trying to fend off a couple of hungry wolves. Where were the parents?

4.3 Construction / general remarks

Unlike the Washburn guitars and mandolins, for which production started during the mid to late 1880s, Washburn banjos were not offered until 1892. New or revised model lines were introduced in 1896, 1910, 1913, 1917, 1923, 1925 and 1928. The less expensive banjo lines made in the Lyon & Healy factories since the mid 1880s were marketed under brand and model names that included Lyon & Healy, Professional, Mystic, Waverly, Olympic, Columbia, Star, Billy Emerson, Robinson, Hamilton, Foster and Thatcher.[99]

Around 1917 four variations of banjo styles were introduced: 'professional' indicated the standard long scale five string 22-fret neck banjo, 'tenor' the shorter scale four string version with a 21-fret extension fingerboard (a few years later reduced to 17 frets), 'tango' stood for a four string banjo with a short (mandolin scale) neck having a 17-fret extension fingerboard and the 'mandolin' version ditto, but with eight strings. After 1923 the different versions were characterized as 'regular' or 'regulation' (indicating an old style five string instrument with a long scale 22-fret neck), 'tenor' (the 'standard' 17-fret neck four string banjo), 'plectrum' (four strings, long scale 22-fret neck), and 'mandolin' (similar to the pre 1923 specs, 17-fret neck). The 1925 line added a short-lived 'guitar' version that sported a six string neck and a slotted headstock with three on a side tuners. The 1928 styles were only available in standard (tenor), 'plectrum' and 'regulation' versions. It seems likely that following the sale of the Washburn manufacturing license to J.R. Stewart Co. in 1928 the Washburn banjos –like the Washburn guitars, mandolins and ukuleles- were still being made by the former Lyon & Healy workers in the Rockwell factory that had been taken over by Stewart. There is no real evidence to suggest that Regal was involved in the manufacturing of Washburn banjos in the 1920s and 1930s. Judging from surviving instruments Regal made relatively few banjos at the time, and none were anywhere as luxurious in their appointments as the Washburns or shared any of their typical constructional features. The fact that not one Washburn banjo with a Tonk stamp or post-1930 serial number has been accounted for seems to indicate that banjo production stopped altogether after the Stewart Co. went bankrupt in 1930, and that Tonk sold off the remaining inventory of Washburns in the next years.

99 Billy Emerson and William H. Hamilton both were managers and star performers of San Francisco based minstrel troupes of the late 1800s. Thatcher was another famed minstrel company of the same period. 'Robinson' likely referred to Bill Robinson, a/k/a Bojangles (1878-1949), an American dancer and entertainer who debuted in minstrel shows. Stephen C. Foster (1826-1864) was a popular songwriter who composed many songs that became staples in the minstrel show repertoire.

Mays & Hunter

Mays & Hunter, 1890s catalog

Endorsement picture of Vess Ossman (1868-1923), one of the greatest ragtime banjoists, in a 1925 Washburn catalog. Already famous during his lifetime, Ossman played for large audiences and luminaries such as King Edward VII and President Theodore Roosevelt (Brian Lydford)

The most prominent early endorsers of Washburn banjos were Mays & Hunter, a popular concert duo formed in 1895 which gave performances in the US and abroad. William 'Parke' Hunter (1876-1912) ranks by all accounts among the greatest classical banjoists of all time. He was a very active performer as well as a frequent recording artist and published over 150 banjo instrumentals during his short life. His musical partner Cadwallader L. Mays was like Hunter a St. Louis based banjoist. In 1897 Mays & Hunter arrived in England for a highly acclaimed concert tour. They performed virtuosic adaptations of well-known classical pieces and were also the first players to present ragtime music to the English audiences.[100] Mays & Hunter's successful partnership was cut short by Mays' untimely death in 1903 at the age of thirty. After Mays' death, Hunter toured for a few years with the Ossman Banjo Trio, which also featured William Farmer and Sylvester "Vess" Ossman (1868-1923), one of the foremost banjo players of the era. Many of the Washburn catalogs around the turn of the 20th century include pictures of and elaborate testimonials by Mays & Hunter, who may have been involved to some extent in the design of Washburn banjos at the time.[101]

100 Robert B. Winans and Elias J. Kaufman, *Minstrel and Classic Banjo: American and English Connections*, in *American Music*, Vol 12, No. 1 (1994).
101 Period catalogs also refer to Style 1050's appointments as "the Mays & Hunter pattern".

4.3.1 Shells

The Washburn banjos manufactured before 1913 did not depart much from the traditional construction methods employed by Lyon & Healy's competitors at the time. The 1892 Washburn catalog however highlighted an ingenious compensating rim consisting of three plies of wood, separated by two small strips positioned next to the head in which tiny metal discs were placed about two inches apart. The purpose of this construction was to create a certain degree of vertical flexibility of the rim which would provide for automatic tension adjustment due to the slight expansions and contractions of the head, and to improve the vibrational qualities of the rim. A patent application was filed for this device during the early 1890s, though it is not known whether a patent was actually granted. The sophisticated 'wood compensating shell' was featured only on Styles 441 and 442.[102] All other models of the 1892 line, including the expensive presentation banjos, had a relatively simple metal clad wooden shell. Likely the disc-fitted rim was discontinued due to production difficulties or stability issues. In 1896 all banjos were fitted with a metal covered maple shell. This rather straightforward design remained in production until the late 1910s.

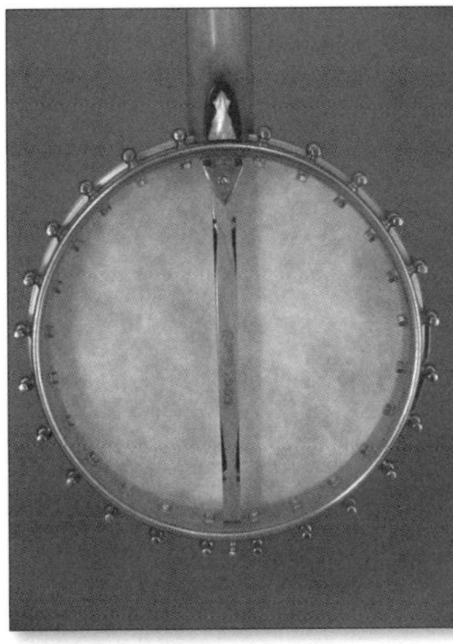

Shell of a Style 430 banjo, mid 1890s (Frank Ford)

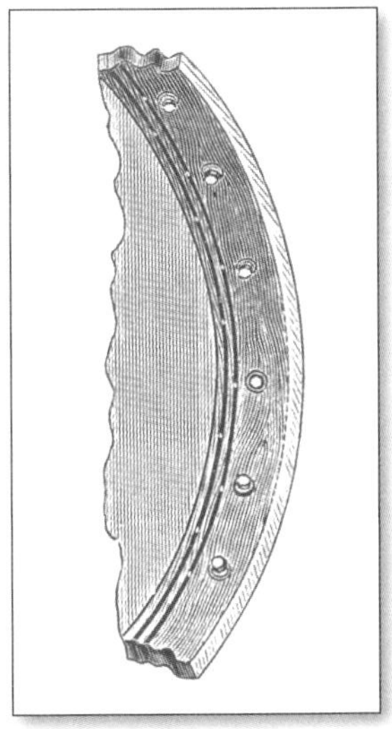

The 'wood compensating shell' of Style 441/442, 1895 catalog

The new banjo styles introduced in 1913 –recognizable by a stamp 'improved' on the dowel stick- were equipped with a new shell, also known as the 'Combination Patent Truss'[103]. This design incorporated a tone ring resting on spikes elevated above the wooden rim, according to period catalogs in order to eliminate "fluty" or "woody" tones. Contrary to the company tradition this feature was not an invention of one of Lyon & Healy's workmen, but had already been patented in 1908 by William D. Bohnenberger of East Orange, New Jersey, who later changed his last name to 'Bowen'.[104] "Banjo Bill" Bowen was a famed performer who at some time was affiliated with New York based Rettberg & Lange and its successor Wm. L. Lange, respectively makers of the well known Orpheum and Paramount banjos. Apparently Lyon & Healy procured a license from Bowen in the early 1910s or purchased his patent. Initially the company may not have been convinced about the success of the new Washburn banjos, as the older styles remained in production besides the new line of 1913 until they were finally phased out around 1917. These older styles (1015, 1025, 1050, 1120, 1130 and 1135) did not receive any of the

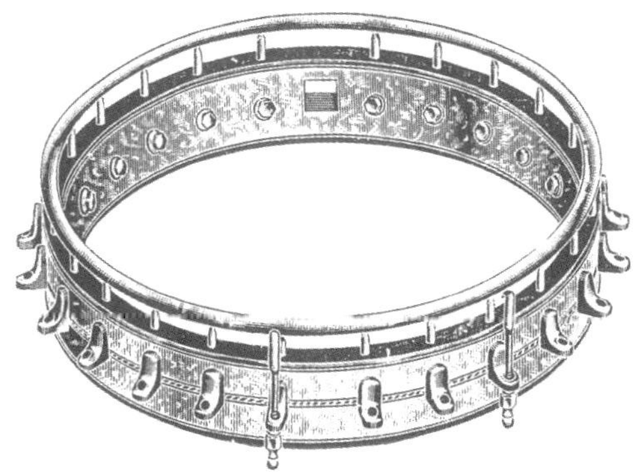

Cut No. 1

Showing construction of New Washburn Patented Truss

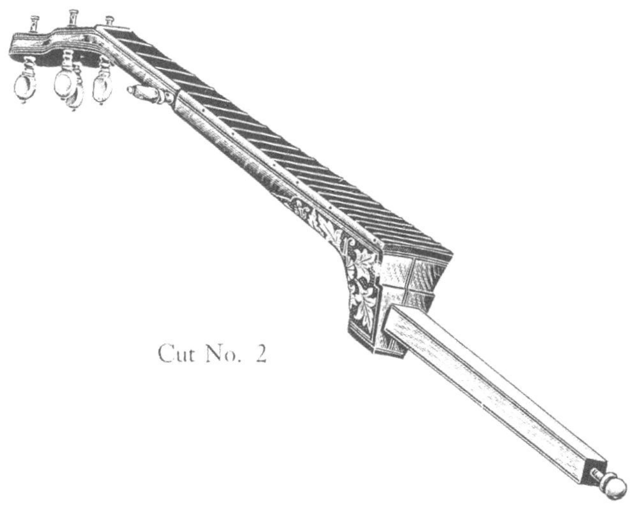

Cut No. 2

Showing center strip reinforcement and strong construction of necks in Washburn Banjos.

1917

Detail of 'Combination Patent Truss' tone ring with patent number stamped inside rim

102 One surviving Style 411 has been found with this shell as well.

103 Style 525, the cheapest new model introduced in 1913, came with a regular shell and was therefore not stamped 'improved'. A 1917 catalog claimed incorrectly that the patent truss tone ring had been introduced on the Washburn line in 1911.

104 Patent number 876,430, which can be found stamped on the shells of Washburn banjos during the 1913-1923 period.

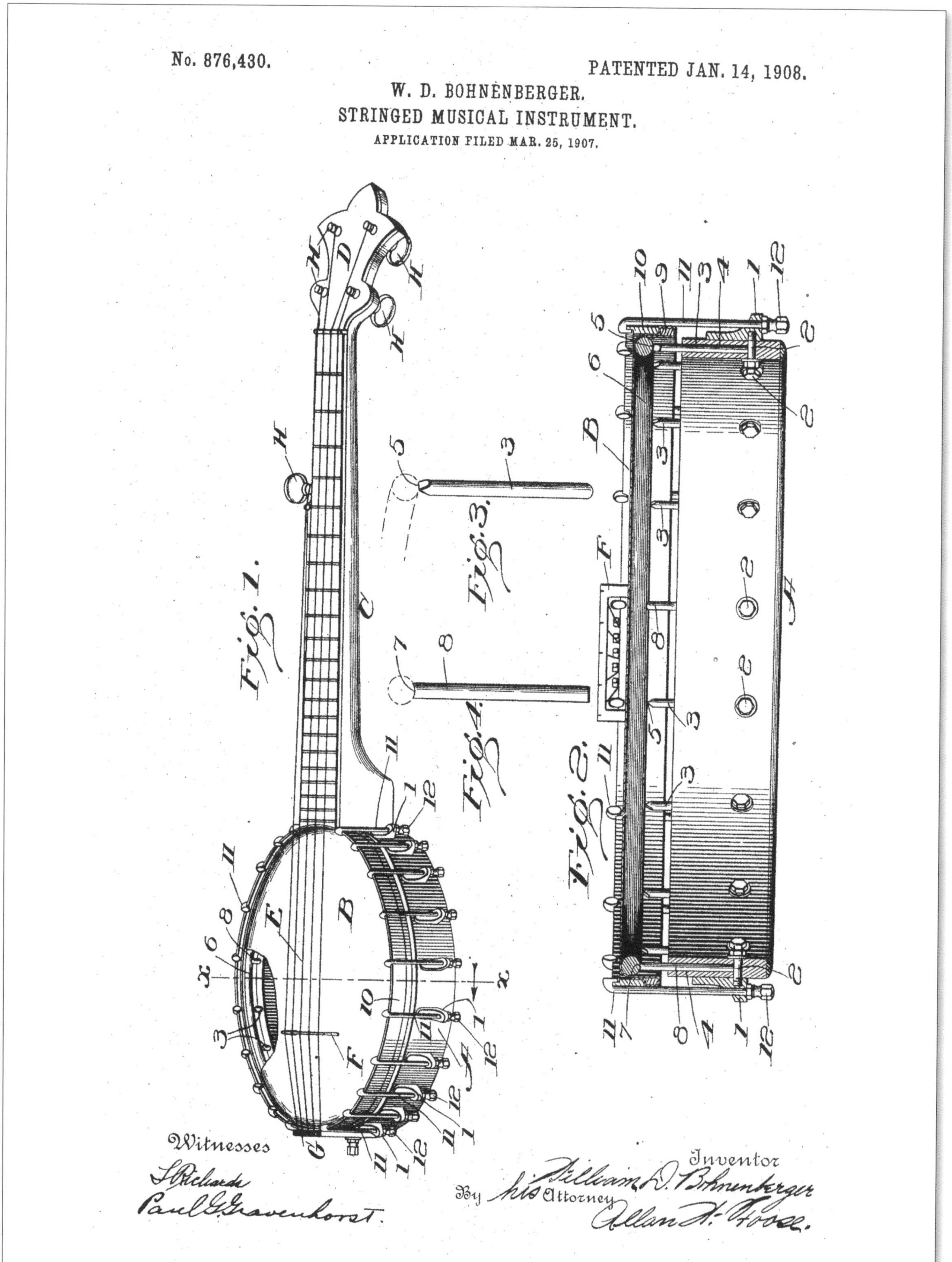

No. 876,430. PATENTED JAN. 14, 1908.

W. D. BOHNENBERGER.

STRINGED MUSICAL INSTRUMENT.

APPLICATION FILED MAR. 25, 1907.

'Banjo Bill' Bowen's 1908 patent for a tone ring resting on spikes as used on the 1913 Washburn banjo line features of the 'improved' models, except for the Elite tailpiece that was fitted on Style 1135.

But did Lyon & Healy actually manufacture their new banjo line? The 1913 Washburn banjo designs were visually and constructionally very similar to the Rettberg & Lange instruments. The marquetry styles, fancy fingerboard inlays and headstock ornamentation of the most expensive Washburns unmasked them as close cousins of the R&L-made Orpheum banjos, which also had an elevated tone ring, the same 'no-knot' tailpiece like the Washburns –and a 9th fret position marker. All banjos designed by Lyon & Healy before 1913 had a position marker at the 10th fret. The catalog pictures of the new 'improved' line showed a 9th fret marker on the five-string banjo models -but the older five-string Washburn styles that Lyon & Healy continued to offer until 1917 strangely kept their 10th fret position marker.[105] Some instruments came with stamped serial and style numbers, while others only received a style number. Inconsistencies like these are typical of the Washburn banjos of the 1910s and early 1920s. The explanation is that Lyon & Healy's banjo manufacturing activities were also partly or wholly farmed out to other makers during the 1910s.[106] Another obvious illustration of this is Style 1135 (1910-1917), a dead ringer for Cole's Eclipse model with its famous 'man in the moon' headstock inlay. Certain other features of style 1135, such as its headstock that was much more rounded than on the other Washburns in the 1910 catalog, differently styled inlays and –again- a 9th fret position fingerboard marker were also definite clues. Lyon & Healy's decision to join forces with competitors Cole and Rettberg & Lange, born out of practical considerations, could also be viewed as a smart business move in view of the lackluster sales figures of the Washburn banjo lines at the time.[107] Given the rarity of surviving instruments, Style 1135 apparently did not much to revive sales, but the new 1913 line was definitely a success and capitalized on the 'tango craze' of the 1910s that brought the banjo back to prominence.

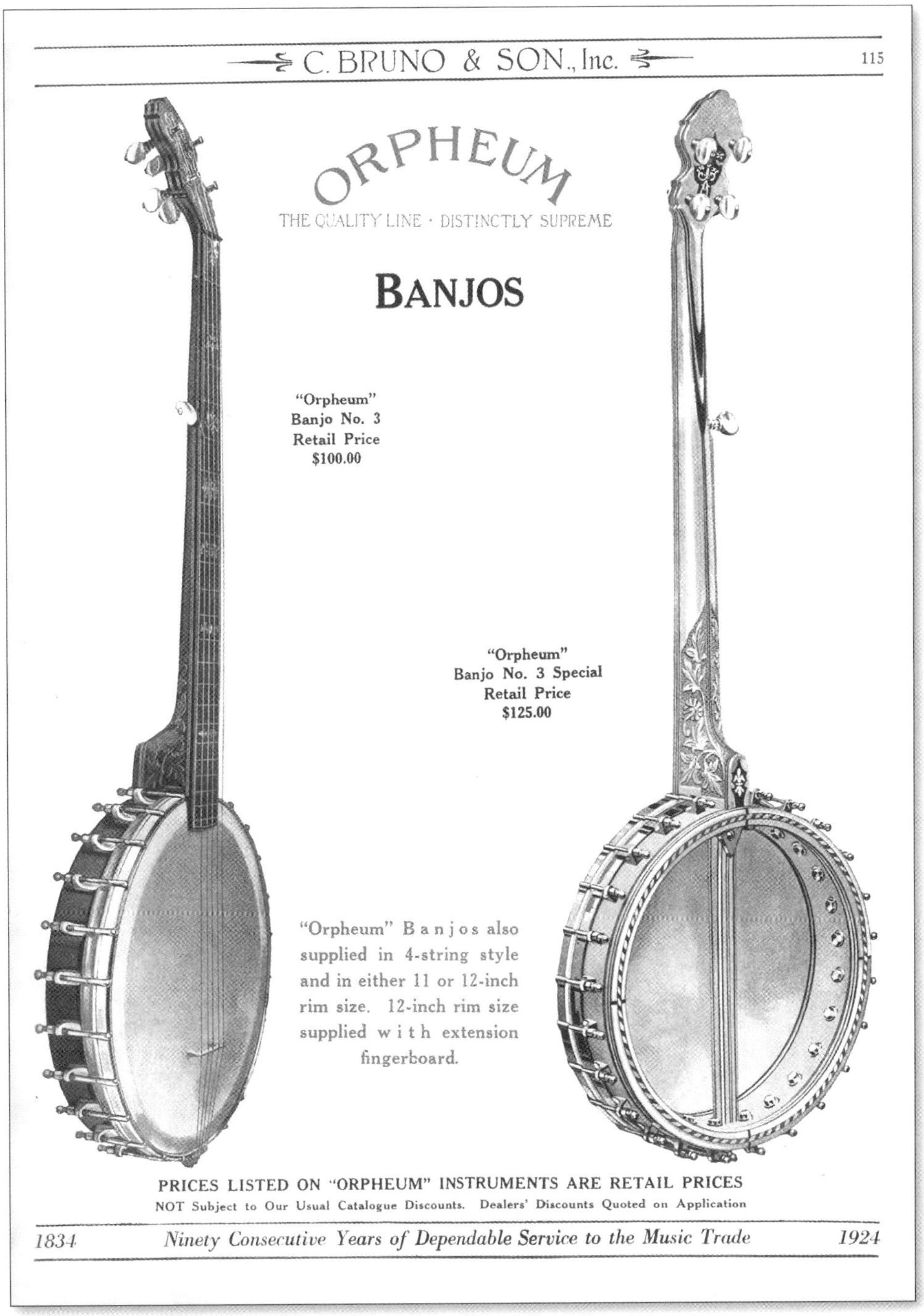

Orpheum #3 banjo in 1924 Bruno catalog (Retrofret.com)

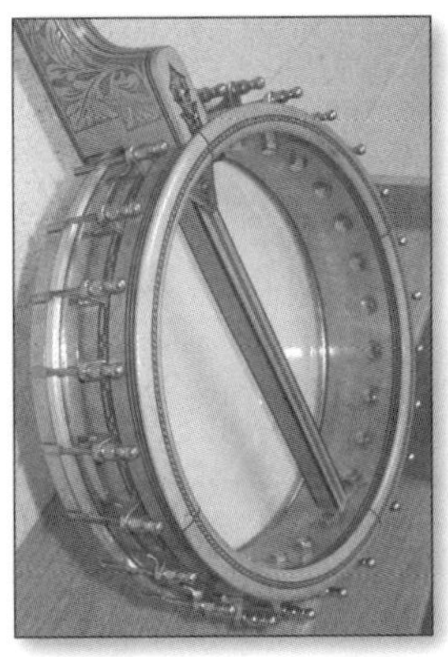
Orpheum #3
(Bill Destler)

Washburn Style 5100
(Bill Destler)

105 This difference is also evidenced by the surviving five-string banjos of the 1913-1923 period.
106 See 1.3.
107 See Chapters 6 and 7.

The Aristocrat of all Banjos

The Lyon & Healy "Own Make"

In designating our "Own Make" Banjo, the aristocrat, we fully recognize the fact that there are many good Banjos on the market, but none is its equal. An unprejudiced judgment will bear us out that it is supreme in the Banjo family. The outstanding feature of any Musical Instrument is, and should be, Tonal quality while preserving its individuality.

Tone, excellence in materials and elegant workmanship, coupled with features not found in any other banjo, place the Lyon & Healy "Own Make" Banjo in a class unrivaled.

To verify these assertions the instrument should be examined and tested.

An important and exclusive feature in the Lyon & Healy "Own Make" Banjo is the Kershner tailpiece, with which these, with the exception of the Mandolin Banjo, are equipped.

By means of a thumb screw, any desired pressure of strings on bridge may be applied, thus making it possible to keep tone bright and snappy in defiance of adverse atmospheric conditions.

The tailpiece is rigid in its alignment with the strings, thereby preventing bridge from slipping sideways no matter how hard strings may be struck.

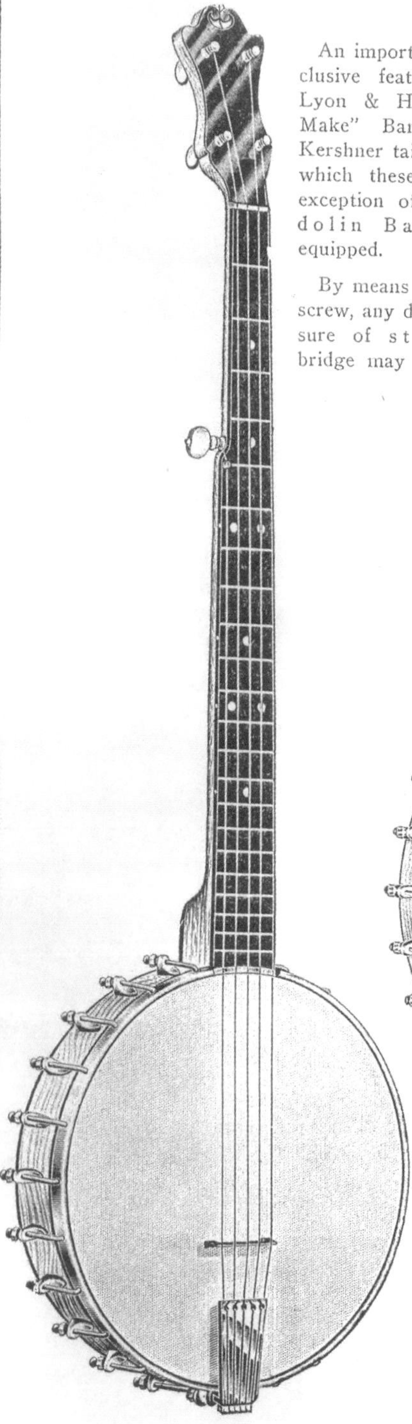

No. 175—Professional

No. 475—Tenor

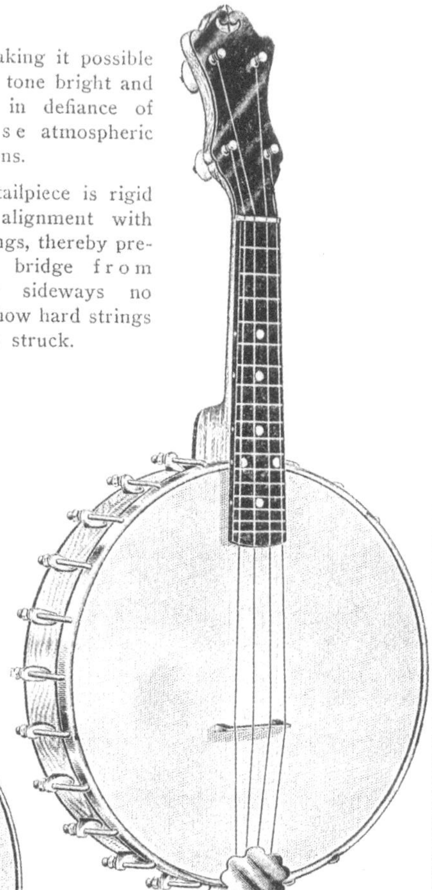

No. 375—Tango

No. 175. Professional Model, 3 octave scale. 10¾-inch shell of heavy laminated maple flanked on both edges with heavy black celluloid, improved combination truss which assures absolute rigidity, 22 nickel plated brackets of graceful design which are fastened to shell with heavy hexagon bolts, heavy N. P. straining hoop drilled longitudinally to receive bolt hooks, thus doing away with the old style of hooking over the top edge of straining hoops, and adding greatly to the beauty of the Banjo, besides permitting of a more even strain of the head. It is equipped with Rogers XXX calf head tucked on a square flesh hoop, thoroughly seasoned maple neck reinforced through center with a strip of hard black fibre, heavy ebony fingerboard bound with black celluloid and inlaid with pearl position dots as shown with an auxiliary set of dots on edge, ebony veneered head and heel, Kershner "sure grip" tailpiece, and a set of our "Own Make" new model "Never Slip" pegs with ivorine buttons. Each.................................**$112.50**

No. 275. Mandolin Banjo, same general description as No. 1100, with 11¾-inch neck, 9-inch fingerboard, ebony bridge, 8 strings. Each.. **112.50**

No. 375. Tango Banjo, same as Mandolin Banjo, but with 4 strings. Each **112.50**

No. 475. Tenor Banjo, same as No. 1100, but with neck 15 inches long, 16 frets, 4 strings. Each.................................. **112.50**

It seems that the business relationship between Lyon & Healy and Rettberg & Lange continued until 1923, when the Chicago firm launched their newly designed Washburn banjo styles. Three years earlier Lyon & Healy had introduced a short-lived premium banjo that was available in tenor, five-string, mandolin and 'tango' versions. Despite their very simple visual appointments these instruments were meant as top-of-the-line items destined to compete in tone with the very best banjos on the market, and were priced higher than all but the most expensive Washburns. These banjos had the elegant 'deco' headstock that was also a feature of the upscale Style B and C mandolins, and the tenor and five-string models came with the 'Kerschner' tailpiece for which Lyon & Healy recently had acquired the manufacturing rights. The mandolin banjo version sported the engraved tailpiece of the carved top mandolin styles.

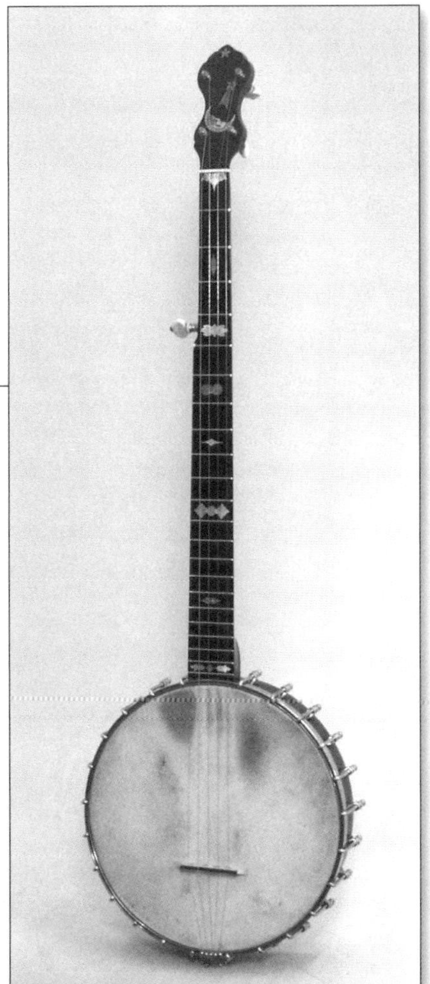

In a 1920 catalog the company proudly advertised their new line as the "Aristocrat of all Banjos", and proclaimed the superiority of the "Lyon & Healy Own Make" instruments. They did not mention the "own make" claim with regard to the any of the Washburn banjos that were described with great detail in the same catalog –and understandably so.

BANJOS—THE WASHBURN.

3-OCTAVE SCALE.

No. 1135. 11-inch German Silver Shell, Both Edges Wired, Ebonized Wood Rim, Double Grooved Hoop, 24 Oblong Brackets with Hexagon Nuts, Joseph Rogers Superior Extra Quality Calfskin Head, Choice Well Seasoned Mahogany Neck, Medium Dark Finish and French Polished. Heavy Ebony Finger-Board, Head and Heel Pieces, Sydney and Japan Pearl Figures Inlaid in Head-Piece, Positions on Finger-Board Handsomely Inlaid with Engraved Pearl, Fancy Engraved Pearl Figures Above and Below String Nut, Ebony Patent Pegs, Strings of the Best Quality, Sure Grip Tail-Piece, Nickel Plated . . . . Each $50 00

No. 1135.

Washburn Style 1135 (1912 catalog), likely made by Cole

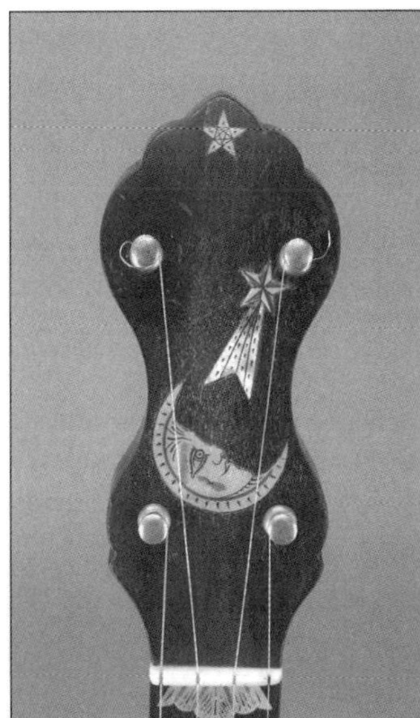

Cole Eclipse banjo with 'Man in the Moon' headstock inlay, 1900s (Retrofret.com, Frank Ford)

features of the Washburn banjo Styles A through C of 1923 and of all subsequent Washburn banjo styles until WWII was a new broad U-shaped tone ring, in the company literature designated as the 'air cushion resonator', but nowadays usually referred to as the 'donut tone ring'. It was a design of Walter Kirk and Louis E. Petersen, for which a patent application had been filed in 1922. A patent was ultimately granted in 1926, which explains the 'pat apld for' notice stamped on the rim of some of the earlier models.[108] Styles D and E of the 1923-1925 period did not have the new tone ring and were equipped with a simple metal clad wooden rim instead. A wooden resonator topped by a brass curved ring, described in the catalogs as 'tone amplifier', was fitted to all Washburn banjos after 1925. The resonator was not a Lyon & Healy design, but had been patented by one of the company's competitors in the banjo market, Weymann & Son of Philadelphia, in 1919.[109] Around 1928 the backs of the resonators were inlaid with colorful geometric marquetry patterns on the cheaper styles, and with an intricate scene depicting a tree standing in a rolling field on the most expensive models.

Gold plated version of the 'donut' tone ring on a Style 5185 banjo, around 1926

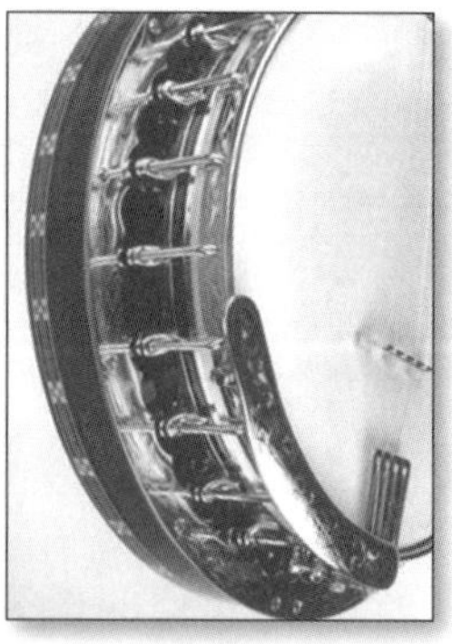

Detail of the brass curved resonator ring, a/k/a the 'patented tone amplifier', on a Style 5187 banjo. According to the Washburn catalogs this ring had a significant impact on tone (National Four-String Banjo Museum, Guthrie, OK)

Resonator marquetry inlay as used for the post-1928 Styles 5183, 5185 and 5187 (Howie Jay Specter, Mill Valley, CA)

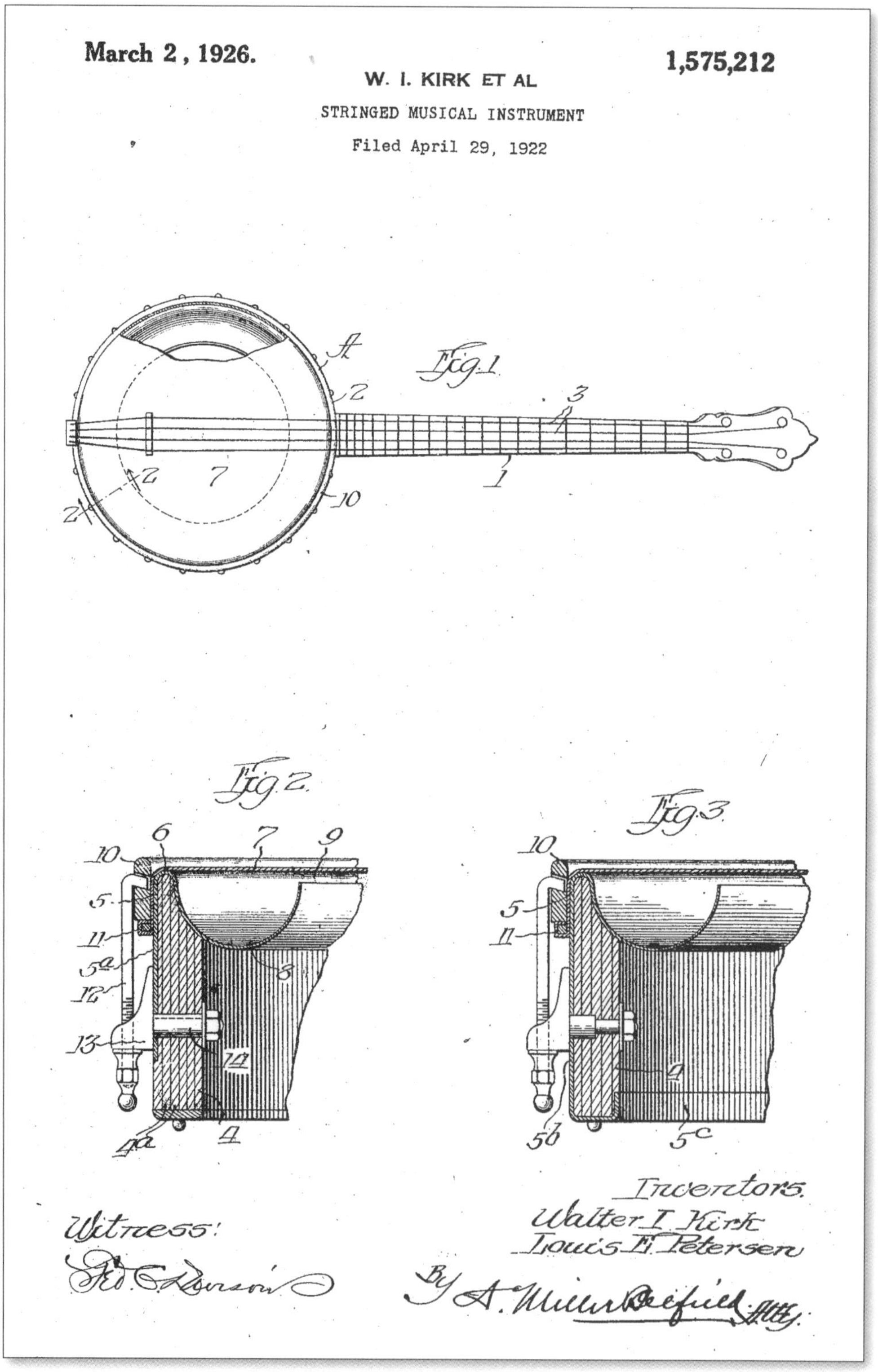

Patent drawing for the 'donut' tone ring

108 Patent number 1,575,212.
109 Patent number 1,312,882.

Without doubt one the most bizarre banjo designs of all time, the Shrine banjo was meant as a companion to the similar shaped guitar, mandolin and ukulele designs introduced around 1927/8. It featured a triangular tone ring apparently inspired by the 'donut' style ring that was a standard appointment of the Washburn banjos at the time, and sported a matching resonator inlaid with colorful marquetry patterns on its sides and back. A design patent was applied for and granted in 1927.[110] The designer listed in the patent documents, Paul Arthur, may well have been the author of the other Washburn shrine instruments.[111] The shrine banjo –which was never catalogued, but apparently positioned as a top of the line instrument- did not appeal to the players at the time and was discontinued together with most of the other triangular shaped Washburns only about a year after their introduction.

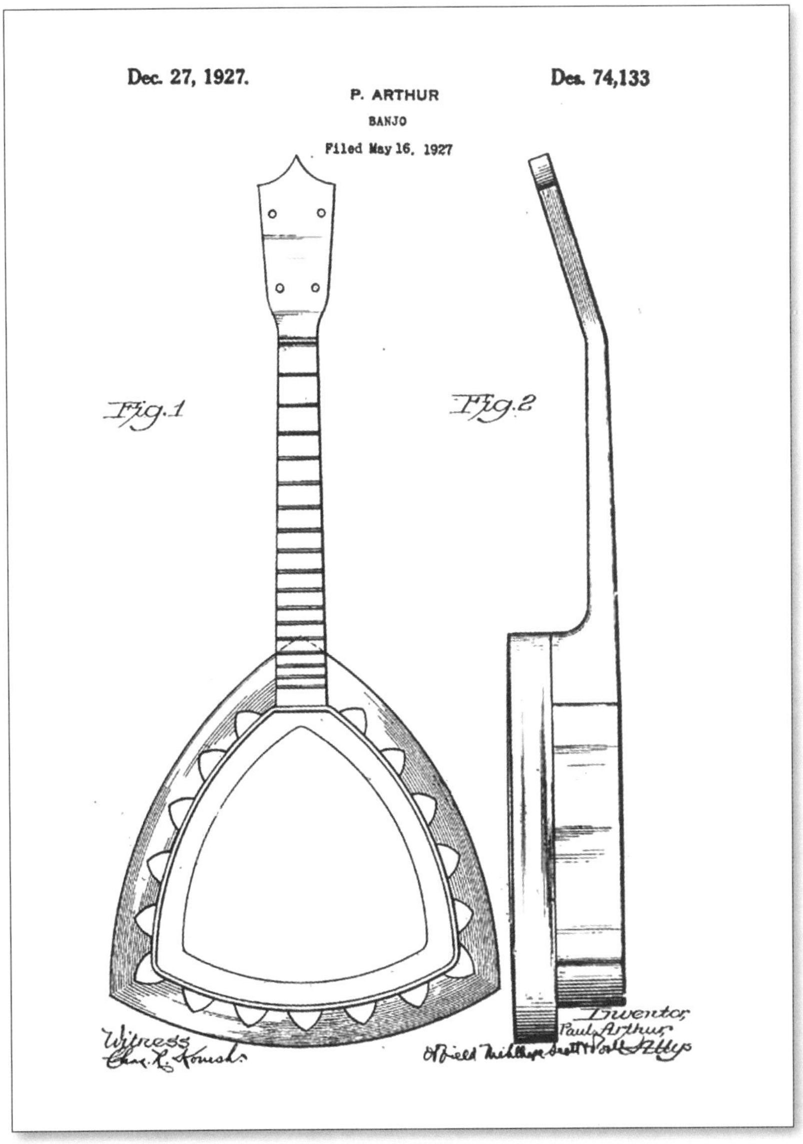

Paul Arthur's 1927 design patent for the Shrine banjo

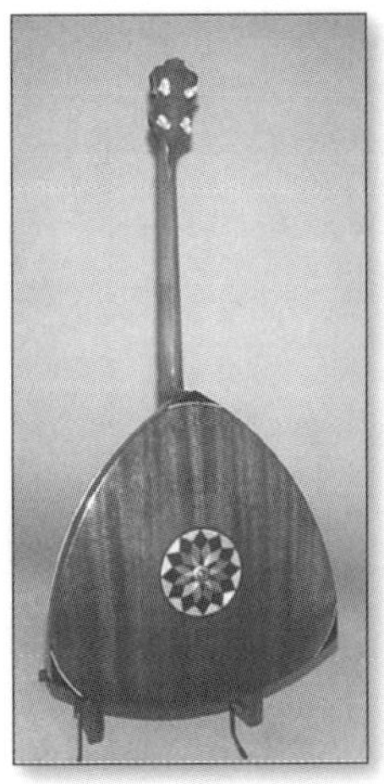

Washburn Shrine banjo with triangular tone ring, 1928. Playing it on your lap could be painful (Bernunzio)

110 Patent number D74,133.
111 The patent description claims this design for banjos, without mentioning other musical instruments.

1892 - Style 430 (Frank Ford)

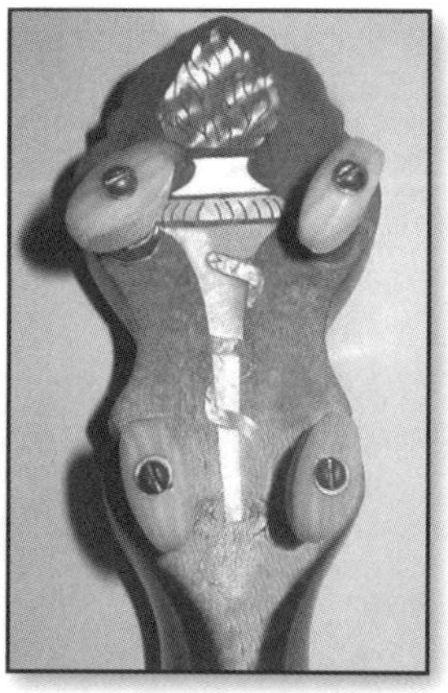

1913 - Style 5100 (Bill Destler)

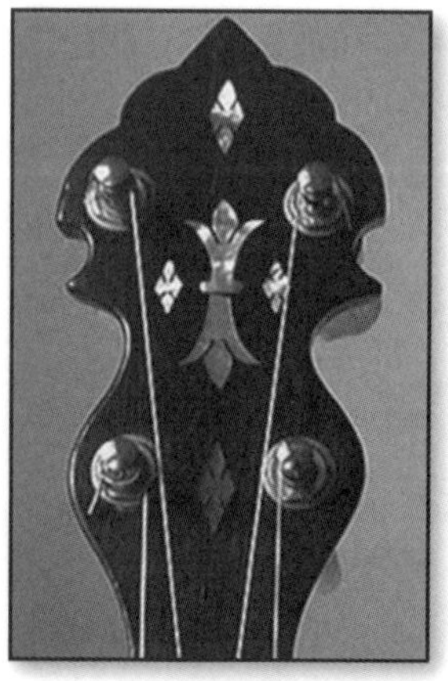

1914 - Style 815

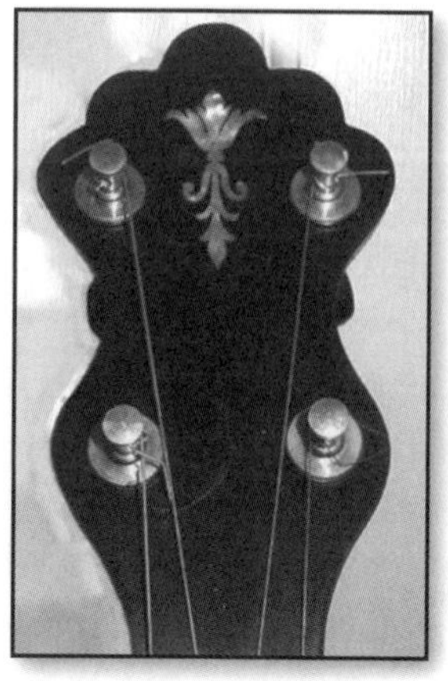

1917 - Style 1535 (Bill Destler)

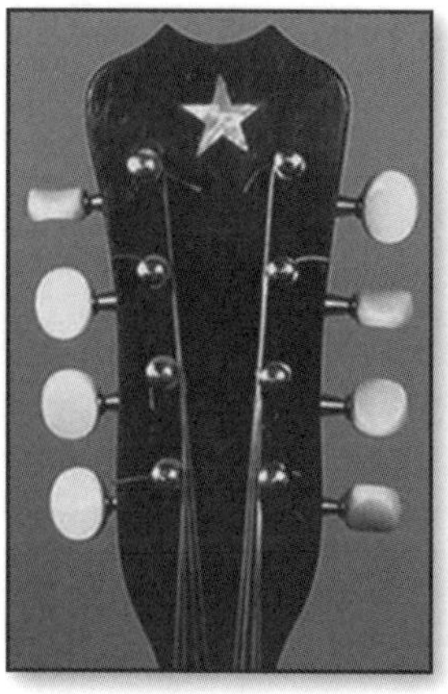

1917 - Style 1930

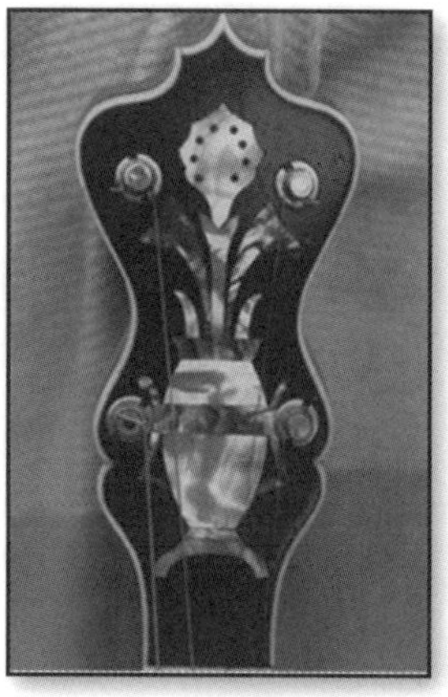

1923 - Style A Special (Guenter Amendt)

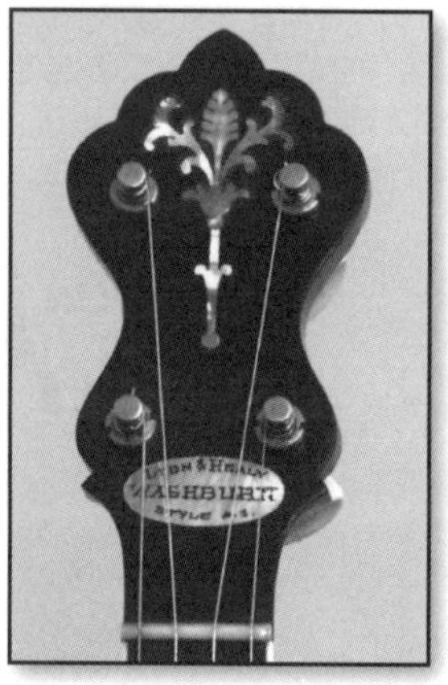

1924 - Style A1 (Retrofret.com)

1925 - Style 5115

Headstock of Regal Esquire archtop guitar, 1930s (Lark Street Music)

Slingerland Troubadour tenor banjo – but the minstrel is playing a guitar (Howie Jay Specter, Mill Valley, CA)

'Wandering minstrel' inlay, Style 5183 (Elderly)

4.3.2 Necks, headstocks, fingerboards, tuning pegs

Necks, headstocks

All Washburn banjos made before 1930 had ebony fingerboards with inlaid pearl position dots or figures. Until 1913 the Washburn banjo styles had one piece five string necks with a sharply cornered headstock pointed at the top. One of the new features of the 'improved' 1913 model line was a three piece neck with a center strip which Lyon & Healy claimed "makes the neck rigid as steel and obviates all danger of warping". On the more expensive styles this center strip consisted of multiple strips of wood. Another change was the slightly smaller headstock with rounded corners and five 'domes' at the top. Two small points were added around the base of the headstock of Style 550 and its later incarnations, Styles 1560-1960. The newly introduced eight string mandolin banjos received a completely different mustache shaped two-pointed headstock. Certain other models retained a one-piece neck after 1913, such as the entry level Styles D and E made between 1923 and 1925 and the cheaper four string 'tango' banjos made prior to 1923.

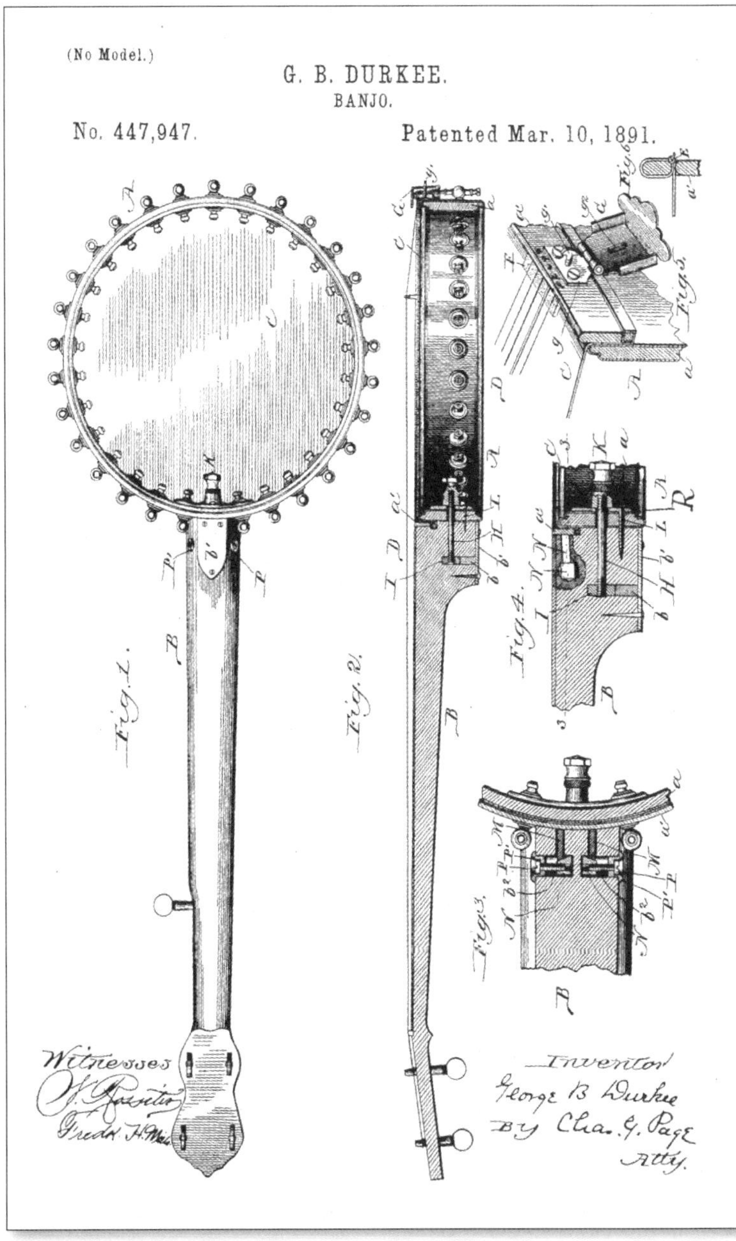

Patent drawing for George Durkee's invention for a banjo neck attachment system without a dowel stick (1891)

The 1923 Styles A-E had a slightly revised headstock with a more pointed end. On the most expensive Styles A and B two small points were also added below the G and E tuner posts. The necks of these two styles also contained a cross-grained piece of maple with a threaded brass insert that was dovetailed into the neck heel. The insert accommodated a large screw that fastened the neck to the shell. This feature in conjunction with the single piece 'donut' tone ring that fitted over the wooden shell made for an extremely rigid structure, eliminating the need for a dowel stick. Interestingly, in 1891 Lyon & Healy's foreman George Durkee had already received a patent for a banjo neck securing mechanism without a dowel stick, which was an exclusive feature of the upscale but short-lived Lyon & Healy 'Star' banjo models of the 1890s.[112] On the 1923/4 Styles A and B a dowel stick could be ordered as an option by those doubting Lyon & Healy's claims. The rigidity of this design is evidenced by a number of period instruments factory made without a dowel stick that have survived in perfect shape and working order. Nonetheless Lyon & Healy fitted all redesigned styles in 1925 again with a dowel stick in order to facilitate the attachment of a resonator that had become a standard feature on all models. The dovetailed neck insert was no longer mentioned in period catalogs and apparently discontinued.

Detail of banjo neck used for Styles A-B (1923-1935) with removed heel cap, showing dovetailed maple insert and neck fastening mechanism (David Hyatt)

The most eye-catching feature of the 1928 Washburn banjo line was the figure of a wandering minstrel, inlaid in pearl on the headstocks of the top-of-the-line Styles 5183, 5185 and 5187. The minstrel inlay was not exclusive to Washburn banjos. It can also be found in slightly different versions on other instruments made during this era, such as the Regal-made Recording King, Prince and Esquire brand archtop guitars and on Slingerland banjos, which suggests that the pearl figure was available in precut form.[113]

112 Patent number 447,947.

113 A late thirties Washburn guitar neck with the minstrel headstock inlay plus a female figure has turned up with pencil markings 'Special' and 'Troubador'. It is unknown if similarly appointed Washburn guitars have ever been built.

Metal Washburn / Lyon & Healy tag

As with other Washburn instruments, the small oval metal Washburn/Lyon & Healy tag was sometimes attached to the back of the headstock or inside the rim of banjos starting around 1923. This practice was continued until 1930 (see 2.4.1).

Tuning pegs

The Washburn banjos of 1892 were equipped with stylish looking friction tuning pegs made of walrus tusk with elaborately carved round or square buttons. These were replaced around the turn of the century by plainer looking molded white celluloid pegs with rounded buttons. The first instruments that were fitted with the patented 'Champion' adjustable friction tuners were Styles 1130 and 1050 of the 1896 model line, followed by Style 1025 during the 1900s.[114] The Champion tuners were also stock equipment on the 'improved' banjo styles of 1913. The plainest Styles 1015 and 1120 kept the celluloid friction tuners until these models were discontinued around 1917. Starting in 1925, all instruments except Style 5175 came with planetary geared tuners, with pearl tuner buttons on the most expensive models.

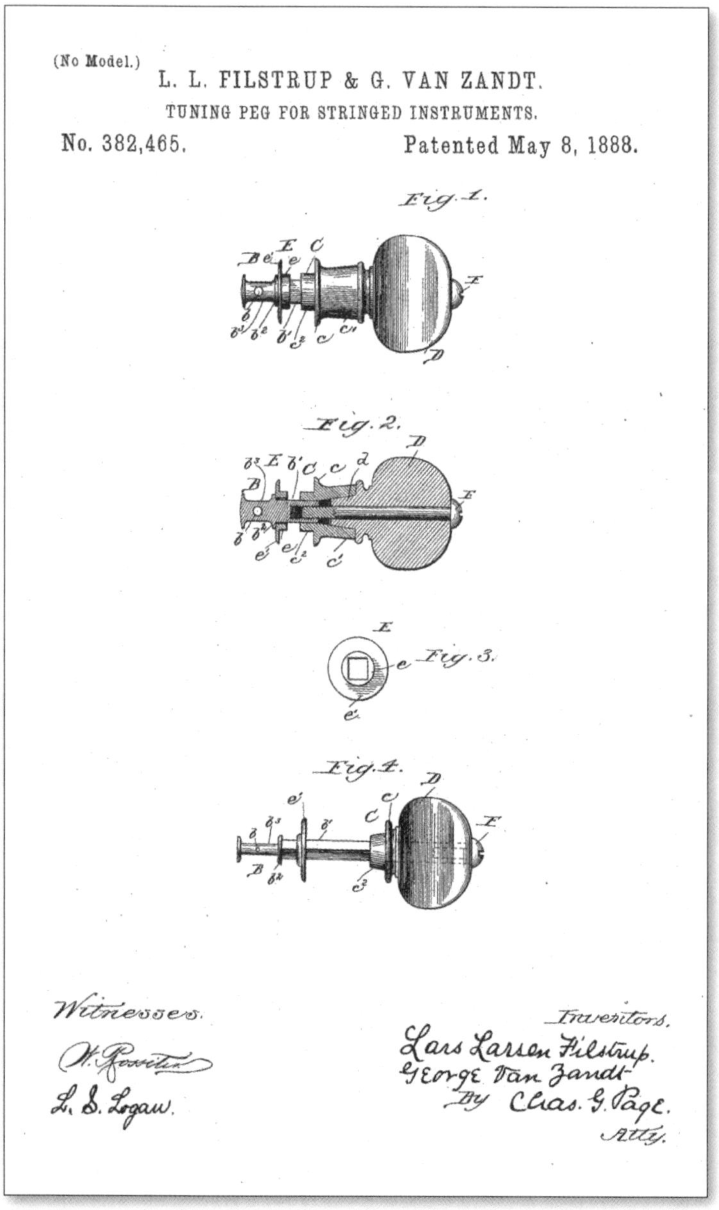

1888 patent for the 'Champion' mechanical friction peg tuners

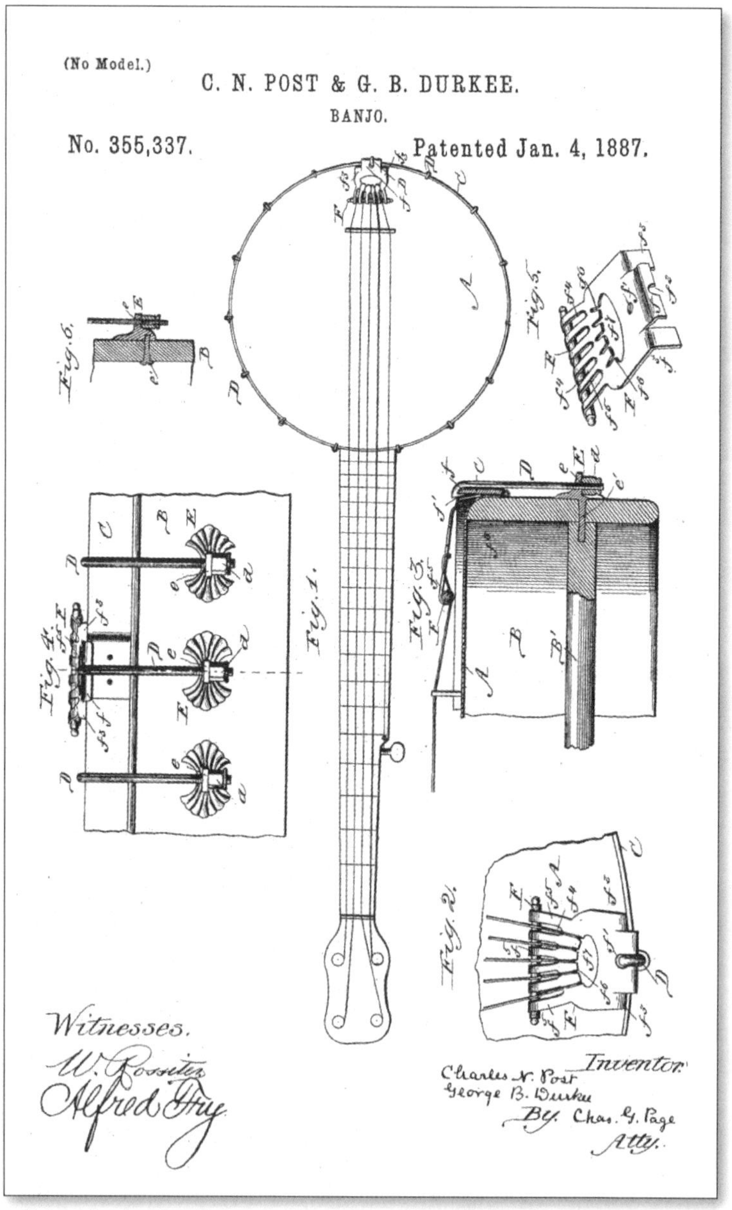

Patent for banjo tailpiece by Durkee and Post (1887)

114 Patent number 382,465, registered in 1888. Whether Lyon & Healy purchased or licensed this patent is unknown. The patent documentation does not mention Lyon & Healy (although inventors Filstrup and Van Zandt had the same patent attorney as L&H at the time, Charles G. Page).

4.3.3 Tailpieces

The Durkee/Post, Son and Elite tailpieces

George Durkee's first patent during his association with Lyon & Healy was granted in 1887 for a banjo tailpiece.[115] This easily identifiable lyre shaped tailpiece was designed by Durkee together with Charles N. Post, who would later become the company president (1905-1908). It was a successful design used on various Lyon & Healy banjos for over three decades and was available in 5, 6 and even 7-string versions, but never became a standard feature on Washburns. The earliest catalogued Washburn banjos came in 1892 with a tailpiece that seemed to be based on a design of Eleanor D. Son patented in 1894.[116] This tailpiece was also featured on the 1896 banjo styles except for Styles 1015 and 1120, which had a simpler tailpiece made of nickel plated brass with five curved 'fingers' holding the strings. It could be ordered separately for the sum of $4.75 per dozen, which was more than twice as much as the price of the cheapest banjo offered by Lyon & Healy around the mid 1890s. The post 1910 Style 1135 and all of the new banjo styles introduced in 1913 were outfitted with the so-called 'Elite tailpiece', a variant of the 'no-knot' tailpieces used by many banjo makers since the 1900s that eliminated the need for tying or knotting the strings. The 1923 instrument line saw the introduction of the Kershner tailpiece on all Washburn banjos except Styles D and E.

Tailpiece as fitted on the 1892 Washburn banjos (Frank Ford)

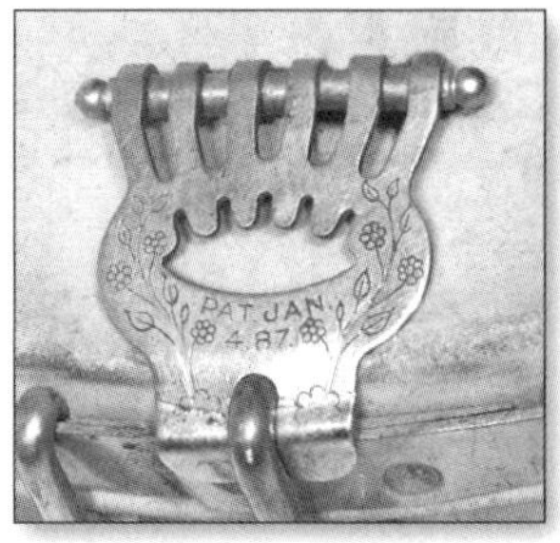

Durkee/Post tailpiece with 1887 patent date stamp

The Kers(c)hner Unique tailpiece

Both names "Kershner" and "Kerschner" can be found stamped on tailpieces of Washburn banjos made after the early 1920s. On the patent documentation for these tailpieces the inventor signed his name as 'Benjamin V. Kershner', probably an Americanized version of his original last name 'Kerschner'.[117] Lyon & Healy, not mentioned in the 1913 and 1915 patent applications, likely later procured an exclusive license for the Kershner tailpiece or acquired the patent. A 1925 catalog claims proudly but unjustly that these tailpieces were "designed, patented and made by Lyon & Healy", since these were

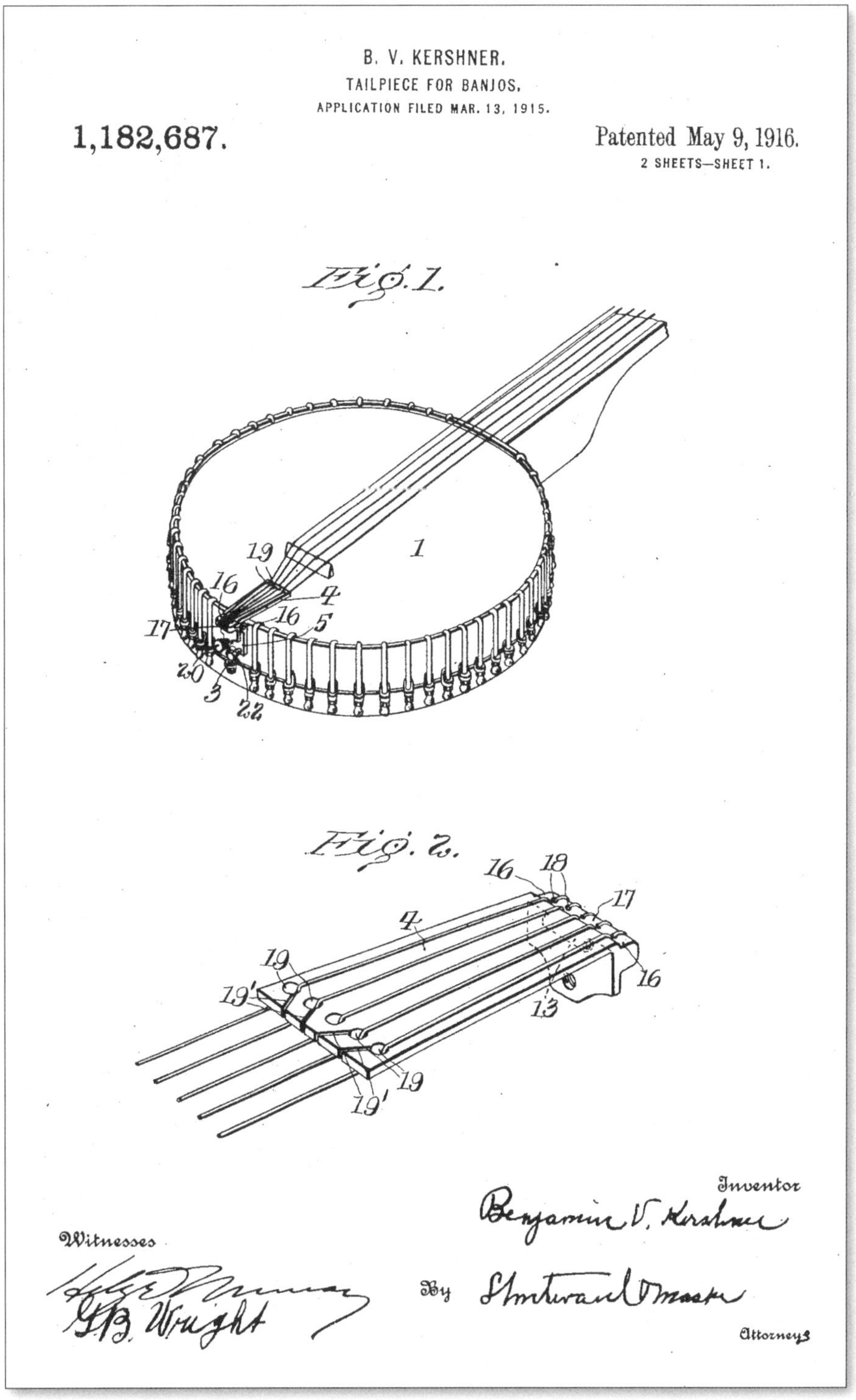

Second patent for the Kershner tailpiece, 1916. The first patent was awarded in 1914

115 Patent number 355,337.
116 Patent number 516,125. It is not known if the inventor was affiliated in any way with Lyon & Healy.
117 Patent nos. 1,122,945 and 1,182,687. The last patent represents an improved version of the original design.

not available on any banjo made by the company prior to the 1920s or offered for sale in the merchandise catalogs during this period. A 1920 catalog picture for the short scale Lyon & Healy "Trijo" banjo showed a novel tailpiece which resembled the Kershner design. Although the description stated that it was a "Kershner" tailpiece, it had in fact been designed in 1919 by Lyon & Healy's Walter Kirk and patented in 1921.[118] Kirk was also the inventor of the special brackets featured on this instrument, which were set into the rim and were claimed to add to the rigidity of the shell.[119]

The Kershner Unique tailpiece was available in four, five and six string versions and became a standard appointment on all Washburn banjos made after 1923. It can also be found on period Gibson and Vega banjos.

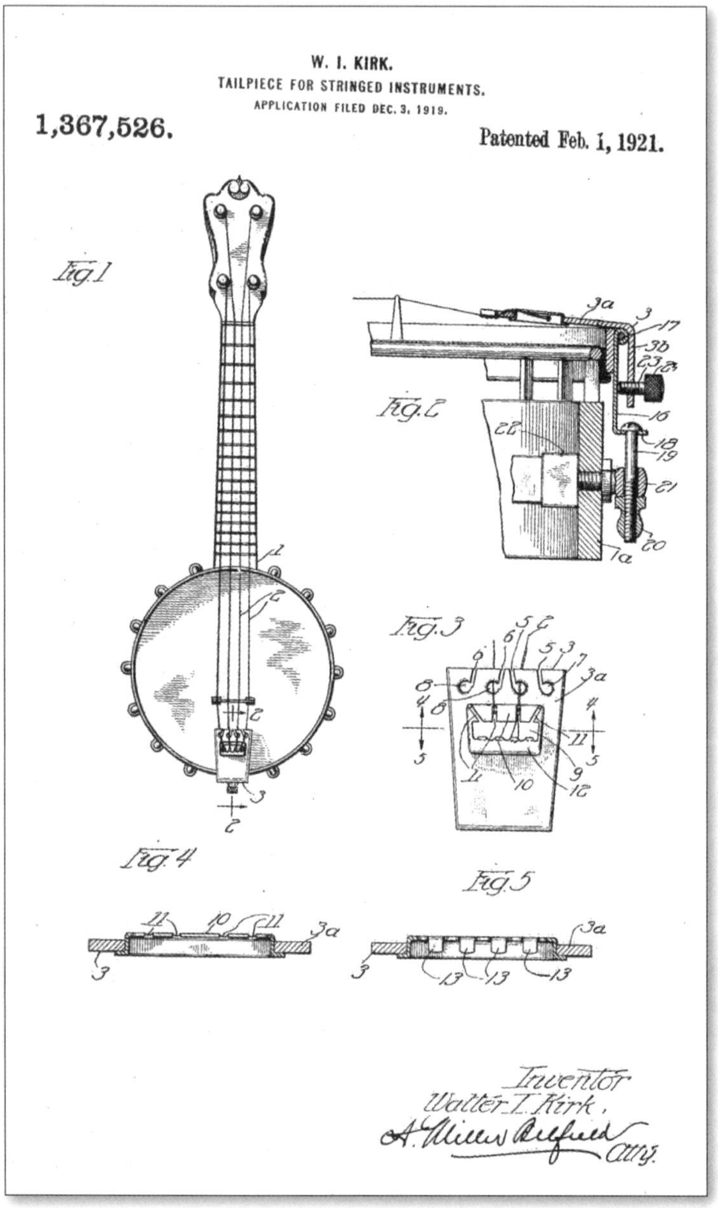

Tailpiece design for Lyon & Healy's 'Trijo Banjo' by Walter Kirk

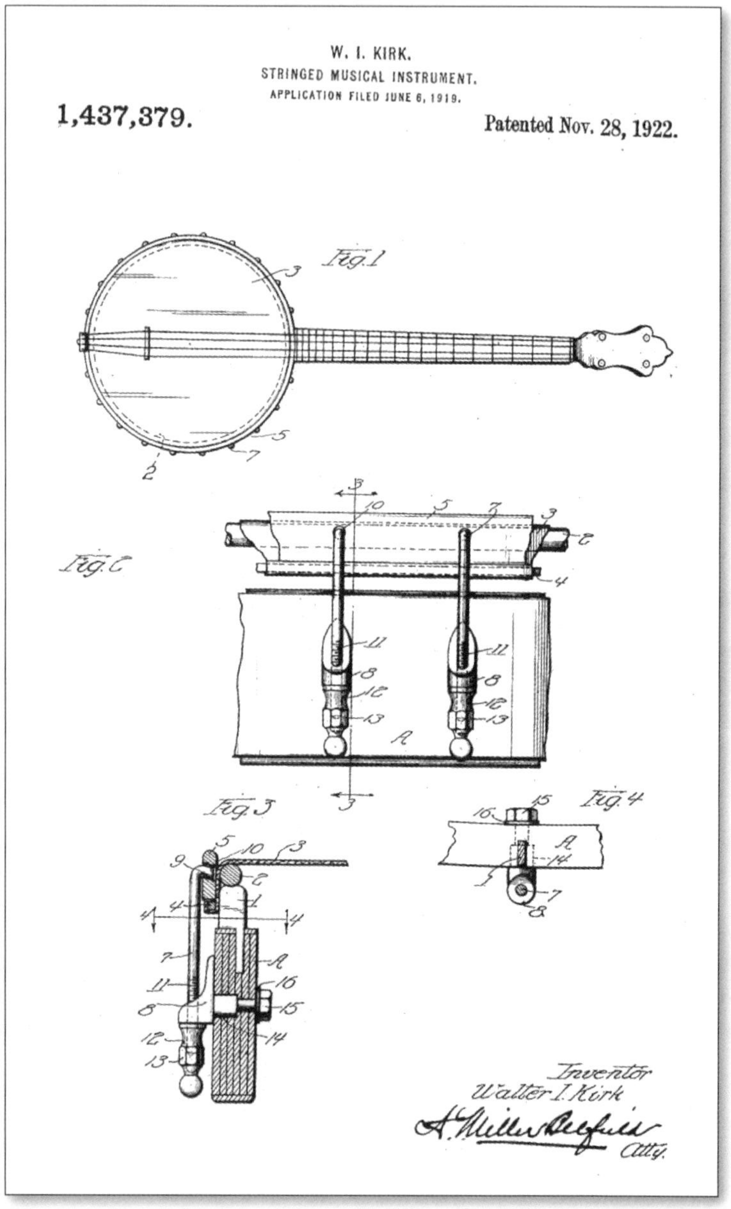

Improved banjo hooks and clamps in Walter Kirk's 1919 patent drawing

118 Patent number 1,367,526
119 Patent number 1,437,379

4.4 Banjo styles 1892-1930

Washburn banjo styles 1892-1896

7″ shell	9″	10″	11″	12″	
407	409	410			nickel plated maple shell, 14 (409: 16, 410: 18) brackets, 5 string neck, 18-fret ebony fingerboard w pearl dots/snowflakes at frets 1, 5, 7, 10, 12 and 17, ebony headstock overlay w pearl star inlay, carved walrus tusk pegs
			411	412	nickel plated maple shell, 24 (412: 30) brackets, 5 string neck, 19 (412: 18) frets, ebony fingerboard w pearl dots/snowflakes at frets 1, 5, 7, 10, 12, 17 and (after) 19 (412: 18), ebony headstock overlay w pearl star inlay, carved walrus tusk pegs, ebony heelcap w pearl flower inlay
		420	421	422	as Styles 410-412, but with engraved shell and elaborate engraved pearl floral inlay on fingerboard and headstock, 18 (421: 24, 422: 30) brackets, ebony overlay on back of headstock w pearl inlay, ebony heelcap w engraved pearl inlay
		430	431	432 (Presentation)	as Style 420-422, but with more elaborate engraved pearl inlays on neck and fingerboard, carved ivory pegs, carved neck, gold plated trimmings
			441	442	'wood compensating shell' w mahogany finish inlaid w wood marquetry, 24 brackets, 5 string neck, 19 (442: 18) frets, ebony fingerboard w engraved pearl figures at frets 1, 5, 7, 10, 12, 18/19 (binoculars at 7th fret), ebony headstock overlay w pearl star inlay, carved walrus tusk pegs
			452 / 462 (Banjorine)		nickel plated wood shell, 5 string neck, 30 brackets, 17-fret ebony fingerboard extending over banjo head w pearl dots/snowflakes at frets 1, 5, 7, 10, 12 and 17, ebony headstock overlay w pearl star inlay, carved walrus tusk pegs

Style 421, #553 (Frank Ford)

BANJOS AND BANJORINES—THE WASHBURN.

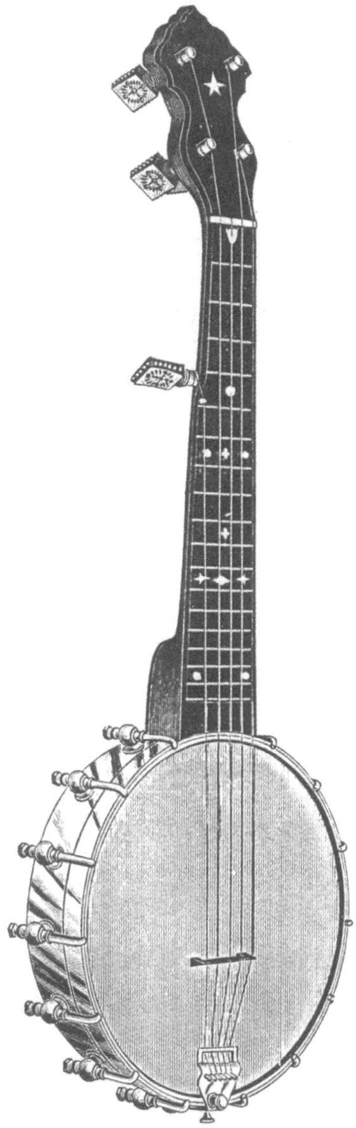

Nos. 407-410.

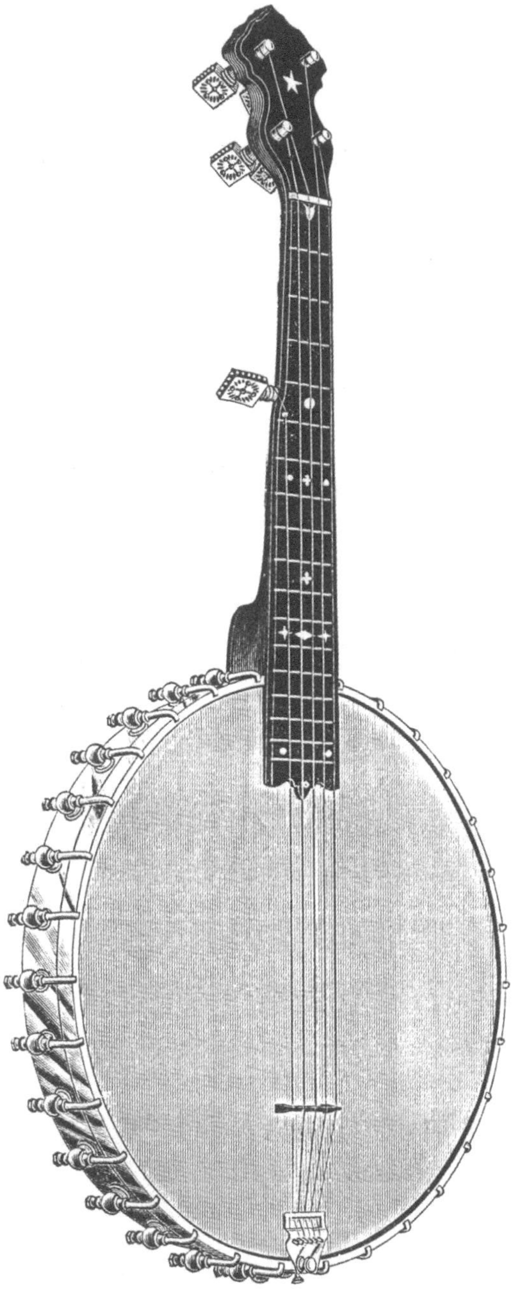

Nos. 452-462.

NICKEL-PLATED ON GERMAN SILVER SHELLS, BOTH EDGES WIRED, HEAVY MAPLE SHELL INSIDE, SHADED AND POLISHED. A BEAUTIFULLY PROPORTIONED NECK, WITH EXTRA HEAVY EBONY FINGER-BOARD, WITH PEARL POSITION DOTS AND ORNAMENTS. CARVED WALRUS TUSK PEGS, NEW AND IMPROVED "NEW DEPARTURE" STRAINER HOOP, ADJUSTABLE TAIL-PIECE, IMPERIAL BRACKETS, HEXAGON-HEAD BRACKET SCREWS, HANDSOME WASHERS INSIDE HOOP. ALL METAL PARTS FINELY NICKEL-PLATED.

No.		Each.
407.	Piccolo Size, 7 Inch Shell, 10 Inch Neck, 14 Brackets	$29 38
409.	Ladies' " 9 " " 16 " " 16 "	33 75
410.	" " 10 " " 17 " " 18 "	37 50
452	Banjorine, 12 Inch Shell, 30 Brackets	52 50
462	" " " same as 452, with elaborately Pearl Inlaid Finger-Board and Head-Piece	67 50

Styles 407, 452 (1892)

BANJOS—THE WASHBURN.

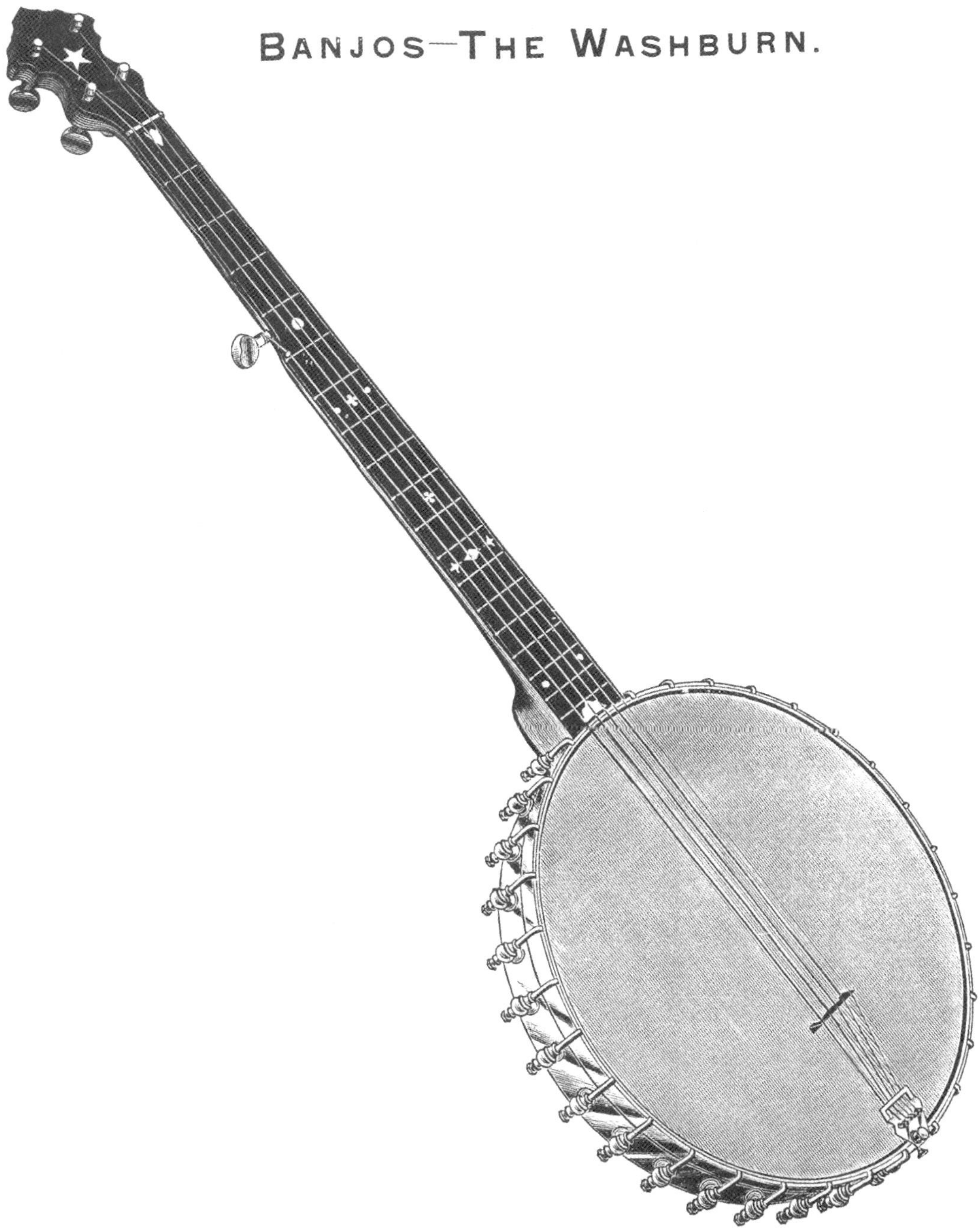

Nos. 411-412.

NICKEL-PLATED ON GERMAN SILVER SHELLS, BOTH EDGES WIRED, HEAVY MAPLE SHELL INSIDE, SHADED AND POLISHED. A BEAUTIFULLY PROPORTIONED NECK, EXTRA HEAVY EBONY FINGER-BOARD WITH PEARL POSITION DOTS AND ORNAMENTS. CARVED WALRUS TUSK PEGS, NEW AND IMPROVED "NEW DEPARTURE" STRAINER HOOP, ADJUSTABLE TAIL-PIECE, IMPERIAL BRACKETS, HEXAGON-HEAD BRACKET SCREWS, HANDSOME WASHERS INSIDE HOOP. ALL METAL PARTS FINELY NICKEL-PLATED.

No.		Each.
411.	Standard Size, 11 Inch Shell, 18 Inch Neck, 24 Brackets	$45 00
412.	Concert " 12 " " 19 " " 30 "	52 00

Style 411 (1892)

Washburn Presentation Banjos.

MADE TO ORDER.

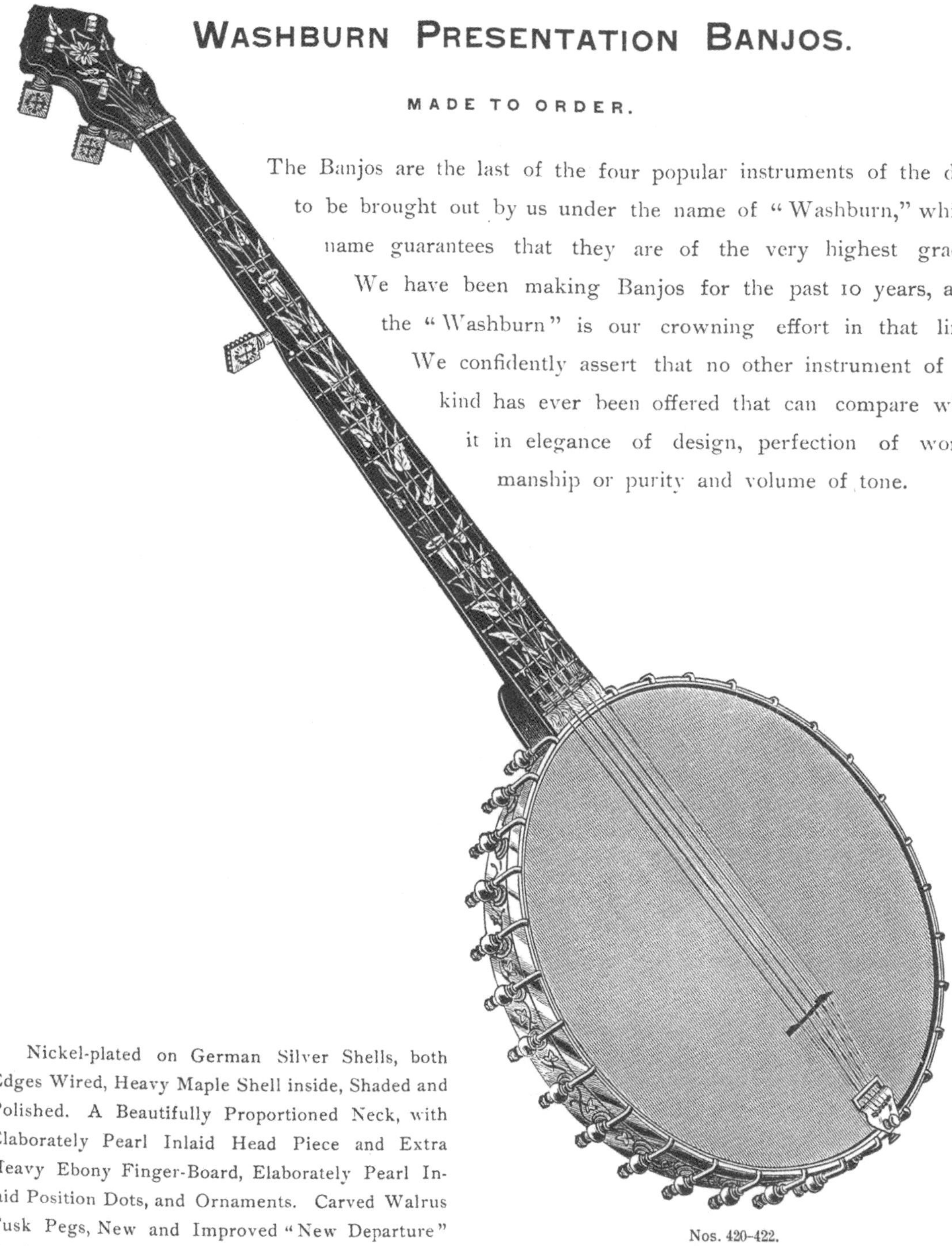

The Banjos are the last of the four popular instruments of the day to be brought out by us under the name of "Washburn," which name guarantees that they are of the very highest grade. We have been making Banjos for the past 10 years, and the "Washburn" is our crowning effort in that line. We confidently assert that no other instrument of its kind has ever been offered that can compare with it in elegance of design, perfection of workmanship or purity and volume of tone.

Nos. 420–422.

Nickel-plated on German Silver Shells, both Edges Wired, Heavy Maple Shell inside, Shaded and Polished. A Beautifully Proportioned Neck, with Elaborately Pearl Inlaid Head Piece and Extra Heavy Ebony Finger-Board, Elaborately Pearl Inlaid Position Dots, and Ornaments. Carved Walrus Tusk Pegs, New and Improved "New Departure" Strainer Hoop, Adjustable Tail Piece, Imperial Brackets, Hexagon-Head Bracket Screws, Handsome Washers inside Hoop, Engraved Shell. All Metal Parts Finely Nickel Plated.

No.					Each.
420.	Ladies' Size,	10 Inch Shell,	17 Inch Neck,	18 Brackets	$65 00
421.	Standard "	11 " "	19 " "	24 "	72 50
422.	Concert "	12 " "	19 " "	30 "	80 00

Style 420 (1892)

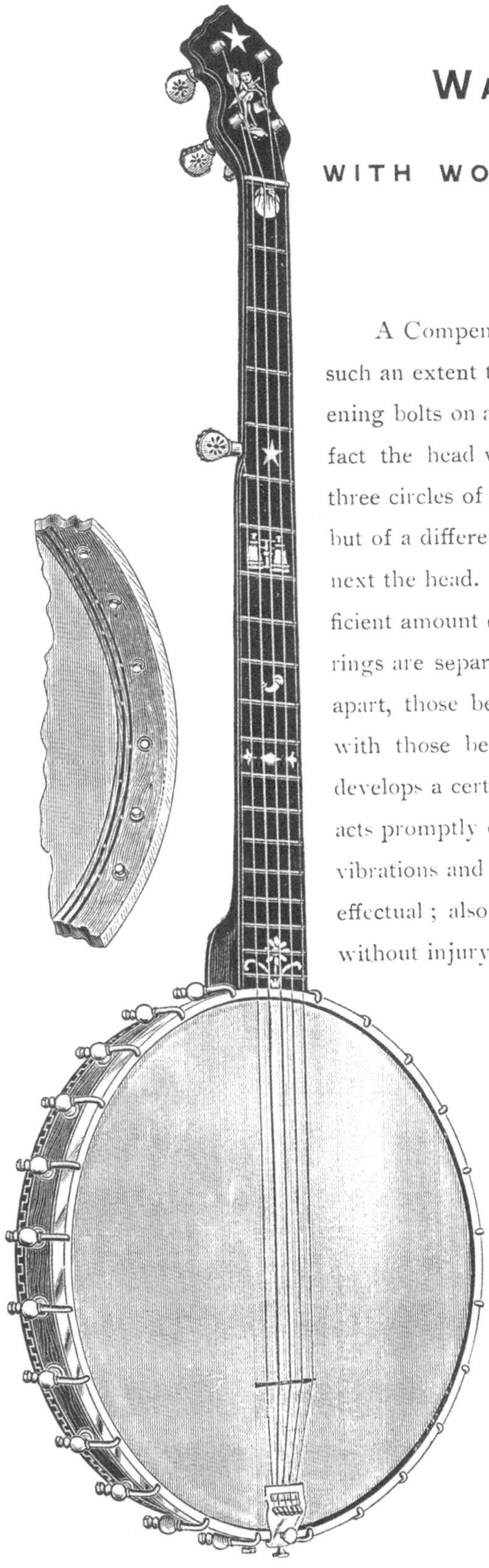

Washburn Banjos.

With Wood Compensation Shell.

Patent Applied For.

A Compensating Rim that will automatically adjust itself to such an extent that it is never found necessary to slacken the tightening bolts on account of the head becoming too tight: from which fact the head will last much longer. This rim is composed of three circles of hardwood, all of the same diameter and thickness but of a different depth, the two compensating rings being on top next the head. These are more or less yielding but retaining a sufficient amount of rigidity to keep the head entirely tight. These rings are separated by small metal discs placed about two inches apart, those between the first and second ring being alternated with those between the second and third. This construction develops a certain amount of activity, so to speak, in the rim, which acts promptly on the head in such a manner as to prolong the vibrations and to render the singing quality of the instrument more effectual; also permits the head to expand and contract slightly without injury.

Wood Rim Finished in Mahogany, inlaid with variegated woods. A beautifully proportioned neck with extra heavy finger-board, inlaid with pearl position ornaments. Carved walrus tusk pegs, new and improved "New Departure" strainer hoop, adjustable tail-piece, imperial brackets, hexagon-head bracket screws, handsome washers inside of hoop. All metal parts finely nickel-plated.

No.		Each.
441.	Standard Size, 11 Inch Shell, 18 Inch Neck, 24 Brackets	$ 59 50
442.	Standard Style, 12 Inch Shell, 19 Inch Neck, 24 Brackets	66 50

Nos. 441–442.

Style 441 (1892)

Washburn Banjo.

Style 1015.

VICTOR MAUREL.
(ABBEY & GRAU GRAND OPERA CO.)

"I had heard the Washburn instruments so freely praised in Europe as well as here that my expectations were very high, but I am free to say that the Washburn Banjo made for me surpasses my fondest expectations."

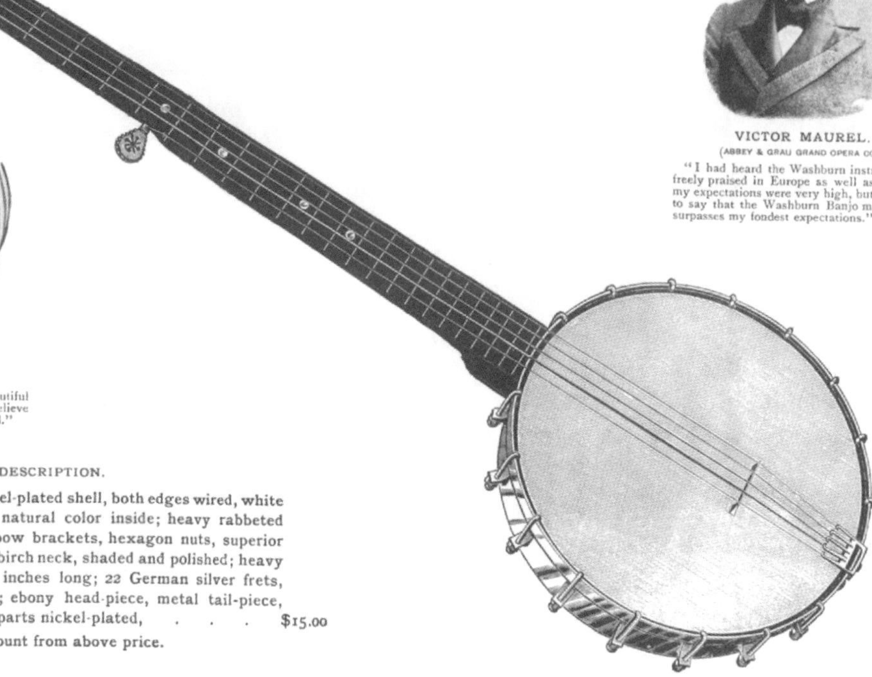

DANTE DEL PAPA.
(ABBEY & GRAU GRAND OP. RA CO.)

"I am more than pleased with the beautiful Banjo I obtained at your place, and believe that I have the best that can be purchased."

DESCRIPTION.

No. 1015—10½-inch brass nickel-plated shell, both edges wired, white maple hoop, finished natural color inside; heavy rabbeted straining hoop; 17 elbow brackets, hexagon nuts, superior quality calfskin head; birch neck, shaded and polished; heavy ebony fingerboard 19 inches long; 22 German silver frets, pearl position marks; ebony head-piece, metal tail-piece, fancy pegs; all metal parts nickel-plated, ... $15.00

No discount from above price.

The scale of all the Washburn instruments is true in all the myriad positions,—more, it is smooth and even.

45

Style 1015 (1896)

Washburn Banjo.

Style 1120.

THOS. P. RYAN.
(TEACHER OF GUITAR AND MANDOLIN, TOLEDO, O.)

"I use and recommend the Washburn instruments, because of their fine tone, correct scales and perfection in finish and workmanship."

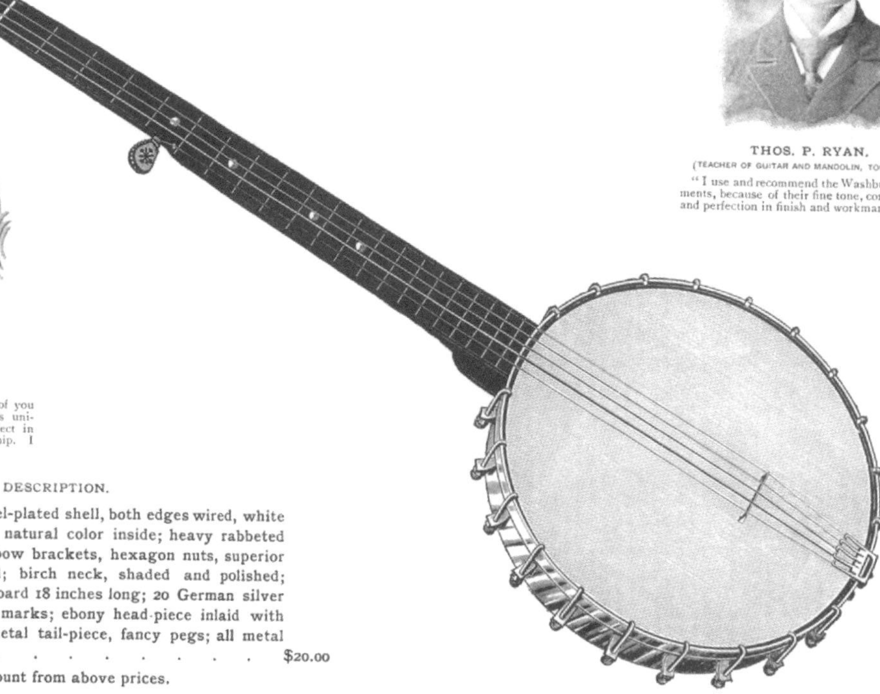

JOSEPH RUSSITANO
(ABBEY & GRAU GRAND OPERA CO.)

"The Washburn Banjo I purchased of you gives most excellent satisfaction. It is universally admired and is certainly perfect in quality of tone, finish and workmanship. I am more than pleased with it."

DESCRIPTION.

No. 1120—11-inch brass, nickel-plated shell, both edges wired, white maple hoop, finished natural color inside; heavy rabbeted straining hoop; 21 elbow brackets, hexagon nuts, superior quality calfskin head; birch neck, shaded and polished; heavy ebony finger-board 18 inches long; 20 German silver frets, pearl position marks; ebony head-piece inlaid with fancy pearl figure; metal tail-piece, fancy pegs; all metal parts nickel-plated, ... $20.00

No discount from above prices.

When Music, or Style, or Economy is sought, the Washburn instrument alone is bought. It leaves nothing to be desired.

47

Style 1120 (1896)

Washburn banjo styles 1896-1913

10 1/2″	11″	banjo mandolins	
1015*	1120		brass nickel plated (around 1910: German silver plated) maple shell, 17 (1120: 21) brackets, 5 string birch neck w ebony heelcap (1120: w pearl inlaid figure), 22 (1120: 20, around 1910 changed to 22) frets, ebony fingerboard w four pearl dots at frets 5, 7, 10 and 12 (1120 around 1910 changed to inlays at frets 1, 5, 7, 10, 12 and 17), ebony headstock overlay (floral inlay around 1910)(1120: w pearl engraved diamond inlay, around 1910 changed to floral inlay), white celluloid friction pegs
1025	1130		German silver plated maple shell, 18 (1130: 24) brackets, 5 string mahogany neck w ebony heelcap inlaid w pearl heart (1130: carved heel), 22 (1130: 20, during the 1910s changed to 22) frets, ebony fingerboard w nine engraved pearl inlays at frets 1, 3, 5, 7, 10, 12, 15, 17 and 22 (1130: 20), ebony headstock overlay w pearl engraved inlay and pearl star and diamond shaped figures, white friction pegs (1130: white mechanical 'Champion' friction pegs, also introduced on Style 1025 after mid 1900s)
1050			German silver plated engraved maple shell, 18 brackets, 5 string mahogany neck w carved heel, ebony fingerboard w nine engraved pearl inlays at frets 1, 3, 5, 7, 10, 12, 15, 17 and 22, ebony headstock overlay w pearl engraved inlay and pearl star figure, white mechanical 'Champion' friction pegs, gold plated straining hoop and brackets
	1135 (introduced around 1910)		German silver plated engraved maple shell w ebonized rim, 24 brackets, 5 string 22-fret mahogany neck w ebony heelcap, ebony fingerboard w seven (eight?) engraved pearl inlays at frets 1, (3?), 5, 7, 9, 12, 17 and 22, ebony headstock overlay w pearl engraved crescent moon and star inlays, mechanical 'Champion' friction pegs w ebony buttons, Elite tailpiece
		5904	(introduced around 1910, discontinued around 1912) 9 ½″ black wood ebony finished shell, 16 brackets, 17-fret rosewood neck w ebony fingerboard and headstock veneer, dot inlays
		5905	(introduced around 1910, discontinued around 1912) 9 ½″ black wood ebony finished shell, 18 brackets, 17-fret rosewood neck w ebony fingerboard and headstock veneer, engraved fingerboard inlays

* In many Lyon & Healy/Washburn catalogs published between 1905 and the early 1920s the style numbers of catalogued instruments and other musical items have a 'G' prefix. This is a reference to Lyon & Healy's Department G, which was responsible for all retail activities

Washburn Banjo.

Styles 1030 and 1050.

FRANCISCO TAMAGNO.
(ABBEY & GRAU GRAND OPERA CO.)

"The Washburn that I selected last week has proven upon thorough trial to be nothing short of a revelation, and I beg that you will send to my hotel one of your best Washburn Banjos with inventory."

EMMA EAMES STORY.
(ABBEY & GRAU GRAND OPERA CO.)

"I send you this note of congratulation upon your Washburn Banjos. My Washburn Banjo is the finest I have ever seen. The volume of its tone is truly surprising and of the most joyous and inspiring quality."

DESCRIPTION.

No. 1025—10½ inch German silver shell, both edges wired, white maple hoop, shaded and polished inside; new Washburn straining hoop; 18 Imperial brackets, hexagon nuts; superior quality calfskin head; fine neck, richly polished, extra heavy ebony finger-board 19 inches long, elaborately inlaid with pearl, 22 German silver frets; ebony head-piece inlaid with pearl figure; patent adjustable tail-piece; fancy pegs; all metal parts finely nickel-plated, ... $25.00

No. 1050—Same description as above, with finely carved neck; elaborately inlaid with variegated pearl, beautifully engraved on finger-board and head-piece; champion pegs; extra fine finish throughout; the "Mays & Hunters" pattern, . $50.00

No discount from above prices.

Washburn instruments are the standard, hence competitors talk of something "as good as the Washburn." Do not be deceived. Look for the well-known brand.

48

Style 1025 (1896)

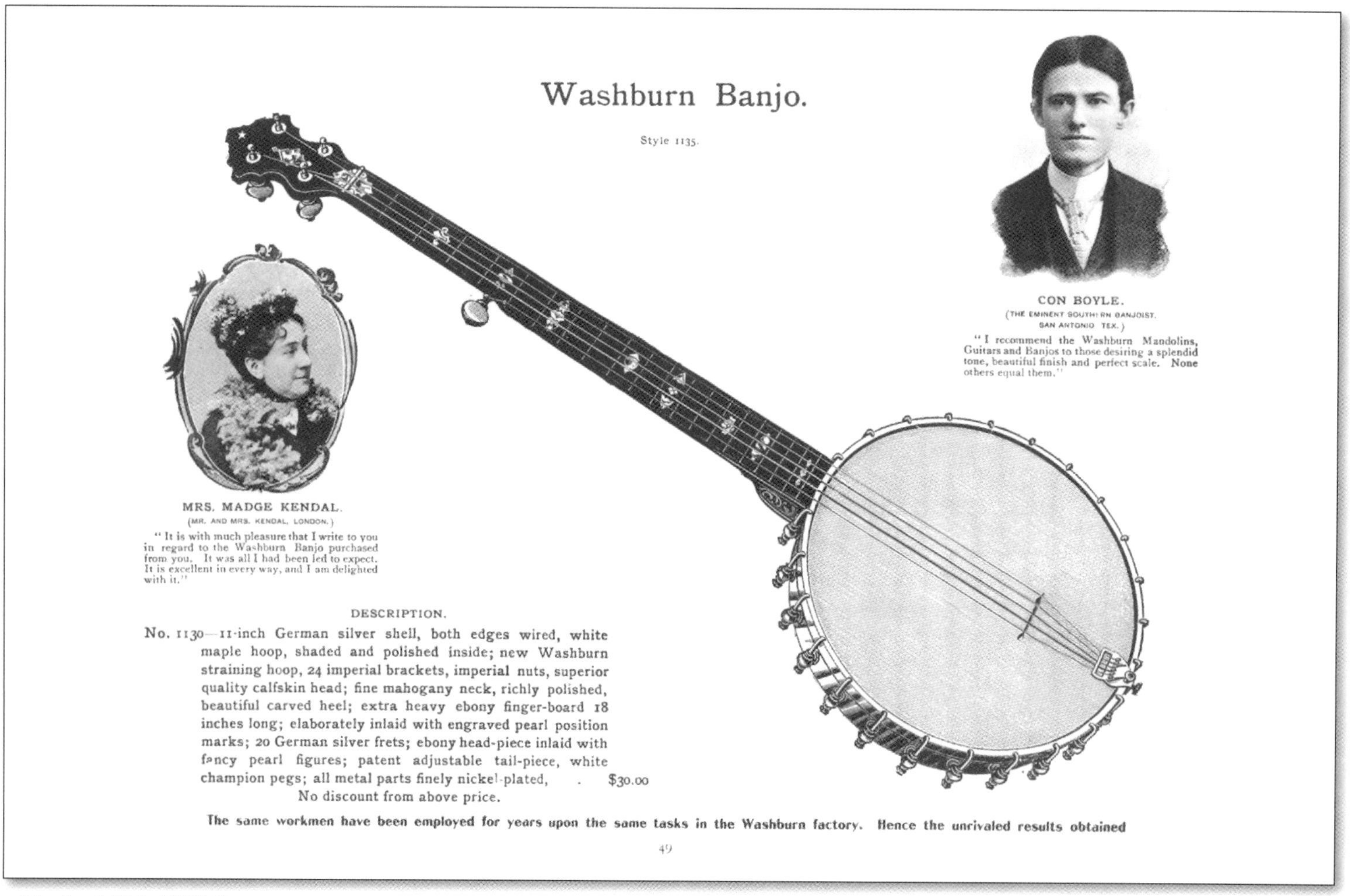

Washburn Banjo.

Style 1135.

CON BOYLE.
(THE EMINENT SOUTHERN BANJOIST, SAN ANTONIO TEX.)

"I recommend the Washburn Mandolins, Guitars and Banjos to those desiring a splendid tone, beautiful finish and perfect scale. None others equal them."

MRS. MADGE KENDAL.
(MR. AND MRS. KENDAL, LONDON.)

"It is with much pleasure that I write to you in regard to the Washburn Banjo purchased from you. It was all I had been led to expect. It is excellent in every way, and I am delighted with it."

DESCRIPTION.

No. 1130—11-inch German silver shell, both edges wired, white maple hoop, shaded and polished inside; new Washburn straining hoop, 24 imperial brackets, imperial nuts, superior quality calfskin head; fine mahogany neck, richly polished, beautiful carved heel; extra heavy ebony finger-board 18 inches long; elaborately inlaid with engraved pearl position marks; 20 German silver frets; ebony head-piece inlaid with fancy pearl figures; patent adjustable tail-piece, white champion pegs; all metal parts finely nickel-plated, . $30.00

No discount from above price.

The same workmen have been employed for years upon the same tasks in the Washburn factory. Hence the unrivaled results obtained

49

Style 1130 (1896)

Style 1120 (1913)

Style 5904 (1913)

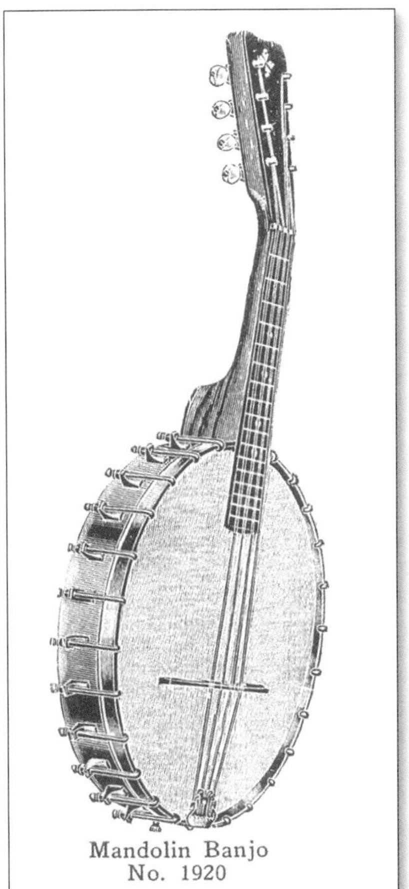

Style 1920 (1913)

3-OCTAVE SCALE.

No. Each.

1135. 11-inch German Silver Shell, Both Edges Wired, Ebonized Wood Rim, Double Grooved Hoop, 24 Oblong Brackets with Hexagon Nuts, Joseph Rogers Superior Extra Quality Calfskin Head, Choice Well Seasoned Mahogany Neck, Medium Dark Finish and French Polished. Heavy Ebony Finger-Board, Head and Heel Pieces, Sydney and Japan Pearl Figures Inlaid in Head-Piece, Positions on Finger-Board Handsomely Inlaid with Engraved Pearl, Fancy Engraved Pearl Figures Above and Below String Nut, Ebony Patent Pegs, Strings of the Best Quality, Sure Grip Tail-Piece, Nickel Plated $50 00

Style 1135 (1913)

Style 1530
(1917)

No. 1530.

Style 1535
(1917)

No. 1535

No. 1548

Style 1548
(1917)

Style 1560
(1917)

10 3/4″	10″	11″	banjo mandolins	
525				nickel plated wood lined shell, 22 brackets, 5 string three-ply birch neck w ebony heelcap, 22 frets, ebony fingerboard w seven pearl snowflake/dot inlays at frets 5, 7 (two), 9, 12 (two) and 17, ebony headstock overlay w pearl star inlay, plain friction pegs, Elite tailpiece
530				nickel plated maple 'patent truss' shell, ebonized inside shell, 22 brackets, 5 string three-ply birch neck w ebony heelcap, 22 frets, ebony fingerboard w seven pearl snowflake/dot inlays at frets 5, 7 (two), 9, 12 (two) and 17 w underlying strip of white holly, ebony headstock overlay w pearl inlay, Elite tailpiece, mechanical friction pegs
540				nickel plated birch 'patent truss' shell, top and bottom edges ebonized, 22 brackets, 5 string three-ply birch neck w ebony heelcap, 22 frets, ebony fingerboard w seven pearl inlays at frets 3, 5, 7, 9, 12, 15, 17 w underlying strip of white holly, ebony headstock overlay w pearl floral inlay, Elite tailpiece, mechanical friction pegs
550				nickel plated birds eye maple 'patent truss' shell w marquetry inlay on sides, top and bottom edges inlaid w ebony and white holly, 22 brackets, 5 string three-ply birds eye maple neck w ebony/white holly edged heelcap, 22 frets, ebony fingerboard w eight pearl inlays at frets 1, 3, 5, 7, 9, 12, 14 and 17 w underlying strip of black/white marquetry, ebony headstock overlay w pearl floral inlay, Elite tailpiece, mechanical friction pegs w white buttons
565				nickel plated birds eye maple 'patent truss' shell, top and bottom edges edged w ebony and white/red holly, 24 brackets, 5 string five-ply birds eye maple neck w white/black/white strip (also on dowel stick), carved heel w ebony/white/red holly edged heelcap, 22 frets, bound ebony fingerboard w nine pearl inlays at frets 1, 3, 5, 7, 9, 12, 14, 17 and 22 w underlying strip of marquetry, ebony headstock overlay w pearl floral inlay, Elite tailpiece, mechanical friction pegs w white buttons

Style 1935
(1917)

No. 1935.

Style 1948
(1917)

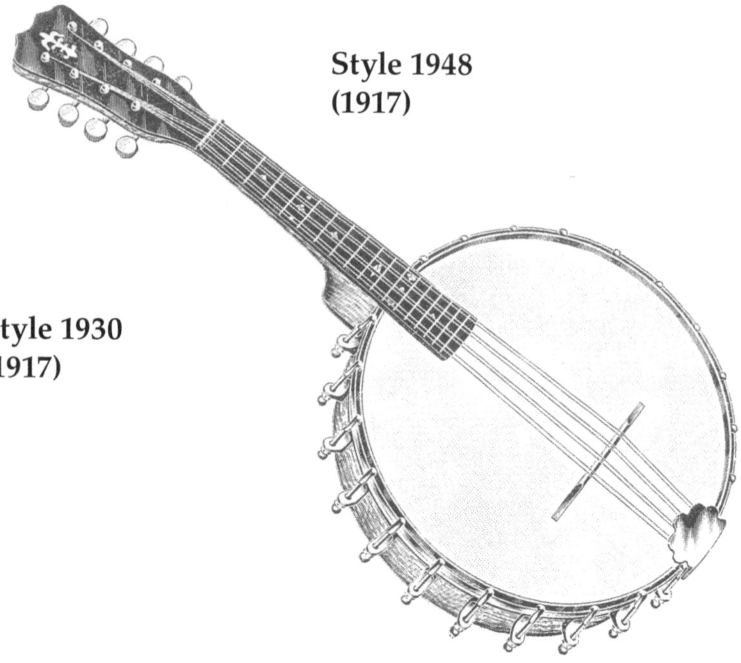

No. G 1948

Style 1930
(1917)

No. 1930

No. G 1748

Style 1748
(1917)

No. G 1735

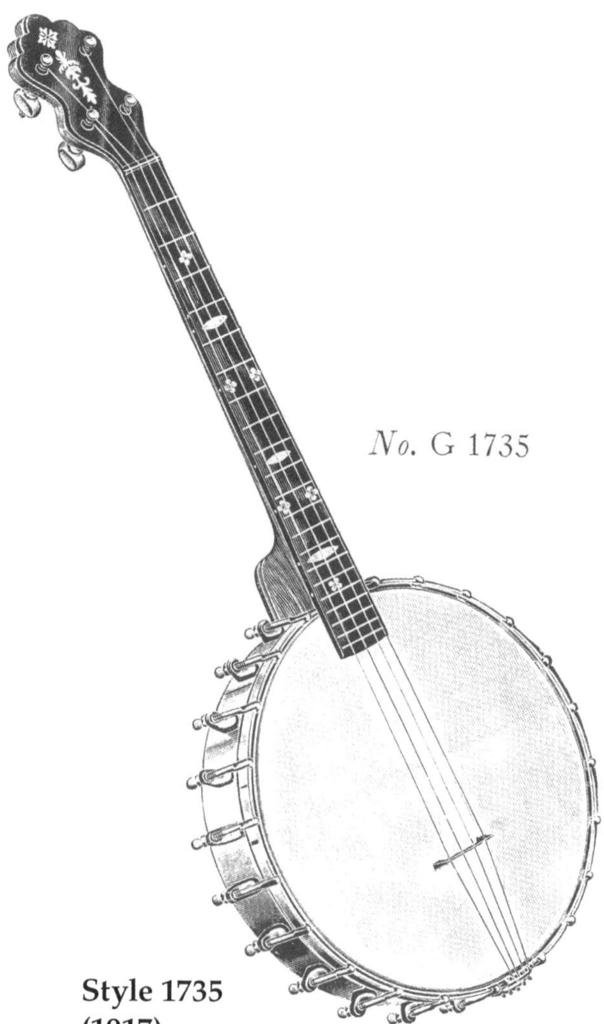

Style 1735
(1917)

Washburn banjo styles 1913-1917 (continued)

10 3/4″	10″	11″	banjo mandolins	
580				nickel plated birds eye maple 'patent truss' shell, top and bottom edges edged w ebony and white/red holly, center and bottom of shell inlaid w marquetry pattern, 24 brackets, 5 string five-ply birds eye maple neck w white/red/white strip, carved heel w ebony/white/red holly edged heelcap, 22 frets, bound ebony fingerboard w nine pearl inlays at frets 1, 3, 5, 7, 9, 12, 14, 17 and 21, three-ply dowel stick w nine inlaid red strips, ebony overlay on top and back of headstock w pearl floral inlay on both sides, Elite tailpiece, mechanical friction pegs w white buttons
5100				nickel plated birds eye maple 'patent truss' shell, top and bottom edges edged w ebony and white/red/green holly, center and bottom of shell inlaid w marquetry pattern, 24 brackets, 5 string seven-ply birds eye maple neck w white/red/green center strip (also on dowel stick), carved heel w ebony/white/red/green holly edged heelcap inlaid w goldfish pearl, dowel stick inlaid w five strips of green, red and white, 22 frets, bound ebony fingerboard w nine goldfish pearl inlays at frets 1, 3, 5, 7, 9, 12, 14, 17 and 22, headstock bound w white celluloid, ebony overlay on top and back of headstock and back of neck w goldfish pearl floral inlay on both sides, Elite tailpiece, mechanical gold plated friction pegs w pearl buttons
	1015	1120		as Style 1015 (1910)
	1025	1130		as Style 1030 (1910), but with headstock overlay w inlaid engraved pearl flower and round shaped figures
		1135		as Style 1135 (1910)
	1050			as Style 1050 (1910)
			615/715/815*	(introduced by or before 1914)
			625/725*	(introduced by or before 1914)
			630/730*	(introduced by or before 1914)
			640/740*	(introduced by or before 1914)
			650/750*	(introduced by or before 1914)

* Though no specifications could be obtained, it is likely that these styles are identical to respectively Styles 1920/1720/1820, 1930/1730, 1935/1735, 1948/1748 and 1960/1760 of 1917

Professional Banjo. Highest Grade

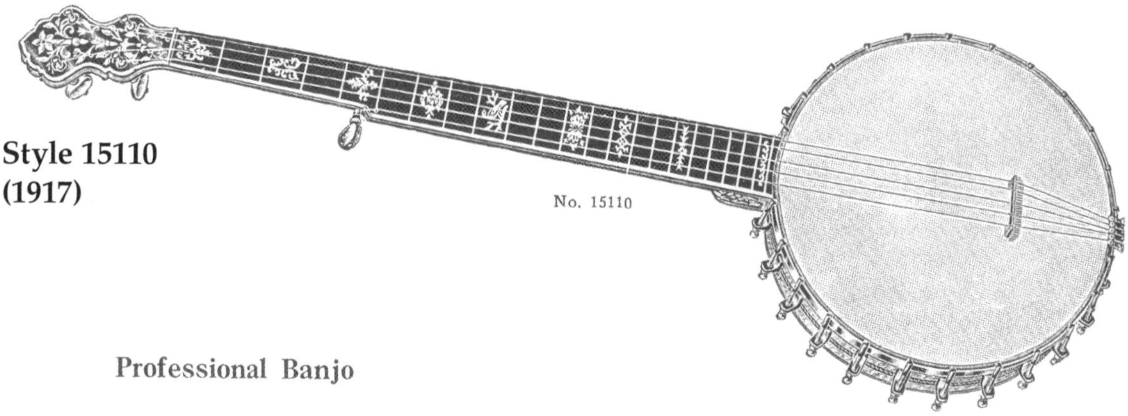

Style 15110
(1917)

No. 15110

Professional Banjo

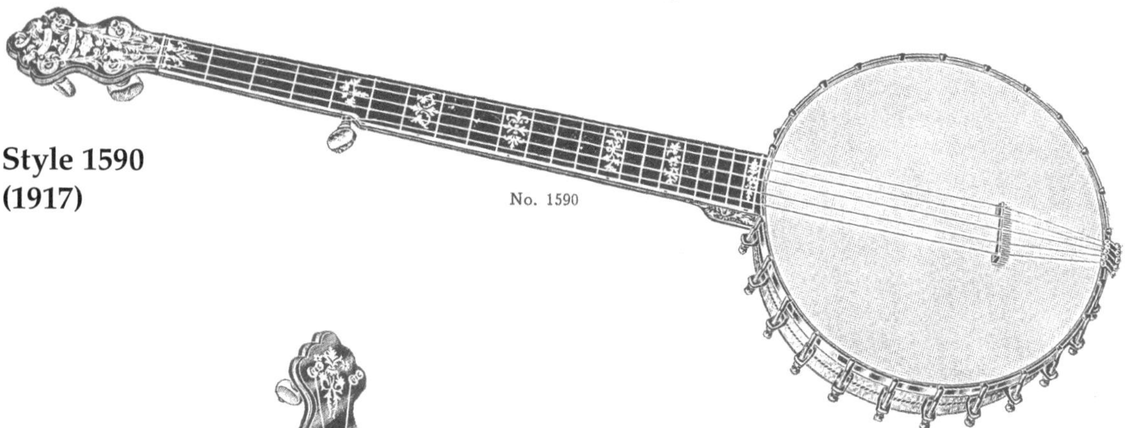

Style 1590
(1917)

No. 1590

Style 1570
(1917)

No. 1570

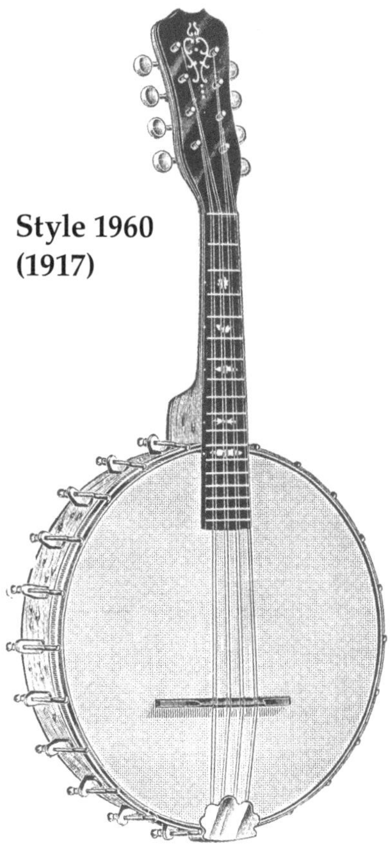

Style 1960
(1917)

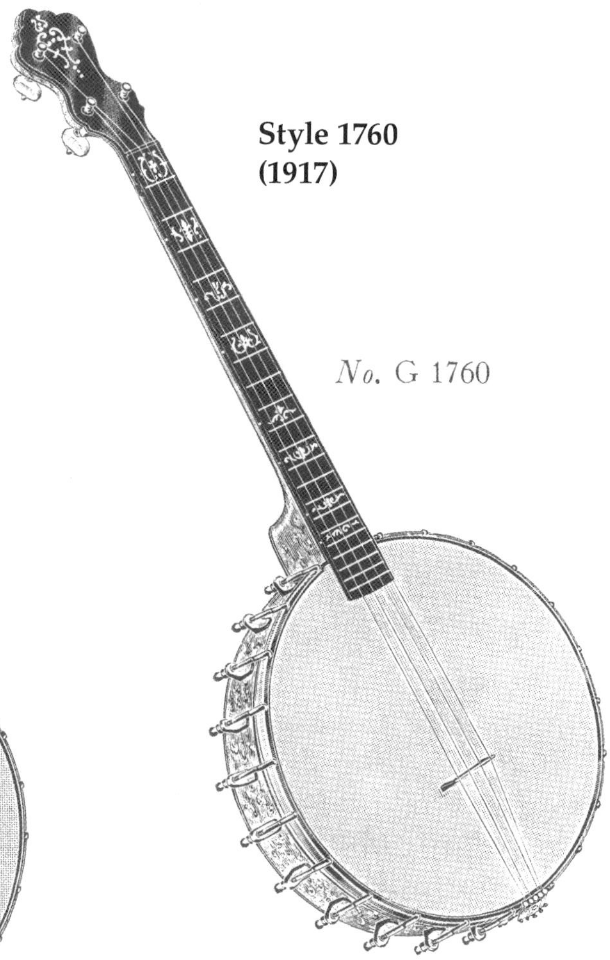

Style 1760
(1917)

No. G 1760

Washburn banjo styles 1917-1920

10 3/4″	11 ½″	Tenor	Tango	Mandolin	
1520*		1720	1820	1920	nickel plated wood lined shell, 22 brackets, 5 (1820: 4, 1920: 8) string three-ply (1820/1920: one piece) birch neck w ebony heelcap, 22 (1720: 21, 1820/1920: 17) frets, ebony fingerboard w seven pearl snowflake/dot inlays at frets 5, 7 (two), 9 (1520) or 10, 12 (two) and 17 (1720: 15, (1820/1920: four pearl dot inlays at frets 5, 7, 10, 12), ebony headstock overlay w pearl star or fleur de lys inlay, plain friction pegs (1820/1920: patent heads), Elite (1820/1920: mandolin) tailpiece
1530		1730	1830	1930	nickel plated maple 'patent truss' shell, ebonized (1830/1930: birch lined) inside shell, 22 brackets, 5 (1830: 4, 1930: 8) string three-ply (1830/1930: one or three piece) birch neck w ebony heelcap, 22 (1730: 21, 1830/1930: 17) frets, ebony fingerboard w seven pearl snowflake/dot inlays at frets 5, 7 (two), 9 (1530) or 10, 12 (two) and 17 (1730: 15) w underlying strip of white holly (1830/1930: five pearl inlays at frets 3, 5, 7, 10, 12), ebony headstock overlay w pearl inlay, Elite (1830/1930: mandolin) tailpiece, mechanical friction pegs (1830/1930: patent heads)
1535	1535**	1735**	1835**	1935**	nickel plated maple 'patent truss' shell, ebonized inside shell, 22 brackets, 5 (1735/1835: 4, 1935: 8) string three-ply birch or walnut neck (1735/1835/1935: one piece or three walnut neck) w ebony/white holly heelcap, 22 (1735: 21, 1835/1935: 17) frets, ebony fingerboard w six pearl inlays at frets 3, 5, 7, 9 (1535) or 10, 12 and 17 (1835/1935: 15) w underlying strip of white holly (1735: nine inlays at frets 3, 5, 7 (two), 10, 12 (two), 15, 17), ebony headstock overlay w floral pearl inlay, Elite (1835/1935: mandolin) tailpiece, mechanical friction pegs (1835/1935: patent heads)
1548	1548**	1748**	1848**	1948**	nickel plated birch 'patent truss' shell, top and bottom edges ebonized, 22 brackets, 5 (1748/1848: 4, 1948 8) string three-ply birch neck w ebony heelcap, 22 (1748: 21, 1848/1948: 17) frets, ebony fingerboard w seven pearl inlays at frets 3, 5, 7, 9 (1548) or 10, 12, 15 and 17 w underlying strip of white holly (1748/1848/1948: pearl snowflake inlays at frets 3, 5, 7, 10, 12, 15), ebony headstock overlay w pearl floral inlay, Elite (1848/1948: mandolin) tailpiece, mechanical friction pegs (1848/1948: patent heads)

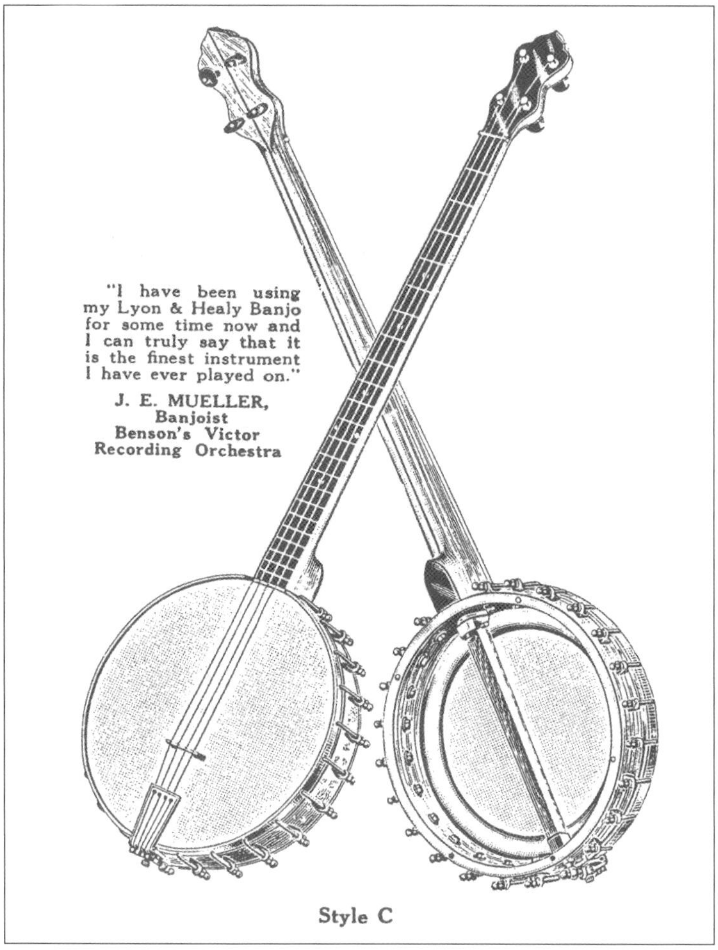

Style C plectrum (1923)

Style B regular (1923)

Style A tenor (1923)

Style A special (1923)

Washburn banjo styles 1917-1920 (continued)

10 3/4"	11 ½"	Tenor	Tango	Mandolin	
1560	1560**	1760**	1860**	1960**	nickel plated birds eye maple 'patent truss' shell w marquetry inlay on sides, top and bottom edges inlaid w ebony and white holly, 22 brackets, 5 (1760/1860: 4, 1960: 8) string three-ply birds eye maple neck w ebony/white holly edged heelcap, 22 (1760: 21, 1860/1960: 17) frets, ebony fingerboard w eight pearl inlays at frets 1, 3, 5, 7, 9 (1560) or 10, 12, 14 or 15 and 17 w underlying strip of black/ white marquetry (1860/1960: five pearl inlays at frets 3, 5, 7, 10, 12), ebony headstock overlay w pearl floral inlay, Elite (1860/1960: mandolin) tailpiece, mechanical friction pegs w white buttons (1860/1960: patent heads)
1570	1570**				as Style 565 (1913)
1590	1590**				as Style 580 (1913)
15110	15110**				as Style 5100 (1913)

* The last two digits of the style numbers reflect the actual retail prices of the respective models in Chicago at the time. Due to changes in price levels between 1915 and the early 1920s, the style numbers stamped on the Washburn banjos were often changed during this period and thus may deviate from the catalog numbers indicated above (e.g. 1738 for a Style 1735 etc.

** 10 ¾" shell prior to 1919, 11 ½" shell 1919-1920

Washburn banjo styles 1920-1923

10 ¾"	11 1/2"	Tenor	Tango	Mandolin	
1528		1728*	1828*	1928*	as Styles 1520-1920 (1917)
1538		1738*	1838*	1938*	as Styles 1530-1930 (1917)
	1542	1742**	1842**	1942**	as Styles 1535-1935 (1917)
	1550	1750**	1850**	1950**	as Styles 1548-1948 (1917)
	1565	1765**	1865**	1965**	as Styles 1560-1960 (1917)
	1590			as Style 1590 (1917)	
	15110			as Style 15110 (1917)	

* 10 ¾" shell

** 11 ½" shell

Style D mandolin banjo (1923)

Style A1 plectrum (Retrofret.com)

Style A special (Guenter Amendt)

Style 5175 (1925)

Style 5177 (1925)

Washburn banjo styles 1923-1925

10 3/4" Tenor	Regular	Plectrum	Mandolin	
Style E	E	E	E	5-ply laminated hardwood shell, mahogany finish, 22 brackets, one piece mahogany finished neck w ebony heelcap, unbound 17-fret (plectrum/ regulation: 22-fret) ebony fingerboard w four pearl dots at frets 5, 7, 10 and 12 (tenor version), ebonized headstock overlay, mechanical friction pegs (mandolin: patent heads) w black buttons, 'no-knot' tailpiece
Style D	D	D	D	5-ply laminated maple shell, natural finish, 22 brackets, one piece neck w ebony heelcap, unbound 17-fret (plectrum/regulation: 22-fret) ebony fingerboard w four pearl dots at frets 5, 7, 10 and 12 (tenor version), ebonized headstock overlay, mechanical friction pegs (mandolin: patent heads) w black buttons, 'no-knot' tailpiece
Style C	C	C	C	6-ply* maple shell w 'donut' tone ring, 22 brackets, maple neck w black center strip and ebony heelcap, 17-fret (plectrum/regulation: 22-fret) ebonized fingerboard w five pearl dots at frets 5, 7, 10 and 12 (2 dots) bound w white celluloid , (plectrum/regulation: six dots at frets 5, 7, 10, 12 (two) and 15) ebony headstock overlay, mechanical friction pegs w black buttons, Kershner Unique tailpiece
Style B	B	B		6-ply maple shell w 'donut' tone ring and inlaid wood strips, bottom edge capped w birds eye maple, 22 brackets, maple neck w black center strip and ebony heelcap, unbound 17-fret (plectrum/ regulation: 22-fret) ebony fingerboard w five pearl inlays at frets 3, 5, 7, 10 and 12, ebony headstock overlay w pearl flowerpot inlay, mechanical friction pegs w white buttons, Kershner Unique tailpiece, dowel stick optional
Style A	A	A		6-ply maple shell w 'donut' tone ring, bottom edge capped w ebony, 30 or 22 brackets**, birds eye maple neck w black center strip and ebony heelcap, 17-fret (plectrum/regulation: 22-fret) ebony fingerboard bound w white celluloid w seven pearl inlays at frets 1, 3, 5, 7, 10, 12 and 15 (tenor version), ebony headstock overlay w pearl floral inlay, mechanical friction pegs w white buttons, Kershner Unique tailpiece, nickel plated parts, dowel stick optional (Style A 'Special': gold plated parts, engraved shell, carved heel, fancier multicolored pearl fingerboard inlays, back rim and heelcap bound with celluloid and inlaid with pearl, oversized pearl/abalone flowerpot inlay on celluloid bound headstock)

Style 5177 (1939)

Style 5179 (1939)

Style 5179 (1925)

Style 5181 (1925)

Washburn banjo styles 1923-1925 (continued)

10 3/4" Tenor	Regular	Plectrum	Mandolin	
Style A1	A1	A1		(introduced around 1924) as Style A, but with added pie-sectioned wooden resonator with marquetry inlay on sides, 22 brackets, geared 'Planet' tuners, oval pearl plaque with 'Lyon & Healy/Washburn/Style A1 on headstock

* In the 1923/4 catalog the shell of Styles A, B and C is incorrectly described as 7-ply

** The 1923-24 catalog specifies 30 brackets, but Style A changed to a 22-bracket rim starting around late 1923. The earliest tenor versions of Style A did not have the 15th fret fingerboard inlay

Washburn banjo styles 1925-1928

10 3/4" Tenor	Plectrum	Regulation	Mandolin	Guitar	
5175/6 (Inspiration)	5150	5100	5125	5115	mahogany finished 10 ¾" (5176, 5115: 12") maple shell w 'donut' tone ring, lower edge bound w tortoise celluloid and capped w ebony veneer, 22 brackets, three-ply mahogany finished maple neck w ebony heelcap, 17-fret ebony fingerboard w five pearl dots at frets 5, 7, 10 and 12 (2) bound w white celluloid, ebony headstock overlay (5115: slotted headstock w three on a side tuners, later changed to a solid headstock w mechanical friction pegs), mechanical friction pegs, open back design, Kershner Unique tailpiece[120], nickel plated parts, gold plated steel strings*
5177 5152 (Dansant)	5102				mahogany finished maple shell w 'donut' tone ring, lower edge bound w tortoise celluloid and capped w ebony veneer, 22 brackets, three-ply neck w ebony heelcap, 17 or 19-fret ebony fingerboard** w twelve pearl inlays at frets 5 (3), 7 (3), 10 (3) and 12 (3) bound w white celluloid, ebony headstock overlay w pearl torch shaped inlay, geared tuners w white buttons, resonator w engraved flange and marquetry inlay on sides, Kershner Unique tailpiece, brass arm rest, nickel plated parts, gold plated steel strings
5179 (Classic)					natural finished birds eye maple shell w 'donut' tone ring, lower edge bound w tortoise celluloid and capped w ebony veneer, three-ply birds eye maple neck w ebony heelcap, 22 brackets, 19-fret ebony fingerboard w pearl inlays at frets 1, 3, 5, 7, 10, 12 and 15, ebony headstock overlay w pearl torch shaped inlay, geared tuners w white buttons, resonator w engraved flange and zigzag marquetry strip inlaid on sides and inlaid backstrip, Kershner Unique tailpiece, brass arm rest, nickel plated parts, gold plated steel strings

120 The 1925 catalog spelling is 'Kerschner' as compared to the earlier 'Kershner'. Both spellings can be found stamped on period tailpieces.

Style 5181 (1939)

Style 5183 (1925)

Style 5183 (1939)

Washburn banjo styles 1925-1928 (continued)

10 3/4" Tenor	Plectrum	Regulation	Mandolin	Guitar	
5181 (Syncopator)	5156	5106			mahogany finished maple shell w 'donut' tone ring, lower edge bound w tortoise celluloid and capped w ebony veneer, three-ply mahogany finish maple neck w ebony heelcap, 19-fret ebony fingerboard w pearl inlays at frets 1, 3, 5, 7, 10, 12 and 15, ebony headstock overlay w pearl inlay, geared tuners, resonator w engraved flange and marquetry inlay on sides, 8 piece pie-sectioned back, Kershner Unique tailpiece, brass arm rest, nickel plated parts, gold plated steel strings
5183 (Aristocrat)					figured black walnut shell w 'donut' tone ring, three-ply figured black walnut neck w ebony heelcap, carved heel 19-fret ebony fingerboard w pearl inlays at frets 1, 3, 5, 7, 10, 12 and 15, ebony headstock overlay w pearl floral inlay, geared tuners w pearl buttons, resonator w engraved flange and marquetry inlay on sides, 8 piece pie-sectioned back, carved heel, Kershner Unique tailpiece, brass arm rest, nickel plated parts, gold plated steel strings
5185 (Aristocrat Special)					as Style 5183 (1925) but with quadruple gold plated parts
5187 (DeLuxe)					as Style 5183 (1925) but with headstock, heelcap and bottom of shell inlaid w abalone pearl designs, gold plated parts

* The later models were equipped with a nickel plated brass arm rest

** Sometime after 1925 a 19-fret fingerboard became standard for this style

Washburn banjo styles 1928-1930

10 3/4" Tenor	Plectrum	Regulation	
5175/6 (Inspiration)			as Style 5175/6 (1925) (discontinued 1930 or earlier)
5177 (Dansant)	5152	5102	as Style 5177 (1925), but with 19-fret fingerboard and round colored marquetry pattern inlaid on back of resonator
5179 (Classic)			as Style 5179 (1925), but with round colored marquetry pattern inlaid on back of resonator
5181 (Syncopator)	5156	5106	as Style 5181 (1925), but with round colored marquetry pattern inlaid on back of resonator
5183 (Aristocrat)	5158	5108	as Style 5183 (1925), but with larger headstock w crown shaped top, square colored marquetry pattern (rolling field w tree) inlaid on back of resonator and pearl wandering minstrel inlay on headstock, eight pearl inlays at frets 1, 3, 5, 7, 10, 12, 15 and 17

Washburn banjo styles 1928-1930 (continued)

10 3/4" Tenor	Plectrum	Regulation	
5185 (DeLuxe)	5161		as Style 5185 (1925), but with larger headstock w crown shaped top, square inlaid colored marquetry pattern (rolling field w tree) on back of resonator and pearl wandering minstrel inlay on headstock, eight pearl inlays at frets 1, 3, 5, 7, 10, 12, 15 and 17
5187 (Super DeLuxe)			as Style 5187 (1925), but with larger headstock w crown shaped top, square colored marquetry pattern (rolling field w tree) inlaid on back of resonator and pearl wandering minstrel inlay on headstock, eight pearl inlays at frets 1, 3, 5, 7, 10, 12, 15, 17
'Shrine' banjo (discontinued around 1929)			triangular tone ring and resonator w round colored marquetry pattern inlaid on back and marquetry inlay on sides, 17-fret ebony fingerboard w seven pearl inlays at frets 1, 3, 5, 7, 10, 12 and 15 bound w white celluloid, ebony headstock overlay w pearl wandering minstrel inlay, Kershner Unique tailpiece

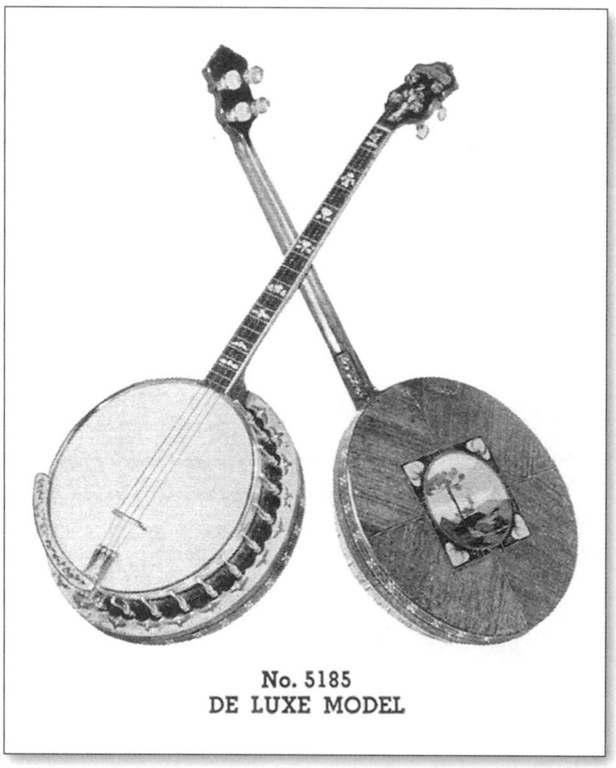

Style 5185 (1939)

Style 5187 (1939)

CHAPTER FIVE

Ukuleles

Washburn ukulele, formerly owned by entertainer Tiny Tim (1932-1996). Note added decals and jack endpin. The koa bodied instrument, used by the artist for over two decades, has a '705' headstock stamp, though 704 was the highest style number catalogued at the time (Collection of Christian Carlson)

Hawaiian Style Guitars

No. 410.

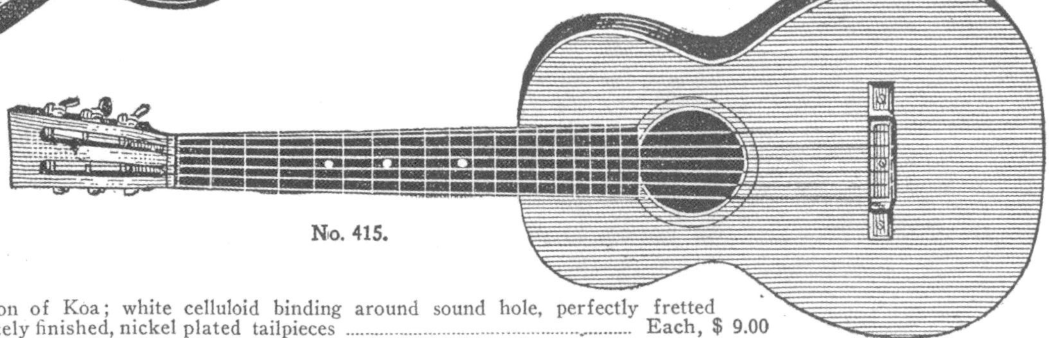

No. 415.

410. Made of birch, imitation of Koa; white celluloid binding around sound hole, perfectly fretted pearl position dots, nicely finished, nickel plated tailpieces .... Each, $ 9.00

415. Standard size, birch back and sides, finished a very fine imitation of mahogany, spruce top, two-ring wood inlaying around sound hole, front and back edges bound with white celluloid, top edge inlaid with wood stripe inside celluloid binding, inlaid stripe in black, ebonized fingerboard, pearl position dots, patent compensating bridge whereby strings can be raised or lowered at will, nicely finished .... Each, 12.25

No. 1715

The Washburn Hawaiian Instruments

The demand for a better grade of Hawaiian instruments—viz: Ukulele, Taropatch and Guitar, has prompted us to add these instruments to our Washburn line. The design of these instruments is most artistic, the finish perfect, and the tone is the same quality that placed the Washburn instrument on the pinnacle of fame it has achieved.

Washburn Ukulele

Dimensions: Length of entire instrument, 21 in. Length of fingerboard 6½ in.

1715. Made of highest grade of flamed Mahogany throughout, beautifully finished and highly polished. Top, back and heel bound with black and white celluloid. Sound hole bound with black and white celluloid and decorated with three rings of wood inlaying. Top and back of sides inlaid with a faint line of white celluloid. Mahogany neck, Koa fingerboard, bridge and headpiece. Champion patent pegs, black buttons. Each........ $22.50

Washburn Taropatch

Dimensions: Length of entire instrument 25½ in. Fingerboard 7¾ in.

1718. Same description as Ukulele No. 1715 but has ebony pegs and eight strings. Each $27.00

No. 1522

Washburn Hawaiian Steel Guitar

No.		Each
1522.	Concert size, six strings. Highest grade of choicest flamed Mahogany. Top, back and sound hole bound with black celluloid with a faint line of white celluloid, producing a decidedly neat, artistic effect. Top edge inlaid with alternating black and white celluloid strips. Sound hole decorated with a three-ring inlaying of white and black celluloid. Top and back edge of sides inlaid with a hair line of white celluloid. Inlaid strip in back. Mahogany neck. Ebony bridge, bone saddle. Ebony fingerboard bound with black celluloid with a faint line of white celluloid. Rosewood veneered head piece. Bone nut. Best quality patent head......	$33.00

1919

5.1 Dating of Washburn ukuleles

Dating Washburn ukuleles based on serial numbers is more complicated because many instruments made after the early 1920s have two different serial numbers, stamped respectively in the headstock back or upper side and inked on the neck block. As with guitars and mandolins from the same era these numbers indicate serial and batch numbers. The numbers found must be compared to the features of the respective instrument to those described under 'General appointments', 'Construction / general remarks' and, lastly, to the style descriptions hereunder. Ukuleles without a serial number or only a stamped style number should be dated based strictly on their visual and constructional features.

5.2 General appointments

1915-1922:
Serial numbers running from 1 into the high 1,000s / low 2,000s are ink stamped together with style numbers on a white, black and red Washburn label inside the instrument, oval shaped with a crown on top, stating '1915 model' and the style number. All ukuleles have 12-fret fingerboards that do not extend over the body and a headstock with curved, wave-shaped sides.

1922-1928:
Most styles have a 17-fret fingerboard extending over the body and a straight sided headstock. The earliest models have a three digit headstock stamp starting with 7XX indicating the style number and no stamped serial or batch numbers. From 1922 up to 1925 serial numbers (1 – 4,000s) are stamped in the back or upper side end of the headstock, while batch numbers (high 6,000s into the low 9,000s) are inked on the neck block. The words 'Washburn' and -until around 1927/8- 'Pat Apld For' are stamped in the headstock back. An oval stamp stating 'Lyon & Healy Makers U.S.A.' is branded inside the body back under the soundhole. Between 1922 and around 1925 additional headstock stamps can be found with the letters UA up to and including UG, or TUA (likely up to TUB), U standing for ukulele, A-G as a style designation (see 5.4), and T for tenor. Starting in 1925 four digit style numbers starting with 53XX are stamped in the headstock back, while serial numbers (1 – 3,000s range) are inked on the neck block. Between 1926-7 and 1928 only batch numbers (8,000s up to the mid 14,000s) are stamped on the instruments, initially inked on the neck block and later impressed in the headstock back. Around the same time four digit style numbers (53XX) are often inked on the neck block, sometimes preceded by 1. or 2. The 'Washburn' and 'Pat Apld For' headstock stamps are discontinued starting around the 12,000 batch number range.

After 1928:
The oval Lyon & Healy Makers stamp inside the instruments is replaced by a stamp stating 'Genuine Washburn Tonk Bros. Chicago Sole Distributors'. Style numbers are inked on the neck block, and serial numbers are sometimes stamped on the instruments.

5.3 Construction / general remarks

The ukulele was introduced in Hawaii by Portuguese immigrants during the late 1870s, but did not become really popular in the United States until the Pan-Pacific International Exposition held in 1915 in San Francisco. During the seven months that the Exposition lasted seventeen million people visited the various events. The music featured in the daily shows hosted by the pavilion of Hawaii created a true sensation, and was the cause for an Hawaiian music craze that immediately captured the U.S. mainland. This led also to an increased demand for Hawaiian instruments, in particular the ukulele and its eight-string cousin, the taropatch. The ukulele fad was born, and it would last for more than a decade.

Lyon & Healy added a ukulele and a taropatch to the Washburn instrument lines in 1915. New or revised lines were introduced in 1920, 1922, 1925 and 1928. Though the interest in Hawaiian music and instruments lasted throughout the 1920s, the company apparently did not spare much time and expense in promoting the ukulele. The advertising campaigns of Lyon & Healy at the time were mainly devoted to selling pianos, mandolins, violins, banjos, saxophones and even tenor guitars, but ukuleles were hardly ever mentioned. The company did not offer aspiring uke players much of a choice either, as only one Washburn ukulele model was available between 1915 and 1920. This may partly explain the relatively small numbers of Washburn ukuleles that were sold in comparison to the models of competitors like Martin.[121]

Tiple

During the 1920s the tiple, a small 10-string instrument that had its origins in South America, was added to the Lyon & Healy product lines. It was tuned in pairs and comparable in size to the tenor ukulele. Washburn tiples were introduced in 1925. Unlike the Washburn ukuleles the tiples were serial numbered together with the Washburn guitars. The bandurria, another small fretted instrument particularly popular in Spain and Latin America, had been offered by the company since the early 1900s. Its pear shaped body is more akin to that of a mandolin, and it has 12 strings that are also tuned in pairs. An upscale version carrying the American Conservatory brand was offered, but a Washburn bandurria was never available.

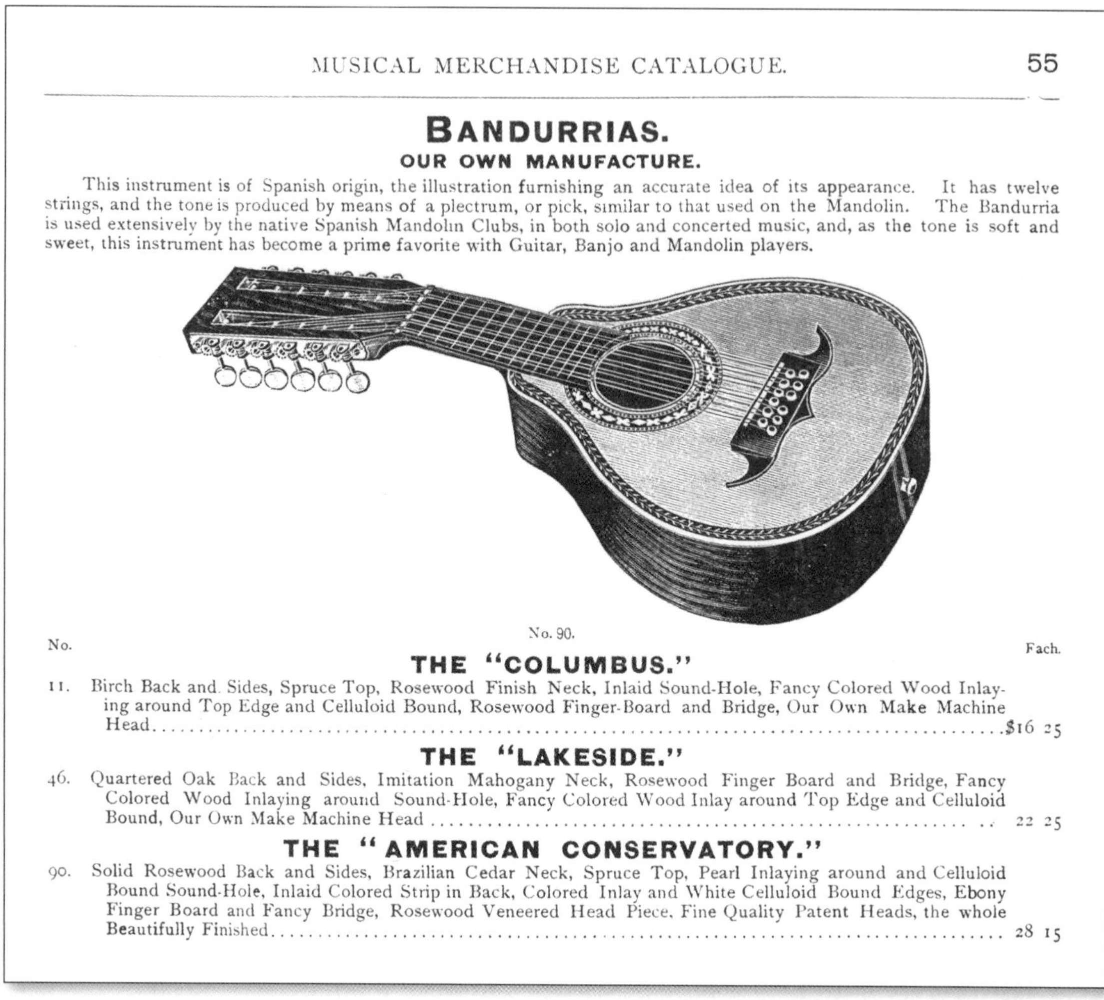

MUSICAL MERCHANDISE CATALOGUE. 55

BANDURRIAS.

OUR OWN MANUFACTURE.

This instrument is of Spanish origin, the illustration furnishing an accurate idea of its appearance. It has twelve strings, and the tone is produced by means of a plectrum, or pick, similar to that used on the Mandolin. The Bandurria is used extensively by the native Spanish Mandolin Clubs, in both solo and concerted music, and, as the tone is soft and sweet, this instrument has become a prime favorite with Guitar, Banjo and Mandolin players.

No. 90.

No.		Each.
	THE "COLUMBUS."	
11.	Birch Back and Sides, Spruce Top, Rosewood Finish Neck, Inlaid Sound-Hole, Fancy Colored Wood Inlaying around Top Edge and Celluloid Bound, Rosewood Finger-Board and Bridge, Our Own Make Machine Head	$16 25
	THE "LAKESIDE."	
46.	Quartered Oak Back and Sides, Imitation Mahogany Neck, Rosewood Finger Board and Bridge, Fancy Colored Wood Inlaying around Sound-Hole, Fancy Colored Wood Inlay around Top Edge and Celluloid Bound, Our Own Make Machine Head	22 25
	THE "AMERICAN CONSERVATORY."	
90.	Solid Rosewood Back and Sides, Brazilian Cedar Neck, Spruce Top, Pearl Inlaying around and Celluloid Bound Sound-Hole, Inlaid Colored Strip in Back, Colored Inlay and White Celluloid Bound Edges, Ebony Finger Board and Fancy Bridge, Rosewood Veneered Head Piece, Fine Quality Patent Heads, the whole Beautifully Finished	28 15

L&H's bandurria line, 1903

5.3.1 Body shapes and sizes

The ukulele styles made between 1915 and 1922 had a slightly smaller body than the post 1922 models. The lower bout of these early styles measured 6 ¼", as compared to the 6 ½" lower bout of the 1922 standard body style. The backs also had a typical small rounded extension that capped the neck heel, which was discontinued in 1922. In general the 1915-1922 styles were more traditional in appearance and features than the post 1922 models. Their design is reminiscent of instruments made by established Hawaiian makers such as Leonardo Nunes, whose products were also sold by Lyon & Healy at the time. A taropatch –an eight-string ukulele- was added to the 1915 line and again dropped from the catalog around 1922.

The 1922 and later lines were based on more original designs and may be viewed as the 'classic' Washburn ukulele styles. Their slightly larger bodies were constructed with three-ply laminated sides for added strength. The newly introduced tenor ukuleles, Styles 710 and 711, had an 8" lower bout, a 6" upper bout and an overall length of 24 ½" in comparison to 20 ¾" of the standard soprano styles. The tuning suggested by Lyon & Healy for the tenor ukuleles was D G B E, one fifth lower than for the soprano ukulele. The ornamentation on the catalog models became more pronounced throughout the 1920s, with gold leaf designs being applied to the tops of the more expensive models. By the late twenties, when the most luxurious abalone-adorned Styles 5319 and 5320 and their tenor counterparts were introduced, the heyday of the ukulele was almost over.

121 See 7.4.

The 'Shrine' and 'Bell' ukuleles

The 'shrine' uke, added to the Washburn line around 1927/8, was a unique design with a body shape reminiscent of a balalaika, tastefully trimmed with green celluloid. It was available in a soprano version with a 9" wide body, and very briefly also in tenor size. Contrary to the other 'shrine' instruments that were introduced during the late 1920s and discontinued very soon thereafter, the shrine soprano uke remained in the catalogs at least for a few more years during the 1930s.[122] Although it was positioned as a mid-priced instrument which listed for $20 in 1930 in comparison to the $55 list price of the top end Style 5320, the shrine uke is in much demand today by ukulele collectors who pay high prices for examples in nice condition.[123] The same applies to Style 5325, the "Bell" ukulele, another unusual design that was available for a much shorter time. It was introduced in 1925 together with the other bell-shaped Washburns: two guitars, a large Hawaiian lap guitar, Style 5260, and a matching tiple, Style 5395. The bell ukulele was heralded in a 1925 catalog as "a new departure in ukulele design, originated by Lyon & Healy", but stringed instruments with similar body shapes were known in Europe as far back as the 17th century. The bell uke was discontinued around 1927/8 and possibly even earlier, making it a very rare bird indeed.

Washburn Style 5395 Bell Tiple, later version with individual bridge saddles, late 1920s (Dave Pasant / Frank Ford)

Patent stamp

The 'Pat Apld For' stamp found on the headstock backs of Washburn ukuleles between 1922 and 1927/8 refers to the raised celluloid soundhole ring designed to prevent the surrounding wood from splitting or becoming frayed (see 2.4.1). It was replaced around 1930 by a plain celluloid soundhole binding flush with the top.

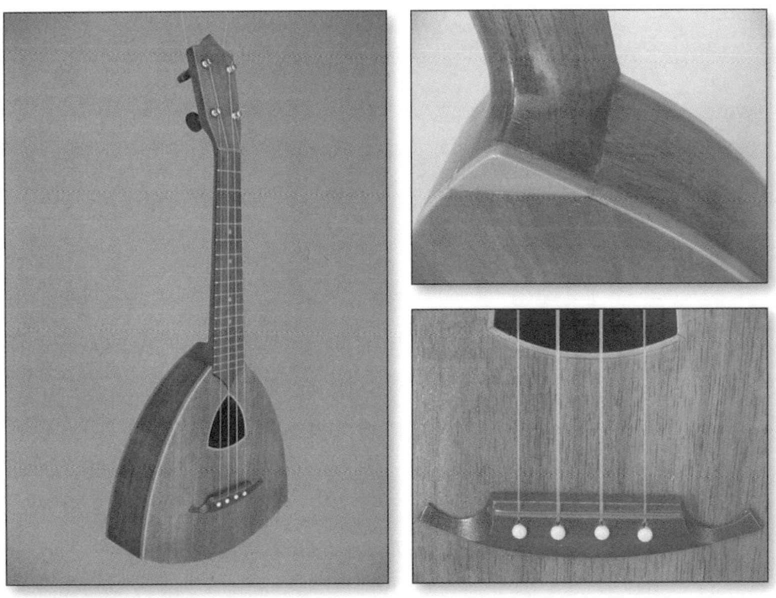

Washburn Shrine ukulele, late 1920s. The 'gondola' bridge was also featured on Style 5260/5273, a/k/a the 'Hawaiian Harp Guitar' (Frank Ford)

122 The 'shrine' instruments featured a guitar, a tenor guitar, a ukulele, a tenor ukulele, a mandolin and a banjo model.
123 A simpler birch bodied version was available for $15 – the matching hardshell case going for $10.50!

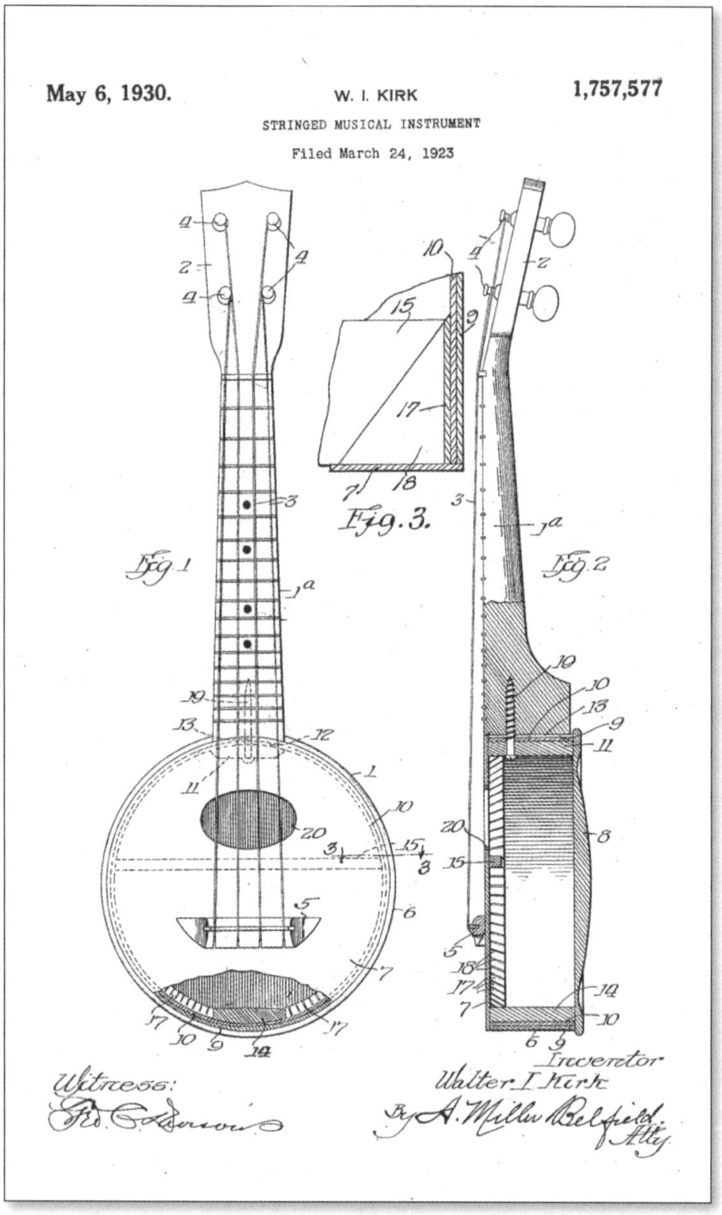

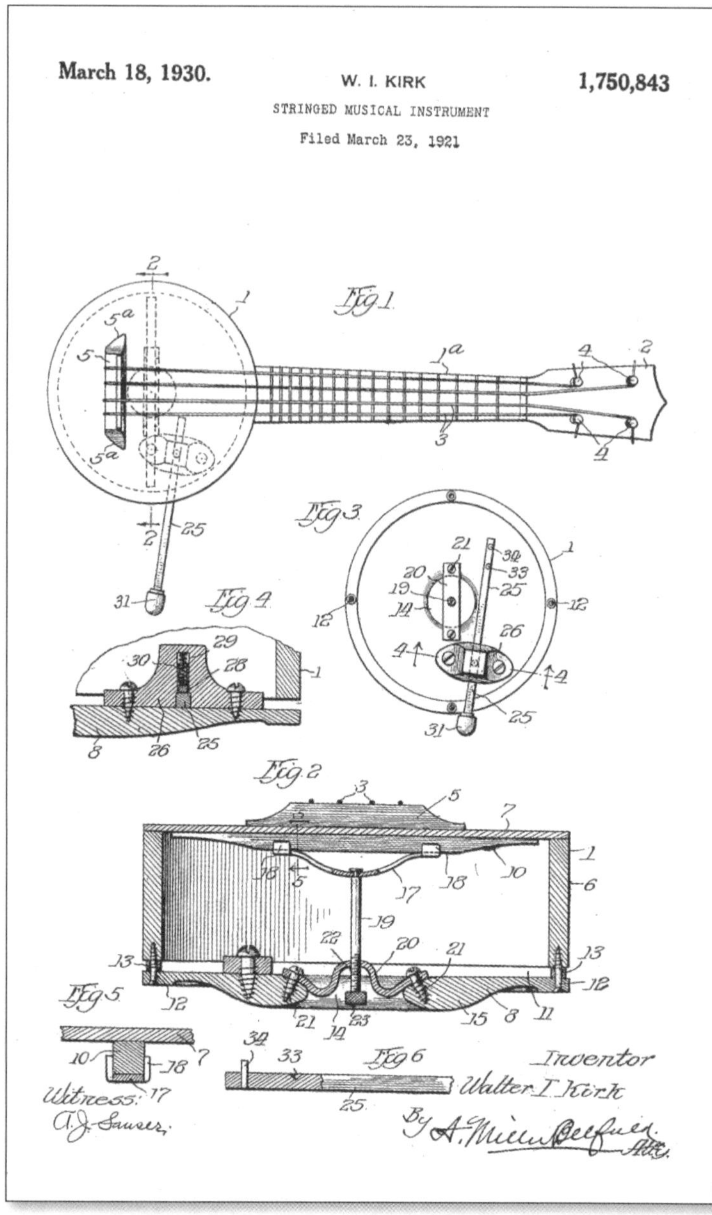

Patent drawings for the Camp Uke and its predecessor, a round bodied ukulele with a soundhole on the back

Batch number stamped in the headstock of a Shrine ukulele (Frank Ford)

Pat Apl For stamp on a Washburn ukulele (1922). The 'UC' stamp stands for a koa bodied Style 703, but without the gold oak leaf pattern on top

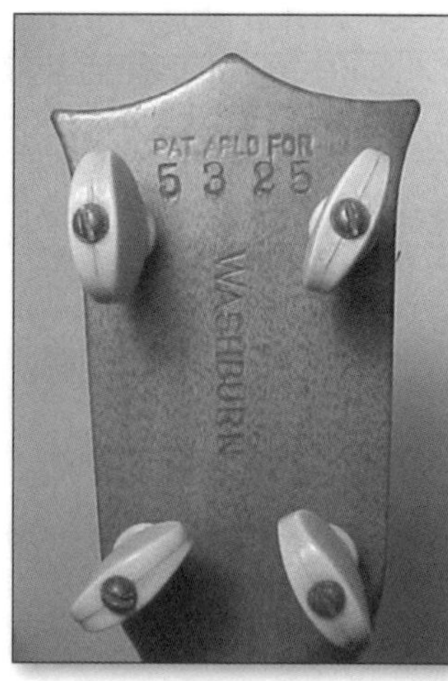

Headstock of Bell uke with stamped style number (1925)

5.3.2 Necks, headstocks, fingerboards

The ukulele line introduced in 1915 featured 12-fret necks that did not extend over the body. Fingerboards were made of mahogany or koa. The headstocks had curved wave-shaped sides and a top with rounded corners ending in a point. All styles were equipped with mechanical friction tuning pegs.[124] The 1922 models came with a redesigned 17-fret rosewood fingerboard with four inlaid pearl dots extending over the body. The new styles also featured a sharply cornered headstock with straight sides and a moustache shaped pointed end. The 12-fret fingerboard was reintroduced a few years later on the cheapest models, Styles 5314 and 5315. The only Washburn ukuleles to feature ebony fingerboards were Styles 5319 and 5320 and their tenor versions Styles 5355 and 5360, all introduced around or before 1928, and a few Shrine ukes.[125]

5.3.3 Bridges

A rather generic rectangular bridge was a standard appointment on the earlier Washburn ukuleles until 1922, when the new 'smile' bridge was introduced. It was described in the catalogs as a "new type extension bridge which allows ultimate vibration and cannot tip or pull off". But it could.... The initial version of the 'smile' bridge did not have bridge pins, which were featured on all but the cheapest styles starting around 1925. Some of the pinless bridges contain a 'Pat Apld For' stamp, but it seems that this refers to the raised soundhole ring for which a patent application had been filed in 1921. Apparently no design patent was ever applied for with regard to the characteristic 'smile' bridge design. The rectangular bridge reappeared briefly on the cheap Style 5315 ('Inspiration') between 1925 and 1928.

5.3.4 Other Lyon & Healy ukulele patents

The Camp Uke

This neat little instrument was designed by Walter Kirk in the early 1920s. A patent was not granted until 1930.[126] Though it was primarily designed as a cheap beginner's uke and never considered worthy of the Washburn name, some fancy versions were made with bindings and even gold maple leaf decals on top similar to those found on the most expensive Washburn ukuleles. Other marketed variants of the camp uke design include eight-string mando ukes and versions with f-holes. Some of these instruments have a stamped serial number. Four and six-string camp guitars were also offered by Lyon & Healy during the mid to late 1920s, but these had a different, pear shaped body. Kirk filed the patent application for the camp uke in 1923, but its basic design dates back at least two years. Another patent application by Kirk filed in 1921 already shows a ukulele with the familiar 'frying pan' shape of the camp uke, equipped with a 'smile' bridge and a new spring-loaded pullout knee rest similar to those found on the Style A and B mandolins.[127] The tension of the top could be adjusted by the player by means of a metal spindle connected to a bow shaped metal top brace. This strange-looking instrument, which had a soundhole at the back of the body and additional 'sound vents' on the side, did not make it to the production stage, although similar looking Lyon & Healy ukes without the metal contraptions mentioned in the patent application have been made.

The 'Marquette Uke'

In 1925 company president Marquette A. Healy, son of founder Patrick J. Healy, also tried his hand at ukulele design. The shape of his oddball creation –which was granted a design patent[128]- certainly invites comparisons to a canoe paddle, making it the ultimate camp uke! In the 1925 catalog it was rather pretentiously referred to as the "Venetian Ukulele". By the time the patent was awarded –in June 1928- Marquette Healy had been replaced as president by Ray Durham, and the company was no longer involved in manufacturing fretted instruments.

124 The 8-string taropatch may have had wooden or celluloid friction pegs.
125 Although the catalog descriptions specify ebony as fingerboard wood, most examined examples of the shrine uke have a rosewood fingerboard.
126 Patent number 1,757,577
127 Patent number 1,750,843
128 Patent number D75,494

Style 1715 (1919)

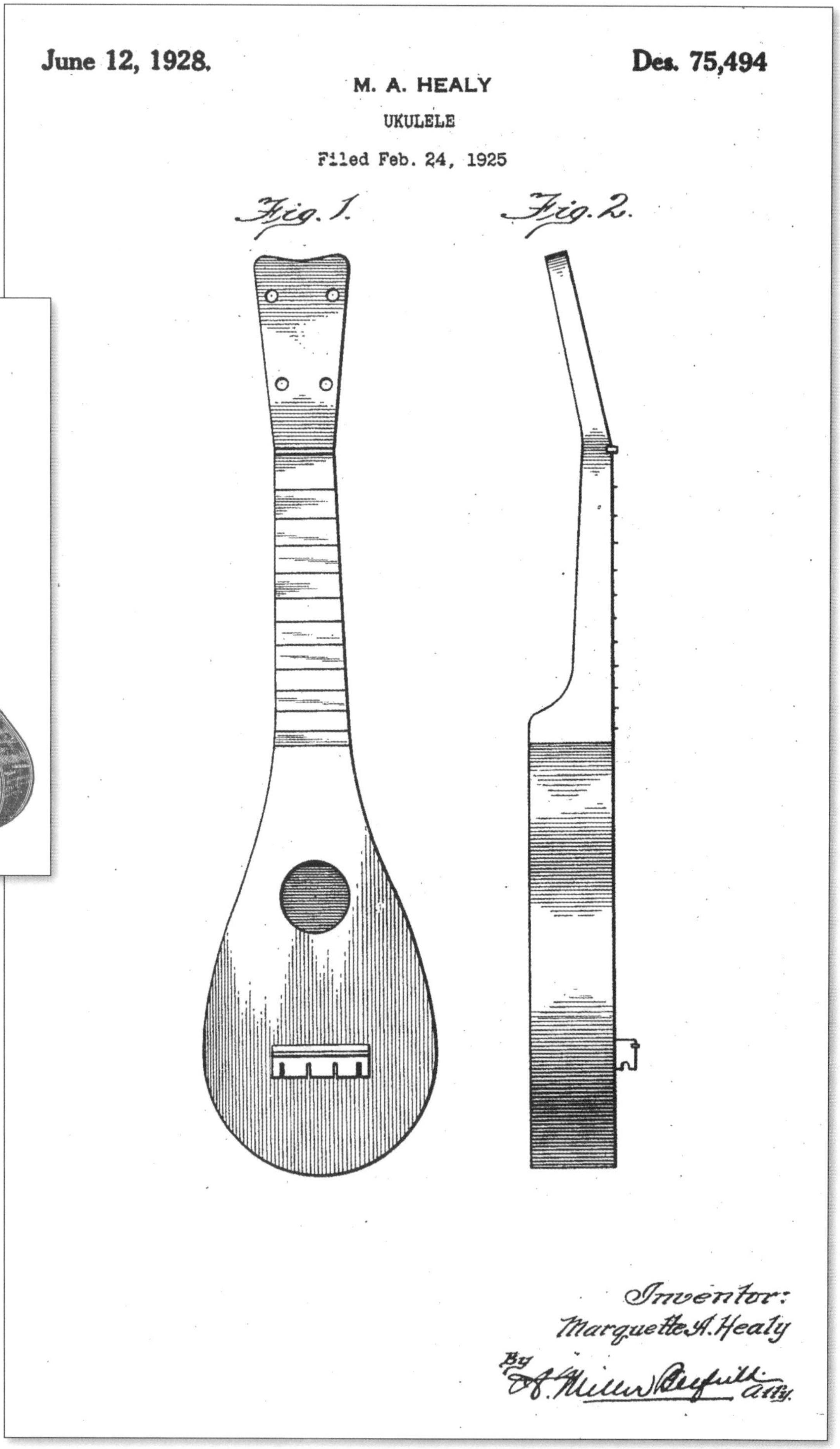

Design patent for the 'Venetian uke' by Marquette A. Healy

5.4 Ukulele Styles 1915-1940

Washburn ukulele styles 1915-1919

Soprano	
1515*	flamed mahogany body, mahogany neck, 12-fret koa fingerboard (not extending over body), koa head piece and koa rectangular bridge, top, back, s/h and heel bound w black and white celluloid, three rings inlaid around s/h, sides inlaid w faint line of white celluloid, Champion patent mechanical friction pegs
1518 (Taropatch)	as style 1715, but with eight strings and ebony or celluloid friction pegs

* In many Lyon & Healy/Washburn catalogs published between 1905 and the early 1920s the style numbers of catalogued instruments and other musical items have a 'G' prefix. This is a reference to Lyon & Healy's Department G, which was responsible for all retail activities

Washburn ukulele styles 1919-1920

Standard	
1715	as Style 1515 (1915)
1718 (Taropatch)	as Style 1518 (1915)

Washburn ukulele styles 1920-1922

	Standard	
	2621	flamed mahogany body, mahogany neck, 12-fret fingerboard (not extending over body), head piece and rectangular bridge, top, back, s/h and heel bound w black and white celluloid, three rings inlaid around s/h, sides inlaid w faint line of white celluloid, rosewood pegs
	2723	flamed mahogany body, mahogany neck, 12-fret koa fingerboard, head piece and rectangular bridge, top, back, s/h and heel bound w black and white celluloid, three rings inlaid around s/h, sides inlaid w faint line of white celluloid, patent pegs w black buttons
	2525 (Taropatch)	as Style 2621, but with eight strings and ebony or celluloid friction pegs
3 (banjo ukulele)		7″ laminated maple shell veneered w nyssawood, 8 brackets, 17-fret nyssawood neck w four black dots at frets 5, 7, 10 and 12, rosewood pegs, nickel plated tailpiece
2 (banjo ukulele)		7″ laminated maple shellcapped w rosewood, 8 brackets, maple neck, 17-fret rosewood fingerboard w four pearl dots at frets 5, 7, 10 and 12, mechanical friction pegs w black buttons, nickel plated tailpiece

WASHBURN UKULELES

1923-24 Series

WASHBURN Ukuleles Are Designed For Solo Playing and Artists' Use.

The "AMERICAN WAY" of playing has lifted the Ukulele to the rank of SOLO instruments and made it the most charming of all Musical Companions—a method so easily mastered that anyone with a little knowledge of music can become adept.

The growth in popularity of the Ukulele and the overwhelming demand for QUALITY prompted us to evolve these beautiful models and add them to our New Washburn Line. We briefly enumerate their points of SUPERIORITY.

1. Larger body with scientifically constructed resonating chamber, affording greatest possible volume.
2. Three-ply laminated sides throughout.
3. Lined and blocked throughout to give unequalled strength.
4. Top and back with minimum thickness and maximum bridging to give utmost freedom of vibration.
5. Extension fingerboard, guaranteed perfect scale, fretted true to the Thousandth of an inch.
6. L. & H. Neverslip pegs of Special design.
7. New Type End Extension bridge which allows ultimate vibration and cannot tip nor pull off.
8. Appearance handsome, Model flawlessly symmetrical, Tone quality superb, Volume unequalled, Material the choicest obtainable—the whole a perfect Solo and Accompaniment Ukulele for discriminating Artists.

Style 702

EVERY MODEL UNIFORM

$20\frac{3}{4}$ inches long, lower bout $6\frac{1}{2}$ inches, upper 5 inches wide, 3-ply laminated sides. Strung with three Gut and one Silk, wire wound, strings.

STYLE 700. Choicest Mahogany throughout, hand rubbed, dull finish, Mahogany neck, Rosewood extension fingerboard, extension bridge, raised mahogany bound soundhole.

Each **$15.50**

STYLE 701. Same as No. 700 but with white celluloid binding around top and back edges and raised soundhole, white buttons. Very attractive appearance.

Each **$19.50**

STYLE 702. Very choicest figured Nyssa wood, a beautiful satin finish. Black celluloid binding on front and back, patented raised soundhole. Black inlay in head and on heel. Attractive decalcomania Maple leaf design below bridge. Rosewood fingerboard. Dainty appearance, beautiful tone.

Each **$21.00**

STYLE 703. Genuine Koawood, Plain, front and back edges bound with white celluloid, patented raised sound-hole. Rosewood fingerboard, diamond design in head, beautiful Maple leaf design below bridge.

Each **$25.00**

STYLE 704. Curly Koawood, chosen for its beautiful figure. Same white trim as on No. 703. A Ukulele any artist will be proud of. A solo instrument of the highest order.

Each **$29.00**

Visualized Instructor for

Playing the "American Way."

With its aid anyone can play easy solos from the beginning.

"DURKEE" VISUALIZED INSTRUCTOR,

Each **$1.00**

WASHBURN TENOR UKULELE

For Accompaniment and Clubwork.

STYLE 710. Enlarged Model. Length over all $24\frac{1}{2}$ inches. Lower about 8 inches, upper 6 inches wide. Strung D, G, B and E—one-fifth lower than the Ukulele—Use Violin A for two outside strings, Violin D gut for the G and a Guitar D compound silk and wire for inside strings. Mahogany top, back and sides.

Each **$30.00**

STYLE 711. Same as Style 710 except Finer Grade Mahogany top, back and sides. Soundhole and edges white celluloid bound. Great volume and tonal beauty.

Each **$40.00**

Style 700

Style 704

1923

Washburn ukulele styles 1920-1922 (continued)

Standard		
1 (banjo ukulele)		7″ laminated maple shell capped w mahogany and bound w white celluloid, 8 brackets, maple neck, mahogany headstock overlay, 17-fret rosewood fingerboard w four pearl dots at frets 5, 7, 10 and 12, mechanical friction pegs w white buttons, nickel plated tailpiece

Washburn ukulele styles 1922-1925

Standard	Tenor	
700*		mahogany body w three-ply laminated sides, mahogany neck, 17-fret rosewood fingerboard w four dots at frets 5, 7, 10 and 12, black nut, mechanical friction pegs w black tuner buttons, mahogany smile bridge w black bridge saddle and no bridge pins, raised soundhole edge
701*		mahogany body w three-ply laminated sides, mahogany neck, headstock w white ivorine square inlay, 17-fret rosewood fingerboard w four dots at frets 5, 7, 10 and 12, black nut, mechanical friction pegs w black tuner buttons, mahogany smile bridge w black bridge saddle and no bridge pins, top and back of body bound w white celluloid, heelcap bound w white celluloid, raised celluloid soundhole ring
702*		nyssawood[129] body w three-ply laminated sides, mahogany neck, headstock w ivorine square inlay, 17-fret rosewood fingerboard w four dots at frets 5, 7, 10 and 12, black nut, mechanical friction pegs w black tuner buttons, mahogany smile bridge w black bridge saddle and no bridge pins, top and back of body bound w black celluloid, heelcap bound w black celluloid, raised black celluloid soundhole ring, gold leaf vine pattern on top
703*		koawood body w three-ply laminated sides, koa or mahogany neck, headstock w white ivorine square inlay, 17-fret rosewood fingerboard w four dots at frets 5, 7, 10 and 12, black nut, mechanical friction pegs w black tuner buttons, mahogany smile bridge w black bridge saddle and no bridge pins, top and back of body bound w white celluloid, heelcap bound w white celluloid, raised celluloid soundhole ring, gold maple leaf pattern on lower top bout

129 Nyssawood indicates pearwood.

Style 5314 (1939)

Style 5315 (1930)

Style 5315 (1939)

Style 5316 (1939)

Style 5317 (1925)

Style 5318 (1939)

Style 5318 (1925)

Style 5319 (1939)

Style 5320 (1939)

Washburn ukulele styles 1922-1925 (continued)

Standard	Tenor	
704*		as Style 703, but with curly koa body
	710*	Tenor Ukulele, appointments as Style 700
	711*	Tenor Ukulele, appointments as Style 701

* Many surviving Washburn ukuleles of the 1922-1925 period have a headstock stamp stating UA, UB etc. These designations are not mentioned or explained in catalogs of the time, but correspond most likely with the following styles: UA: 704, UB: 703, UD: 702, UE: 701, UF: 700. UC stamped instruments are identical to a koa bodied Style 703 without the gold leaf pattern on top, UG indicates an entry level instrument identical to Style 5315 of the 1925 line. TUA is stamped on a Style 711, and (likely) TUB on Style 710. Obviously, the T stands here for 'Tenor'

Washburn ukulele styles 1925-1940

Sml size	Concert*	Tenor	
5314 (Junior) (introduced 1928 or earlier)			mahogany neck and body (slightly smaller in size than the concert models), three-ply laminated sides, 12-fret rosewood fingerboard w three pearl dots at frets 5, 7 and 10, mahogany smile bridge w ebony saddle, ebony nut
	5315 (Inspiration)		figured mahogany neck and body, three-ply laminated sides, 12-fret rosewood fingerboard w three pearl dots at frets 5, 7 and 10, ebony nut, mahogany rectangular bridge w ebony saddle and no bridge pins (replaced by 'smile bridge' around or before 1928), s/h bound w black and white celluloid, mechanical friction pegs w black tuner buttons
	5316 (Collegian)		figured mahogany neck and body, three-ply laminated sides, 17-fret rosewood fingerboard w four pearl dots at frets 5, 7, 10 and 12, ebony nut, mahogany smile bridge w ebony saddle and no bridge pins, raised mahogany ring around s/h, mechanical friction pegs w black tuner buttons
	5317 (Solo)		figured mahogany neck and body, three-ply laminated sides, 17-fret rosewood fingerboard w four pearl dots at frets 5, 7, 10 and 12, bone nut, ivorine square inlaid in headstock, mahogany smile bridge w bone saddle and bridge pins, s/h, body top and back bound w white celluloid, (around or before 1928: gold maple leaf pattern on top at lower bout), mechanical friction pegs w white tuner buttons
	5318 (Superb, Deluxe prior to 1928)		figured koa neck and body, three-ply laminated sides, 17-fret rosewood fingerboard w four pearl dots at frets 5, 7, 10 and 12, bone nut, ivorine square inlaid in headstock, koa smile bridge w bone saddle and bridge pins, s/h, body top and back bound w white celluloid, gold maple leaf pattern on top at lower bout, mechanical friction pegs w white tuner buttons

The WASHBURN "Bell" Ukulele

Made in the Lyon & Healy Factory

This instrument is a new departure in ukulele design, originated by Lyon & Healy. It has a superb quality of tone, peculiarly its own, of unusual mellowness and of great volume. The unique shape appeals immediately to the purchaser who is seeking the novel and individual. The professional finds the WASHBURN "BELL" exceptionally suited to concert and stage work.

The WASHBURN "BELL" Ukulele is made of a beautifully figured genuine mahogany, hand rubbed, satin finish all over; top and back edges bound with ivorine; patented raised sound-hole bound with ivorine; new type end extension mahogany bridge which allows freest possible vibration and cannot tip or pull off; polished bone bridge pins and fret; beautifully finished genuine rosewood extension fingerboard with 17 accurately placed German silver frets and 4 pearl position dots; polished bone fingerboard nut; artistically shaped head equipped with Lyon & Healy special model patent pegs; ivorine design inlaid in head; patent pegs have nickel-plated brass posts mounted with ivorine buttons. Strung with finest quality gut strings.

No. **5325** .... *Each $25.00*

Style 5325 (1925)

Shrine Model

This is a professional instrument of the highest order, unique in shape, convenient to handle, and, above all, possessing a tone quality sweeter, more resonant and far-carrying than any ukulele you have ever heard. You will be amazed at the tone quality of this instrument. Scientifically built in every respect, and pronounced by discriminating players everywhere as in a class by itself.

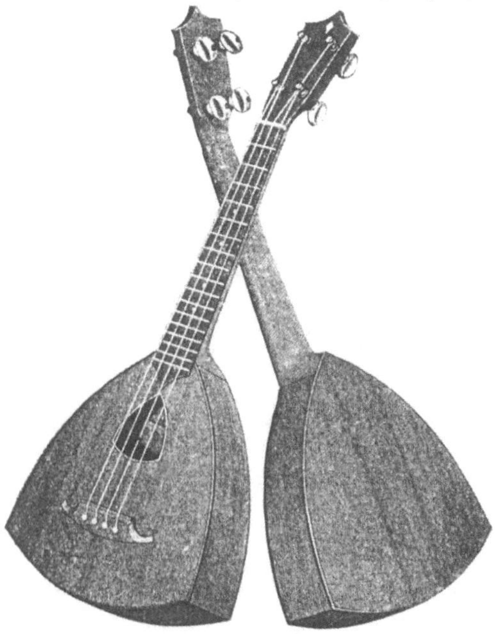

Description

The body is made of extra fine genuine mahogany in beautiful satin finish; width of lower bout, 9 inches; length of entire instrument, 21½ inches. Top, back and sound hole edges bound with green celluloid, giving a very pleasing appearance; new model end extension bridge which allows freest possible vibration; genuine ebony fingerboard with 17 German silver frets and 4 round green celluloid position marks; genuine mahogany neck, beautifully modeled and finished; rosewood veneered headpiece with inlaid green celluloid design; equipped with special model patent pegs of our own exclusive design; strung with finest quality gut strings. This instrument absolutely possesses the last word in tone quality. Highly recommended for solo work.

No. 5330 Made of mahogany. Price, each **$20.00**

No. 5331 Same as No. 5330, except made of specially selected birch, mahogany finish. Each 15.00

Shrine Model Ukulele Cases

Made of 3-ply veneer covered with walrus grain waterproof black Keratol; steel valance; side opening; velvet lined; nickel plated brass lock, clasps and protectors; leather handle; durable workmanship throughout.

No. 6412 Price, each **$10.50**

No. 6410 Black walrus grain Keratol; fiberboard body; side opening; flannel lined. Each 6.00

Style 5330 (1930)

Sml size	Concert*	Tenor	
	5319 (DeLuxe)		(introduced 1928 or earlier) figured koa body, three-ply laminated sides, three-ply mahogany neck w black fiberoid center strip, 17-fret ebony fingerboard** w six pearl dots at frets 5, 7 (2 dots), 10 and 12 (2 dots), bone nut, ivorine square inlaid in headstock, ebony smile bridge w bone saddle and bridge pins, s/h, body top and back and heelcap bound w white celluloid, wood purfling inlaid around top and back and backstrip, s/h inlaid w abalone pearl ring, mechanical friction pegs w white tuner buttons
	5320 (Super DeLuxe)		(introduced 1928 or earlier) figured koa body, three-ply laminated sides, three-ply mahogany neck w black fiberoid center strip, 17-fret ebony fingerboard bound w white celluloid w five pearl inlays at frets 1, 5, 7, 10 and 12, bone nut, headstock bound w white celluloid, pearl fleur de lys inlaid in headstock, ebony smile bridge w bone saddle and bridge pins, s/h, body top and back bound w white celluloid and inlaid pearl line, backstrip inlaid w pearl, heelcap bound w white celluloid and ebony, mechanical friction pegs w white tuner buttons
	5325 (Bell)		(discontinued 1928 or earlier) figured mahogany bell shaped body, three-ply laminated sides, mahogany neck, 17-fret rosewood fingerboard w four pearl dots at frets 5, 7, 10 and 12, ivorine square inlaid in headstock, mahogany smile bridge w bone bridge pins and saddle, bone nut, body top and back bound w white celluloid, mechanical friction pegs w white tuner buttons
	5330 (Shrine)***	Shrine Tenor	(introduced 1927/8, tenor version discontinued 1930 or earlier) triangular mahogany body, three-ply laminated sides, mahogany neck, 17-fret rosewood or ebony fingerboard w four green celluloid dots at frets 5, 7, 10 and 12, green celluloid nut and heelcap, rosewood headstock overlay w inlaid green ivorine square, mahogany gondola shaped bridge w green celluloid saddle and white bridge pins, top, back and s/h bound w green celluloid, black tuner buttons
	5331 (Shrine)		(introduced 1927/8) as Style 5330 (1925), but with birch body without binding on back and standard 'smile' bridge
		5350	(Grand Symphony model, introduced 1928 or earlier) appointments as Style 5317 (1925)
		5355 (DeLuxe)	(introduced 1928 or earlier) appointments as Style 5319 (1925)

Style 5355 (1939)

Style 5360 (1939)

Style 5350 (1932)

Style 5395 (1925)

Washburn ukulele styles 1925-1940 (continued)

Sml size	Concert*	Tenor	
		5360 (Super DeLuxe)	(introduced 1928 or earlier) appointments as Style 5320 (1925)
	5375 ("Duke", tenor banjo ukulele)		8" walnut shell w marquetry inlay on side, 12 brackets, three-ply walnut neck, 17-fret ebony fingerboard w four pearl dots at frets 5, 7, 10 and 12 bound w white celluloid, veneered headstock w pearl fleur de lys inlay, mechanical friction tuners w white buttons, walnut resonator and bridge, brass arm rest****
	5394 (tiple, introduced 1930 or later)		mahogany b/s, spruce top, slotted headstock w five on a side tuners, mahogany neck, 18-fret ebony fingerboard w four pearl dots at frets 5, 7, 10 and 12, ivorine square inlaid in headstock, black celluloid headstock overlay w "Washburn" inlaid in pearl, rectangular bridge, top, back and s/h bound w black celluloid
	5395 (Bell Tiple)		(discontinued 1930 or earlier) figured mahogany bell shaped body, spruce top, slotted headstock w five on a side tuners, mahogany neck, 17-fret ebony fingerboard w four pearl dots at frets 5, 7, 10 and 12, ivorine square inlaid in headstock, ebony headstock overlay and heelcap, ebonized rectangular bridge w nickel saddle, bone nut, body top and s/h bound w black and white celluloid, back bound w white celluloid, inlaid backstrip

* 'Concert' size is identical to the pre-1925 standard (soprano) size

** Styles 5319 with rosewood fingerboards have also been reported

*** Surviving examples exist of a deluxe shrine ukulele model with identical appointments as Style 5320, likely introduced around 1928-9

**** At least three other versions with fancier appointments are known: 1) five snowflake fingerboard inlays at frets 5, 7, 10, 12 (2) and inlaid round marquetry pattern on resonator back; 2) seven large pearl fingerboard inlays, abalone 'troubadour inlay on headstock; 3) eight large pearl fingerboard inlays, pearl flower motifs on headstock, pearloid covering on resonator sides and top

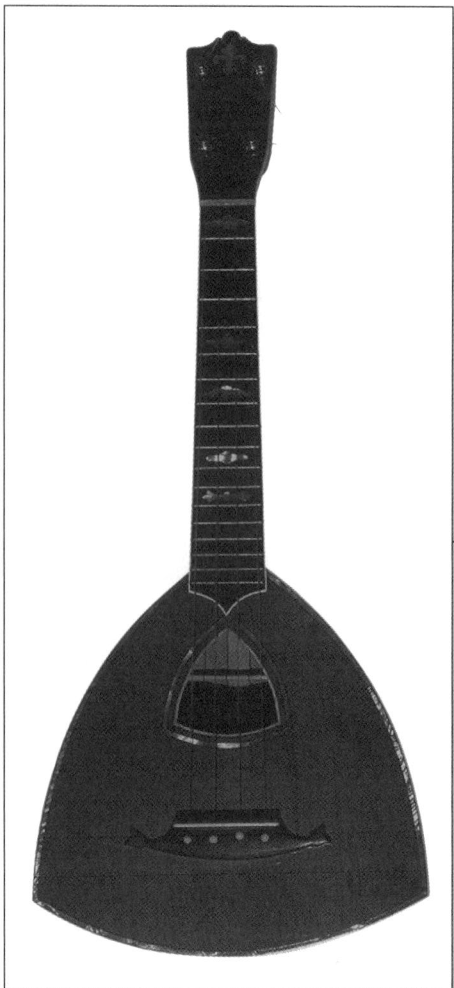

Jim Beloff

Style 5375 w post-1928 resonator inlay (Gruhn Guitars)

Style 5375 (1925)

CHAPTER SIX

Notes on production totals 1883-1940

Woman playing a custom made Washburn Lyre Terz guitar with an added neck, late 1890s (from the Collection of Barry Trott)

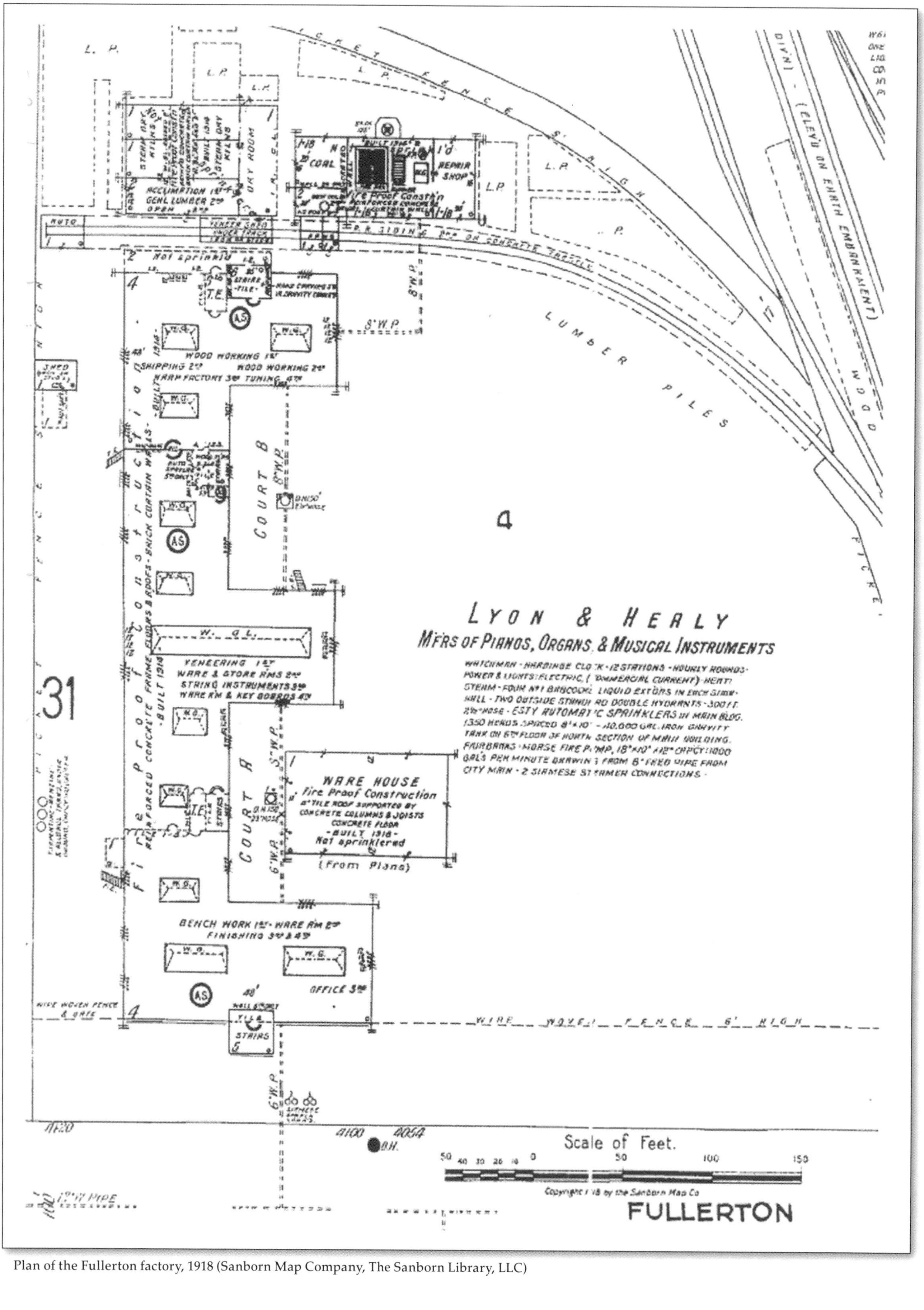

Plan of the Fullerton factory, 1918 (Sanborn Map Company, The Sanborn Library, LLC)

General notes

In merchandise catalogs and advertisements of the 1890s Lyon & Healy's boasted that the annual output of their factories was 100,000 instruments. It is evident that this figure should not be equated with the actual production totals of the Washburn brand instruments at the time, or at any time before WWII. Before making an attempt towards a more realistic estimate, a number of relevant factors and preliminary assumptions are discussed briefly. The conclusions in this and the following chapter are based on research data regarding the Washburn instrument lines and Lyon & Healy in general and serial numbers found on more than 2,000 prewar instruments.

The Washburn brand name was used for a number of instrument lines manufactured in the Lyon & Healy factories. The Washburns -guitars, mandolins, zithers, banjos, ukuleles, harps, violins, pianos and parlor organs- represented in most cases top of the line instruments made of premium woods and hardware that were competitively priced but nonetheless costly.[130] The most expensive guitar offered in the Sears Roebuck merchandise catalogs from the mid to late 1890s was a Washburn Style 101, the cheapest model of the Washburn line. It retailed for $22, while most of the other guitars offered by Sears were priced under $10. In today's currency that cheap Washburn would cost between $400 and $500. In the 1890s $22 was a substantial amount for such a plain guitar, especially taking into account that labor and materials were relatively cheap. The most affordable Martin guitar at the time, the small rosewood bodied Style 3-17, was considerably more expensive at $36.

Production figures for the Washburn instrument lines reached a peak between 1890 and the early 1900s, and were by all means huge in comparison to the output of any of Lyon & Healy's competitors at the time. The 1889 Washburn catalog boasted that the "manufacturers of the Washburn instruments (....) carry in stock at least five times the amount of seasoned material and the number of instruments in process of construction, owned by any other makers in the world". Since the 'manufacturers' referred to here were Lyon & Healy, this claim was undoubtedly true as many other instruments were made in the company's factories besides the Washburns. Period photos of the Lyon & Healy factory show impressive looking racks with finished guitars, mandolins and banjos that were claimed to contain between hundreds and thousands of instruments each. The pictured workmen are employed in assembly line fashion, working with machinery specially developed for instrument building. Some of this equipment was innovative enough to receive a patent, such as the jig used for building the early cross-braced Washburn mandolins.

According to Lyon & Healy machines were employed for cutting fret slots, graduating tops, backs and sides, turning the necks, cutting for inlay and shaping and bending parts. The rationale behind this was to make it "possible for the manufacturers of the Washburns to more accurately duplicate their instruments than for other makers, the others depending to a large extent on their workmen, (...) frequently trusting to luck, and often making dismal failures."[131] In spite of this contention there was a downside to the high production figures, as evidenced by substandard workmanship displayed on some surviving instruments, resulting in sloppy inlaying or engraving work, visible glue residue around braces, et cetera. Lyon & Healy also claimed that their factories made all component parts for the Washburn and other instrument lines, including machine heads, pearl ornaments and marquetry. The company's cheaper instrument lines accounted for the bulk of Lyon & Healy's fretted instrument output, and greatly outnumbered the Washburns.

Nonetheless the company's manufacturing totals for fretted instruments decreased during the first decades of the 20th century. By the time Lyon & Healy sold the manufacturing rights for the Washburns to the J.R. Stewart Co. in 1928, the company's guitar and mandolin production figures had dwindled to a fraction of the output during the heyday of the mandolin craze. The reason for this decline in production is unclear, but the success of Chicago based competitors Harmony and Regal -who had become a major force on the market for cheap instruments- may have been an important factor. Gibson and Martin, Lyon & Healy's rivals in the premium guitar and mandolin market, also fared well during the first decades of the 20th century, though Gibson found itself temporarily in financial straits in the early 1920s. Martin experienced a tremendous boost in guitar sales in the years following the First World War and saw its annual output rapidly climb from a few hundred to thousands of guitars. During the same period production figures for the Washburn guitars did not show significant growth.

130 Washburn violins were imported from Europe. Like the Washburn harps and pianos, they were mid priced instruments and not top of the line models as the other Washburns.
131 1889 Washburn catalog.

Gibson's early successes were fueled to a large extent by its aggressive marketing and advertising strategies, for which Lyon & Healy had set the example in the 1890s. Gibson went much further in trying to convince the public about the superiority of its products than Lyon & Healy had ever done, and did not eschew the use of the most nonsensical arguments and claims in their catalogs and advertising campaigns. But the Gibsons were also fine and innovative instruments that set new standards, which swayed players more than any sales pitch could have accomplished.

For some reason, Lyon & Healy gradually lost interest in promoting fretted instruments after the turn of the 20th century. The frequent guitar and mandolin advertising campaigns of the 1890s were not continued with the same intensity during the early 1900s and thereafter. Instead, the company redirected its marketing efforts to possibly more profitable instrument lines such as pianos, violins and band instruments, which all were advertised much more often than guitars, mandolins and banjos. Tonk Bros followed suit and hardly advertised the Washburn line after 1928 outside of the merchandise catalogs that were sent to dealers.

During the depression years the Washburn production figures hit an all-time low. The bankruptcy of the J.R. Stewart Co. in March 1930 resulted in the closing down of the Washburn manufacturing facilities, and temporarily halted instrument production. Though things got better after the mid 1930s, the Washburns were doomed to obscurity with annual guitar production figures of less than half of those of Martin. Three decades earlier, Lyon & Healy's sales of Washburn guitars had been between five and ten times the number of Martin's annual output. Times had changed, and for good.

A mysterious factory fire

One often heard story about Lyon & Healy is that the company suffered a factory fire in the 1920s or earlier[132] that allegedly resulted in the loss of the company archives and also may have caused production to be outsourced to other manufacturers. The location of the factory at the time was 4100 W Fullerton Avenue, also referred to at the time as "Healy Station" after a railroad station with the same name situated at 4014 W Fullerton. Today a Metra railway station called "Healy" is still located at this site.

Lyon & Healy moved into the newly built factory in 1914. Earlier Chicago factory buildings were situated during the early to late 1880s at 1-13 Madison Street and 213-217 S. Canal Street, and since the late 1880s at the corner of Randolph and Ogden Avenue, in period company literature often referred to as the "Union Park" factory. A smaller building at the Randolph & Ogden block located behind this factory was employed by Lyon & Healy after the mid teens, initially as a warehouse for finished pianos. It was enlarged around 1920 and has housed the headquarters of the Lyon & Healy harp company since 1928 until the present day. The Union Park factory was vacated by Lyon & Healy in 1914 and remained in use by various companies until the early 1920s, at which time it had to make way as Ogden Avenue was extended onto Lake Street. Consequently most of the original structure was demolished.

The new Healy Station factory was pictured in various period promotional materials between 1914 and the mid 1920s, which all show a free standing four-story building with one central 'tower' in the midst of its façade. A promotional company envelope postmarked 1913 contains a picture of "the new Lyon & Healy piano and harp factories" with a façade that looks almost three times as wide, containing two towers.[133] Was this the initial architectural design that was downsized later or did it reflect the actual original size of this building, later reduced as a consequence of a large fire? The last theory is refuted by photographs of the finished building that were published in 1914. The possibility of a later fire is also unrealistic in view of the complete lack of mention thereof in period publications regarding the company or elsewhere. A number of articles and books about Lyon & Healy's history published between 1900 and 1925 mention the two store fires of 1870 and 1871, but are silent on a later fire. Neither can it be found in a more recent commemorative booklet published by Lyon & Healy on its centennial that covers the period from the company's early years up to the 1960s.[134] If there had been a third serious fire, that event certainly would have deserved mention. Period insurance maps reveal moreover that the 1914 structure was substantially enlarged in 1927 and 1928, and that the main building –where the various manufacturing divisions were housed- had been equipped with an automatic sprinkler system in the 1910s. Fireproof construction was used for all buildings including the warehouses. It is unknown if the Healy Station factory was closed in 1926, at which time Lyon & Healy opened another Chicago factory located at 22nd and Rockwell Streets, or in May 1928, when

132 *Wheeler*, p. 361.
133 Fretted instruments were also made in the Healy Station factory, as evidenced by period insurance maps.
134 See note 1.

the company ceased most of its manufacturing activities. A 1928 telephone directory shows Lyon & Healy no longer being listed at the Fullerton Ave. address. The Mills Novelty Co, a manufacturer of coin operated machines, since used the building for a number of decades. The company gained notoriety because of its documented ties with organized crime in Chicago in the 1920s and early 1930s, and manufactured illegal slot machines commissioned by Al Capone at the site where Lyon & Healy had made such world class instruments as the Style A mandolin, the Washburn Deluxe guitar and the Lyon & Healy harp. The enlarged and modified structure has survived to this day and currently houses a number of companies.

1913

Nowadays Lyon & Healy Harps, Inc. only has a very small fraction of the original pre-1928 archive materials in their possession. Among these are reportedly notes indicating that certain records dating prior to 1910 were lost in a fire. It therefore cannot be ruled out that there was in fact a fire at some point -possibly with a relatively small impact, which could have involved the room where the archives were kept. But even if this actually happened, it still does not explain why the company's factory records after 1910, and the large amounts of paperwork produced at its downtown offices, are also completely gone. Either these have once been stored somewhere and are since awaiting their rediscovery, or were destroyed.

The Fullerton factory, 2002

Serial numbering systems

Until the early 1920s the Washburn guitars, mandolins, banjos, ukuleles, zithers, violins and harps were serial numbered individually per instrument category and separately from the other Lyon & Healy instrument lines, using consecutive numbering systems.[135] Washburns were the only fretted instruments considered worthy by Lyon & Healy to receive stamped serial numbers, with the exception of certain models of the American Conservatory line, and a limited number of other upscale instruments such as the College Line 'Monster Bass' guitars and the Lyon & Healy carved top A-C mandolin styles. The cheaper instrument lines manufactured by the company –including the Lakeside, Marquette, Columbus and Arion guitar and mandolin brands- usually did not have stamped serial numbers.[136]

Between the late 1880s until 1907 Lyon & Healy used consecutive numbering systems that reflected the overall production totals of their various guitar and mandolin lines, while only the Washburns and a few other top of the line instruments received stamped serial numbers, thus reflecting their superior status. A claim by Lyon & Healy in the 1896 Washburn catalog that they had made 100,000 guitars in the previous ten years corresponds with the serial numbers found on Washburn and American Conservatory brand guitars, which had reached the 120,000s range

135 Washburn pianos shared a numbering system with Lyon & Healy brand pianos (see 7.5).
136 A few late 1880s or early 1890s Arion guitars and some of the post 1900 Columbus and Jupiter guitars have stamped serial numbers.

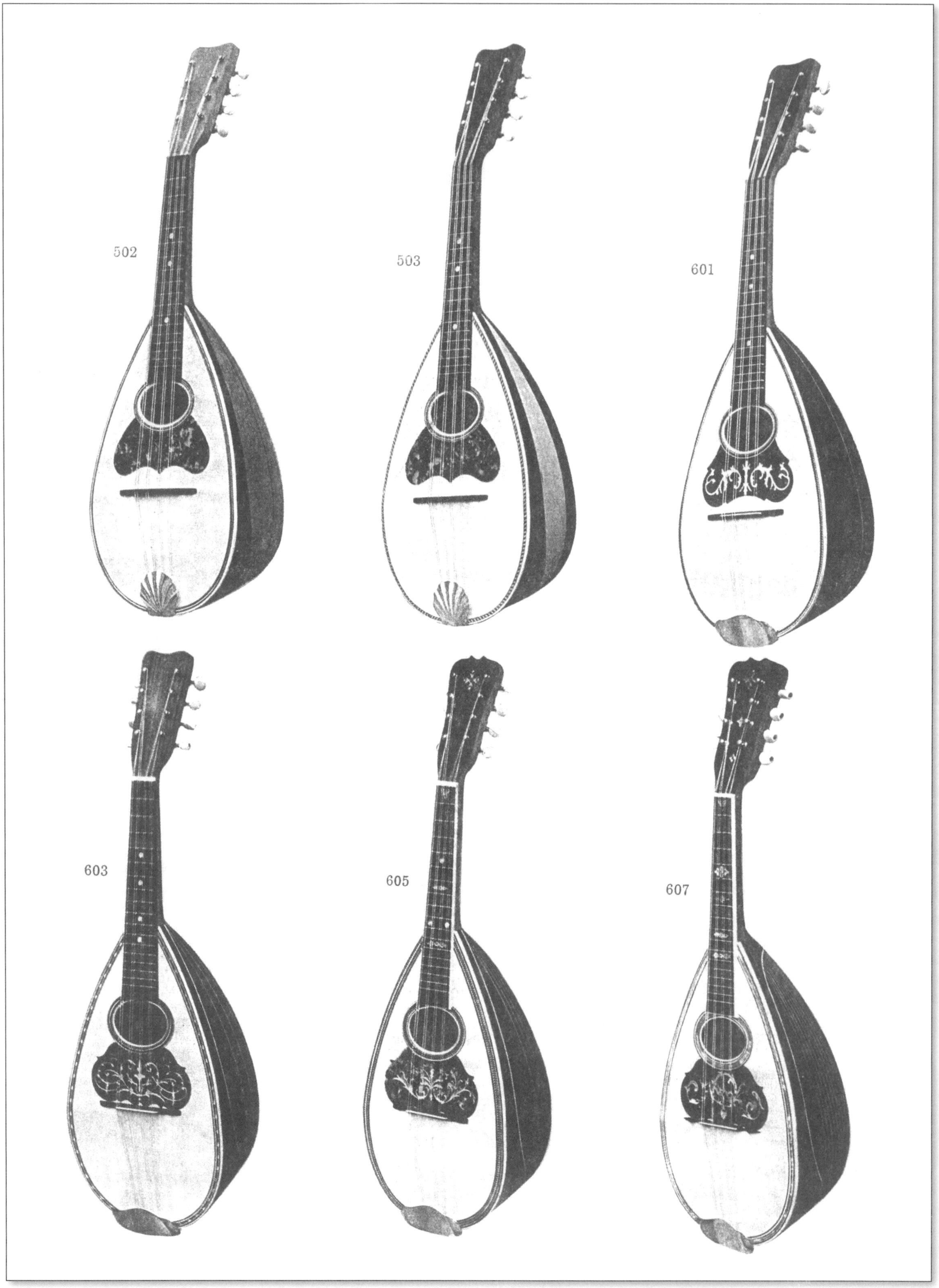

American Conservatory mandolins, 1903 catalog

by the end of 1896. In the 1905 Washburn catalog the company claimed a total of 300,000 guitars made, while the actual guitar serial numbers had reached the 275,000s by 1905. At the same time the company did not make it clear that the claimed production figures did not relate to just Washburns. Similar mystifications were not uncommon to Lyon & Healy. In various early 1890s advertisements the company claimed that the Lyon & Healy factories put out 100,000 instruments annually. Later this claim was attributed to the 'Washburn factories' which, although true in a sense, incorrectly suggested that enormous numbers of Washburns were made. Lyon & Healy even went so far to retouch the company name on the factory banner in the ad into 'Washburn'! The wrongful impression that this little ad created has persisted for over one hundred years and is the main cause of many misconceptions about prewar Washburn instruments today – quite a feat!

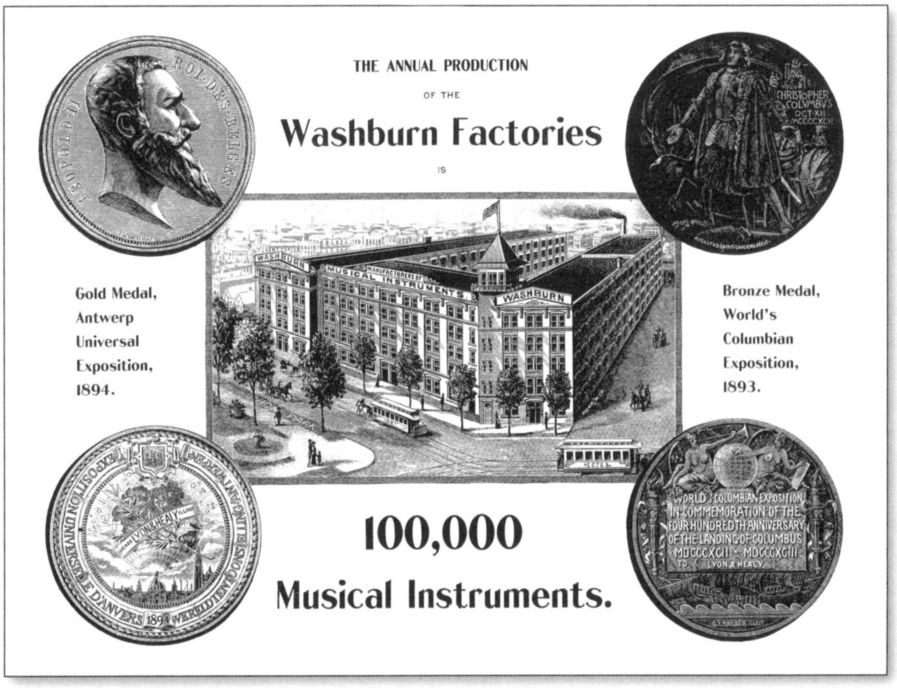

1896

The serialization schemes introduced by Lyon & Healy after 1907 were used almost exclusively for Washburns and indicate more accurately the actual number of these instruments that were made. Between 1922 and 1930 batch numbers were also stamped on many Washburn guitars, mandolins, banjos and ukuleles, making it not always clear which of both sets of digits represent the actual serial number. Around 1926-7 inconsistencies seem to occur in the numbers found on the Washburn fretted instrument lines. The reason therefore is that the company started stamping batch numbers in the headstocks of guitars, mandolins and ukuleles and in the dowel stick of the Washburn banjos, while serial numbers were no longer indicated on the instruments. This change happened around the same time that Lyon & Healy opened a new Chicago factory at Rockwell and 22nd streets (June 1926). Starting in 1930 the batch numbers were no longer stamped on the instruments that were now being manufactured by Regal, and the Washburn guitars and mandolins shared the same serial number sequence. Some of the Gibson-made Washburns of the late thirties received a stamped batch number on the neck block besides a serial number on the label.

The rise of the guitar – a new theory

Based on the serial numbers found on surviving instruments Lyon & Healy had made a total of approximately 275,000 guitars and 200,000 mandolins by the start of 1905, an average of around 22,000 instruments per year over the 1885-1905 period. This implies that the aforementioned 1890s claim of an "annual production upward of 100,000 musical instruments" appears quite feasible in view of the many other product lines manufactured by the company at the time such as harps, zithers, banjos, violins, band instruments, drums, church and parlor organs, et cetera. Lyon & Healy certainly did not concentrate on selling just guitars and mandolins –or any specific instrument for that matter. The large period musical merchandise catalogs published by the company until the 1920s contained hundreds of pages with a plethora of musical instruments. Separate catalogs were also available for specific items as pianos, organs, violins and band instruments.

The total production figures for mandolins and guitars as evidenced by their serial numbers also cast a different light on established notions about the impact of the mandolin craze that had started in the 1880s and continued for a few decades. The same applies to the generally presumed smaller popularity of the guitar before the 1930s in comparison to the five string banjos of the 1800s, the mandolin (after the 1880s) and the tenor banjo (after 1920).[137] Since Lyon & Healy arguably was the world's largest manufacturer and importer of musical instruments between the 1890s and the mid 1920s and sold a myriad of different instrument lines, their instrument output may provide important –if not decisive- clues on these subjects.

137 *Gruhn & Carter (I)*, p. 8, 164/5, *Carter*, p. 123.

Serialization data shows that even during the heyday of the mandolin the Lyon & Healy factories produced more guitars than mandolins. Around the start of 1897 the company had manufactured approximately 70,000 mandolins (since 1886) and 120,000 guitars (since 1884). Between 1897 and 1905 Lyon & Healy produced an additional 155,000 guitars and 130,000 mandolins, even though the mandolin craze was at its peak.

Since the overall guitar and mandolin output of Lyon & Healy after 1907 is unknown due to a change of the serial numbering systems used, the production totals for the Washburn guitars and mandolins need to provide clues for this period. These show that slightly more guitars than mandolins were manufactured between 1907 and 1922, and that mandolin production figures dropped steeply after the mid twenties. It is also clear that in spite of the renewed interest in banjos during the 1910s and 1920s the Washburn banjo output in this period only briefly surpassed the annual production totals of the Washburn guitars.[138] The foregoing strongly suggests that the guitar, though it was not as 'fashionable' as the mandolin around the turn of the 20th century, had gained a much larger popularity at the time than usually is assumed, and had already become *the* most popular fretted instrument in the United States. The soaring popularity of the guitar in the post-Civil War era[139] is also illustrated by the 1880 Lyon & Healy catalog, which listed twenty six guitar styles and nineteen banjo styles (mandolins were not yet offered by the company in 1880 because their tremendous surge to public fervor was yet to begin). An 1895 article about Lyon & Healy's Union Park factory states that in the previous year the company had made approximately 13,000 guitars, 7,000 mandolins and 12,000 banjos –the latter mostly destined for export to England.[140] This illustrates that the prominent role of the five-string banjo in the United States, originally popularized by the blackface minstrel shows that had caught on big after 1830, had ceased by the 1890s. This all implies that from a historical perspective, the 'most popular' status of the guitar which it likely had already attained by the late 1870s was first challenged in the late 19th century and the following decades by the mandolin, and subsequently by the ukulele and the tenor banjo during the 1910s and 1920s, without these instruments posing a lasting threat to that status.[141]

During the 1930s guitar design evolved rapidly. The typical larger bodied and louder instruments with their 14-fret necks definitely brought the flattop guitar out of the parlor to the concert stage. The big archtop guitars of the Swing Era were a staple in many jazz bands and orchestras, and the first electric guitars were introduced to accommodate the players' demands for more volume. The increased popularity of the guitar more firmly cemented its dominant position among the other fretted instruments, which it still holds today.

---

138 See Chapter 7.3 for more detailed information on production figures for these instruments.

139 Philip F. Gura, *C.F. Martin and His Guitars*, 1796-1873 p. 162.

140 W.S.B. Mathews, *A Morning in a Musical Instrument Factory*, in *Music, Volume VIII, 1895* p 351-360. At the time the banjo had become a very fashionable instrument in Britain.

141 Only between 1925 and 1926-7 average annual production figures for the Washburn ukuleles exceeded those for the Washburn guitar.

CHAPTER SEVEN

Serial numbers and estimated production totals

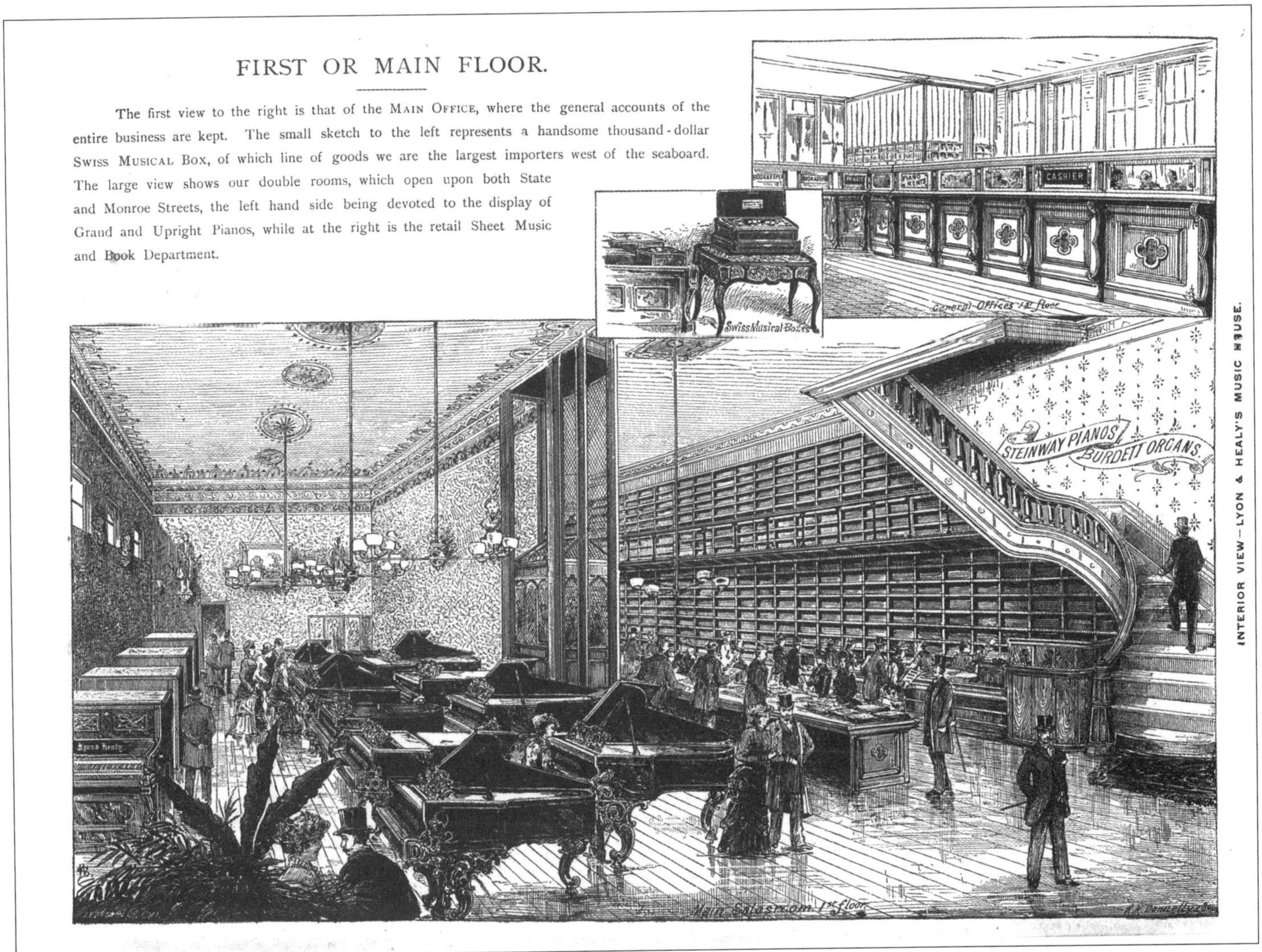
FIRST OR MAIN FLOOR.

The first view to the right is that of the MAIN OFFICE, where the general accounts of the entire business are kept. The small sketch to the left represents a handsome thousand-dollar SWISS MUSICAL BOX, of which line of goods we are the largest importers west of the seaboard. The large view shows our double rooms, which open upon both State and Monroe Streets, the left hand side being devoted to the display of Grand and Upright Pianos, while at the right is the retail Sheet Music and Book Department.

View of one of the floors of Lyon & Healy's offices at State and Monroe Streets, 1889 catalog (Frank Nordberg, www.musicaviva.com)

7.1 Guitar serial numbers and estimated production totals

Serial no.	Starting at year
1	1884 or later (numbers not stamped in instruments until around 1887)
low 10,000s	1889 or earlier
low 120,000s	1897
275,000s	1905
316,000s	around 1907
A-1 (restart numbering)	around 1907
A-14,000s	around 1910
A-28,000s	around 1910
A-36,800s	around 1915
37,000s (no A-prefix)	around 1915
42,000s	around 1920
45,000s	around 1923
high 46,000s-low 47,000s	around 1925
1 (restart numbering)	around 1922
low 2,000s	around 1925 (note: headstock numbers)
3,500s	around 1926-7 (note: neck block numbers)
mid 14,000	around late 1929 (note: numbers stamped on guitars between 1926-7 and 1930 represent batch numbers)
1 (restart numbering)	around 1930
2,000s	around 1935
1 (restart numbering)	around 1935
high 2,000s –low 3,000s	around 1937
low 7,000s	around 1940

As explained earlier the numbering system used in the pre-1907 period indicates the total number of Lyon & Healy-made guitars, not just Washburns. After 1907 up to the mid 1920s serial numbers were used practically exclusively for Washburn guitars. During the Regal era (1930-1940) the serial numbers used for Washburn guitars no longer reflect the actual number of guitars made, since the numbering sequence was used also for the Washburn mandolins.

Guitar production totals 1907-1940 based on serialization data

1907-1910	8,000 (2,600 per year)[142]
1910-1915	8,500 (1,700 per year)
1915-1922	7,000 (1,000 per year)
1922-1925	3,000 (1,000 per year) [143]
1925-1930	5,000 (1,000 per year)[144]
1930-1935	1,800 (350 per year)[145]
1935-1940	5,700 (1,150 per year)
Total	39,000 (averaging around 1,200 guitars per year)

142 This figure cannot be derived from serial numbers alone due to certain numbering inconsistencies, likely caused by Lyon & Healy's outsourcing of instrument production at the time, and is therefore estimated as being equal to mandolin production figures during the same period.

143 This includes the estimated totals of Styles F and G (1923-1925), which were numbered according to the pre-1922 serialization schemes. All other guitar styles were renumbered starting at 1 around 1922.

144 Estimated figures for this period are assumed to be equal to the 1925-1926-7 average production totals.

145 The calculations for the 1930-1940 period are based also on the number of reported Washburn guitars vs. mandolins from this period.

The production drop after 1915 may be explained by a number of factors, including the lack of success of a new guitar line introduced in that year. On the 1915 guitar styles the colorful and abundant marquetry and pearl ornamentation of the earlier models had made way for an almost spartan look, which may not have appealed to the guitar buying public at the time. Lyon & Healy may also have concentrated its production efforts during the wartime years on other product lines due to important government contracts, e.g. for band instruments and uniforms. A third factor may be the move of production facilities during 1914 to the newly built factory at Fullerton Avenue. Besides, promotion of the Washburn brand was lacking. Few of the various ad campaigns by Lyon & Healy between around 1913 and 1923 featured Washburn instruments.

The post 1929 figure clearly shows the profound effects of the depression era combined with the temporary shutdown of the Washburn production facilities in 1930 following the bankruptcy of J.R. Stewart Co., the manufacturer of Washburn instruments at the time. The annual average of around 1,150 guitars in the post-1935 period is in the same league as the Gibson flattop production figures of the late thirties. The total production for all Gibson flattop models between 1937 and 1941 period was 7,379 instruments, averaging 1,475 guitars per year. Martin did much better with a yearly average output of slightly over 3,000 guitars in the 1935-1941 period.[146]

Estimated guitar production totals 1884-1907

How many guitars were made prior to 1907, probably the era of peak instrument production for Lyon & Healy? In the 1889 Washburn catalog Lyon & Healy claimed that nearly 20,000 Washburns were in use. It is likely from serial number data that this figure also included other guitars and mandolins manufactured by Lyon & Healy and marketed under the company name and other 'house brands'. The true total number of Washburn guitars and mandolins that had been produced by the late 1880s may have been closer to 10,000.[147]

An average of 2,600 Washburn guitars a year -as during the 1907-1910 period- would translate into approximately 60,000 Washburns. If we use the post 1907 estimated totals, divide this figure by the number of instruments found from this period and project this on the number of researched pre-1907 guitars, a total of 44,000 guitars would result. Applying the average annual production of the 1907-1940 period to the pre-1907 years yields a total of 27,000 instruments, which, in view of the small output of Washburn guitars during the depression years, must be considered a low-end estimate. The true figure likely lies somewhere in between. This means that 45,000 Washburn guitars, or slightly less than 2,000 instruments manufactured annually, could be considered a realistic estimate for the period 1884-1907. This figure equals 14% of Lyon & Healy's total guitar production between 1884 and 1907 of around 317,000 instruments, which means that approximately one out of seven guitars made by the company was a Washburn.

This average of 2,000 Washburns per year, or six or seven Washburn guitars per working day, may not turn heads in today's music industry dominated by computerized mass-manufacturing processes, but in the late 1800s this was an impressive figure for such an expensive guitar. The Washburn production totals around the turn of the 20th century dwarfed those of C.F. Martin & Co, one of Lyon & Healy's competitors in the upscale guitar market, whose output typically averaged between 150 and 250 guitars per year. Fortunately for Martin this soon would change. By the early 1920s Martin's guitar output had surpassed the Washburn totals, and would eclipse Lyon & Healy's overall guitar production in the following years. The sale of the Washburn manufacturing license to the J.R. Stewart Co. in 1928 therefore seemed a logical step for Lyon & Healy, because the company had no outlook on regaining its position of leading contender in the upscale guitar market.

Based on the serial numbers used by Lyon & Healy, an estimated total number of around 84,000 Washburn guitars were manufactured between 1884 and 1940. By comparison, Martin had made around 75,000 guitars by the end of 1939.

146 *Washburn & Johnston*, p. 248 (for the Martin figures), the Gibson totals are derived from Larry Meiners, *Gibson Shipping Totals 1937-1979*, (2001) p. 40. It should be noted that unlike Martin, Gibson also manufactured large numbers of cheap instruments during the 1930s under other brand names.

147 The relative large share of Washburns vs other Lyon & Healy-made guitars can be explained by the fact that only a few budget styles and brands had been introduced by Lyon & Healy by the late 1880s in comparison to the mid and late 1890s.

7.2 Mandolin serial numbers and estimated production totals

Serial no.	Starting at year
1	1889 or earlier
high 50,000s – low 60,000s	mid 1896
115,000s-120,000s	1900
mid 190,000s	1905
low 230,000s	around 1907
A-1 (restart numbering)	around 1907
mid A-8,000s	around 1910
low 19,000s (no A-prefix)	around 1915
mid 22,000s	around 1920
low 24,000s	around 1923
mid 27,000s	around 1925
1 (restart numbering)	around 1922
mid 14,000s	around late 1929 (note: numbers stamped on mandolins between 1926-7 and 1930 represent batch numbers)
(no serial numbers are stamped on instruments between 1930 and 1935)	
1 (restart numbering)	around 1935
high 2,000s –low 3,000s	around 1937
low 7,000s	around 1940

As with guitars, serial numbers prior to 1907 period indicate the total number of Lyon & Healy mandolins that were manufactured.

Serial numbers for the Lyon & Healy/Washburn A-C styles between 1917 and the mid 1920s are in the 1-2,300s range. Research data from surviving instruments suggests that Styles A-C were each numbered separately prior to 1925, and that Style A mandocellos and mandolas were also numbered separately from the standard A Style mandolins.

Mandolin production totals 1907-1940 based on serialization data

1907-1910	8,000 (2,600) per year)
1910-1915	10,000 (2,000 per year)
1915-1922	4,500 (650 per year)
1922-1925	2,500 (850 per year)[148]
1925-1930	2,500 (500 per year)
1930-1935	200 (40 per year)
1935-1940	300 (60 per year)
Total	30,000 (averaging 900 mandolins per year)

Interestingly, the post 1915 production drop equally applies to mandolins as to guitars. In this respect it should be noted that the cosmetics of the new mandolin line of 1905 were as understated as that of the guitar line introduced in the same year.

It is likely that in spite of the various mandolin styles advertised in the Washburn section of the Tonk Bros catalogs throughout the 1930s, actual sales must have been marginal during this period as only a few mandolins from this period have surfaced.

148 The calculations for the mandolin totals in the 1922-1940 period are also based on the number of reported Washburn guitars vs. mandolins from this period.

Estimated mandolin production totals 1886-1907

Reference is made to the calculation methods explained under 7.1 for guitars manufactured during this period. The estimated totals according to these methods are respectively 55,000, 44,000 and 19,000. Since it is certain that Lyon & Healy manufactured more guitars than mandolins during this period[149], a feasible estimate should be lower than the 45,000 figure established for Washburn guitars. A total of 40,000 Washburn mandolins for the 1886-1907 period –i.e. averaging 1,900 instruments per year- may therefore be reasonably accurate.

The foregoing leads to an estimated total number of around 70,000 Washburn mandolins manufactured between 1886 and 1940. The Lyon & Healy A-C mandolin styles made before the early 1920s –during which period they were not marketed under the 'Washburn' brand- are not included in this figure.

7.3 Banjo serial numbers and estimated production totals

Serial no.	Starting at year
1	1892
900s-1,000s	around 1896
low 3,000s	around 1913
5,000s	late 1915
high 9,000s-low 10,000s	late 1922
1 (restart numbering)	around 1923
4,200s	around 1925
9,000s-11,000s	around 1928 (note: numbers stamped on banjos between 1926-7 and 1930 represent batch numbers)
mid 14,000s	around late 1929 (batch numbers)
Banjo production totals 1892-1940 based on serialization data	
1892-1913	2,800 (130 per year)
1913-1923	6,400 (640 per year)
1923-1925	3,800 (1,900 per year)
1925-1930	5,000 (1,000 per year)[150]
Total	18,000 (averaging around 475 banjos per year over the 1892-1930 period)

Since the Washburn banjos shared their serial numbering system with a few other Lyon & Healy premium banjo styles, their serial numbers approximate but are not identical to the actual total of Washburn banjos made (about 10% of all reported serial numbers were found on Lyon & Healy banjos other than Washburns).

From the collected serialization data it becomes clear that the Washburn banjos –and possibly banjos in general- enjoyed relatively little popularity from the 1890s up to the early 1910s. The 'tango craze' that started in the early 1910s clearly accounted for a boost in Lyon & Healy's banjo sales, which triggered the need for the introduction of the 1913 banjo line with its much larger palette of available styles. During the 'jazz age' until the early 1930s banjo sales reached a peak. The new Washburn banjos introduced in 1923 sporting the 'donut' tone ring turned out to be successful, which was likely aided by the 1924 advertising campaigns by Lyon & Healy that highlighted the features of the new Washburn styles.

The numbers of Washburn banjos made between the mid and late twenties were not quite in the same ballpark as Gibson's banjo output at the time. Between 1925 and 1929, Gibson's peak production period for banjos in the prewar era, an estimated total of 8,200 banjos were made. This implies an average of a little over 2,000 instruments per year, twice as much as the Washburn annual average production figures that are estimated around 1,000 units in the 1925-1930 period.[151]

149 See chapter 6.
150 This calculation is also based on the number of reported Washburn guitars vs. mandolins vs. banjos from this period.
151 Gibson figures derived from Joe Spann, *Analysis of Pre-War Gibson Banjo Production*, http://home.cfl.rr.com/tbiggs/Serial_nos/Spann.html.

7.4 Ukulele serial numbers and estimated production totals

Serial no.	Starting at year
1	1915
high 1,000s – low 2,000s	1922
1 (start renumbering)	1922
low 4,000s	1925 (note: headstock numbers)
1 (start renumbering)	1925 (note: neck block numbers)
low 3,000s	1926-7 (note: neck block numbers)
mid 14,000s	late 1929 (note: headstock numbers stamped on ukuleles between 1926-7 and 1930 represent batch numbers)
(no sufficient data after 1930)	

Ukulele production totals 1915-1930 based on serialization data

1915-1922	2,000 (300 per year)
1922-1925	4,000 (1,300 per year)
1925-1926-7	3,000 (2,000 per year)
1926-7-1930	3,500 (1,000 per year)[152]
After 1930	500 (50 per year)[153]
Total	13,000 (averaging around 850 ukuleles per year over the 1915-1930 period)

In view of the popularity of the ukulele between 1915 and the early 1930s it might be expected that Lyon & Healy's sales for these instruments would have been very high in comparison to mandolins and guitars during the same period. Martin sold tens of thousands of ukuleles at the time –14,000 in 1926 alone.[154] Surprisingly, the serialization data and the number of surviving Lyon & Healy-made instruments reported and researched both seem to indicate otherwise. Even though the average annual production figures for ukuleles surpassed the guitar and mandolin output for a brief period around the mid 1920s, the estimated totals seem nonetheless rather moderate. The relative rarity of the Washburn ukuleles is also reflected by the much smaller numbers of these instruments turning up on the vintage market in comparison to prewar Washburn guitars, mandolins and banjos.

Only three Washburn ukuleles have been reported to date that have a 'Tonk Bros' stamp. This seems to indicate that sales of Washburn ukuleles after 1928, the Regal/Tonk Bros era, were minimal. An explanation for the relative small ukulele production figures in comparison to Martin may be that Lyon & Healy did not adequately react to the ukulele fad, as only two Washburn ukulele styles were offered before 1922, and also did not sufficiently promote these instruments. In retrospect the failure to sufficiently capitalize on the fashionable Hawaiian instruments may have been an important strategic mistake of Lyon & Healy. For Martin's successful venture into the ukulele market did not just mean extra income for the company. The added brand recognition and customer appreciation resulting from the many thousands of Martin ukuleles that were sold each year led also to a large and permanent increase in guitar sales, and turned the expanding company from a smaller fish into the leading contender on the premium flattop guitar market, all at a time that the production figures of Lyon & Healy's Washburn guitars and mandolins were dropping to unprecedented lows.

152 The calculations are also based on the number of reported Washburn guitars vs. mandolins vs. banjos vs. ukes from this period.
153 Estimate – only three post 1929 Washburn ukuleles have been reported to date.
154 *Washburn & Johnston*, p. 95.

7.5 Pianos, organs, zithers, harps, violins

The Washburn pianos appeared for the first time in Lyon & Healy ads in the early 1910s but were already being made in the 1890s. They were not numbered separately from the other Lyon & Healy piano models. In 1909 Lyon & Healy claimed to have sold 100,000 pianos of various brands since the opening of their first store in 1864. According to the company the Union Park factory was annually turning out between 1,500 and 2,000 Lyon & Healy and Washburn pianos at the time. It is unknown how many Washburn pianos have survived to this day, but thousands must have been made between the 1890s and the 1920s. The Washburn parlor organs were offered briefly during the 1890s. As none of these have turned up in recent years, likely only very few instruments were manufactured.

Washburn zithers were available from the late 1880s through the 1910s. Based on serial number information only between 2,000 and 3,000 of these instruments were made. The Washburn harps and violins were briefly listed in Lyon & Healy catalogs during the 1910s. Contrary to most Washburn brand instruments the Washburn violins were not made by Lyon & Healy craftsmen but were imported from Europe. It is estimated that approximately 400 Washburn harps and less than one thousand Washburn violins were manufactured during their respective production runs.

7.6 Overall Washburn production totals (1884-1940) based on serialization data

In view of the missing Lyon & Healy company records it will likely never be possible to establish definite production figures for the prewar period Washburn instruments, but approximations can be derived from serial numbers. Based on the aforementioned findings for the separate categories of Washburns, the overall production total for the period 1884-1940 is estimated at approximately 185,000 instruments, consisting of 84,000 guitars, 70,000 mandolins, 18,000 banjos and 13,000 ukuleles, averaging 3,300 instruments per year. This figure does not include Washburn pianos, organs, zithers, harps and violins.

Conclusion

Though the primary purpose of this book is to describe the Washburn fretted instrument lines made prior to 1940, a number of popular theories about Lyon & Healy and the Washburns have been challenged here as well. Often writers wrongfully assume that humongous numbers of Washburns were made around and before the 1900s and go on claiming that the relatively few examples that have survived must prove their inferior construction as compared to Gibsons and Martins.[155] That Lyon & Healy played second fiddle to these makers with regard to innovation in instrument design[156] is another myth that can be put to rest in view of the many different, original and sometimes experimental instrument styles marketed by Lyon & Healy before the 1930s and the various utility and design patents awarded to the company over a forty year period. The appreciation for vintage Washburns still seems to be affected negatively by these ill-conceived notions, which have led to their perception by many as mass-produced instruments that are nicely decorated though musically not on a par with the products of Martin or Gibson. But there are also other signals. Many owners of old Washburn instruments will testify that the good examples rival their counterparts from Kalamazoo and Nazareth tone wise. Eric Schoenberg, guitar designer and longtime connoisseur of fine vintage acoustics, particularly holds the 1930s Regal-made Washburn guitars in high esteem and recently praised a rosewood bodied Style 5237 as "possibly the most amazing sounding vintage guitar". Contemporary artists who have recorded or performed with prewar Washburns include Ricky Skaggs, Roy Book Binder, Laurence Juber, Paul Simon, Jackson Browne, and Duke Robillard. The Lyon & Healy/Washburn carved top mandolins are widely regarded as the standard for performing classical music and are favored by notable players such as Norman Blake and David Grisman. Slowly the Washburns have begun to shed their 'sleeper' status on the vintage market, and more players and collectors have discovered the true value of these fine instruments.

It has been over a century since George Lyon and Patrick Healy have died, but the name and heritage of the small store they founded in 1864 lives on until the present day. Lyon & Healy Harps, Inc., based in Chicago, is still acknowledged as the one of the world's premier makers of concert harps. Fretted instruments bearing the Washburn brand are available in practically every music store and are played by amateur and professional musicians all over the world. As more facts are being unearthed about the early years of the house of Lyon & Healy and their wide range of product lines, existing myths are dispelled and recognition grows for the important historical role of the company as trendsetter within the music industry, pioneer in the development of original and adventurous fretted instrument designs, and manufacturer of many great instruments.

155 *Dangerous Curves, the Art of the Guitar (2000)*, p. 89.
156 See previous note.

Bibliography

The following abbreviations are used in this book:

Carter	Walter Carter, *Gibson: 100 Years of an American Icon* (1994), General Publishing Group
Gruhn/Carter (I)	George Gruhn & Walter Carter, *Acoustic Guitars and Other Fretted Instruments: a photographic history* (1993), GPI
Gruhn/Carter (II)	George Gruhn & Walter Carter, *Gruhn's Guide to Vintage Guitars, an Identification Guide for American Fretted Instruments (2nd Ed)* (1999), Miller Freeman
Teagle	John Teagle, *Washburn: 100 Years of Fine Stringed Instruments* (1994), 20th Century Guitars
Washburn & Johnston	Jim Washburn & Richard Johnston, *Martin Guitars: an Illustrated Celebration of America's Premier Guitarmaker* (1997), Rodale Press
Wheeler	Tom Wheeler, *American Guitars, an Illustrated History* (1982), Grafton

Other books and publications:

Achard, Ken	*The History and Development of the American Guitar* (1979), Musical News Services Ltd
Bacon, Tony	*The History of the American Guitar: from 1833 to the Present Day* (2001), Friedman/Fairfax
Carter, Walter	*The Martin Book: a Complete History of Martin Guitars* (1995), Balafon
Gura, Philip F.	*C.F. Martin and His Guitars, 1796-1873* (2003), Chapel Hill, University of North Carolina Press
Gura, Philip and	*America's Instrument: The Banjo in the Nineteenth Century* (1999),
Bollman, Jim	Chapel Hill: University of North Carolina Press
Johnston, Richard	*Vintage Guitars: the Instruments, the Players, and the Music* (2003), (and others) String Letter Publishing
Kuronen, Darcy	*Dangerous Curves, the Art of the Guitar* (2000), MFA Publications
Lyon & Healy	*A Century of Music in Chicago – the Story of Lyon-Healy's First One Hundred Years 1864-1964* (1964), Lyon & Healy
Lyon & Healy	*Patrick Joseph Healy, founder of the house of Lyon & Healy – an appreciation* (1907)
Meiners, Larry	*Gibson Shipping Totals 1937-1979* (2001), Flying Vintage
Sparks, Paul	*The Classical Mandolin*, Oxford University Press (1995)
Tyler, James and Sparks, Paul	*The Early Mandolin*, Oxford University Press (1989)
Whitford, Eldon, Vinopal, David and Erlewine, Dan	*Gibson's Fabulous Flat-Top Guitars, an Illustrated History and Guide* (1994), GPI

Style 6 (1884-1887) pictured with its original coffin case. This guitar, one of the earliest X-braced Washburns, was also available with a solid headstock sporting the 'Champion' friction tuners

Style 1 (1887) with replacement bridge (Eltjo Haselhoff)

Style 503 Contra Bass Guitar (1892) (Retrofret.com)

Style 804 Lyre Terz Guitar (1895). Note fingerboard dots, replaced bridge pins and lack of f-holes. The photo (below) shows the original owner of this guitar with her instrument (Elderly)

Style 108, early 1890s. Note earlier 10th position fingerboard inlay (Mike Gazay)

Style 308 with replica 'Durkee' bridge, mid 1890s (Blazer & Henkes, Antique Acoustics.de)

Style 188, around 1900 (Elderly / photo Dave Matchette)

American Conservatory Style 1210 Harp Guitar,
around 1905 (Retrofret.com)

Style 355 (1905), formerly owned by Dan Fogelberg (Gruhn Guitars)

One of a kind Washburn 10-string guitar, around 1907. Its cosmetic features are derived from Styles 175-380, but with a size 4 (auditorium) body (Palm Guitars/Jurgen Te Rijdt)

College Line Style 2090 twelve-string 'Monster Bass' guitar, around 1910 (Gregg Miner / photo: Gregg Miner)

Carl Sandburg (1878-1967), Illinois-born poet and two-time Pulitzer Prize laureate, with his Washburn Style 5271 Bell Guitar. The photo at left shows the guitar in its current state (Dr. John Steichen)

19-fret Style 5238 made by J.R. Stewart, 1929-30
(Elderly / photos Dave Matchette)

Unusual 19-fret guitar with abalone trim, likely made by J.R. Stewart. It was originally a Hawaiian guitar and has a 5246 stamp on the neck block. The bridge is a replacement (Lowell Levinger, Players Vintage Instruments)

One of the last 20-fret Style 5234 guitars, Regal-made, around 1935 (Elderly / photos Dave Matchette)

1936 Style 5257 ½, Full Auditorium size
(Terry O'Laughlin)

1937 Style 5244, dreadnought version in natural finish, replaced tuners (Alan Fisher / photos Rick Singer)

A pair of Style 5246 dreadnoughts (around 1937) with consecutive serial numbers. The guitar at left has lost its orginal tuners, the other has had its 'smile' bridge replaced (Mark Demaray)

1939 Regal-made Style 5244, Extra Super Auditorium size (Mark Demaray)

Gibson-made Style 5249 #4211, shipped on May 19, 1939. This rosewood beauty was used by former owner Roy Book Binder for many concerts and recordings. The Waverley tuners are not original (Mike Rivamonte)

Style 80, 1892 (Richard Myers / photo Dan'l Terry © 2006)

Style 80 (1896), transitional model with unusual pearl fingerboard and post-1896 tailpiece (Richard Myers / photo Dan'l Terry © 2006)

Style 1125, 1896 (Richard Myers / photo Dan'l Terry © 2006)

Style 275, 1905 (Richard Myers / photo Dan'l Terry © 2006)

Very early Lyon & Healy Style A mandolin, 1917
(Kieron Seamons)

Washburn Style A mandolin, 1920s
(Elderly / photo Dave Matchette)

Style 5183 'Aristocrat' banjo, 1925 (Gruhn Guitars)

Style 5183 (1928), non-original resonator
(Elderly / photo Dave Matchette)

Detail of Style 5187 Super DeLuxe banjo, late 1920s
(National Four-String Banjo Museum, Guthrie, OK)

A pair of extremely rare Shrine banjos
(National Four-String Banjo Museum, Guthrie, OK)

Style 5318 DeLuxe ukulele, mid 1920s
(Dave Pasant / photos Dan Waltz)

Style 5325 Bell ukulele, mid 1920s
(Dave Pasant / photos Dan Waltz)

Style 5395 Bell tiple, later version with 'gondola' bridge, late 1920s (Dave Pasant / photos Dan Waltz)

Style 5319 DeLuxe ukulele, around 1928 (Dave Pasant / photos Dan Waltz)

Style 5320 Super DeLuxe ukulele, late 1920s
(Dave Pasant / photos Dan Waltz)

Style 5360 Super DeLuxe tenor ukulele, late 1920s
(Dave Pasant / photos Dan Waltz)

An impossibly rare grouping of 'shrine' family instruments: guitar, tenor guitar, mandolin and ukulele, late 1920s (Elderly / photo Dave Matchette)